VERSE BY VERSE

THE BOOK OF MORMON

VOLUME ONE

VERSE BY VERSE

THE BOOK OF MORMON

VOLUME ONE
1 NEPHI THROUGH ALMA 29

D. KELLY OGDEN
ANDREW C. SKINNER

DESERET
BOOK

SALT LAKE CITY, UTAH

First hardbound printing in 2011
First paperbound printing in 2023

Library of Congress Cataloging-in-Publication Data

Ogden, D. Kelly (Daniel Kelly), 1947– author.
Verse by verse : The book of Mormon. Volume 1, 1 Nephi through Alma 29 / D. Kelly Ogden and Andrew C. Skinner.
    p. cm.
Includes bibliographical references and index.
ISBN 978-1-60908-740-1 (hardbound : alk. paper) | ISBN 978-1-63993-184-2 (paperbound)
1. Book of Mormon—Commentaries. I. Skinner, Andrew C., 1951– author. II. Title.
BX8627 .O33 vol. 1 2011
289.3'22—dc23   2011019588

Printed in the United States of America
University Press, Provo, UT

10   9   8   7   6   5   4   3   2   1

CONTENTS

PREFACE

The series Verse by Verse, which began with *The Four Gospels* and *Acts through Revelation,* continues with *The Book of Mormon,* a verse-by-verse commentary that is one book in two volumes. This division reflects the way in which courses on the Book of Mormon are structured in seminary, in the institutes of religion, and on the various campuses of Brigham Young University: 1 Nephi 1 through Alma 29, and Alma 30 through Moroni 10.

The introduction to the two volumes appears, of course, in the first volume, and the index to both volumes is found at the end of the second. Each volume contains its own table of contents, notes, and sources. Occasionally, cross-references between the two volumes appear in the text.

We acknowledge the assistance of many colleagues and students at Brigham Young University for their helpful suggestions during the years of preparation of these books. We express gratitude to Dennis L. Largey for permission to use several maps from *Book of Mormon Reference Companion.* We extend particular appreciation to the production team at Deseret Book Company: Cory Maxwell, director of publishing; Suzanne Brady, senior editor; Shauna Gibby, designer; and Rachael Ward, typographer.

We dedicate these writings to Marcia Hammond Ogden and Janet Corbridge Skinner, our dear wives, who are also ardent students and teachers of the Book of Mormon, and to our children and grandchildren.

Most of all, we thank our Heavenly Father and his Son,

Jesus Christ, and all the prophets and other faithful record-keepers for their dedicated attention to preserving eternal truths that they knew would be crucial for us in these last days.

INTRODUCTION

There is no book like the Book of Mormon. It is the most correct of any book on earth; it is the keystone of Latter-day Saint faith (Book of Mormon, Introduction). Indeed, The Church of Jesus Christ of Latter-day Saints stands or falls with the truthfulness of the Book of Mormon.[1] The Lord himself testifies of its truthfulness (D&C 17:6). He acted as one of its editors (3 Nephi 23:7–14), and it stands as a supreme witness of him (Book of Mormon, Title Page). More than half of the verses in the Book of Mormon refer to Jesus Christ. The book presents one hundred name-titles of our Lord and testifies of the reality of God the Father and his interest in his children. It is a primer on the Father's great plan of happiness.

President Ezra Taft Benson declared: "The Lord Himself has stated that the Book of Mormon contains the 'fulness of the gospel of Jesus Christ' (D&C 20:9). That does not mean it contains every teaching, every doctrine ever revealed. Rather, it means that in the Book of Mormon we will find the fulness of those doctrines required for our salvation. And they are taught plainly and simply so that even children can learn the ways of salvation and exaltation."[2]

The Book of Mormon was of inestimable value in laying the foundation for the restoration of the gospel in these latter days. President Benson explained that a "powerful testimony to the importance of the Book of Mormon is to note where the Lord placed its coming forth in the timetable of the unfolding Restoration. The only thing that preceded it was the First Vision. . . . Think of that in terms of what it implies. The

1

coming forth of the Book of Mormon preceded the restoration of the priesthood. It was published just a few days before the Church was organized. The Saints were given the Book of Mormon to read before they were given the revelations outlining such great doctrines as the three degrees of glory, celestial marriage, or work for the dead. It came before priesthood quorums and Church organization. Doesn't this tell us something about how the Lord views this sacred work?"[3]

The Book of Mormon is of immense value to each of us personally. It serves as a personal scriptural tutor, no matter what our station or situation might be—prophet or Primary child, Saint or unrepentant sinner, scholar or simple student. President Benson continued: "The Book of Mormon . . . was written for our day. The Nephites never had the book; neither did the Lamanites of ancient times. It was meant for us. . . . Each of the major writers of the Book of Mormon testified that he wrote for future generations. . . . If they saw our day, and chose those things which would be of greatest worth to us, is not that how we should study the Book of Mormon? We should constantly ask ourselves, 'Why did the Lord inspire Mormon (or Moroni or Alma) to include that in his record? What lesson can I learn from that to help me live in this day and age?'"[4]

The Book of Mormon teaches us to hear the voice of inspiration (1 Nephi 18:3; Enos 1:2–4, 10; Helaman 5:30; 3 Nephi 11:3). It teaches us how we should live and how we will be judged (Moroni 10:32–34). It reveals to us the enemies of Christ and his gospel: false doctrines, false educational philosophies, characteristics of false teachers, pride, apathy, and Lucifer, the chief enemy of Christ.[5] It serves as a guide concerning the future. It discloses the pattern of the Second Coming and how to prepare for it (Acts 1:11; 3 Nephi 1–11). It brings the Spirit of the Lord into the lives of those who study it. "There is a power in the [Book of Mormon] which will begin to flow into your lives the moment you begin a serious study of the book," President Benson testified, "You will find greater power to resist temptation. You will find the power to avoid deception. You will find the power to stay on the strait and narrow path. . . . When you begin to hunger and thirst after those words, you will find life in greater and greater abundance."[6]

Years ago, Elder Marion G. Romney of the Quorum of the Twelve (later of the First Presidency) promised the following, based on his experience: "I feel certain that if, in our homes, parents will read from the Book of Mormon prayerfully and regularly, both by themselves and with their children, the spirit of that great book will come to permeate our homes and all who dwell therein. The spirit of reverence will increase, mutual respect and consideration for each other will grow. The spirit of contention will depart. Parents will counsel their children in greater love and wisdom. Children will be more responsive and submissive to the counsel of their parents. Righteousness will increase. Faith, hope, and charity—the pure love of Christ—will abound in our homes and lives, bringing in their wake peace, joy, and happiness."[7]

This commentary is written to help us as families and individual students of the Book of Mormon study this great volume of scripture in a personal fashion, suggesting ways its messages can be likened to our own circumstances. Other excellent commentaries exist; this one is not a replacement for them. Rather, it emphasizes applying the Book of Mormon to our lives as individuals and families in this age just before the Second Coming. It also combines the best interpretive information from many sources—including matters doctrinal, historical, geographical, and linguistic—in a simplified manner to help each of us make the most of our time with the Book of Mormon.

Some might ask, "Do we need another study guide for the Book of Mormon?" We would answer yes! We can never do too much with the Book of Mormon. President Benson reminded us of this when he stated, "The Book of Mormon is studied in our Sunday School and seminary classes every fourth year. This four-year pattern, however, must *not* be followed by Church members in their personal and family study. We need to read daily from the pages of the book that will get a man 'nearer to God by abiding by its precepts, than by any other book.' (*History of the Church*, 4:461.)"[8]

In the early days of the Church in this dispensation, missionaries returning home were reproved by the Lord because they had treated lightly the Book of Mormon. As a result, their minds and spirits became darkened. This slight to the Book of Mormon brought the whole Church under condemnation. "And," said the Lord, "they shall remain under this condemnation until they repent and remember the new covenant, even the Book of Mormon" (D&C 84:57). Years ago, President Benson asked, "Are we still under that condemnation?"[9] All of us may answer for ourselves. Each one must do all we are capable of doing to bring the Book of Mormon to the attention of the world. We have prepared this commentary not only to help us to remember "the new covenant" but to learn its teachings and live them.

OPENING PAGES OF THE BOOK OF MORMON

TITLE PAGE

The Prophet Joseph Smith said the title page of the Book of Mormon is a literal translation of the last leaf of the plates written by Moroni.[1] It is really a synopsis of the book and Moroni's final testimony.

In Joseph Smith's day, the question of writing on metal plates was huge—a claim thought by some to disprove the book's ancient provenance. Not anymore! Examples of inscribed metal plates in museums and libraries from Europe to Asia number literally in the hundreds. The languages on these plates range from Akkadian (dating to around 2450 B.C.) to comparatively recent ancient languages like Greek and Latin. Several examples of engraved plates have also been discovered in Central and South America.[2] One of the most interesting recently discovered instances of inscribed metal plates is housed in the Bulgarian National Museum of History in Sofia, Bulgaria. It is an ancient book, comprising six pages composed of almost 24-karat gold, bound together by gold rings. The language on the plates is Etruscan, and the book was prepared about the time Lehi and his family left Jerusalem. It generally fits the description of the Book of Mormon plates given by Joseph Smith in his letter to John Wentworth: "These records were engraven on plates which had the appearance of gold, each plate was six inches wide and eight inches long, and not quite so thick as common tin. They were filled with engravings, in Egyptian characters, and bound together in a volume as the leaves of a book, with three rings running through the whole. The volume was something near six inches in thickness, a part of which was sealed. The characters on the unsealed part were small, and beautifully engraved. The whole book exhibited many marks of antiquity in its construction, and much skill in the art of engraving."[3]

The title page makes clear that the Book of Mormon is a *gift* of God and an interpretation of sacred events—not merely a translation. We do not know exactly how Joseph Smith's work of translation proceeded. All of the witnesses to the process thought that the Prophet somehow saw words and dictated them to his scribes. The witnesses are also unanimous that Joseph did not have any helps or prompts with him during the translation process—no books or manuscripts or papers. Emma Smith, who acted as scribe for a short time, insisted Joseph had no text with him during the work of translation. And there was no great secrecy, pretense, or flowery display of spiritual power exhibited during the period of translation. "The plates," said Emma, "often lay on the table without any attempt at concealment, wrapped in a small linen table cloth, which I had given him to fold them in."[4] Truly, the translation was by the gift and power of God, as the title page indicates, through the efforts of a humble man called to be a prophet.

David Whitmer repeatedly asserted that the work of translation took place in full view of Joseph Smith's family and associates. The sometimes-repeated description of a curtain hanging between Joseph and his scribe (also represented in some illustrations of the story of the Book of Mormon) is based on a misunderstanding. There was a curtain, at least in the later stages of translation. However, it was not suspended between translator and scribe but hung close to the front door of the Peter Whitmer home to prevent curious onlookers and visitors from interfering with the work of translation.[5]

At least five purposes of the book are summarized by Moroni on the title page:

- To show unto the remnant of the house of Israel

what great things the Lord has done for them
through their fathers
- To teach the remnant of the house of Israel the covenants of the Lord
- To show the house of Israel that they are not cast
off forever
- To convince Jew and Gentile that Jesus is the Christ,
the eternal God
- To convince Jew and Gentile that Jesus manifests
himself to all nations

In our day, President Ezra Taft Benson emphasized that
"the Book of Mormon was designed by Deity to bring men to
Christ and to His church."[6] We who live in these last days are
part of the remnant of the house of Israel of whom Moroni
spoke (D&C 86:8–9; Abraham 2:9–11).

Moroni also emphasized that the Book of Mormon is an
abridgment of other records. The following chart may help to
show how our current Book of Mormon is related to the various groups of plates spoken of in the record and in historical
sources.

THE TESTIMONY OF THREE WITNESSES AND THE TESTIMONY OF EIGHT WITNESSES

Included in the front matter of the Book of Mormon are
The Testimony of Three Witnesses and The Testimony of
Eight Witnesses. Doctrine and Covenants 17 is a revelation
given to the Three Witnesses prior to their viewing the engraved plates that contained the Book of Mormon record.[7]
These witnesses were foreknown anciently (Ether 5:2–4;
2 Nephi 11:3; 27:12). The Lord emphasized that it was by
their faith and the power of God that the witnesses would
obtain a view of the plates, and he charged them to testify of
the things they would see. Also noteworthy, evident from the

ORIGINS OF THE BOOK OF MORMON

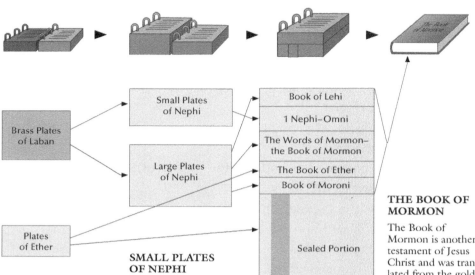

SMALL PLATES OF NEPHI

A religious record kept by Nephi and his people while in the promised land. Contains the teachings of the Nephite prophets and leaders and writings of Isaiah preserved and taught by Nephi.

LARGE PLATES OF NEPHI

A historical record kept by Nephi while in the promised land. Mostly a genealogical record with information about wars and contentions and Nephite leadership. The book of Lehi constituted the 116 pages of the translated record lost by Martin Harris.

BRASS PLATES OF LABAN

Retrieved by the sons of Lehi from Jerusalem. Lehi and his family carried the plates with them to the promised land in order to preserve the language and genealogy of their fathers for their children, to have a record of the books of Moses, and to preserve the words spoken by the prophets to the time of Jeremiah (1 Nephi 3:19-30; 5:11-16).

PLATES OF ETHER

Plates found by Nephites while in the promised land. Contain a record of the Jaredites, who came to the promised land from the Tower of Babel at the time the languages were confounded.

SEALED PORTION OF THE PLATES

The sealed portion, approximately two-thirds of the records received by Joseph Smith, includes the vision of the world, from beginning to end, by the brother of Jared. He received this vision before coming to the promised land and was commanded by the Lord (whom the brother of Jared saw) to write the things he witnessed but to seal them up because another prophet, John, would behold the same vision and would write it for the world (1 Nephi 14:18-27; Ether 3:19-28).

THE BOOK OF MORMON

The Book of Mormon is another testament of Jesus Christ and was translated from the gold plates by Joseph Smith Jr. It was published in 1830, only a short time before The Church of Jesus Christ of Latter-day Saints was organized under the direction of the Lord. The plates given to Joseph Smith consisted of the large and small plates of Nephi, the book of Ether, and the sealed portion. The Prophet was commanded not to open or translate the sealed portion at that time. He was able to translate the Book of Mormon by the gift and power of God through the use of the Urim and Thummim.

names of the Eight Witnesses, is that the restoration of the gospel rested on the shoulders of a few righteous families, which was also true of the establishment of the Church of Jesus Christ in the Savior's day.

THE FIRST BOOK OF NEPHI

The First Book of Nephi relates the ministry of Nephi from his family's departure out of the land of Jerusalem to their arrival in the promised land. The first part of his journal-history is a synopsis of his father's record: "I make an abridgment of the record of my father, upon plates which I have made with mine own hands; wherefore, after I have abridged the record of my father then will I make an account of mine own life" (1 Nephi 1:17). His own account begins in chapter 10. Nephi shows us how important journal-keeping really is.

Twenty years before the Book of Mormon begins, the kingdom of Judah was experiencing its last period of greatness. The Assyrian Empire was rapidly disintegrating, and the righteous King Josiah expanded the political borders of Judah, instigated rigorous religious reforms, and established relative peace. Josiah's life ended tragically at Megiddo, where he had gone at the head of his armies to attempt to stop the Egyptian advance under Pharaoh Nechoh II toward the Euphrates. Nechoh wanted to support the last Assyrian king in a stand against the new Babylonian Empire, and after Josiah's death pharaoh flexed his military muscle to control all of Judah's political life. That situation lasted for about four years, until the Babylonian invasions began. Josiah's death marked the beginning of the end for the kingdom of Judah (2 Kings 22–23).

Josiah's son Jehoahaz was made king after his father's death in 609 B.C., but Pharaoh Nechoh took him away to

Egypt and put his brother Eliakim on the throne. Eliakim's name was changed to Jehoiakim.

Jehoiakim reigned for eleven years, until 598 B.C., after which Nebuchadnezzar bound him and carried him away to Babylon along with thousands of others, including Ezekiel. Jehoiakim's son Jehoiachin was allowed to rule as a vassal or puppet king of the Babylonians. He reigned only three months, and then Nebuchadnezzar summoned him to Babylon along with "ten thousand captives, and all the craftsmen and smiths" (2 Kings 24:14). His uncle Mattaniah, whose name was changed to Zedekiah, began to reign. Book of Mormon history begins in the first year of Zedekiah's reign, which, according to Bible chronology, was 598 or 597 B.C. The Book of Mormon designates the year of its beginning, and the first year of Zedekiah's reign, as six hundred years before the coming of Christ into the world.

Lehi and his family were living *at* Jerusalem (1 Nephi 1:4, 7; 2 Nephi 25:6). The preposition *at* in this case could mean in, within, close by, or near. Lehi could have lived several miles away and still lived at Jerusalem. It is recorded at least thirty-three times throughout the Book of Mormon that Lehi and Nephi went out from "the *land* of Jerusalem." Any satellite towns or villages that surrounded larger population or political centers were regarded in ancient times as belonging to those larger centers. That Lehi and his family lived outside of Jerusalem proper is also evidenced in the account of the sons' attempt to obtain the plates with their abandoned wealth: "We went down to the land of our inheritance, and we did gather together our gold, and our silver, and our precious things. And after we gathered these things together, we went up again unto the house of Laban" (1 Nephi 3:22–23).

1 Nephi 1:1–3

Nephi began his record with a note about his goodly parents. The adjective *goodly* may mean distinguished, esteemed, or respected—an allusion to both moral and spiritual status.

These days we might consider using the term *awesome*. Nephi gave particular credit to his father, from whom he had received a proper education and learned of the goodness and mysteries of God. Generations of writers following Nephi bore similar testimony of the valuable instruction of their fathers. For example, the first sentence inscribed on the plates by Enos was a eulogy of his father, Jacob, for having planted some seeds of eternal consequence deep in his heart: "I, Enos, knowing my father that he was a just man—for he taught me in his language, and also in the nurture and admonition of the Lord" (Enos 1:1). The revered King Benjamin caused his three sons to be "taught in all the language of his fathers, that thereby they might become men of understanding; and that they might know concerning the prophecies" (Mosiah 1:2). It appears to be a characteristic of goodly parents to spend significant time and energy teaching their children the things of God. In promising great blessings to Abraham, the father of hundreds of millions, the Lord said that "Abraham shall surely become a great and mighty nation. . . . For I know him, that he will command his children and his household after him, and they shall keep the way of the Lord, to do justice and judgment; that the Lord may bring upon Abraham that which he hath spoken of him" (Genesis 18:18–19).

All of these Book of Mormon passages refer to the *language* of the fathers. Language facility, the ability to communicate with others, is the life-breath of any civilization. We see its importance as Lehi's sons were required to make a lengthy trek to secure some metal plates, which would ensure their emigrant colony some cultural stability and continuity. Lehi's sons were taught in the learning of the Jews and the language of the Egyptians. The sons had likely been educated in Hebrew and Aramaic grammar and vocabulary (Aramaic being the language of diplomacy and commerce at the time), but it appears that they had learned to express their thoughts in written form in Egyptian characters. Lehi had been "taught in the language of the Egyptians therefore he could read [the brass plates'] engravings, and teach them to his children" (Mosiah 1:4). Perhaps Lehi mastered the Egyptian language, as Joseph and Moses before him. There appears to have been considerable commercial and cultural interchange between Judah and Egypt in the late 7th century B.C. Archaeological excavations show great Egyptian influence in this period, rising out of that nation's rule over the land of Judah for some years prior to the opening of the Book of Mormon record. Egyptian soldiers, merchants, and travelers were present and active during that period.

Nephi said that he had seen many afflictions during his growing-up years, but also he had been "highly favored," or highly blessed. Blessings and afflictions are part of a normal mortal life. Couldn't all of the noble and great ones start out their life's record with those same observations? Couldn't Abraham, Moses, Isaiah, Peter, Paul, and Joseph Smith have summarized their life with the words—"having seen many afflictions in the course of my days"? Perhaps some of us could summarize our lives the same way. This is not a bad thing, for it means the Lord is working in our lives. He thinks enough of us to send us refining experiences.

1 Nephi 1:4

Nephi wrote that "there came many prophets, prophesying unto the people that they must repent, or the great city Jerusalem must be destroyed." Amos taught that the Lord God would do nothing "but he revealeth his secret unto his servants the prophets" (Amos 3:7). The Lord always gives sufficient warning; "never hath any of them been destroyed save it were foretold them by the prophets of the Lord" (2 Nephi 25:9). For such a dramatic and devastating destruction as was coming, the cast of prophets was indeed, as the Book of Mormon says, "many." Lehi, Jeremiah, Huldah, Zephaniah, Habukkuk, Ezekiel, and one Urijah of Kirjath-jearim (Jeremiah 26:20) were all contemporaries.

"And the Lord God of their fathers sent to them by his

messengers, rising up betimes, and sending; because he had compassion on his people, and on his dwelling place: but they mocked the messengers of God, and despised his words, and misused his prophets, until the wrath of the Lord arose against his people, till there was no remedy" (2 Chronicles 36:15–16).

1 Nephi 1:5–20

The Book of Mormon begins with the story of a family and a people in crisis. While Lehi was out teaching in the city, he prayed earnestly in behalf of his family and his people. As he prayed he saw and was taught many things through a spiritual manifestation that caused his whole body to tremble. He was physically exhausted by the spiritual work (see also 1 Nephi 17:47; 19:20; Alma 27:16–18; Daniel 8:27; Moses 1:10; Joseph Smith–History 1:20); he cast himself upon his bed and was overcome by the Spirit. He saw a heavenly court full of brilliant beings. One of them handed Lehi a book with the judgment to be passed upon Jerusalem: death, destruction, and deportation to Babylon. This represents Lehi's call to be a prophet; his experience parallels that of others, including Ezekiel (Ezekiel 1:1), Alma (Alma 36:22), and Joseph Smith (D&C 137:1).

Lehi was to the people of his day what Joseph Smith is to our day. As with other prophets, Lehi then went forth to boldly declare what he had seen and heard. He detailed for Jerusalem's citizens a lengthy catalog of their sins; the result was mockery, anger, and violence. That the city of Jerusalem was doomed to destruction could not have been such shocking news to the Jews, as other prophets had issued the same warning. Jeremiah had been sounding that warning for nearly three decades already. What could be so difficult about believing that people would be taken captive to Babylon when thousands had already been taken? Surely someone would now be ready to listen! But people do not like to hear about their sins, especially when they are enjoying them and have no inclination to change. Lehi's hearers wanted to remove his antagonizing, grating voice.

Another significant witness Lehi bore to his Jerusalem audience was of the coming of a Messiah, for "none of the prophets have written, nor prophesied, save they have spoken concerning this Christ" (Jacob 7:11; see also 3 Nephi 20:24). John later exclaimed that "the testimony of Jesus is the spirit of prophecy" (Revelation 19:10); that is, testifying of Jesus is the essence of prophecy. Even six hundred years before he would come in the flesh, the people needed to know to whom they should look for a remission of their sins. Lehi was a special witness of Jesus Christ.

1 Nephi 1:6

During Lehi's first vision there came a "pillar of fire and dwelt upon a rock," and he "saw and heard much" (so did Joseph Smith; see Joseph Smith–History 1:20, 41, 54). The pillar of fire "dwelt upon" a rock—the Hebrew verb *shakhan* means to be situated or rest upon (compare Deuteronomy 33:16, "dwelt in the bush"). Another form of the word is *Shekhinah*, which refers to the divine Presence. The pillar of fire was actually the presence and glory of the Lord. Joseph Smith also saw a pillar of fire, or "a pillar of light" (Joseph Smith–History 1:16).[1]

1 Nephi 1:8–11

Nephi reported in idiomatic terms that his father, Lehi, saw God sitting upon his throne. ("He thought he saw" means "it seemed to him that . . ."; compare "methought" in 1 Nephi 8:4 and Alma 36:22.) Others have also envisioned the throne room of Deity (Isaiah 6:1–4; Revelation 4:1–4; D&C 76:20–21). Lehi's vision included a book. The same happened later to John the Beloved (Revelation 10:9) and to Joseph Smith (Joseph Smith–History 1:30–34). The book from which Lehi was instructed to read contained scenes of the future of God's people, including judgments to be poured out on Jerusalem.

1 Nephi 1:15

"His whole heart was filled"—in many cultures, ancient and modern, the heart has been considered the center of emotion and affection, and figurative language has centered around the feelings of the heart. Lehi's heart being full is an idiomatic expression for his whole being swelling with deep sentiment of praising and rejoicing.

1 Nephi 1:20

This verse provides comforting assurance to all those who earnestly seek true discipleship: "The tender mercies of the Lord are over all those whom he hath chosen, because of their faith, to make them mighty." The Lord is merciful to the chosen—that is, to those who choose him—to deliver them from whatever challenges they will encounter; faith brings power to be delivered from any negative influence bearing down on us.

1 Nephi 2:1–3

Lehi was faithful in fulfilling his calling to teach of the Messiah and call his people to repentance. They wanted to kill him because of his teachings. Objections to true teachings are usually a cover-up for not wanting to abandon sins.

The Lord warned Lehi in a dream to take his family and depart into the wilderness. Why Lehi? What qualified this citizen of the kingdom of Judah, a descendant of Manasseh, to lead a colony of Israelites through the wilderness to a new promised land? Lehi understood and could guide a diverse society. Members of tribes other than Judah had taken up residence in the land of Jerusalem years before. First Chronicles 9:3 notes, "In Jerusalem dwelt of the children of Judah, and of the children of Benjamin, and of the children of Ephraim, and Manasseh." Lehi, Laban, and Ishmael were all from the tribes of Joseph.

The scriptural record contains hints that Lehi was wealthy (1 Nephi 2:4; 3:16, 22). The Mediterranean world was alive with mercantile activity in this period of time, with Syria and Canaan serving as a hub of sea and land commerce at the place where continents and cultures came together. Caravans traversed Judah from all directions: side roads off the coastal highway and the King's Highway; the distant Frankincense Trail; pilgrims' highways and trade routes connecting Moab, Edom, and Arabia with Gaza and Egypt. Lehi could have been a trained and experienced caravaneer and trader. He knew what provisions to prepare and what route to take. Knowing how God has worked in other periods of history, we believe it is not unlikely that he selected a man who, in addition to his spiritual maturity and responsiveness, was already adapted to the particular task at hand, in this case desert travel and survival. He was the right man for the right time.[2]

1 Nephi 2:4–5

Lehi and his family abandoned all unnecessary possessions and gathered together appropriate provisions for an indefinite period of travel in the desert. Besides the tents especially mentioned, they would need food, emergency water, extra clothing, bedding, cooking equipment and eating utensils, weapons, and pack animals, probably camels.

Lehi and some family members were willing to live the law of sacrifice, as outlined in *Lectures on Faith:* "A religion that does not require the sacrifice of all things never has power sufficient to produce the faith necessary unto life and salvation. . . . The faith necessary unto the enjoyment of life and salvation never could be obtained without the sacrifice of all earthly things."[3]

The word *wilderness* occurs more than three hundred times in the Book of Mormon and may at some later time in the Western Hemisphere refer to the thick forests or jungle, but it does not mean lush vegetation in reference to Judah and its neighboring deserts. Two Hebrew terms for wilderness are *midbar* and *jeshimon*. *Midbar* is generally land to the east of the central hills, east of the agricultural fields, out into the rain shadow, with a sparce vegetation. These are tracts for pasturing flocks. *Jeshimon* is the desolate wasteland beyond, where little rain falls. The Judean desert through which Lehi and his family journeyed is at first *midbar* and then *jeshimon*. It is known scripturally as a place of flight and refuge. It is a frightening place for the uninitiated.

In recent years, researchers have ventured to describe the route Lehi and his family took from Jerusalem to the Red Sea. Gospel scholar Sidney B. Sperry wrote as follows: "As for a route to the Red Sea, they had two choices: they could go either directly south of Jerusalem by the road through Hebron and Beersheba and thence through the great wilderness to the northern tip of what is now the gulf of Aqaba, or they could go directly east across the Jordan until they struck the ancient 'King's Highway' and then proceed south, or nearly so, until the Gulf of Aqaba was reached. Lehi probably used the western route."[4] Lynn and Hope Hilton expanded the possibilities to three: (1) eastward from Jerusalem through the Judean wilderness to the plateau on the eastern side of the Rift Valley to the King's Highway; (2) southward from Jerusalem, past Hebron and Beersheba, and then eastward to join the Rift Valley, called the Arabah; or (3) straight east to the northern end of the Dead Sea, past Qumran, En Gedi, Masada, and on south to the Red Sea.

The Hiltons considered the first option, the King's Highway, unlikely because of passage through foreign lands with border complications, taxes, and so on. They also saw the second option as improbable because the route remains in the hill country, near population centers, instead of entering the wilderness as the account says. The Hiltons, therefore, concluded that the third option was the likely route.[5]

Based on our personal experience of walking from Jerusalem to the Red Sea, it seems unlikely to us that Lehi's family would have used the King's Highway or that they

Possible route of Lehi's journey.

would have journeyed straight southward through populated centers, such as Hebron and Beersheba. The account specifically points to immediate entry into the wilderness. The Hiltons' preferred route (east to the area of Qumran and then south) is also unlikely, however, as the fault escarpment of the Rift Valley drops down dramatically to the waters of the Dead Sea and allows no passage to the south. There was no evidence of a road along the northwestern shore of the Dead Sea before the Israelis cut and paved one in 1967.

19

We believe that a more likely course for Lehi's journey is southeast out of Jerusalem toward Tekoa and then along an ancient road to En Gedi (called the cliff or ascent of Ziz in 2 Chronicles 20:16), and thence southward through the Rift Valley and Arabah. An alternate route could have been from Tekoa southward, passing between the villages of Juttah and Carmel, down into and across the eastern Negev eastward to the Arabah.

1 Nephi 2:6

Having arrived at the shores of the Red Sea, Lehi and his party decided to continue on for another three days, after which they established camp "in a valley by the side of a river of water." The phrase "river of water" seems redundant to western ears, since we are accustomed to thinking of rivers as consisting only of water. In the Near East, however, most rivers are not perennial but contain water only in the rainy season, for relatively few days of the year. Usually such a riverbed is dry and sandy and quite passable for travel. If Lehi's family pitched their tents near a flowing stream, that may tell us something about what time of year it was; perhaps it was spring, the time of winter runoff.

1 Nephi 2:7–9

Lehi, along with all other prophets, held the Melchizedek Priesthood.[6] Lehi's family had no Levitical or Aaronic Priesthood holders among them. Such priesthood functions as offering sacrifices (Hebrew *corban*), though usually executed under the direction of Aaronic or Levitical Priesthood in biblical times, could also be carried out by those who held the higher priesthood, which comprehends all lower powers (D&C 107:8). Lehi was authorized to perform sacrifices by virtue of the Melchizedek Priesthood he held.

Lehi built an altar of stones to make an offering and give thanks. It was an altar of unhewn stones as stipulated in Exodus 20:25. The wording is intentional, again showing the

Book of Mormon to be translated from an ancient Semitic record. It was not a "stone altar," which might allow for cut, fitted stones, but an "altar of stones."

Lehi then began naming various geographical features around the camp. All hills, rock outcroppings, valleys, and other topographical details were and are given names in the Near East. The ancient Hebrew people loved imagery and figures of speech. The most powerful way to illustrate a truth was to find something in the human experience or conduct that corresponded to something in nature. If only Laman could be like this temporary river, or even better, like a perennial river, continuously flowing toward the source of righteousness! Many parents have wished that blessing for children experiencing difficulties. Likewise, the prophet Amos pleaded with northern Israelites to "let judgment run down as waters, and righteousness as a mighty [or everflowing] stream" (Amos 5:24). The two prophets wished that their people would be more constant and stable in their devotion and loyalty to God and his purposes.

1 Nephi 2:10

Three of our favorite words in the Book of Mormon are *firm, steadfast,* and *immovable.* On 31 May 1994, hurricane-force winds swept through Utah's Wasatch Front with destructive results, especially in Provo. Brigham Young University equipment clocked the winds at 121 miles per hour. Though only five minutes in duration, the winds ripped apart or felled upwards of five thousand trees. Provo City announced within a few days that the total loss approached $9 million. One house had four very tall pine trees lying flat in the yard and out into the street, with huge but shallow root systems exposed. There's the gospel lesson: it is not enough to grow tall and broad and beautiful. Shallowness is perilous. We must sink *deep roots* and be solidly planted to withstand the storms of life; be firm, steadfast, and immovable—enduring, solid, and stable.

1 Nephi 2:11–24

These verses give us insights into the character of Lehi's four sons. Laman and Lemuel are portrayed as stubborn, hard-hearted, lovers of money, faithless, and spiritually weak. Nephi and Sam, on the other hand, are humble seekers of knowledge and of God, faithful, and obedient to parents. The latter two sons are exemplary, deserving of being emulated, which, since we all need role models, is one of the main purposes for the painstaking engraving of the metal plates—to preserve for us in modern times some examples or patterns for our lives. President Heber J. Grant wrote: "I read the Book of Mormon as a young man and fell in love with Nephi more than with any other character in [secular] or sacred history that I have ever read of, except the Savior of the world. No other individual has made such a strong impression upon me as did Nephi. He has been one of the guiding stars of my life."[7]

Consider the four brothers. The marvel is not that some complained about the hardships in leaving all and journeying into the wilderness but that others did not! Conditions were such that *anyone* could have murmured. *Murmuring* may be defined as half-suppressed or muttered complaint, grumbling behind the scenes rather than being openly critical, or disloyal.

What was the reason for Nephi's amazing ability to press forward positively and not join in the grumbling and rebellion? Nephi wanted to know the things of God; he prayed, and the Lord visited him and softened his heart—which suggests the possibility that his heart was somewhat hard before.

God raises up the young, those malleable and teachable, not set in their ways, to accomplish tasks that will confound the wise—allowing the "weak things of the world" to "break down the mighty and strong ones" (D&C 1:19).

Faith and faithfulness are always rewarded. Nephi and all the others were called upon to make a great sacrifice, to leave

behind practically all they had known; but the Lord promised that they would eventually possess more and greater
blessings. We of modern times struggle with that principle
also. One of the most dangerous problems we face is wanting immediate gratification. Few people, it seems, believe in
postponement—if we want something, we want it now. Adam
and Eve sacrificed a pleasant existence in the Garden of Eden
for something ultimately and infinitely better, though immediately harder. Moses sacrificed prestige in a kingly court for
the noble task of suffering the sands and complaints of Sinai.
Elijah, Amos, Isaiah, Jeremiah, and all the other prophets sacrificed comfort and security to fulfill a difficult duty with eternal rewards.

In the Lord's economy, whenever we give up something
or go without, we find ourselves in eventual possession of
more and *greater*. During the tests of his faithfulness, Job lost
almost everything he had; his story concludes, however, with
a simple note that he was blessed in the end with more than
he had in the beginning. Lehi's family sacrificed their possessions, their riches, to follow the old patriarch into the great
Arabian desert and over the sea; but after their journey, they
possessed a land of amazingly abundant wealth. The promises
of the Lord to Lehi and to Nephi, as with our own patriarchal
blessings, must have encouraged and sustained them through
the sometimes bitter trials they had to endure along the way.

As Lehi and his family traveled through the Rift Valley
and near the Red Sea, perhaps they were inspired by the
example of the prophet-hero Moses, who led their ancestors
through some of the same terrain to their promised land.
Lehi's wilderness journeys were shorter in time but greater in
distance.

1 Nephi 2:24

Because God is a personal God, tailor-made pains, hardships, trials, obstacles, or adversities may come into our lives
to stir us up to remember God. See also Helaman 12:1–3.

1 Nephi 3:1–6

The Lord commanded Lehi in a dream to send his sons back to Jerusalem for the plates of brass, then in the possession of an elder of the Jews named Laban. Lehi and his family did not have their own copy of the scriptures—roughly equivalent to our Old Testament—and Lehi did not want his children growing up without them, so the brothers had to go back.

Those plates were of such importance that the prophet was willing to risk all of his sons' lives to obtain them. There's a lesson on the significance of scripture study: the Lamanites continued without prophets and without scripture, and their society rapidly deteriorated.

We might ask, why did the Lord wait until they were more than two hundred miles away from home to command Lehi to get the plates? Could not arrangements have been made for them before the family left Jerusalem? One more test! The older brothers immediately protested. We may suppose that their foremost reason for not wanting to go was their fear of Laban; but there is no doubt that the distance and topography also had some bearing on their resistance. The Book of Mormon itself and most Book of Mormon commentaries say little, if anything, about the distance and terrain involved.

We have learned by walking it that the distance between Jerusalem and the Red Sea is two hundred miles. An agreeable pace for a group of people on camels would be between twenty and thirty miles a day. So the journey was a minimum of seven or eight days. Add to that the three days they traveled after reaching the Red Sea, and the figures are up to 260 to 290 miles in ten or eleven days. That is one direction only. The round trip that the Lord and father Lehi were asking of the four sons was more than 500 miles and at least three weeks through some of the most rugged terrain in the Near East. And they had no idea how they were going to obtain the plates. Having the advantage of "knowing the end from the beginning," we are amazed to think ahead and realize that Lehi, soon after his sons returned from their first assignment, would command them to go back again. That is over a thousand miles and many weeks on those desolate tracts of land—and we have often looked down on Laman and Lemuel for being chronic complainers.

1 Nephi 3:2

In the early chapters of the Book of Mormon we are introduced to fascinating linguistic phenomena arising out of the Hebrew language and culture from which the record came. These expressions are called Hebraisms, sets of words or phrases that appear in English but with Hebrew-like construction. The small plates of Nephi especially, written mostly by Nephi and Jacob, who knew Hebrew, would understandably feature many examples of Hebraisms.

One of the most common Hebraisms is the cognate accusative, in which Hebrew verbs and their related nouns are used in the same phrase, something writers try to avoid in English. Old Testament examples with which these migrating Israelites would be familiar are "bloom blossoms" (Numbers 17:8); "sacrificed sacrifices" (1 Samuel 11:15); "divine divinations" (Ezekiel 13:23); and "preach the preaching" (Jonah 3:2).

Book of Mormon examples include "curse . . . with a curse" (1 Nephi 2:23); "dreamed a dream" (1 Nephi 3:2); "yoketh . . . with a yoke" (1 Nephi 13:5); "work a . . . work" (1 Nephi 14:7); "write the writing" (2 Nephi 3:18); "build buildings" (2 Nephi 5:15); "desire which I desired" (Enos 1:13); "taxed with a tax" (Mosiah 7:15); "peopled with a people" (Mosiah 8:8); "judge . . . judgments" (Mosiah 29:43); "warred a . . . warfare" (Alma 1:1); "number . . . not numbered" (Alma 3:1); "sing the song" (Alma 5:26); and "die a . . . death" (Alma 12:16).

These and many other examples corroborate the fact that

the Book of Mormon originated from ancient Semitic cultures and languages.

1 Nephi 3:3

The Book of Mormon continually refers to the "plates of brass," whereas in English they would be called the "brass plates." In 1 Nephi 8:19 we learn about the "rod of iron," what we would normally call the "iron rod." This particular manner of expression, called the construct state, utilizes two nouns. There are many interesting examples: "mists of darkness" (1 Nephi 12:17); "works of darkness" (2 Nephi 25:2); "words of plainness" (Jacob 4:14); "words of soberness" (Jacob 6:5); "plates of ore" (Mosiah 21:27); "ornaments of gold" (Alma 31:28); "houses of cement" (Helaman 3:7); and "plans of wickedness" (Ether 13:15).

1 Nephi 3:7–8

Having already worked things out with the Lord, Nephi responded positively to the Lord's command. In one of the most inspiring outpourings of faith in all of scripture, Nephi assured his father that he would go and do the things the Lord had commanded because he knew that the Lord never gives a command without providing some way to fulfill it. A believing attitude is a characteristic of every great soul. "As the Lord liveth, and as we live, we will not go down unto our father in the wilderness until we have accomplished the thing which the Lord hath commanded us" (1 Nephi 3:15).

1 Nephi 3:9–31

The brothers set out with their tents to go *up* to the land of Jerusalem. Approaching Jerusalem from any direction requires an ascent in elevation. All the locative adverbs (the "downs" and "ups") in the next pages of scripture accurately depict the topography of Judah and the deserts to the south.

After Laman's attempt to talk Laban out of the plates, the brothers agreed to go *down* to the land of their inheritance (which suggests that their holdings were outside the city proper), gather the gold, silver, and other valuable objects they had left behind, and offer them to Laban in exchange for the plates. They went *up* again to Laban's house in Jerusalem, and upon their failure to secure the plates by that means, they fled for their lives and hid in a cave, or "cavity of a rock." Caves are numerous in the Judean hills and desert.

Having exhausted their resources and their patience, Laman and Lemuel had some hard words for their younger brothers. They resorted to physical violence and even questioned the Lord's ability to resolve the situation, until stopped by an angel. The angel again commanded them to go up and get the plates, saying that the Lord would deliver Laban into their hands. After all human effort was expended, the Lord himself would help them accomplish the task. This is a life-lesson for each of us.

1 Nephi 3:29–30

The witness of the Spirit is more powerful and indelible than seeing a messenger from heaven, a truth poignantly illustrated by President Wilford Woodruff:

"One of the Apostles said to me years ago, 'Brother Woodruff, I have prayed for a long time for the Lord to send me the administration of an angel. I have had a great desire for this, but I have never had my prayers answered.' I said to him that if he were to pray a thousand years to the God of Israel for that gift, it would not be granted, unless the Lord had a motive in sending an angel to him. I told him that the Lord never did nor never will send an angel to anybody merely to gratify the desire of the individual to see an angel. If the Lord sends an angel to anyone, He sends him to perform a work that can be performed only by the administration of an angel.

"Now, I have always said, and I want to say it to you, that the Holy Ghost is what every Saint of God needs. It is far more important that a man should have that gift than he should have the ministration of an angel."[8]

ANGELS ARE COMING TO VISIT THE EARTH

The Hebrew word for angels is *malachim,* meaning "messengers." The role of angels is to call men to repentance, to help fulfill the covenants of the Father, and to prepare the way for the Savior by declaring his words to his chosen vessels so they can bear sure testimony of him (Moroni 7:31). Angels sometimes have to speak with the "voice of thunder" (when people are spiritually hard of hearing; see 1 Nephi 17:45; Mosiah 27:11; Alma 36:7). Other times they speak not with a "voice of thunder" or a voice of "great tumultuous noise" but with a "pleasant voice," a "still voice of perfect mildness, as if it had been a whisper . . . [to] pierce even to the very soul" (Helaman 5:46, 30).

During Jesus' mortal life there was frequent contact between him and his heavenly home. Angels announced his birth (Luke 1:26–38; 2:8–15) and his forerunner's birth (Luke 1:11–20); they were present at the Transfiguration (in the form of translated beings; Matthew 17:3; Luke 9:30–31); at least one angel ministered to him in Gethsemane (Luke 22:43); angels attended his sepulcher and bore witness of his glorious resurrection (JST, Matthew 28:2–4; Luke 24:4–7; John 20:11–13); and they appeared at his ascension into heaven (Acts 1:10–11).

Angelic messengers were also involved in the work of God in the Western Hemisphere during Book of Mormon times. Following are examples:

- 1 Nephi 3:29–30. An angel appears to Lehi's sons.
- 1 Nephi 11–14. An angel guides Nephi through a vision of the future.
- 2 Nephi 10:3; Jacob 7:5. Angels teach Jacob.
- Mosiah 3:2–27; 4:1. An angel teaches King Benjamin and testifies of Christ (possibly Abinadi; see commentary at Mosiah 15:1).
- Mosiah 27:11–18. An angel appears to Alma and the four sons of Mosiah.

- Alma 8:14–18. The same angel appears to Alma again.
- Alma 8:20; 10:7. An angel appears to Amulek.
- Alma 13:24–26; 19:34; 39:19. Angels appear and teach many in the land.
- Moroni 7:17. The devil and his angels also appear to some (see also Sherem in Jacob 7:17 and Korihor in Alma 30:53).

Elder Jeffrey R. Holland testified of the role of angels: "I believe we need to speak of and believe in and bear testimony of the ministry of angels more than we sometimes do. They constitute one of God's great methods of witnessing through the veil, and no document in all this world teaches that principle so clearly and so powerfully as does the Book of Mormon."[9]

President Joseph F. Smith taught: "We are told by the Prophet Joseph Smith, that 'there are no angels who minister to this earth but those who do belong or have belonged to it.' Hence, *when messengers are sent to minister to the inhabitants of this earth, they are not strangers, but from the ranks of our kindred, friends, and fellow-beings and fellow-servants.* The ancient prophets who died were those who came to visit their fellow creatures upon the earth. . . . In like manner our fathers and mothers, brothers, sisters and friends who have passed away from this earth, having been faithful, and worthy to enjoy these rights and privileges, may have a mission given them to visit their relatives and friends upon the earth again, bringing from the divine Presence messages of love, of warning, or reproof and instruction, to those whom they had learned to love in the flesh."[10]

---

1 Nephi 4:1–38

One more time they went *up* to Jerusalem. Nephi drew some parallels with Moses. The great deliverer from Egypt was backed up with his people against a wall of water. He had no further human recourse, so the Lord took over. If the Lord could deliver all those Israelites from the pharaoh, He could also deliver these Israelites from Laban. The four approached the walls of Jerusalem at night. Nephi "crept into the city and went forth towards the house of Laban." He had no plan in mind but was led by the Spirit.

Finding Laban lying drunk in the road, Nephi was told by the Spirit to kill him. Hugh Nibley wrote of Laban: "A few deft and telling touches resurrect the pompous Laban with photographic perfection. We learn in passing that he commanded a garrison of fifty, that he met in full ceremonial armor with 'the elders of the Jews' (1 Nephi 4:22) for secret consultations by night, that he had control of a treasury, that he was of the old aristocracy, being a distant relative to Lehi himself, that he probably held his job because of his ancestors, since he hardly received it by merit, that his house was the storing place of very old records, that he was a large man, short-tempered, crafty, and dangerous, and to the bargain cruel, greedy, unscrupulous, weak, and given to drink."[11]

Nephi was repulsed by the idea of slaying Laban. Nevertheless, the Spirit again counseled him: The Lord delivered Laban to Nephi; it was in answer to a prayer; Laban was a thief and a murderer; and there were precedents for the Lord's slaying wicked people to accomplish his righteous purposes (the Flood, the conquest of Canaan, and so on). As Joseph Smith taught, "Whatever God requires is right, no matter what it is, although we may not see the reason thereof till long after the events transpire."[12] It would be better for this one man to die than for an entire (future) nation to dwindle and perish in unbelief, which would happen without those records. Slaying one man to preserve a people seems to have been an ancient oral legal tradition in Judaism because it surfaces again when Jewish leaders were contemplating a rationale for executing Jesus of Nazareth. Said Caiaphas, the high priest, "Ye know nothing at all, nor consider that it is expedient for us, that one man should die for the people, and that the whole nation perish not" (John 11:49–50).

Nephi continued to reason that future generations would

need the commandments on the plates and the Lord had devised this method for Nephi to obtain them. Having reasoned this out, Nephi obeyed the Spirit and carried out the unpleasant job of dispatching Laban into the next world by cutting off his head. He then disguised himself and imitated Laban well enough to convince Laban's servant to open the treasury, get the plates, and follow Nephi outside the walls of the city.

Along the way there was talk about what the elders of the Jews had been discussing that night, possibly including the delicate political turmoil in which they were enveloped. Nephi reassured his frightened brothers that he was not Laban. He also convinced Zoram that he could stay with them and be a free man, and he bound him with an oath to do so. Then the five set out *down* through the wilderness on the long journey back to the main camp.

On the matter of oath-taking and the trust Nephi and others placed in Zoram, an example from modern times is instructive. It comes from W. F. Lynch and his team from the United States Navy who conquered the wilds of the same Rift Valley in the mid-nineteenth century:

"Sometime after the agreement was made, Akil [their Arab guide] returned and expressed a wish to be released. I ascertained that some of his timid followers had been dissuading him, and held him to his obligation. . . . At our former meeting I advanced him money for his expenses and the purchase of provisions, for which he refused to give a receipt or append his seal. . . . I had, therefore, nothing but his word to rely upon, which I well knew he would never break. 'The bar of iron may be broken, but the word of an honest man never,' and there is as much honour beneath the yellow skin of this untutored Arab, as ever swelled the breast of the chivalrous Coeur de Lion. He never dreamed of falsehood."[13]

Nephi and his brothers could trust Zoram because of the sanctity of oaths in those cultures, ancient and modern. In the gospel sense, an oath is a solemn declaration or absolute promise, calling on someone or something considered

31

sacred by the oath-maker (often God) to witness the truth of the declaration or the binding nature of the promise being made. Throughout the ancient world, oaths carried an added measure of sanctity beyond a mere promise. In ancient Israel oaths were regarded as extraordinary promises, binding the oath-maker's very soul: "If a man vow a vow unto the Lord, or swear an oath to bind his soul with a bond; he shall not break his word, he shall do according to all that proceedeth out of his mouth" (Numbers 30:2). We have reason to believe that even among dishonorable persons, oaths were regarded as inviolable. When the daughter of Herodias danced before Herod the tetrarch and his entourage, Herod "promised with an oath to give her whatsoever she would ask" (Matthew 14:7; see also Mark 6:23). She asked for the head of John the Baptist. "And the king was sorry: nevertheless for the oath's sake . . . he commanded it to be given her" (Matthew 14:9).

1 Nephi 4:13

A pair of missionaries in Santiago, Chile, wrote to their president about a woman they were teaching: "She started reading the Book of Mormon, and she got to the part where Nephi killed Laban. She didn't understand how God could command someone to kill another. It bothered her, and she went to bed with that doubt. During the night a bolt of lightning woke her up, and she immediately thought of David and Goliath. She thought that if God could command David to kill Goliath, then why not Nephi? Then, she said, a feeling of peace and tranquility came over her."

1 Nephi 5:1–9

During the long weeks of her sons' absence, Sariah mourned for them, thinking that the worst had probably happened. She complained against her husband (a touch of marital conflict that occurs with even the most righteous couples), telling him that he was a visionary man; they had lost their home, then lost their sons, and were now going to lose their own lives. The normal response to accusation is defense and counteraccusation. Lehi, however, responded to Sariah's complaint with comfort. When people complain, they often need comfort. Lehi's faith was Sariah's comfort. He had been promised that his sons would return, and he believed the promise. When the sons finally returned, Sariah's faith in her prophet-husband was confirmed, and the family rejoiced and gave thanks by offering up burnt offerings; then everyone's attention turned to examining their new treasure, the plates of brass.

Incidentally, the plates could actually be referred to as the plates of *bronze*. Brass is an alloy of zinc (unknown to the ancients) and copper, but bronze is an alloy of copper and tin (both known and used). The centuries before the Israelites arrived in the land of Canaan are known archaeologically as the Bronze Age.

1 Nephi 5:10–22

The plates that Lehi's sons had obtained at the peril of their lives would prove of inestimable value to prophets, historians, and numberless righteous people for a thousand years. The plates of brass were preserved for the Nephites just as the Book of Mormon was preserved for us. Thus Lehi prophesied that "these plates of brass should go forth unto all nations, kindreds, tongues, and people who were of his seed." He further prophesied "that these plates of brass should never perish."

As Lehi's family and Zoram scrutinized the plates in their tent-camp on the shores of the Red Sea, they learned that the plates contained the five books of Moses—presumably Genesis, Exodus, Leviticus, Numbers, and Deuteronomy—including an account of the creation of the world and of Adam and Eve, their family's genealogy (Lehi was a descendant of Joseph, who was a great-grandson of Abraham), a record of the Jews, and the prophecies of the holy prophets from the beginning down to the commencement of the reign of Zedekiah, even prophecies that had been spoken by Jeremiah. Laban also was a descendant of Joseph. Either he or some scribal assistants had been interested in recording two decades of Jeremiah's prophecies.

1 Nephi 6:1–6

We know from later writings that it was not easy to inscribe on metal plates. Yet Nephi worked at it earnestly because his whole intent was to "persuade men to come unto the God of Abraham, and the God of Isaac, and the God of Jacob, and be saved." Nephi followed the example of the great patriarch Abraham, who noted in his own writings, "I shall endeavor to write some of these things upon this record, for the benefit of my posterity that shall come after me" (Abraham 1:31).

1 Nephi 7:1–6

Then Lehi had another revelation: the sons must go back to the land of Jerusalem once again. Yet another test! But the record does not say that they murmured about having to return for their future brides; that was a fairer proposal—bringing marriageable women into the growing colony was apparently worth the aching bones and muscles of an additional long journey.

We might wonder how another family, without direct revelation from the Lord, would be so willing to abandon their home and all they had known to join these refugees in the wilderness. We can only surmise from the record of Nephi that Ishmael believed the words of the Lord that Jerusalem would soon be destroyed by the enemy armies who already occupied the city. Besides, Lehi's sons had quite a story to tell about how an angel had appeared and how the Lord had miraculously made it possible to secure their genealogical and scriptural records. The one reason given in Nephi's account for the family's willingness to go was that "the Lord did soften the heart of Ishmael, and also his household, insomuch that they took their journey with us down into the wilderness."

Our tradition that Ishmael's ancestry went back to Ephraim, son of Joseph, is based on a discourse given by Elder Erastus Snow in Logan, Utah, on 6 May 1882. He said, "The prophet Joseph informed us that the record of Lehi was contained on the 116 pages that were first translated and subsequently stolen, and of which an abridgement is given us in the first Book of Nephi, which is the record of Nephi individually, he himself being of the lineage of Manasseh; but that Ishmael was of the lineage of Ephraim, and that his sons married into Lehi's family, and Lehi's sons married Ishmael's daughters."[14]

From Elder Snow's statement and from 1 Nephi 7:6 we may suppose that two of Ishmael's sons had married daughters of Lehi and Sariah. That would mean the two families were already related by marriage, which might explain Lehi's seeming nonchalance about instructing his sons to bring Ishmael's family down into the wilderness. Those married children of Lehi and Ishmael could already have had some daughters of their own who could later marry Lehi's sons, Jacob and Joseph, born in the wilderness. There might already have been additional marriage plans between the two families—only the setting for the ceremonies would now have to change from the city to the desert. Another reason why Ishmael's family in particular was elected to join Lehi's was that Ishmael had five unmarried daughters; the four sons of Lehi along with Zoram would in time marry Ishmael's daughters—a perfect five-way match set up in advance by the Lord.

1 Nephi 7:4–5

Here is an application for modern missionaries finding a whole family prepared by the Lord: (1) "We went up unto the house of Ishmael," the investigator; (2) "we did gain favor in the sight of Ishmael" by establishing a relationship of trust and confidence; (3) "we did speak unto him the words of the Lord"; (4) "the Lord did soften the heart of Ishmael, and also his household"; and (5) "they took their journey with us"; they were willing to join with them.

1 Nephi 7:6–22

The final journey from Jerusalem to the Red Sea was not without the usual friction, and even open conflict, between Nephi and his elder brothers. Laman and Lemuel again vented their anger on Nephi to the point of physical violence.

Why didn't Laman and Lemuel just get up one morning and make the hike back to Jerusalem? Why their incessant efforts to kill Lehi and Nephi and *then* go back to Jerusalem? Isaiah 53:9 may give us insight by describing why Jesus was crucified: "because he had done no violence [or evil], neither was any deceit in his mouth." Few things can stir up anger in the unrighteous as much as confronting the truth. Laman and Lemuel knew that their father and brother were telling the truth, and they were angry because of it. They were jealous and envious and proud. Some of the Jewish leaders had the same problem with Jesus. Nobody welcomed them into the city by throwing down palm fronds in their path. Nobody was being healed by them. There were no great crowds flocking around them to hang on their every word. Something had to be done about this righteous person who always spoke the truth. They had him crucified. The two oldest sons of Lehi had in their hearts to do likewise: slay their father and brother.

The rebels were finally pacified only by the pleading of some of Ishmael's family. Their hearts were actually softened enough that they bowed down and asked Nephi's forgiveness. The greatness of Nephi's soul is again revealed in his terse summation of the episode: "I did frankly forgive them all that they had done." Even after such rebelliousness, belligerence, rudeness, harshness, and spite, Nephi could frankly forgive. Is not this our own great charge?

The Lord had now warned at least eighteen people to flee

from the wrath to come over Jerusalem: Lehi, Sariah, Laman, Lemuel, Sam, and Nephi; Zoram; Ishmael, his wife, five daughters, and two sons with their wives. We do not know, but there may also have been children from the latter four.

In some ways it must have been a sacrifice for Lehi and his family to leave Jerusalem, but their lives were spared by doing so. What about the other two trips? The main reasons the four men were commanded to trek a thousand miles through the inhospitable desert were (1) records—for knowledge of ancestry and prophecy and (2) marriages—for posterity. What they were doing was tied to the past as well as to the future. They needed to preserve the knowledge and memory of one nation while producing with their wives another, so that the covenants of the Lord might be fulfilled.

1 Nephi 8

Do we, like Lehi, want our family and close friends to partake of God's love? What are we doing every day to help them get to the tree of life? In the first issue of the *Ensign*, President Joseph Fielding Smith asked these provocative questions about our investment in our families: "Do you spend as much time making your family and home successful as you do in pursuing social and professional success? Are you devoting your best creative energy to the most important unit in society—the family? Or is your relationship with your family merely a routine, unrewarding part of life?"[15]

1 Nephi 8:5–8

Lehi saw a man dressed in a white robe, Christ or his representative, who invited Lehi to follow him. The prophet saw himself in a dark and dreary waste; after many hours in darkness, he prayed. When we are in darkness resulting from our pride or that of others, sin, or contention, we, too, must pray. That is what Joseph Smith did: he was in doctrinal darkness and then in the darkness of Satan's personal attack, but after he prayed, the greatest Light came.

1 Nephi 8:9–12

Lehi saw a large and spacious field. Usually in the scriptures the field is the world (see also Matthew 13:38). He saw a tree, whose fruit could make one happy. When he partook, it turned out to be the sweetest thing he had ever tasted, and it filled him with the greatest joy. It was more desirable than any other fruit. We note that Lehi partook first. President Harold B. Lee once said we can't lift another until we ourselves are on higher ground. Lehi then wanted his family also to partake of this fruit that represents the love of God (1 Nephi 11:22). That is the main message of the Book of Mormon: Come unto Christ, be filled with his love, and learn to love others as he does.

1 Nephi 8:13–18

Lehi invited Sariah, Sam, and Nephi to come and partake. Note that the righteous were invited first and their place secured. Lehi then invited Laman and Lemuel, but they refused to come. Imagine the personal pain he felt. Did Lehi fail as a parent? The record is clear that he had taught them and showed them how to live, but they exercised their agency to deny themselves the blessings of righteous living. Nevertheless, as a dedicated father, Lehi refused to give up on them. He continued to minister to them and exhorted them "with all the feeling of a tender parent."

Elder Robert D. Hales taught: "We too must have the faith to teach our children and bid them to keep the commandments. We should not let their choices weaken our faith. Our worthiness will not be measured according to their righteousness. Lehi did not lose the blessing of feasting at the tree of life because Laman and Lemuel refused to partake of its fruit. Sometimes as parents we feel we have failed when our children make mistakes or stray. Parents are never failures when they do their best to love, teach, pray, and care for their children. Their faith, prayers, and efforts will be consecrated to the good of their children."[16]

President Henry B. Eyring observed: "In some cases . . . parents are desperately trying to bring back some in their family who have wandered. I am confident that there will be, increasingly, a reward given by God for their efforts. Those who never give up will find that God never gave up and that He will help them."[17]

1 Nephi 8:19–32

Influences that keep people away from the most desirable fruit are mists of darkness; shame, scorn, embarrassment, mockery, and scoffing; forbidden paths or strange roads; and the fountain of filthy water (see also 1 Nephi 12:16–18).

Influences that encourage people toward the most desirable fruit are the strait and narrow path and the rod of iron to hold onto (see also 1 Nephi 11:25; 15:23–24). Since one cannot necessarily see the tree—the end is *not* in plain sight—faith is required.

1 Nephi 8:23, 32

Mist consists of thousands of tiny water particles that obscure our view and confuse us. Examples of the world's "mists of darkness" and the "strange roads" that many people take include distractions offered by the sports and entertainment worlds; the vile allurements of the pornography producers; the enticements of money and its power to obtain the things of this world; the seductions to satisfy, even in perverse ways, the lusts of the flesh through substance abuse, illicit sexual relations, and so on. The master of evil knows no bounds for deceiving, blinding, covering up, justifying, misguiding, and keeping us—in every way possible—from clearly seeing and pressing forward to the fruit that gives life. The only sure way of holding steady on the path to the tree of life is to hold to the rod. We have been reminded that the iron rod does not pass through the lobby of the great and spacious building.

The iron rod is the word of God, especially the Book of Mormon. By continually holding onto the iron rod—the daily habit not just of reading but of searching, pondering, and treasuring up—our path is made secure. Holding onto the word of God cannot be loose or haphazard but must be a tight grip, a constant grasp.

1 Nephi 8:26

Of this passage one student of the scriptures wrote: "I was reading in 1 Nephi, the part when Nephi received his own vision of the tree of life. . . . Have you ever wondered how the wicked get into the building if it doesn't touch ground? Well, they're *lifted up* in the pride of their hearts," and they have no foundation.

Elder Neal A. Maxwell commented on worldly people mocking the righteous: "The laughter of the world is merely loneliness pathetically trying to reassure itself."[18] Inhabitants of the great and spacious building use some of Lucifer's greatest tools—scorn, mockery, and peer pressure—to defeat the weak (those not thoroughly committed to God's kingdom) who were partaking of the fruit but became ashamed because the world made fun of them. The adversary will use the ways of the world to draw away disciples after him. President Daniel H. Wells presciently stated, "There will come a time, . . . in the history of the Saints, when they will be tried with peace, prosperity, popularity and riches."[19]

See also commentary at Helaman 12:1–3.

1 Nephi 8:30

The many people who pressed forward, holding fast to the word of God, finally arrived at the tree and *fell down* and partook of the fruit. Note that in 11:24, Nephi says he "saw many fall down at [Christ's] feet and worship him." They fall to their knees out of pure respect and adoration. Notice the contrast: the wicked are lifted up in pride; the righteous are falling down in humility.

1 Nephi 8:36

Lehi "exceedingly feared for Laman and Lemuel . . . lest they should be cast off from the presence of the Lord." One mission president provided a modern example of Lehi's concern:

"A rock group performed a concert in the area last night, in a big stadium right in the middle of our mission. Seventy thousand people attended. When we heard that the group was coming, we wondered if any of our missionaries would defile themselves with a heavy dose of worldliness and attend it (totally against mission rules). To their credit, as far as we know, almost all of them just kept on working, and obeying. Except two. One missionary finished his mission last week but is still in the country, touring with his parents who came to pick him up. This afternoon he went back to his last proselyting area, and invited his last companion (still fairly young in the mission, and a potential leader), and he agreed to go to the concert with him.

"I was so tired last night that I went to bed about 11 P.M., then at 1 A.M. was awakened by a call from the young missionary's current companion, who felt horrible that he had allowed his companion to go to the concert without calling the president and saying something. Today I called them all in, including the returning missionary and his parents. I lovingly chastised the young missionary and called him to repentance. He was quite remorseful and anxious to be forgiven.

"The missionary who leaves tonight for the States, who has been Spiritless for several months, told me he regretted having taken his former companion to the concert, but he had not an ounce of regret for having gone himself. He doesn't care at all whether someone thinks he is disobedient or not. I was appalled at his attitude. As kindly as I could, I also called him to repentance and warned him that he was heading for big trouble. I asked him if he honestly desired someday to live with Heavenly Father and his Son, our Savior. He said, with a somewhat defiant grin on his face, 'Well, I'm not really sure.' 'You mean to tell me,' I replied, 'that you've been teaching and testifying for two years, and you admit you're not even sure you want to be with God yourself?' 'Yes, I guess that's what I'm saying.' I told him that I feared for him and once again called on him to examine himself and consider seriously if he really wants to pursue the path to misery. It all reminds me of Lehi's fearful concern for his sons, Laman and Lemuel. I next had a talk with his parents and commiserated with them, for they, too, fear for their son."

1 Nephi 9

No question it was hard work making a set of smooth metal plates to engrave. When commanded to make a second set, even without knowing the reason why, Nephi was obedient and went right to work. He was convinced the Lord knows all things, prepares the way to accomplish whatever he commands, and has all power to follow through on every word he utters. We now know the Lord required Nephi to make another record because part of Mormon's abridgment of Nephi's other record would be lost by Martin Harris.[20] See also the commentary at 1 Nephi 19:1–6 and Words of Mormon 1:7.

1 Nephi 10:1–3

Nephi, giving his own account, continued to quote his father. Lehi prophesied, as had Isaiah, that his people would be exiled to Babylon but that they would return again to their homeland. Though the tribes of Israel were carried off and lost to Israelite history, the tribe of Judah would not be completely destroyed. A remnant must return, for the Messiah was to come though Judah, and he had to be born in the land of Jerusalem.

NAMES AND TITLES FOR GOD

God the Father

Heavenly Father

Elohim (2,500 times in Hebrew Bible)

Man of Holiness (Moses 6:57)

Ahman (in *Journal of Discourses,* 2:342)

God the Son

Firstborn Son in the spirit; Only Begotten Son in the flesh

Jehovah (6,800 times in Hebrew Bible)

Lord

Son of Man (of Holiness)

Son Ahman (D&C 78:20)

Many name-titles—all teaching of his divine attributes: Creator, Redeemer, King, Judge, Immanuel, Good Shepherd, Lamb of God, Bread of Life, Living Water, True Vine, Light of the World, Rock, and many more

Jesus Christ: "Anointed Savior"—most frequently used name

Jesus (Hebrew, *Yeshua*): "Salvation" or "Savior"

Christ (Greek, *Christos*) and Messiah (Hebrew, *Mashiakh*): "Anointed One"

1 Nephi 10:4–6

Lehi and his sons prophesied plainly of the Holy One who would come six hundred years after their departure from Jerusalem. To be sure their message was unequivocally clear, they labeled and described him using several divine titles: prophet, Messiah, Savior, Redeemer, Lamb of God, Lord, and Son of God.

"The Book of Mormon prophets often made reference to 'God' or 'the Lord' without any indication of whether Elohim or Jehovah was intended. [Verse 4] has obvious reference to the fact that Elohim our Father (here designated 'the Lord God') would raise up and send his Only Begotten Son (Jesus Christ, also sometimes designated as 'the Lord God'). Elder Bruce R. McConkie taught: 'Most scriptures that speak of God or the Lord do not even bother to distinguish the Father from the Son, simply because it doesn't make any difference which God is involved. They are one. The words or deeds of either of them would be the words and deeds of the other in the same circumstance. Further, if a revelation comes from, or by the power of the Holy Ghost, ordinarily the words will be those of the Son, though what the Son says will be what the Father would say, and the words may thus be considered as the Father's.' ('Our Relationship with the Lord,' [*1982 Brigham Young University Fireside and Devotional Speeches,* Provo: Utah, BYU Publications, 1982], p. 101)."[21]

1 Nephi 10:7–10

Of the prophet who would come to prepare the way for the Messiah, the Prophet Joseph Smith taught:

"The question arose from the saying of Jesus—'Among those that are born of women there is not a greater prophet than John the Baptist; but he that is least in the kingdom of God is greater than he.' How is it that John was considered one of the greatest prophets? His miracles could not have constituted his greatness.

"First. He was entrusted with a divine mission of preparing the way before the face of the Lord. Whoever had such a trust committed to him before or since? No man.

"Secondly. He was entrusted with the important mission, and it was required at his hands, to baptize the Son of Man. Whoever had the honor of doing that? Whoever had so great a privilege and glory? Whoever led the Son of God into the waters of baptism, and had the privilege of beholding the Holy Ghost descend. . . .

"Thirdly. John, at that time, was the only legal administrator in the affairs of the kingdom there was then on the earth, and holding the keys of power. The Jews had to obey his instructions or be damned, by their own law; and Christ Himself fulfilled all righteousness in becoming obedient to the law which he had given to Moses on the mount, and thereby magnified it and made it honorable, instead of destroying it. The son of Zacharias wrested the keys, the kingdom, the power, the glory from the Jews, by the holy anointing and decree of heaven, and these three reasons constitute him the greatest prophet born of a woman."[22]

1 Nephi 10:9

"These things were done in Bethabara beyond Jordan, where John was baptizing" (John 1:28). "Beyond Jordan" is the name of a region on the east side of the Jordan River (Greek *Perea*). According to Lehi's prophecy, Bethabara was the name of the site of John's baptizing. Bethabara appears on the Medeba Map at the natural fording place east of Jericho entering Perea. (The Medeba Map is a sixth-century mosaic map in Medeba, Jordan; it is the oldest known cartographic representation of the Holy Land in existence.) In Hebrew, *Beth-abara* or *Beth-avara* means "place of crossing." At such an important juncture along a major east-west travel route, John could have taught souls coming from the regions of Judea, Perea, Galilee, Decapolis, and Phoenicia. "They came unto John, and said unto him, Rabbi, he that was with thee beyond Jordan [Perea], to whom thou barest witness, behold, the same baptizeth, and all men come to him" (John 3:26). Just across the Jordan opposite Jericho is where the closing scenes of the ministries of the great prophets Moses and Elijah occurred—an appropriate location for the opening scenes of the ministries of the great Forerunner and the Messiah.

1 Nephi 10:11

The gospel (glad tidings of great joy) would be preached among the Jews; they would reject it and reject their Messiah. They would have him killed, and after he rose from the dead he would make himself manifest, by the Holy Ghost, to the Gentiles—which manifestations are recorded in the New Testament books of Acts through Revelation.

The term *Gentiles* is used many times from this point on in the Book of Mormon, so it would be wise to define its meaning: "During the meridian dispensation . . . the gospel went preferentially to the Jews first and to the Gentiles second. In the final dispensation the order would be reversed. Note again that to the Nephites, *Jews* were nationals, persons from the kingdom of Judah. In this sense, the Nephites and Lamanites—though genealogically of the tribe of Joseph— were Jews (see 2 Nephi 30:4; 33:8). *Gentiles* were all other peoples, including those who were of the house of Israel but who would be found among other nations on earth. . . . In this sense, the Latter-day Saints are called Gentiles (see D&C 109:60)."[23]

1 Nephi 10:12–14

The house of Israel is compared to an olive tree, whose branches are broken off and scattered worldwide; the Lehite colony's migration to the New World is part of the fulfillment of the prophecy that the house of Israel would be scattered upon *all* the face of the earth. The comparison to an olive tree is an affirmation of the authentic ancient provenance of the text of the Book of Mormon. Israelite tradition equated the house of Israel with an olive tree. Jeremiah 11:16 indicates that Jehovah called Israel "a green olive tree, fair and of goodly fruit." Later rabbinic commentary expounded on that symbolism, calling Israel a leafy and fair olive tree that shed light on all others. This imagery possibly came from the coloration of the underside of the olive leaf (silvery and light) as well as the fact that olive oil was burned for light. It is not happenstance in the Bible that when Gideon's youngest son, Jotham, climbed Mount Gerizim and proclaimed a parable to the citizens of Shechem, the olive tree was given priority of place (Judges 9:7–11).

After the prophesied scattering of Israel comes a prophesied gathering. Read verse 14 carefully, noting the little word *or*. This is a classic example of plainness, continually clarifying to make sure no one misses the message. Notice also that the *or* signals wanting to add to or rephrase something that has already been written; it is hard to erase something that has been carved into metal plates!

1 Nephi 10:15–22

Nephi wanted to see and hear and know the things that had been revealed to his father, and he asserts that others may also know if they are willing to diligently seek to know them. The Prophet Joseph Smith taught that "God hath not revealed anything to Joseph, but what He will make known unto the Twelve, and even the least Saint may know all things as fast as he is able to bear them."[24] Nephi testified that God is unchangeable—the same yesterday, today, and forever—and that he is willing to unfold his mysteries to anyone willing to diligently seek him, in modern times as in ancient times.

1 Nephi 10:20–22

Every soul will be taken back to God's presence for judgment (2 Nephi 2:10; 9:22, 38; Alma 11:41, 44; 42:23; Helaman 14:15–17; Mormon 9:12–14). Those who sought to do wickedly and refused to repent will be found unclean and because "no unclean thing can dwell with God," they will have to be escorted right back out of his presence—permanently. "All men, everywhere, must repent, or they can in nowise inherit the kingdom of God, for no unclean thing can dwell there, or dwell in his presence" (Moses 6:57).

1 Nephi 11:1–33

Nephi desired to see what his prophet-father saw, and he had faith that the Lord could and would show him the vision. Nephi sat pondering these heavenly things and then was caught away by the Spirit of the Lord, who would be his guide during a grand, panoramic tour down through the centuries: chapter 11 (Christ in Israel—New Testament), chapter 12 (Christ in America—Book of Mormon), chapter 13 (apostasy, restoration), and chapter 14 (last days).

The condescension of two Gods—the Father and the Son—reveals the depth of their love for us, as symbolized in the tree of life. "For God so loved the world that he gave his only begotten Son" (John 3:16), and "we love him, because he first loved us" (1 John 4:19).

1 Nephi 11:1

Nephi explained: "After I had *desired* to know the things that my father had seen, and *believing* that the Lord was able to make them known unto me, as I sat *pondering* in mine heart I was caught away in the Spirit" (emphasis added). Then follows the grand panoramic vision the Lord gave to Nephi, chapter after chapter, of many centuries of what we call "history" but he would have called "prophetic preview." All this was opened up to him because he desired it, was believing, and took time to ponder upon the things of the Lord.

As a boy, Joseph Smith enjoyed studying the Bible. One day he was reading the letter of James, where the ancient Church leader encouraged anyone who lacked wisdom to ask of God, and God would respond (James 1:5). Young Joseph wrote what happened to him after he read those words: "Never did any passage of scripture come with more power to the heart of man than this did at this time to mine. It seemed to enter with great force into every feeling of my heart. I reflected on it again and again" (Joseph Smith–History 1:12). Notice that the Prophet's history does not say that he read that powerful verse, closed his Bible, and dashed across the road to enter a grove of trees and immediately kneel to pray. It was some time later that he went to pray, because he said that he "reflected on it again and again"; the words just kept working their way into his consciousness, and he could not get them out of his mind. The Spirit of the Lord carried those words deep into young Joseph's heart and influenced him to act on them. The great Visitation occurred, followed by many other visits and revelations from the heavenly world, along with conferral of power (the priesthood), the translation and publication of more of the Savior's words, and the beginning of the restoration of all things. All of that happened because of the boy's initial desire, his believing heart, and his ponderings over a single verse of scripture.

On 16 February 1832, Joseph Smith and Sidney Rigdon were working on the Prophet's inspired revision of the biblical text, specifically in the Gospel of John. As they came to a particular verse (John 5:29), they stopped to ponder the meaning of the Lord's teaching. "And while we meditated upon these things, the Lord touched the eyes of our understandings and they were opened, and the glory of the Lord shone round about" (D&C 76:19). Then opened up to them the grand vision of the degrees of glory, one of the greatest of all the revelations that have come in our day. All this happened because they desired it, were believing, and paused to meditate upon the words of scripture.

There have been several men by the name of Joseph Smith in our dispensation. One of them, a nephew of the Prophet Joseph Smith, was Church president Joseph F. Smith. He was sitting in his home in Salt Lake City on 3 October 1918, pondering over the scriptures and reflecting particularly on the words of Peter about Christ's visit to the spirit world between his death and resurrection (1 Peter 3:18–20; 4:6). President Smith recorded: "As I pondered over these things which are written, the eyes of my understanding were opened, and the Spirit of the Lord rested upon me, and I saw the hosts of the dead" (D&C 138:11). He described in greater detail than anyone has in all of scripture the world of spirits, who is there, and what they are doing. He specifically noted what the Savior did in organizing the hosts of the righteous to carry on the teaching of the gospel and the preparing of the dead to receive their saving ordinances. All of that was opened up to him because he desired it, was believing, and had paid the price to stop and ponder the teachings of the scriptures.

The Lord seldom encourages or commands us to merely read the scriptures. He and his prophets use such terms as "search" (John 5:39; 3 Nephi 23:1, 5; D&C 1:37); "meditate" (Joshua 1:8; 1 Timothy 4:15; D&C 76:19); "study" (D&C 11:22; 26:1; 88:118); "ponder" (2 Nephi 4:15; 3 Nephi 17:3; D&C 88:62, 71; 138:1, 11); "reflect upon" (D&C 138:2; Joseph Smith–History 1:12); "feast upon" (2 Nephi 31:20; 32:3; Alma 32:42); and "treasure up" (D&C 84:85; Joseph Smith–Matthew 1:37). The Lord will indeed show unto us great things, as we do our part: praying over and studying and reflecting upon the words of scripture, and taking the time to be "in the Spirit."

1 Nephi 11:5–6

"I believe all the words of my father"—glorious words for a father to hear who was devastated because of the behavior of other sons. Even more important, notice that the Spirit rejoiced because he had found someone (Nephi) who believed not in a tree but rather in Jesus Christ. As the Spirit said, "Blessed art thou, Nephi, because thou believest in the Son of the most high God." In other words, the tree spoken of represents Jesus Christ. Because Nephi believed in Christ, he would see all that he desired, thus confirming that the testimony of Jesus is the spirit of prophecy (Revelation 19:10).

1 Nephi 11:11–12

Elder James E. Talmage taught: "That the Spirit of the Lord is capable of manifesting Himself in the form and figure of man, is indicated by the wonderful interview between the Spirit and Nephi, in which He revealed Himself to the prophet, questioned him concerning his desires and belief, instructed him in the things of God, speaking face to face with the man. . . . However, the Holy Ghost does not possess a body of flesh and bones, as do both the Father and the Son, but is a personage of spirit.

"Much of the confusion existing in human conceptions concerning the nature of the Holy Ghost arises from the common failure to segregate His person and powers. Plainly, such expressions as being filled with the Holy Ghost, and His falling upon persons, have reference to the powers and influences that emanate from God, and which are characteristic of Him; for the Holy Ghost may in this way operate simultaneously upon many persons even though they be widely separated, whereas the actual person of the Holy Ghost cannot be in more than one place at a time."[25]

1 Nephi 11:13–26

Nephi envisioned six centuries ahead of his time, seeing Jerusalem in Judea and Nazareth in Galilee. In Nazareth he saw a most beautiful young Jewish girl, a virgin, who had never known intimately a mortal man (see also Alma 7:10).

Many Saints skip over the question in verse 16, viewing it as an interruption to the flow of the text, often because they don't know what *condescension* means. *Condescension* derives from Latin words meaning "to descend or come down to be with."

Nephi teaches here the marvelous doctrine of the condescension of God. Verses 16–21 speak of God the Father, a resurrected, exalted, glorified Being, who condescended to sire a Son in this world with a mortal woman, Mary (to "sire" means to beget or procreate). There is nothing figurative about the paternity of Jesus Christ; he is literally the Son of an immortal Man and a mortal woman. Jesus Christ, the premortal Jehovah, the Firstborn of all the Father's spirit children, thus became the Only Begotten in the flesh—that is, the only mortal Son whom the Father ever had in this world.

This is a fundamental doctrine of true Christianity. The Jews do not believe God (Elohim) would have a Son; the Muslims do not believe God (Allah) would have a Son in this world; and many Christians these days likewise deny the Savior's unique birth. Nevertheless, the doctrine of the Divine Sonship of Christ is the foundation of our religion. With his unique parentage, he literally had power over life and death. He said: "I lay down my life, that I might take it again. No man taketh it from me, but I lay it down of myself. I have power to lay it down, and I have power to take it again" (John 10:17–18). He could, and did, give his life and take it up again, providing the way for all of us to be resurrected.

Verse 16 speaks of God the Father condescending to sire a Son. Footnote 16*a* refers to the Topical Guide, "Jesus Christ, Condescension of" because that is where all passages referring to any kind of condescension are collected, but the verse is specifically referring to the condescension of the Father, as evidenced by the next verse recording Nephi's comment, "I know that he loveth his children."

Verse 26 speaks of God the Son, who created worlds without number, then condescended to the manger in Bethlehem. He not only descended to our condition but also descended below it (D&C 88:6; 122:8).

President Ezra Taft Benson wrote: "The most fundamental doctrine of true Christianity is the divine birth of the child Jesus. This doctrine is not generally comprehended by the world. The paternity of Jesus Christ is one of the 'mysteries of godliness' comprehended only by the spiritually minded. . . .

" . . . The testimonies of appointed witnesses leave no question as to the paternity of Jesus Christ. God was the Father of Jesus' mortal tabernacle, and Mary, a mortal woman, was His mother. He is therefore the only person born who rightfully deserves the title 'the *Only* Begotten Son of God.' . . .

"The Church of Jesus Christ of Latter-day Saints proclaims that Jesus Christ is the Son of God in the most literal sense. The body in which He performed His mission in the flesh was sired by that same Holy Being we worship as God, our Eternal Father. Jesus was not the son of Joseph, nor was He begotten by the Holy Ghost. He is the Son of the Eternal Father!"[26]

"He was the Only Begotten Son of our Heavenly Father in the flesh—the only child whose mortal body was begotten by our Heavenly Father. His mortal mother, Mary, was called a virgin, both before and after she gave birth. (See 1 Ne. 11:20.)"[27]

1 Nephi 11:17

Prophets do not automatically know everything; they also learn line upon line. Compare commentary at Alma 7:8.

1 Nephi 11:18

Mary, whose Hebrew name was Miriam, was the mother of the Son of God, "after the manner of the flesh," meaning the way babies are naturally born.

1 Nephi 11:19

The language of this verse provides a respectful shroud of silence regarding the details of the relationship. On Mary's being carried away by the Spirit and conceiving, Elder Bruce R. McConkie wrote: "Without overstepping the bounds of propriety by saying more than is appropriate, let us say this: God the Almighty; the Maker and Preserver and Upholder of all things . . . who is infinite and eternal, elects, in his fathomless wisdom, to beget a Son, an Only Son, the Only Begotten in the flesh.

"God, who is infinite and immortal, condescends to step down from his throne, to join with one who is finite and mortal in bringing forth, 'after the manner of the flesh,' the Mortal Messiah."[28]

"There was only one Christ," Elder McConkie also wrote, "and there is only one Mary. Each was noble and great in preexistence, and each was foreordained to the ministry he or she performed. We cannot but think that the Father would choose the greatest female spirit to be the mother of his Son, even as he chose the male spirit like unto him to be the Savior."[29]

1 Nephi 11:20–25

After showing Nephi these scenes of holy cities and condescension and conception and birth, the angel asked him if he now understood the meaning of the tree. Yes, Nephi responded, "it is the love of God . . . the most desirable above all things." And the angel added, "And the most joyous to the soul." All of what he had thus far seen was to help him understand how great is the love of both Gods—Father and Son—for the children of men, making available mortality, the Atonement, resurrection, and eternal life. The latter is the greatest of all the gifts of God (D&C 6:7, 13).

Nephi saw that the iron rod was the word of God and that it led to the waters of life and the tree of life—both representing the love of God, which is manifested in the coming of Jesus in the flesh. In other words, the scriptures lead us to Christ. And we need to come to him daily through the scriptures.

1 Nephi 11:27

The Prophet Joseph Smith explained about the Holy Ghost coming down and abiding on Jesus: "The sign of the dove was instituted before the creation of the world, a witness for the Holy Ghost, and the devil cannot come in the sign of a dove. The Holy Ghost is a personage, and is in the form of a personage. It does not confine itself to the *form* of the dove, but in *sign* of the dove. The Holy Ghost cannot be transformed into a dove; but the sign of a dove was given to John to signify the truth of the deed, as the dove is an emblem or token of truth and innocence."[30]

See also commentary at 2 Nephi 31:8.

1 Nephi 11:28–36

The mortal mission of the Redeemer, before his actual redeeming atonement, was to "minister unto the people." He came not to be ministered to but to minister. He came to be the servant of all, "as he that serveth" (Luke 22:27), and his unique service was with "power and great glory." So the Lamb of God had love and power and glory, yet the people cast him out. Nephi saw Jesus' ministry, his crucifixion, the fight of the house of Israel and the proud world against the Twelve Apostles and the early Church, and the fall and destruction of the world's pride. This passage is one of the most frightening in scripture, for we see that no one is immune to the influence of the world. The "house of Israel" gathered to "fight against the twelve apostles." Church members today must be ever vigilant.

1 Nephi 12:1–23

Nephi saw the following in the land of promise, the ancient Americas: "wars, and rumors of wars," "mist of darkness," and "vapor of darkness," suggesting temptations and evils that are encircling, entangling, and all-pervasive; twelve disciples over the Church of God; "the fountain of filthy water," or "depths of hell"; and "the large and spacious building," or "vain imaginations and pride" of mortals. Nephi also saw that his posterity was overpowered by the posterity of his brothers (ca. A.D. 385).

1 Nephi 12:10–11

"Garments are made white in his blood": this seemingly incongruous image powerfully teaches that the atoning blood symbolically cleanses, purifies, whitens, and sanctifies the garments of those who apply that blood (see also Alma 5:27;

34:36). White garments typify the purity of those who are clothed with righteousness.

1 Nephi 13:1

The words "look" and "behold" are used repeatedly, and each time Nephi looked, he beheld a new scene. An angelic messenger from God escorted him through the vision.

1 Nephi 13:2–9

Regarding the formation of the great and abominable church described in these verses, we note Joseph Smith's axiom: "In relation to the kingdom of God, the devil always sets up his kingdom at the very same time in opposition to God."[31] Is it any wonder, then, that godless humanistic philosophies would surface in the same century as the restoration of the kingdom of God on earth?

Former dean of religion at Brigham Young University David H. Yarn Jr. wrote: "There has never been a single century like the nineteenth in the history of thought when so many ideas, concepts, and systems of thought have emerged which are destructive to faith and righteousness. In addition to the discipline of Biblical Criticism came the atheistic philosophies of Schopenhauer, Comte, Darwin, Marx, Nietzsche, and Freud. Aside from any positive value that might be attributed to any or all of them, the collective force of their materialism, naturalism, humanism, and atheism has burst upon the twentieth century and its fruit—the hellish immoralities of our time—seem to be all but omnipresent in our contemporary world. As regards the testimony of Jesus Christ, perhaps Nietzsche might appropriately be chosen as the spokesman for that faith-destroying coterie. He impudently boasted, 'I am the Antichrist' (Nietzsche, *Ecce Homo*, "Why I Write Such Excellent Books," paragraph 2)."[32]

The great and abominable church is always set up to oppose the great and marvelous work the Lord establishes. The great and abominable church is plainly defined in Nephi's writings:

The devil is the founder of it; it is otherwise called "the mother of harlots"; it has caused people to stumble because of plain and precious parts of the gospel which it kept back. "There are save two churches only; the one is the church of the Lamb of God, and the other is the church of the devil; wherefore, whoso belongeth not to the church of the Lamb of God belongeth to that great church, which is the mother of abominations; and she is the whore of all the earth" (1 Nephi 14:10). "All churches which are built up to get gain, and all those who are built up to get power over the flesh, and those who are built up to become popular in the eyes of the world, and those who seek the lusts of the flesh and the things of the world, and to do all manner of iniquity . . . [are] those who belong to the kingdom of the devil" (1 Nephi 22:23). "He that fighteth against Zion, both Jew and Gentile, both bond and free, both male and female, shall perish; for they are they who are the whore of all the earth" (2 Nephi 10:16).

1 Nephi 13:4–6

On the matter of every soul standing either with the great and abominable church or with the true Church of Jesus Christ, Brigham Young University professor of ancient scripture Stephen Robinson noted that it depends more on who has your *heart* than who has your *records*.[33]

1 Nephi 13:7–9

The great and abominable church, or the church of the devil, is organized with priestcraft instead of priesthood. Nephi characterized it by precious metals, gold and silver; precious clothing, silks, scarlets, and fine-twined linen; immoral men and women; efforts to secure the praise of the world by destroying the Saints of God and bringing them down to captivity in religion as well as in politics. Thus, the great and abominable church has been known by many names over the centuries and has been led by various institutions and individuals. The list of institutions leading the charge of the devil's program on this earth might include apostate Christianity, secularism, Nazism, Communism, radical religions and groups in the Near East, as well as others.

1 Nephi 13:10–11

The Atlantic Ocean separated the nations and kingdoms of the Gentiles, the European countries, from the descendants of Book of Mormon-era Lamanites who were living in abject apostasy and, as the angel said, "the wrath of God" was upon them.

1 Nephi 13:12

Christopher Columbus understood that he was directed in his ventures by the God of heaven. "Who can doubt but that the Holy Ghost inspired me?"[34]

The *Encyclopedia of Mormonism* states: "Nephi appears to give an accurate account of Columbus's motives. . . . Columbus apparently . . . felt himself spiritually driven to discover new lands. Newly acknowledged documents show that medieval eschatology, the scriptures, and divine inspiration were the main forces compelling him to sail. His notes in the works of Pierre d'Ailly and his own unfinished *Book of Prophecies* substantiate his apocalyptic view of the world and his feelings about his own prophetic role. . . .

"He believed himself chosen by God to find that land and deliver the light of Christianity to the natives there. . . . He believed that he was to help usher in the age of 'one fold, and one shepherd,' citing John 10:16 (cf. 3 Ne. 15:21), and spoke of finding 'the new heaven and new earth.'

"Writing to King Ferdinand and Queen Isabella to gain financial support, Columbus testified that a voice had told him he had been watched over from infancy to prepare him for discovering the Indies. He felt that he was given divine keys to ocean barriers that only he could unlock. . . . In a second letter, he emphasized his prophetic role: 'Reason, mathematics, and maps of the world were of no use to me in the execution of the enterprise of the Indies. What Isaiah said [e.g., Isaiah 24:15] was completely fulfilled' (Watts, p. 96). Unknowingly, Columbus also fulfilled Nephi's prophecy."[35]

1 Nephi 13:13–16

The Pilgrim Fathers, also called Puritans and Separatists, sought to break away from the political and religious oppression in the British Isles and continental Europe. They migrated, driven by the "Spirit of God" or the "Spirit of the Lord," and settled the "land of promise," at the same time scattering the descendants of ancient Book of Mormon peoples, whom they called Indians.

The Gentiles, who included the Pilgrims and America's Founding Fathers, "did humble themselves before the Lord; and the power of the Lord was with them." Doctrine and Covenants 101:80 says God established the Constitution of the United States of America "by the hands of wise men whom I raised up unto this very purpose." His power, of course, would then be with them.

In the mid-1970s, Brother Ogden learned that the Church was going to close the St. George Utah Temple for two years for major remodeling, so he traveled to St. George to attend the temple in one of the final sessions before closing. After the session, he stopped at the temple recorder's office, explained who he was and what he did, and asked if he could see the temple's records of the visit of the signers of the Declaration of Independence, the United States' presidents, and other famous men and women. The recorder went immediately to a specific volume on a particular shelf in a relatively small room with wall-to-wall shelves and many big, handwritten ledgers of a hundred years of temple work. He said that Brother Ogden could look and remember all he could, but he was not permitted to make copies of the pages. (These records were later moved to the Church archives in Salt Lake City.)

Glancing through the book, Brother Ogden saw that temple president Wilford Woodruff and assistant president John D. T. McAllister had done the ordinances for all the signers of the Declaration, except John Hancock, whose work had already been done by his descendant Levi Hancock; all the United States presidents up to that date except three— Buchanan, who sent Johnston's Army to Utah in 1857; Van Buren, who said, "Your cause is just, but I can do nothing for you"; and Grant, who was then living; and other renowned men, such as Christopher Columbus, Amerigo Vespucci (Americus Vespucius), John Wesley, William Makepeace Thackeray, Washington Irving, Michael Faraday, David Farragut, Louis Agassiz, Benjamin Franklin, Daniel Webster, William Seward, Henry Clay, and John C. Calhoun. Wilford Woodruff's diary records that the ordinance work was also performed for the following: Napoleon Bonaparte, Johann Wolfgang Goethe, William Wordsworth, and Sir Walter Scott.[36] Sister Lucy B. Young helped do the work for Martha Washington and seventy other eminent women of the world.

1 Nephi 13:17–19

The Revolutionary War, between the American colonies and the British Empire and others, was the great prologue to the Restoration. The American colonists "were delivered by the power of God out of the hand of all other nations." In fact, the God of this land has declared that he "redeemed the land by the shedding of blood" (D&C 101:80)—just as he redeems all worthy souls by the shedding of his own blood. Thus, it seems to be a true principle that redemption relative to God's plan comes by the shedding of blood. Our lives, our salvation, were redeemed, or purchased, by the shedding of the blood of God. The land of the latter-day restoration was purchased by the shedding of the blood of patriots. The future of our Church, our religious future, was purchased by the shedding of the blood of pioneers. There is no redemption in the eternal scheme of things, it seems, without the shedding of blood.

The establishment of a free land, with guarantees of religious liberty, was a necessary prelude to the glorious latter-day restoration of the Church, the gospel, and the new and everlasting covenant. The hand of God was in it! When the work of the framers of the U.S. Constitution was completed, James Madison wrote, "It is impossible for the man of pious reflection not to perceive in it a finger of that Almighty hand which has been so frequently and signally extended to our relief in the critical stage of the revolution."[37]

Many have had the sobering experience of visiting Valley Forge and remembering how General Washington encouraged the ten thousand soldiers of the Continental Army in desperate conditions during the winter of 1777–78. Many have paid tribute to his leadership genius and his humility in calling upon God. Many have probably also read from Nephi's visionary description, which ties together all the momentous events of Plymouth, Salem, Boston, and Philadelphia with the restoration of the gospel (1 Nephi 13). The Revolution and the Restoration were integrally connected in God's great plan for laying foundations for the permanent establishment of his kingdom on this earth.

1 Nephi 13:20–42

Nephi saw a book among the Gentiles, a book that "proceeded forth from the mouth of a Jew"—the Holy Bible, as we call it, or "the book of the Lamb of God," as he called it, which contains the covenants and prophetic promises of the holy prophets. Its contents were similar to those of the plates of brass but "not so many," suggesting that the plates of brass had a fuller record of the people than does our current Bible, although our Bible is still "of great worth" to us "Gentiles."

1 Nephi 13:24–25

Regarding the condition of the prophets' writings before precious things were lost, Joseph Smith wrote: "I believe the Bible as it read when it came from the pen of the original writers. Ignorant translators, careless transcribers, or designing and corrupt priests have committed many errors."[38] That is to say, the biblical record was at first pure and "contained the fulness of the gospel of the Lord."

1 Nephi 13:26–28

Many truths that were plain and precious are now missing, having been deleted or corrupted, and many covenants of the Lord have been omitted. Why? With malice aforethought, the church of the devil has done it to "pervert the right ways of the Lord" and to "blind the eyes and harden the hearts of the children of men."

1 Nephi 13:29–42

The phrase "plain and precious" appears nine times in a span of fifteen verses. Taking away plain and precious things perverts the correct understanding of the nature of God and causes people to stumble doctrinally. Biblical examples include "No man hath seen God at any time" (John 1:18) and "God is a spirit" (John 4:24).

To help remedy these losses and misunderstandings, God has brought forth "other books," and "these last records [Book of Mormon, Doctrine and Covenants, Pearl of Great Price, and the Joseph Smith Translation of the Bible] . . . shall establish the truth of the first [the Bible], . . . and shall make known the plain and precious things which have been taken away." For example, latter-day scripture has restored the truth that "the Lamb of God is the Son of the Eternal Father, and the Savior of the world; and that all men must come unto him, or they cannot be saved."

The prophecy "the words of the Lamb shall be made

known in the [Book of Mormon], as well as in the [Bible]; wherefore they both shall be established in one" is certainly accomplished in the publication of the Book of Mormon, the Doctrine and Covenants, the Pearl of Great Price, and the Latter-day Saint edition of the King James Bible. They have become literally one in our hand in testifying of the divine Sonship of Jesus Christ (see 2 Nephi 3:12).

We see again in this passage how the term *Gentile* is used. It can refer to anyone, even an Israelite, who is not of the house of Judah, or it can refer to those raised in a non-Israelite, or Gentile, culture.

1 Nephi 13:37

This verse is a blessing on those who seek to bring forth Zion, who publish peace and tidings of great joy—"how beautiful upon the mountains shall they be." See further commentary on the latter expression at Mosiah 15:14–18.

1 Nephi 14:1–17

Not only do we see how extensive Lehi's and Nephi's visions were, we see that they beheld the latter days—our days—and the end of the world. This sweeping vision was seen by many prophets (see commentary at 1 Nephi 14:26).

The great war between the forces of good and the forces of evil that began in the premortal world has changed battlefields, but the war rages on. The mother of abominations, the whore of all the earth or the church of the devil seems omnipresent (see commentary at 1 Nephi 13:2–9); it has infiltrated organizations and movements and has pervasive power and influence.

In 1845 the Council of the Twelve Apostles proclaimed: "As this work progresses in its onward course, . . . no king, ruler, or subject, no community or individual, will stand *neutral*. All will . . . take sides either for or against the kingdom of God."[39] President Ezra Taft Benson declared: "I testify that as the forces of evil increase under Lucifer's leadership and as the forces of good increase under the leadership of Jesus Christ, there will be growing battles between the two until the final confrontation. As the issues become clearer and more obvious, all mankind will eventually be required to align themselves either for the kingdom of God or for the kingdom of the devil."[40]

The kingdom of the devil is described as a whore. The image is a foil, or a contrasting opposite, to the kingdom of God, which is described in the most sacred relationship of husband and wife. The Lord is married to his people; he is the Bridegroom and she, his Church, is the bride. If there is ever any infidelity, it is always on the part of the wife, because the Lord is faithful eternally. That is why the wife is cast in the role of the whore or the harlot; she has prostituted the holiest of all relationships. In this case, the devil and his companions have violated or prostituted all the covenants of eternity. Nephi saw that the whore "sat upon many waters," meaning that her influence was far and wide, as the next phrase indicates: "she had dominion over all the earth, among all nations, kindreds, tongues, and people." The waves of her wickedness were washing up on all the shores of humankind.

The power and influence of the true Church, comparatively speaking, seems meager. Nevertheless, the numerically minor power of the Church and the Saints is manifested in strong and impressive ways because righteousness is power, and God's power is glorious.

God's anger is poured out as the great and abominable church engages in constant wars and war-mongering efforts. When we see all this happening in our day, we know that the Father's work of fulfilling his covenants to Israel is in progress.

1 Nephi 14:3

The devil and the church established by him work to lead the souls of men to hell. Hell is part of the postmortal world of spirits where the wicked suffer but have the opportunity to repent. The other part of the postmortal spirit world is called paradise. Both paradise and hell have an end in the resurrection. When Nephi says that hell "hath no end," he is undoubtedly referring to the fact that the punishment suffered in hell is endless because God is endless and, therefore, God's punishment is endless (D&C 19:10–12). An endless hell of never-ending torment is reserved for the sons of perdition, who inherit no kingdom of glory (D&C 76:44–48). All but the sons of perdition are saved in the sense that all receive a kingdom of glory (D&C 76:43). Nephi also teaches that hell is a place (1 Nephi 15:35).

1 Nephi 14:18–30

Nephi's sweeping vision of the future continues with a glimpse of the grand mission of John, one of Jesus' twelve apostles, otherwise known as John the Beloved or John the Revelator. John would write of the things that Nephi saw and many things of the past, "and he shall also write concerning the end of the world." The angel guiding Nephi bore testimony of the justice and truth of John's writings, exclaiming that his writings were "plain and pure, and most precious and easy to the understanding of all men."

Wait! you say. Is this referring to John's Revelation, the final and great apocalyptic book of the New Testament— "plain" and "easy to the understanding of all men"? That is not the way most people view those writings. Joseph Smith actually declared, "The book of Revelation is one of the plainest books God ever caused to be written."[41] True, Joseph Smith may have seen the whole vision also, but with the Spirit and some serious study, we too can understand much of what John wrote. It is meant to be understood in order to help us comprehend events of the last days and prepare ourselves for the final day.

1 Nephi 14:24–25

Nephi was permitted the expansive view of past and future but was instructed not to write about the end time. That assignment was given to the Beloved Apostle, to write it and publish it to the world; John, in a sense, was granted the copyright on those prophetic things.

1 Nephi 14:26

Others have written what the Lord showed them in a grand panoramic vision of the history of the world: Adam, Enoch, the brother of Jared, Abraham, Moses, Isaiah, Daniel, John the Revelator, and Joseph Smith (see commentary at 2 Nephi 27:6–11). With the exception of John, however, the Lord instructed them to seal up their writings until the time of the end of the world (see, for example, Daniel 12:4 and Ether 3:27; 4:5).

1 Nephi 14:27

The name of John the Revelator was known and recorded centuries before he was born, as were the names of Moses (2 Nephi 3:9–10), Cyrus (Isaiah 44:28; 45:1), Mary (Mosiah 3:8; Alma 7:10), Joseph Smith (2 Nephi 3:11, 15), and especially Jesus Christ (Moses 6:52, 57; 7:50; 2 Nephi 25:19; Mosiah 3:8).

John's record of the sweeping vision seen by Lehi, Nephi, and others is called the book of Revelation. Nephi and John saw the same things, and their accounts contain many of the same images: tree of life, great and abominable church, the restoration of the gospel, and so forth. However, Nephi's account emphasizes the first coming of Jesus Christ and the meridian dispensation, while John's account emphasizes the second coming of Jesus Christ, the end of the final dispensation, and the Millennium.

1 Nephi 14:28

Like Nephi, the Prophet Joseph Smith declared, "I could explain a hundred fold more than I ever have of the glories of the kingdoms manifested to me in the vision, were I permitted, and were the people prepared to receive them."[42]

1 Nephi 14:30

Nephi wrote about what he saw while carried away in the Spirit, as did John (Revelation 1:10) and Joseph Smith and Sidney Rigdon (D&C 76:11–12, 116–18).

1 Nephi 15:1–5

When you have had a profound experience with the Spirit, it is hard to come back down from that "mountaintop" you have been on. Coming "down" or re-engaging the fallen world, only to find less spiritually inclined persons arguing, is distasteful.

There are many great things that are hard to understand unless you ask God. If you harden your heart you will not ask, and tragedy is inevitable for those with hard hearts (see commentary at 1 Nephi 17:41–42; Alma 12:31–37).

Because of the prophetic preview Nephi had just witnessed of the disastrous destiny of his descendants, he felt that his afflictions were "great above all."

1 Nephi 15:6–9

Of course Laman and Lemuel did not understand the doctrine; they had not asked God. And they had not asked because they were certain he would not reveal anything to them. With that attitude, they were right.

1 Nephi 15:10–11

You can miss out on the great things of the Lord simply because you fail to ask. Could it be that you don't really believe the Lord would make such remarkable things known to "little old me"? If you desire to experience the mighty things of the Spirit, here is the formula, from verse 11 and the end of verse 14: *Inquire with faith + obey the commandments = receive revelation.* If you do his will, you can know the doctrine is true (John 7:17). This passage teaches the same grand message as James 1:5–6 and Moroni 10:4–5. If you sincerely ask of God, with real intent, having faith in Christ, he will manifest the truth to you by the power of the Holy Ghost. The patriarch Abraham is a superb example of one who actively inquired of the Lord and relentlessly sought to claim blessings that God promises to all who seek him in righteousness (Abraham 1:1–4).

1 Nephi 15:12–16

Israel is compared to an olive tree, and the Nephites were a branch of Israel that was broken off from the rest of Israel. Rock, vine, fold, and tree are all meaningful images of the Redeemer and his doctrine; they denote stability, nourishment, security, and fruitfulness.

1 Nephi 15:24

Here is one of the great promises in all of scripture, a guarantee of safety during the tumultuous last days—safety and salvation. Whoever will hold fast to the word of God, especially the Book of Mormon, will "never perish." What does it mean to "hold fast" to the rod? If you are in a river, sinking and about to drown, and someone extends you a branch, how do you hold onto it? You grab it tightly and cling to it for dear life. That is how you must hold firmly to the word of God.

In Nephi's analogy, in a sense we are all dartboards and Satan is a professional dart thrower. What are the "fiery darts" he is hurling at us? Immoral and violent movies, pornographic Internet sites, worldly music, profane and crude language, sexual perversions and deviations, the allure of materialism, and many more.

If you are treasuring up the word, you will not have to debate whether or not to indulge in these things; they will be repulsive to your spirit. You will not be blinded by the world's example. "Whoso treasureth up my word, shall not be deceived" (Joseph Smith–Matthew 1:37). The adversary will not overpower you; he will have "no power over you" (Helaman 5:12). That is a sure promise, and a comforting one.

1 Nephi 15:25–27

As demonstrated in these verses, family members are not to give up on one another. Nephi did not give up on his wayward brothers. He encouraged them "with all the energies of [his] soul," continually clarifying the teachings of his father.

The river of water represents the filthiness of the world, but Lehi was so "swallowed up" or so preoccupied with better things that he didn't particularly notice how filthy the water was. Later, we encounter missionaries who were so "swallowed up" in the joy of Christ that they didn't notice the depth of their own afflictions and deprivations (Alma 31:38). It is good to be "swallowed up," or caught up, in the things of God.

1 Nephi 15:31–36

Temporal or spiritual—it is all the same. Everything temporal is also spiritual to God and to all those who are godly (D&C 29:34). The wicked or filthy cannot enter the kingdom of God because there cannot be anything filthy in a place where a totally clean Being lives. The wicked cannot enjoy the most precious and desirable fruit of the tree of life—the love of God that results in eternal life—which is the greatest of his gifts (D&C 6:13).

1 Nephi 16:1–4

The evil-minded brothers concluded that Nephi's beautiful teachings were hard and unbearable. The young prophet responded that they are hard only for the wicked, who feel guilty in their dark sins and want to avoid the light. Indeed, our experience has shown that the manifestation of gospel truths in the face of wickedness causes great divisions and brings guilt, embarrassment, and anger to the less righteous. Truth cuts the wicked to the very center because the word of the Lord is "sharper than a two-edged sword" (D&C 11:2). The Savior said he would bring not peace but a sword (Matthew 10:34–37). John's Gospel records that "there was a division among the people because of him" (John 7:43).

What does a righteous person do who has to live with someone who is wicked and rebellious? Persist in encouraging the lost one to keep the commandments, and refuse to give up. Let the rebellious one keep hearing that encouragement with love and kindness.

1 Nephi 16:7

Nephi "took one of the daughters of Ishmael to wife." How wonderful to have a prophet in the family to perform the sealing.

1 Nephi 16:10

It is interesting that the Lord would provide a hand-held device to guide Lehi and his family (consider today's technology for accessing global positioning systems). The more ancient Israelites had a cloud and fire to guide them, but now the Lord provided an apparatus that needed no outside power source because it operated through inner power sources: faith and diligence. A label or title for this ball, director, or compass—"Liahona"—is noted in Alma 37:38.

The word *curious* has changed meanings over the past nearly two centuries. In Joseph Smith's day the word meant "made with care, skillfully wrought with art, elegant, and exactness of workmanship."[43]

1 Nephi 16:18–27

There was plenty of cause to murmur: broken bows, lack of food, fatigue, suffering—sounds like life! The similarities here to the Israelite exodus are striking: fatigue, lack of food, and great murmuring against the Lord (Exodus 16:8; Numbers 11:1). Instead of sitting around groaning and complaining about their plight, Nephi got up and did something constructive. He devised a solution to their dilemma and then went to his father for direction. He himself could have sought guidance from the Lord, but he sustained and honored the priesthood leadership of his father, even though his father, a prophet, had also been complaining and was chastened and humbled.

Elder Richard G. Scott taught: "Just when all seems to be going right, challenges often come in multiple doses applied simultaneously. When those trials are not consequences of your disobedience, they are evidence that the Lord feels you are prepared to grow more (see Prov. 3:11–12). He therefore gives you experiences that stimulate growth, understanding, and compassion which polish you for your everlasting benefit. To get you from where you are to where He wants you to be requires a lot of stretching, and that generally entails discomfort and pain."[44]

1 Nephi 16:28–29

The Liahona is a profound example of how great things come about by small means (see also Alma 37:6). This seems to be a powerful and important lesson for individuals and families to learn. Our daily "pointers" are prayer, scripture study, and obedience—small means that bring about great results. The gift of the Holy Ghost, like the Liahona, functions only upon our faith, diligence, and obedience. We also receive the word of the Lord from time to time according to our faith and attention. The whole program is so simple but can produce great results. The Lehites received greater understanding of gospel doctrine and spiritual things through the Liahona, and we receive such understanding through the gift of the Holy Ghost, the scriptures, and patriarchal blessings.

The phrase "and thus we see" is used at least twenty-one times in the Book of Mormon and signals some important lesson that we should not miss. The lesson in this first instance is that the Lord by small and simple means can bring about great things. It is not a matter of walking back to Jackson

County; it is walking or driving over to visit and lift those we home teach or visit teach. It is not whether you are willing to die for the cause of Christ but whether you will daily study his words and daily talk with Heavenly Father in humble prayer.

1 Nephi 16:30–38

When we can see immediate and dramatic results of true faith and diligence, we are prone to humbly acknowledge them and give thanks to the great Provider.

Every time something went wrong in the traveling group and every time something hurt, it was time to complain and criticize. Just like Lot's wife, they wanted to go back. They obviously did not have a testimony and feel gratitude that they had escaped destruction, or they would not have desired to return. We have to trust the prophet.

Those who don't have a believing heart will probably have a critical heart, which can lead to anger, then to murderous feelings. Liars accuse others of lying. Because of the lies, they stir up people to anger, which comes from Satan (3 Nephi 11:29–30).

1 Nephi 16:39

The Lord himself had to intervene and chasten the rebellious sons and brothers, which caused them to admit their wrong, eradicate their anger, and repent, all of which resulted in blessings flowing again. It seems that Laman and Lemuel were constantly vacillating back and forth, up and down, between aggressive rebellion and then contrite pleading for forgiveness and acknowledging God.

1 Nephi 17:1–3

Travel is fatiguing, and a wilderness has such primitive conditions for giving birth. The women grew physically tougher and endured conditions without complaint.

If we are willing to keep God's commandments, he assures us of strength, nourishment, and success in continuing in the path of obedience. He will provide the way, and we are guaranteed success—if not immediately, then eventually. "Thus we see" what God will do if we obey.

1 Nephi 17:3, 13, 49–50

God has commanded us to do certain things, and he provides the way to do them. We have to study it out in our mind and make decisions, but *he provides the means* for accomplishing whatever he commands. The following words in a letter from a missionary caught the president of the Missionary Training Center by surprise: "Take care of yourself and your family, and never give in to temptation. I hope that you will have many trials so you can continue progressing and be able to teach us all the better." That was a rather unusual desire, but the missionary was right. We do learn a lot from our trials, and we are then able to teach others more effectively.

For the previous three days the MTC president had been living with a little cloud of darkness hanging over him—and confusion, agitation, perplexity, and bewilderment—because of another elder who wanted to go home. Although that missionary fully participated, with outward enjoyment, in all the studies and activities with the other missionaries, he said he was terribly homesick and couldn't learn. He insisted he had no knowledge of the gospel whatever, because he had skipped out on his church classes over the years, and he felt inferior to all the other missionaries. Through hours of interviews with the MTC president and with his wonderful branch president, he kept saying, "I just can't do it; I can't do it; I can't do it." President Ogden reminded him that "can't" is a denial of the Holy Ghost. With God all things are possible, especially learning to serve as a servant of the Lord.

It was a challenging situation for the missionary. His father had left the country and had lived for many years in the States, and his mother, who remained in her country, had recently been excommunicated. The missionary was allowed to call his stake president and his mother; his mother and all three members of his stake presidency tried to dissuade him from abandoning his mission. The area president asked why the elder wanted to leave: "Why did he prepare and send in all the papers, and why did he write an acceptance letter to Church leaders and the Missionary Department?" The young missionary said he hadn't done any of those things.

The hours and hours of interviews and phone calls were spiritually draining for everyone. Finally the young man confessed to immorality with his girlfriend. That explained the depressing darkness through which he had put himself. He could not learn, he could not love, and he could not feel the Spirit because he was not clean. Soon after his confession and an honest beginning to repentance, he began to feel lighter and happier and more determined to resolve this sin.

Not long afterward another elder lamented to the MTC president how unprepared he felt and how he questioned whether he could learn enough to succeed on the mission. A rush of counsel came for him—the encouragement literally poured into President Ogden's mind, and he just opened his mouth and passed it on to the young elder.

After all that, President Ogden collapsed, exhausted, into his favorite big chair, wanting to soak up a little Book of Mormon for the first time in almost three days. He opened to where his marker was and started reading 1 Nephi 17. The third verse says: "And if it so be that the children of men keep the commandments of God he doth nourish them, and strengthen them, and provide means whereby they can accomplish the thing which he has commanded them."

Within seconds the revelation came that he didn't have to do this work alone. It was not his work; it was the Savior's work. He would encourage the missionaries. President Ogden got a notebook and started writing:

Are you struggling, discouraged, wondering if you can make it?

Here is some encouragement from Nephi (liken his words to yourself):

- 1 Nephi 3:5–7, 15
- 1 Nephi 4:6
- 1 Nephi 9:6
- 1 Nephi 15:11
- 1 Nephi 17:3, 13
- 1 Nephi 18:3
- 1 Nephi 18:16
- 1 Nephi 18:21—"I prayed . . . and there was a great calm"
- 2 Nephi 10:20 (first half)
- 2 Nephi 10:23 (first line)
- 2 Nephi 32:3 (second half)
- 2 Nephi 4:17–35 (!)

1 Nephi 17:4–6

We wonder if disobedience contributed to the length of the wilderness experience of Lehi's family, as it did for ancient Israel (Alma 37:40–42). Even though the colony had suffered tremendously, and they couldn't even list and describe all the difficulties along the way, in the end the Lord prepared a reward for them—a fruitful, temporary campground.

1 Nephi 17:7–8

Again Nephi went into the mountain (for us, the mountain of the Lord, the temple) to commune with God and receive revelation.

"Thou shalt construct a ship." The Lord preempted Nephi's surprise by saying, in effect, I already know you have never constructed a ship before and you don't know how—"after the manner which I shall show thee." In other words, the Lord was going to tell Nephi step-by-step how to do it.

The archaeology of the ancient Near East confirms that

Nephi lived during the Iron Age (1200–539 B.C.), so it is little wonder that he sought ore to make tools.

1 Nephi 17:11

Noting that he made a bellows, we wonder if Nephi might have been a goldsmith or a blacksmith. He found ore and made tools, swords, and plates on which to engrave the records of his people.

1 Nephi 17:13–14

The Lord is literally the light of the universe (D&C 88:6–13). He will also be our light while we are passing through this wilderness of mortality, and he will "prepare the way" before us—if we keep his commandments—and he will lead us toward the ultimate promised land, the celestial kingdom. In the end, we will know it is he who did it. When we arrive in the eternal world, we will know with a perfect knowledge that the Lord delivered us out of destruction, out of the hand of the destroyer.

1 Nephi 17:17–18

Earlier, Laman and Lemuel didn't believe the Lord could deliver Laban and the plates into their hands; now they didn't believe Nephi could build a ship. The excuses continued: we don't believe Nephi can cross these great waters, and we don't believe the Lord told him to do it. Therefore, we are not going to work.

1 Nephi 17:19–22

Nephi felt bad, and his brothers were glad that he felt bad. It is typical of the fallen man to rejoice in a righteous person's sadness. The wicked use name-calling, labels, and false accusations.

"And why are they not chosen? Because their hearts are set so much upon the things of this world" (D&C 121:34–35). "We might have enjoyed our possessions," they lamented. Of course. Life could have been more comfortable and more pleasurable—and shorter! They might have been facing imminent death or exile back in Jerusalem. They were short-sighted indeed. The same attitude that afflicted the citizens of Jerusalem also blinded Laman and Lemuel: "What is our sin that we have committed against the Lord our God?" (Jeremiah 16:10). Laman and Lemuel probably acquired their attitude from the Jerusalemites of their day.

Laman and Lemuel denounced Nephi: You have unjustly accused our friends back home. They are strictly observant; they are meticulous observers of the Mosaic rituals, and you and our father are guilty of misjudging them.

1 Nephi 17:23–43

All right, brothers, Nephi said in effect, it is time for some history lessons. You are already aware of these facts of our forefathers' history and their miraculous deliverance in these same wilderness areas centuries ago.

Again, we are struck by the parallel between Lehi's family and the Exodus of the children of Israel:

- Murmuring over their hardship (1 Nephi 16:20)
- Journeying toward the promised land (17:13)
- Deliverance from destruction by the Lord (17:14)
- The prophet-leader receiving direction on a mountain (17:7)
- Nephi's use of the Exodus story to teach and inspire (17:23–43)

The last parallel is much like the practice of Jews today in recounting the Exodus story on the eve of Passover. Lehi and Nephi were following the Mosaic injunction to teach the children of the family the Passover miracles and God's goodness to the house of Israel (Exodus 12:26–27; 13:8, 14). Nephi used the phrase "ye know" eight times in five verses. Laman and Lemuel "knew" the Exodus story and its lessons because they had been taught before. Out of Nephi's discussion of the Exodus experience come profound doctrines: the Lord esteemeth all flesh in one, but the righteous receive his favor; the Lord speaks in a still small voice, but continual rebellion can put individuals in a condition "past feeling," where the Spirit of the Lord can no longer be recognized; and thus God raises up righteous peoples, but he "destroyeth the nations of the wicked."

God is just and fair. Those who want to disobey and be wicked bring destruction upon themselves. Those who are righteous are favored of God; he will love them and bless them.

1 Nephi 17:35, 40

It is fashionable these days to speak of God's unconditional love. Do the scriptures teach that God has unconditional love for everyone, or does God favor some over others? The Book of Mormon clearly answers those questions. "He that is righteous is favored of God. . . . And he loveth those who will have him to be their God." See also Psalm 145:18–20; John 14:21; 15:10; Acts 10:34–35; Romans 10:12–13; Helaman 3:27–28; 15:3–4.

1 Nephi 17:39

Dr. Robert J. Matthews explained why this earth is the Savior's footstool: "'Did Jesus have to suffer and die on any other worlds to redeem them, as he did on this earth?' The answer, based on the provisions of Alma 11 . . . can only be, 'No.' The fact that he was born, died, and resurrected on this earth—these being one-time events—demonstrates that he had never done these things elsewhere, or he would not have been able to do them here. And having done them on this earth, he cannot repeat them anywhere else. We see how unique our own world is in the universe. This earth is called God's footstool (D&C 38:17). On this earth Jesus Christ obtained his only physical body, and on this earth he was resurrected with that same body, and on this earth he will stand again and reign in his body throughout eternity (see D&C 130:9)."[45] See also Moses 6:44.

1 Nephi 17:41–42

Verse 41 notes that God straitened the Israelites with his rod. To *straiten* means to restrict their freedom, to subject them to distress, or in other words, to chasten them. The chastening or disciplining was done by sending "fiery flying serpents" among them. Upon being bitten by the serpents, all they had to do to be healed was look to the serpent Moses raised up on a pole (a type or symbol of Christ, who was also raised up; see John 3:14; Helaman 8:14–15). Because the way to be healed was so simple, many ignored it and would not look and live. Alma, while teaching about Moses' testimony of the Son of God, gave the best explanation of why many would not look:

"Behold a type was raised up in the wilderness, that whosoever would look upon it might live. And many did look and live.

"But few understood the meaning of those things, and this because of the hardness of their hearts. But there were many who were so hardened that they would not look, therefore they perished. Now the reason they would not look is because they did not believe that it would heal them" (Alma 33:19–20; see also commentary at Alma 33:19–20).

When people are living in sin, they harden their hearts and complain and condemn and criticize true, honest leaders and even God.

1 Nephi 17:44–46

Laman and Lemuel's anger had turned to murderous thoughts. The wicked cannot leave the righteous alone. It is clear that miraculous, other-worldly manifestations cannot change a stubborn, recalcitrant heart. The Spirit's calm, quiet, peaceful voice was trying to reach them, but the noise of their sinful lifestyle and mind-set was obstructing the voice. The wording here suggests that even if they could hear, they could not feel. The tragic message was that they were past feeling. Sometimes if a person cannot be reached by that quiet, gentle voice of the Spirit, the Lord will employ other methods such as thunder, lightning, tempests, and earthquakes (compare D&C 88:88–90).

President Boyd K. Packer warned of a growing trend in modern society that also leads to hard-heartedness, a loss of Spirit, and becoming past feeling:

"The world grows increasingly noisy. Clothing and grooming and conduct are looser and sloppier and more disheveled. Raucous music, with obscene lyrics blasted through amplifiers while lights flash psychedelic colors, characterizes the drug culture. Variations of these things are gaining wide acceptance and influence over our youth. . . .

"This trend to more noise, more excitement, more contention, less restraint, less dignity, less formality is not coincidental nor innocent nor harmless. . . .

"Irreverence suits the purposes of the adversary by obstructing the delicate channels of revelation in both mind and spirit."[46]

1 Nephi 17:47

Nephi, spiritually sensitive as he was, felt anguish and pain for his brothers, and he feared for their eternal lives. Being so full of the Spirit—the workings of the Spirit in him—caused him to feel totally debilitated physically (see commentary at 1 Nephi 1:5–20).

1 Nephi 17:48, 52

Nephi was so filled with the power of God—the Spirit of God—that he was untouchable. That is the same power that made the holy ark of the covenant untouchable (2 Samuel 6:6–7) and that protected Shadrach, Meshach, and Abednego (Daniel 3:17–27) and Nephi and Lehi (Helaman 5:23–24) in otherwise lethal circumstances.

1 Nephi 17:49–51

Don't complain, don't be lazy, just get busy and obey. Whatever God commands is right *and possible*. God knows all things, and he is the Master Teacher; of course he can instruct Nephi how to build a ship. There is a precedent: Noah already did it, and his ship must have been bigger.

1 Nephi 17:52

Righteousness and spirituality generate a palpable, physical power. Light and truth are an actual force in the universe (D&C 84:45–46; 88:6–13). Priesthood power is demonstrable. The brothers didn't dare touch Nephi, and they couldn't succeed in being argumentative. There must have been a few days of peace.

1 Nephi 17:53–55

It is interesting how the Lord provided a testimony *at the brothers' level*. Let's just give them a little shock treatment so they will know that God and his power are real. The testing was successful. They were convinced. Then they launched into a little misguided adoration of their brother; they couldn't seem to get it right. It is a measure of Nephi's integrity that he did not claim any special honor or glory. Rather, he directed others to the Lord. He said, in effect, Worship God! And honor your parents if you want to live a long time in the land where you are going. This absence of pride is seen in Jesus, Moses, and all the Lord's true servants.

1 Nephi 18:1–3

Nephi received blueprints and technical revelation from the Master Shipbuilder. The young prophet made frequent hikes to his private spot on the mountain, poured out his soul in prayer, and was blessed with great views. "I, Nephi, did go into the mount oft, and I did pray oft unto the Lord; wherefore the Lord showed unto me great things." That passage has at least two meanings: in the temple, the mountain of the Lord, God opens up to all of us the views of great things. Also, when we climb our personal mountains—challenges, trials, difficulties, struggles, hardships, afflictions—he can teach us great things.

Matthew 8:1 says, "When he was come down from the mountain, great multitudes followed him." We must also climb to the mountaintop (for example, the temple), where the Lord will also show us great things. Then we must go back down among the people, and because we are full of the Spirit, others will desire to follow us into the kingdom. We must desire with all our heart to go to the mountaintop and then go back down to lead others up.

1 Nephi 18:9–16

Singing and dancing can be either good and uplifting or evil and degrading. The word of the Lord at Winter Quarters, given during the Saints' modern exodus westward, states, "If thou art merry, praise the Lord with singing, with music, with dancing, and with a prayer of praise and thanksgiving" (D&C 136:28). In the case of Nephi's brothers and Ishmael's sons, the merriment was carried on with such "rudeness" that it offended the Spirit of the Lord. And, as usual, Nephi's cautions were met with Laman and Lemuel's anger. They bound Nephi and treated him so roughly that his wrists and ankles became greatly swollen. The traveling party also suffered the consequences of unrighteousness on the high seas. However, the most powerful lesson comes in Nephi's magnificent response to all of that: "Nevertheless, I did look unto my God, and I did praise him all the day long; and I did not murmur against the Lord because of mine afflictions" (1 Nephi 18:16). To remain loyal to God, especially through trials clearly not of our own making, and resist the temptation to become bitter over the Lord's nonintervention is the great test and lesson of life—"to serve Him at all hazards," thus guaranteeing our exaltation.[47]

1 Nephi 18:17–25

Lehi and Sariah in their old age had "suffered much grief because of their [rebellious] children" and now once again were sickened by their behavior, which nearly brought them to "a watery grave." Only the fear of death caused the rebels to soften their rudeness, crudeness, and ill tempers. Released from bands, Nephi fervently prayed and again took up steering toward the promised land.

In their new land of inheritance they planted seeds and discovered that the seeds grew prolifically. Having left some wealth back in Jerusalem, they now found themselves in possession of a wealth of valuable flora and fauna and ores and precious metals (see also 2 Nephi 5:15). These bounteous blessings were a direct fulfillment of part of the blessing their ancient ancestor Joseph had received from his father, Jacob (whose names, not incidentally, were given to the two sons born to Sariah and Lehi in the wilderness): "Blessed of the Lord be his land, for the precious things of heaven, . . . and for the precious fruits brought forth by the sun, . . . and for the chief things of the ancient mountains, and for the precious things of the lasting hills, and for the precious things of the earth and fulness thereof" (Deuteronomy 33:13–16).

1 Nephi 19:1–6

The Lord instructed Nephi to make two sets of plates. Nephi said, "Wherefore I did make plates of ore," that is, the first, or large, plates of Nephi. The first set recorded Lehi's ministry, his genealogy, the family's travels, and other historical events, especially political and military history. The second set recorded Nephi's ministry, prophecies, and other matters of a more sacred nature. He continued, "And I knew not at the time when I made them [the large plates] that I should be commanded of the Lord to make these plates [the small plates]." He then certified, "I do not write anything upon [the small] plates save it be that I think it be sacred." As noted already in the commentary at 1 Nephi 9, the prophet didn't know all of the Lord's wise reasons for making two different records, but he was willing to be exactly obedient.

Note the wisdom in engraving on metal plates so the record would endure far longer than ancient papyrus and even parchment (animal skin) or our modern paper and plastic materials on which we engrave or "burn" records.

1 Nephi 19:7–9

Nephi's discussion of the sets of plates and their different purposes led him to talk about value systems, which then led to his prophetic testimony of Christ. Some people esteem the sacred things as of great worth, whereas others set them "at naught." Some even trample the sacred things under their feet, as it were, and go so far as to trample God himself under their feet (a shocking image, to be sure). Twice in verse 7, Nephi mentioned setting God "at naught," the same God who would condescend to become mortal "six hundred years from the time [Lehi] left Jerusalem."

Verse 9 describes the sinful world judging God, the Savior, as "a thing of naught." Other passages of the Book of Mormon define this concept: that which is just and good is considered "of no worth" (2 Nephi 28:16); the words of God are esteemed "as things of naught" (2 Nephi 33:2); the commandments of God are "set at naught" (Helaman 4:21); the counsels of God are "set at naught" (Helaman 12:6); and the atonement of God is set "at naught" (Moroni 8:20). In these contexts God and his eternal principles are ignored, disregarded, avoided, rejected, disobeyed, and reviled against. "Set at naught" means they are considered worthless, regarded as unimportant.

Imagine men, in their *nothingness* (see Mosiah 4:5, 11; Helaman 12:7; Moses 1:10), deeming God, in his greatness and power, as worthless and unimportant. Nephi described the Savior's magnanimous response to this insulting ignorance of men: "They scourge him, and he suffereth it; and they smite him, and he suffereth it. Yea, they spit upon him, and he suffereth it, because of his loving kindness and his long-suffering towards the children of men" (1 Nephi 19:9). It will be remembered that this earth, upon which Jesus lived, is one of the most wicked of all those created (Moses 7:36), and the Savior's own people, especially their leaders, were the only group who would crucify their God (2 Nephi 10:3). What a glorious Being we revere, who is willing to suffer the offensive abuse of men and still extend his loving kindness and forgiveness! "O Savior, Thou Who Wearest a Crown," a powerful Latter-day Saint hymn, declares:

> No creature is so lowly,
> No sinner so depraved,
> But feels thy presence holy,
> And through thy love is saved.
> Tho craven friends betray thee,
> They feel thy love's embrace;
> The very foes who slay thee
> Have access to thy grace.[48]

That truly is amazing grace.

1 Nephi 19:10

The great God who miraculously led Israel out of Egypt and preserved the Israelites in the Sinai desert, the same great God worshipped by the patriarchs, yielded himself into the hands of wicked men to be crucified and then to be buried in a borrowed sepulcher. The sign of his death would be three days of darkness. All of these events, Nephi recorded, were prophesied by three otherwise unknown prophets, Zenock, Neum, and Zenos. (Zenos and Zenock are frequently mentioned together as Israelite prophets who detailed the ministry, death, and resurrection of the Savior; see also Alma 33:15; 34:7; Helaman 8:19–20; 3 Nephi 10:16. They lived and taught sometime between Abraham and Lehi.)

1 Nephi 19:11–24

Nephi engraved some prophecies of "the prophet," whom he mentions nine times in these verses (though mentioning his name—Isaiah—only once). It is clear in context that Nephi is referring to the prophet Isaiah (see, for example, 1 Nephi 22:2). These verses constitute Nephi's introduction to Isaiah, whose words are some of the greatest ever written by a prophet (3 Nephi 23:1).

1 Nephi 19:11–12

The phrase "at that day" generally refers to the last days and Jesus' second coming. To their great joy and salvation, the righteous will be visited with the voice of the Lord God. Others will be visited with a different voice of God (D&C 88:88–90), actually various natural catastrophes, what we call "acts of God"—thunderings, lightnings, tempests, fires, smoke, vapors of darkness, and earthquakes—as a testimony against them.

1 Nephi 19:13–14

The inhabitants of Jerusalem will be scourged by people worldwide because, as a people, they reject their Deliverer and his awesome use of priesthood power to perform numerous signs and wonders. His people at Jerusalem, for the most part, will turn their hearts away from the Holy One of Israel and despise him, so in that generation they will "wander in the flesh, and perish, and become a hiss and a byword, and be hated among all nations." And the persecution and hatred will continue in succeeding generations (including centuries of persecutions, inquisitions, pogroms, and the Holocaust) because, as a people, they continue to reject their God (see commentary at 2 Nephi 25:9).

1 Nephi 19:15–17

After all the doom, desolation, and destruction will come the restoration, reinstatement, and redemption. When the Jews turn back (Hebrew *lashuv*, means "turn or repent"), the Holy One will remember the covenants made with their fathers, the patriarchs. Then the gathering begins, when they will come to a knowledge of their true Messiah. All the earth shall see the salvation of the Lord. Jesus' name (Hebrew *Yeshua*) means "Savior" or "salvation."

1 Nephi 19:18–21

Nephi advised future readers that his overall purpose in writing the words of Isaiah into the record is to persuade people, the whole house of Israel (plus all who would be adopted into the house of Israel), to remember the Lord, their Redeemer.

Once again Nephi called attention to the physical weakness he felt when full of the workings of the Spirit (see also 1 Nephi 1:5–20; 17:47). Nephi's comment about the workings of the Spirit leaving him weary was not a complaint but rather an expression of gratitude that the Lord had watched over him so carefully. Intense experiences with the Spirit and power of God do leave mortals feeling weakened. Even the mortal Jesus experienced this when a woman touched the hem of his garment and was healed. Mark recorded that Jesus felt strength go out of him (Mark 5:27–30).

Ancient prophets foresaw the future Jews at Jerusalem at around 600 B.C., and they foresaw groups broken off from the olive tree of Israel, such as the Lehite colony ("ye who are a remnant of the house of Israel, a branch who have been broken off"; 1 Nephi 19:24). The testimonies of these prophets of old were engraved on the plates of brass.

1 Nephi 19:22–24

Nephi taught the teachings of former prophets so his people could visualize the active role the Lord has played in other lands, too. He cited much from the Torah, the books of Moses (at least some of which we have in our present books of Genesis, Exodus, Leviticus, Numbers, and Deuteronomy), but to "more fully persuade them to believe in the Lord their Redeemer [he] did read unto them that which was written by the prophet Isaiah." Few prophets have ever lived on earth who wrote more pointedly and powerfully about the Savior, the Lord Jesus Christ, than did Isaiah. As we will see, the Lord himself recommended Isaiah's words in order for us to become truly acquainted with Him. Jesus commanded us to search the prophet's words diligently and to do as Nephi did: "liken all scriptures unto us, that it might be for our profit and learning." Like many Book of Mormon prophets, Isaiah wrote to us and for us—to bring us to Christ. Even his name is his message: *Isaiah* (Hebrew *Yesha-Yah*) means "Jehovah saves."

All of us who are of the house of Israel are encouraged to liken Isaiah's words to our situations in these latter days, that in these tumultuous times we "may have hope," for our Savior is indeed the Hope of Israel.

INTRODUCTION TO ISAIAH

Isaiah is the most frequently quoted prophet in the New Testament, in the Book of Mormon, and in the Doctrine and Covenants. The Book of Mormon: Another Testament of Jesus Christ contains the oldest copy of Isaiah extant. It is the best text of Isaiah and the best commentary. The Book of Mormon is host to over thirty pages of Isaiah's writings, quoting about one-third of the prophet's book. There are passages from twenty-four of Isaiah's sixty-six chapters (nineteen complete; two others almost complete). Of 425 separate verses of Isaiah quoted in the Book of Mormon, 196 are identical but 229 are quoted differently. Of 425 verses, 391 teach something about the attributes or mission of the Lord Jesus Christ.

The book of Isaiah is not a sequential narrative; it is more like sections in the Doctrine and Covenants. Isaiah 1:1 is a heading or introduction to the entire book of Isaiah. Other headings that apply to whole books, such as Amos 1:1, Hosea 1:1, Micah 1:1, and Zephaniah 1:1, are similar in form to Isaiah 1:1.

The prophet's forty-year ministry spanned the reigns of at least four kings, from approximately 740 to 700 B.C. We have no scriptural information about Isaiah's birth, childhood, maturation, personal appearance, or death, though Jewish rabbinical writings (*Yebamoth* 49b; *Sanhedrin* 103b) do record traditions about the manner of his death in the reign of Manasseh, king of Judah, ca. 700 B.C., and the apocryphal book called The Ascension of Isaiah records Manasseh's killing the prophet by sawing him asunder. Isaiah was the son of Amoz, whose name is not the same as that of Amos the prophet.[49]

For understanding the social background of Isaiah we may compare also the writings of his contemporaries Amos, Hosea, and Micah. During the century 830–730 B.C. an incessant parade of internal conflicts and overthrowing of kings, military threats and invasions of foreign powers, and general apostate conditions prevailed. The people among whom God had established his covenant and to whom he had promised his divine protection had, as a people, abandoned him. Politically they were trusting in the arm of flesh, and spiritually they were gone awhoring after other gods. In the midst of Israelite military victories and territorial expansion and resultant pride and sense of security, the prophets began to appear to condemn the moral and spiritual failings of their people.

It had been two hundred years since the Davidic kingdom was divided; northern and southern kingdoms had often been at odds with each other and sometimes had united to withstand a common enemy. In the days of Isaiah and Amos, Israel was enjoying considerable stability and prosperity (due, of course, to the fact that there was no great power—Assyria or Egypt—pressing at their border). Removal of the threat of Ben-hadad III of Damascus allowed Israel at least partial control of territory as far as sixty miles north of Damascus. Jeroboam and Uzziah both carried on vigorous campaigns of expansion and extended their southern and eastern frontiers to equal the former kingdom of David and Solomon.[50] Assyria was becoming an increasing political threat, but Tiglath-pileser III was still on the distant horizon, and Israel, Judah, Syria, and Egypt were all united in their opposition to Assyrian advances westward.

The material prosperity of Israel showed no signs of waning, but it was a hollow prosperity at best. The people could not long conceal their injustices and corruptions. Baalism had worn threadbare the moral fabric of the people. When the prophet Amos had finished with his summary treatment of the sins of Israel's neighbors, the northern Israelites discovered that his prophecy against them was not to be "for three transgressions and for four," but an extensive enumeration of the social and religious ills of the people to whom Jehovah had sent him. The dark list of sins began: the sale into slavery of innocent people, mistreatment of the poor, sexual abuse of young women which profaned God's name (cultic prostitution), exaction of unjust fines, corruption of the court and legal processes, enticing of Nazarites to break their vows, and prohibiting prophets from delivering their messages. The charges continue throughout Amos's writings: violence and robbery, oppression of the needy, greed, drunkenness, hypocrisy in cultic ordinances, disdain of honest judges, cheating the poor, bribery, idolatry, gluttony and revelry, pride, vainglory, false sense of security, deceitful business practices, and desecration of the spirit of the Sabbath. All in all, not a very flattering catalog of sins for God's people. They needed to listen to a prophet's voice. Isaiah's catalog of criminal and sinful behavior would exceed that of Amos.

WHY STUDY ISAIAH

3 Nephi 23:1–3

The first and best reason to study Isaiah is that we have been commanded to search his writings, and the commandment has been repeated several times (see also 3 Nephi 20:11–12; Mormon 8:23). A commandment, of course, is something for which we will all be held accountable, for our God demands that we make special study of the words he gave to this particular prophet.

Isaiah gave revelations concerning all things and all stages of the great plan of salvation. His prophecies have been and will be fulfilled; they have dual and, in some cases, multiple fulfillment. Things which have been and will be are often called "types."

Time, rather than being linear, is circular: "one eternal round" (Ecclesiastes 1:9; 1 Nephi 10:19). The creation and population of worlds are cyclical, doing that which has been done over and over again. The work of dispensations is also cyclical, each having a beginning, an apostasy, a warning period, and "latter days."

Apocalyptic revelation (such as Lehi's and Nephi's dreams and some writings of Isaiah, Ezekiel, Daniel, Zechariah, and John) can often be seen in terms of timelessness. For a brief moment all things are before the prophet—past, present, and future.

Typical actors, in all ages, are a dragon, a beast, a serpent, a great and abominable institution, a "spiritual Babylon," a mother of harlots, a pit, darkness, angels, stars, servants, saints, sheep, water, light, those arrayed in white, and so forth.

Zion and Babylon, the righteous and the wicked, are foils or contrasts; "Assyria" and "Egypt" are superpowers at the end of time.

The use of symbols is important. They can *conceal* meaning, but understanding the symbols can *reveal* meaning.

1 Nephi 19:23

Jesus Christ is the central message of Isaiah—recall that the prophet's name means "Jehovah saves." Isaiah provides a greater testimony of the Redeemer, and the study of him is certainly for our profit and learning (see also 2 Nephi 25:23, 26).

2 Nephi 6:4–5

By searching the writings of Isaiah we learn about God and glorify him. Isaiah's teachings apply to us. They are not just history lessons but lessons from history. As someone has said, history is what happened; literature is what happens. And the book of Isaiah is great literature. Isaiah gives us views of what lies ahead.

2 Nephi 11

We can learn much from eyewitnesses of the Redeemer. Joseph Smith wrote, "Could you gaze into heaven five minutes, you would know more than you would by reading all that ever was written on the subject."[51] Isaiah is one of the great prophets who have gazed into heaven, and he can teach us much. We can come to more fully believe in the God of heaven and delight in his coming; we can learn the typologies and attributes of him—all of which will enable us to lift up our hearts and rejoice for all men.

HOW TO UNDERSTAND ISAIAH

1 Nephi 19:23

Reading Isaiah is a spiritual workout. Proper study of his writings can sharpen us mentally and spiritually. We are encouraged to liken his writings to our own personal situations, for our profit and learning.

THE FIRST BOOK OF NEPHI

2 Nephi 25:1, 5

We can become acquainted with the manner of writing among the Jews, coming to understand their literary mechanisms for better comprehension. Isaiah in particular wrote with sophisticated artistry; over 90 percent of his writings is in poetic form (poetry is saying one thing and meaning another). Types, figures, and symbols usually have a surface meaning but also a deeper, underlying meaning. Coming to understand the form is important—for example, the similes, metaphors, personification, and parallelisms (couplets).

Knowing King James English helps; the more we read and study it, the more familiar it becomes. Knowing Hebrew helps also. We are grateful for the English (IE) and Hebrew (HEB) language notes in the Latter-day Saint edition of the King James Version of the Bible.

2 Nephi 25:4

Understanding Isaiah requires us to be filled with the spirit of prophecy, which, according to John, is "the testimony of Jesus" (Revelation 19:10). There is an obligation of personal worthiness for every student of Isaiah. Only when we sincerely inquire of the Lord, in faith, and keep his commandments will the comprehension of his writings be opened to us. Each one must pay the price (1 Nephi 10:19; Alma 12:9–10; 26:22).

2 Nephi 25:6

Learn something of the history and geography of the Holy Land. Goethe said, *"Wer den Dichter will verstehen, muss in Dichter's Lande gehen"* ("Whoever wants to understand a poet, must go to the poet's homeland"). If you want to understand Wordsworth, go to his homeland, and you will understand his writings better. If you want to understand Isaiah, who is a poet par excellence, you can go to his homeland and relate better than ever to his imagery. Nephi lived in the same land and city as Isaiah, so he understood Isaiah's figurative language. The land is a natural commentary on the writings that come from it. Just as Jesus did in his mortal ministry, Isaiah constantly drew

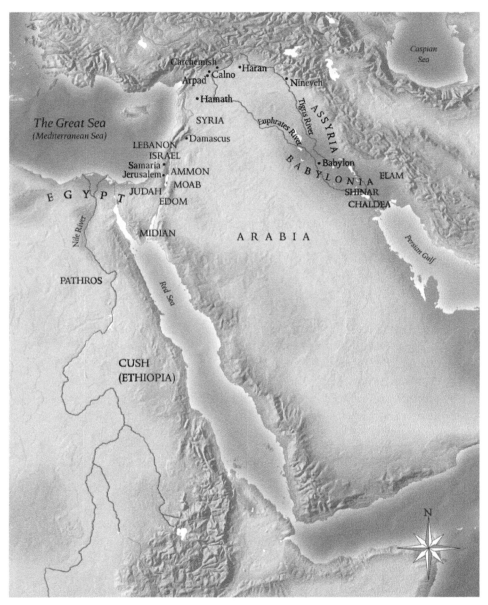

Places in the Near East mentioned in Isaiah's writings in the Book of Mormon.

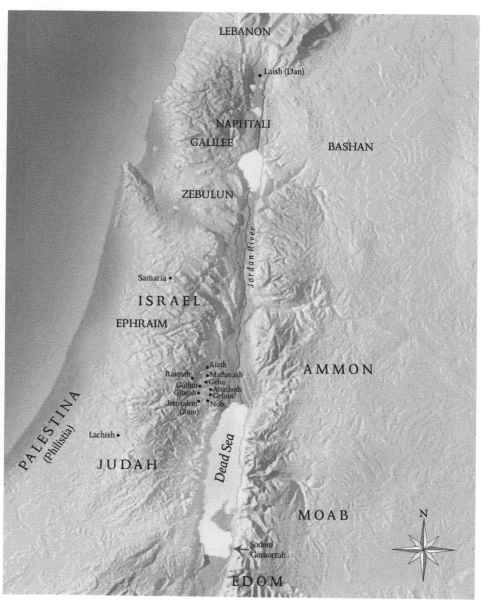

Places in the Holy Land and environs mentioned in Isaiah's writings in the Book of Mormon.

examples and illustrations from the objects of daily living and from the "regions round about."

2 Nephi 25:7–8

We can benefit from Nephi's plainness, in which "no man can err." Nephi intentionally avoided the manner of prophesying among the Jews; the Book of Mormon does not follow all the Hebraic literary styles. Isaiah is difficult only because the Jews desired it (compare Jacob 4:14–18). Knowing the prophecies in our day we can see them fulfilled (for example, Isaiah 29 [2 Nephi 27], including a conversation between two men in New York City, seen, heard, and recorded twenty-five hundred years before it happened!). Isaiah's prophecies are of great worth particularly to us in the last days. The phrase "in that day" appears forty-three times in Isaiah. His teachings are recorded for our good, to help us be prepared and involved in bringing about the great purposes of God.

1 Nephi 20 (Isaiah 48)

1 Nephi 20 and 21, the first two chapters of Isaiah quoted in the Book of Mormon, describe Nephi's reading of Isaiah 48 and 49 to his brothers. Isaiah 48 (1 Nephi 20) is largely a discussion of ancient Israel's waywardness and disloyalty to the Redeemer of Israel. Isaiah 49 (1 Nephi 21) is the prophet's announcement of a special servant to come forth, who would possess several significant and special characteristics and would fulfill unique roles. Three things become obvious: first, Isaiah possessed a panoramic perspective of Israel's history and destiny; second, Nephi knew well and appreciated this section of Isaiah because of the parallel it presented between Israel and his own brothers, Laman and Lemuel; third, only two beings fit Isaiah's very specific and unusual qualities: the Savior Jesus Christ and the Prophet Joseph Smith (see "A Special Servant," accompanying the commentary at 1 Nephi 21:14, 21, 24).

Notice that after hearing these two chapters Nephi's brothers came to him and asked, "What do these things mean?" (1 Nephi 22:1). Fortunately, Nephi gave further explanation.

Isaiah scholar Claus Westermann claimed that Isaiah 48 has serious textual difficulties, "and so far editors have not succeeded in finding any convincing solution."[52] Now we have a solution: the Book of Mormon.

1 Nephi 20:1

Notice that the very first word in this first chapter of Isaiah that Nephi quotes is not *hear* but *hearken*—supplementing the passive hearing with active obeying.

In the 1840 printing of the Book of Mormon, the Prophet Joseph Smith added after "the waters of Judah" the phrase "or out of the waters of baptism." This refers to those who have taken on themselves the covenant of baptism, thus indicating that baptism was an essential ordinance performed in Old Testament times (though known more by the term *immersion* than by the later Greek term *baptism*).

1 Nephi 20:2

"They call themselves of the holy city"—as hypocrites said in Jesus' day, "we have Abraham [for] our father" (Luke 3:8); "we be Abraham's seed" (John 8:33). They thought themselves worthy of some preferential status, but they did not stay themselves on (that is, depend on, rely on, trust in) the God of Israel.

Of this verse professors McConkie and Millet wrote: "Salvation is not obtained by living in a particular place, but rather by living in a particular way. There are no holy cities without a holy people."[53]

1 Nephi 20:3–9

The Lord revealed future things before his wayward people could claim that idols did them.

Verse 7 addition in the Book of Mormon: "Even before the day when thou heardest them not *they were declared unto thee.*"

Verse 9 addition: "For my praise will I refrain *from* thee."

1 Nephi 20:10

The phrase "but not with silver" in Isaiah disrupts the meaning of the verse, and the Book of Mormon omits it.

This is great doctrine, this idea of being refined and chosen in the furnace of affliction. Just as gold is smelted in the fire to remove impurities, so God has tried his people with fire to remove impurities. The Lord is working hard to draw impurities out of us. Just as a diamond is carefully faceted and polished to reveal its inner beauty, so has Israel been shaped and polished. Trials are not punishment inflicted by a vengeful God but tests by a loving Father who wants us to be refined and polished. Our impurities (weaknesses, faults) get burned away *if* we can withstand the heat and pressure of our trials. Refineries heat up the metal to its melting point, at which time the impurities separate. In a similar way God "turns up the heat" until we reach the point where we become refined so we can be of use to him. The temperature necessary to refine each of us is different. Refinement is customized for each of us by a perfect and omniscient Father. And it helps to know that troubles and trials are purposeful; we endure them for good reasons.

We are here on earth to be refined, and this earth is one big furnace! All of these metaphorical expressions about the refiner's fire give new meaning to the statement of the prophet Brigham Young: "Learn everything that the children of men know, and be prepared for the most refined society upon the face of the earth."[54]

1 Nephi 20:11

Book of Mormon change from the King James Version: "for I will not suffer my name to be polluted."

1 Nephi 20:13

Right hand: "Showing favor to the right hand or side is not something invented by man but was revealed from the heavens in the beginning. . . . There are numerous passages in the scriptures referring to the right hand, indicating that it is a symbol of righteousness and was used in the making of covenants."[55]

1 Nephi 20:14–15

The pronouns *he* and *him* are somewhat confusing; it seems to be Jehovah speaking but talking about himself. He is delivering the message of the Father about himself, so the prophecy is about Jesus, who is using the third-person form.

1 Nephi 20:18

See commentary about topographical imagery at 1 Nephi 2:7–9.

1 Nephi 20:20

"Go ye forth of Babylon"—in one of our hymns we sing about the importance of bidding Babylon farewell; on the eve of Babylon's destruction we have a new exodus, a type of the old. Doctrine and Covenants 133:14 certainly refers to a spiritual exodus, but could it also be referring to a physical exodus? Unlikely. Our God wants us to flee from the spiritual wickedness around us but not isolate ourselves physically from the rest of humankind. We have to stay among them to show them the way, to be a light to all people. Ralph Waldo Emerson made an interesting observation: "It is easy in the world to live after the world's opinion; it is easy in solitude to live after our own; but the great man is he who in the midst of the crowd keeps with perfect sweetness the independence of solitude."[56]

1 Nephi 20:22

Book of Mormon addition: "And notwithstanding he hath done all this, and greater also."

There is no peace for the wicked. The Holy Ghost does not comfort the wicked. No one comforts the wicked. See also Alma 41:10: "wickedness never was happiness."

1 Nephi 21 (Isaiah 49)

The best way to study this chapter is alongside the inspired commentary and interpretations of Nephi (in 1 Nephi 22:1–12) and Jacob (in 2 Nephi 6:4–18; 10:1–22).

This chapter is directed to the modern covenant people of Israel: "The revelations that are in the Bible, the predictions of the patriarchs and prophets who saw by vision and revelation the last dispensation and fulness of times plainly tell us what is to come to pass. The 49th chapter of Isaiah is having its fulfillment."[57]

1 Nephi 21:1–6

This is one of the great Servant Songs of Isaiah, speaking of an individual or a group who will make salvation accessible for those who diligently seek it. Possibilities for the servant are Isaiah himself; Jehovah (Jesus Christ); Israel, particularly Ephraim; and Joseph Smith. Maybe all of the above are applicable, but especially Jesus Christ and Joseph Smith.

1 Nephi 21:1

The first half of the verse is missing in the King James Version; Nephi adds, "And again: Hearken, O ye house of Israel, all ye that are broken off and are driven out because of the wickedness of the pastors of my people; yea, all ye that are broken off, that are scattered abroad, who are of my people, O house of Israel."

Isles means habitable ground or dry land as opposed to

water, or in other words, islands and continents (see 2 Nephi 10:20–21).

America is referred to (see 1 Nephi 22:7–8).

"Called me from the womb"—that is, the servant was foreordained.

All servants of the Lord are foreordained (compare Jeremiah 1:5).

1 Nephi 21:2

"Mouth like a sharp sword"—to the wicked the servant's words are cutting like a sword (1 Nephi 16:2; D&C 6:1–2).

Elaborating on the concept of a polished shaft, the Prophet Joseph Smith exclaimed: "I am like a huge, rough stone rolling down from a high mountain; and the only polishing I get is when some corner gets rubbed off by coming in contact with something else, striking with accelerated force against religious bigotry, priestcraft, lawyer-craft, doctor-craft, lying editors, suborned judges and jurors, and the authority of perjured executives, backed by mobs, blasphemers, licentious and corrupt men and women—all hell knocking off a corner here and a corner there. Thus I will become a smooth and polished shaft in the quiver of the Almighty, who will give me dominion over all and every one of them, when their refuge of lies shall fail, and their hiding place shall be destroyed, while these smooth-polished stones with which I come in contact become marred."[58]

"In his quiver hath he hid me"—the servant is hidden or protected until the appropriate time for the Lord to pull him out to fight in the cause of righteousness. The arrow of truth will be shot out into the world and will pierce the hearts of the wicked.

1 Nephi 21:5

Of Joseph Smith the Lord said: "Fools shall have thee in derision, and hell shall rage against thee; while the pure in heart, and the wise, and the noble, and the virtuous, shall seek counsel, and authority, and blessings constantly from under thy hand" (D&C 122:1–2). And "God shall exalt thee on high" (D&C 121:8).

1 Nephi 21:6

The mission statement of the covenant people of Israel is identified: to be a light to the Gentiles, to bring them to salvation. "Salvation" is Hebrew *Yeshua* (Jesus). The Savior, the prophet, and every true servant of the Lord are lights to the Gentiles.

1 Nephi 21:7

The world despised the Lord Jesus Christ and the Prophet Joseph Smith, but kings and princes will indeed bow and honor these noble and great ones.

1 Nephi 21:8

" . . . have I heard thee, *O isles of the sea*"—isles, again, are the far islands or continents beyond Asia.

" . . . and give thee *my servant* for a covenant of the people"—that is, Joseph Smith.

1 Nephi 21:9

Salvation for the dead is taught also in the Old Testament. How do we know that Isaiah understood this vital doctrine? "And Isaiah, who declared by prophecy that the Redeemer was anointed to bind up the broken-hearted, to proclaim liberty to the captives, and the opening of the prison to them that were bound, [was] also there" (D&C 138:42).

1 Nephi 21:14, 21, 24

Israel remonstrates with a series of complaints:

Verse 14—complaint 1: The Lord forsook and forgot Israel. Some in Israel felt wronged by the Lord. They felt severely punished through their sufferings due to political oppression, exile, famine, plague, and more.

Verses 14–16—answer: "*but he will show that he hath not.*" A powerful attachment is expressed: graven on palms of hands are the nail wounds in the Savior's hands. Far from forsaking them, he gave his all for them. "Greater love hath no man than this, that a man lay down his life for his friends" (John 15:13). Christ paid the ultimate price for our sins. He cannot forget us because he has the evidence of that price in his hands and feet (D&C 6:36–37).

Verse 18: The covenant people of Israel will eventually be clothed and ornamented (that is, prepared) as a bride for the Bridegroom, as reflected in various scriptures; see, for example, Matthew 25:1–10; D&C 33:17; 133:10, 19.

Verse 21—complaint 2: Israel has lost all her children.

Verses 22–23—answer: The Lord will raise a standard or ensign (for example, the Church, the Book of Mormon, and the everlasting covenant) and bring the children of Israel back to their promised inheritance.

Is the Lord talking about Jews in the Holy Land or the Israelites broken off inhabiting the Americas? See 1 Nephi 22:6. Isaiah speaks to *all* Israel, which assures multilevel fulfillment.

Kings and queens and other political leaders will be nursing fathers and mothers in helping restore the remnants of Israel. Note one fulfillment of this prophecy in the following excerpt from Orson Hyde's dedicatory prayer given 24 October 1841 on the Mount of Olives in Jerusalem:

"Let the land become abundantly fruitful when possessed by its rightful heirs; let it again flow with plenty to feed the returning prodigals who come home with a spirit of grace and supplication. . . . Incline them to gather in upon this land according to Thy word. Let them come like clouds and like doves to their windows. Let the large ships of the nations bring them from the distant isles; and let kings become their nursing fathers, and queens with motherly fondness wipe the tear of sorrow from their eye.

"Thou, O Lord, did once move upon the heart of Cyrus to show favor unto Jerusalem and her children. Do Thou now also be pleased to inspire the hearts of kings and the powers of the earth to look with a friendly eye towards this place, and with a desire to see Thy righteous purposes executed in relation thereto. Let them know that it is Thy good pleasure to restore the kingdom unto Israel—raise up Jerusalem as its capital, and constitute her people a distinct nation and government."[59]

Verse 24—complaint 3: Israel is prey; she is held captive.

Verses 25–26—answer: Read 2 Nephi 6:16–18. The Mighty God shall deliver his covenant people.

A SPECIAL SERVANT

Isaiah announced a special servant of God who would come forward in the future, possessing several significant and unusual characteristics. Originally recorded in Isaiah 49, Nephi describes again this prophetic figure. He would be someone—

- whom "the Lord hath called . . . from the womb" (1 Nephi 21:1).
- who would say that the Lord "formed me from the womb" to do a special work, or in other words, someone who *knew* he had been foreordained (21:5).
- whose "mouth [was] like a sharp sword," or in other words, someone who spoke with authority (21:2).
- who was hidden "in the shadow of [the Lord's] hand" (21:2).
- who was "made . . . a polished shaft; in his quiver hath he [the Lord] hid [him]" (21:2).
- who would say, "I have labored in vain" (21:4).
- who would authoritatively say, "And now, saith the Lord" (21:5).

- whose life's work would be "to bring Jacob again to [the Lord]—though Israel be not gathered" (21:5).
- who would be the Lord's "servant to raise up the tribes of Jacob, and to restore the preserved of Israel" (21:6).
- whom the Lord would "give . . . for a light to the Gentiles" (21:6).
- "whom man despiseth," but at the same time, someone whom "kings shall see and arise, princes also . . . worship" (21:7).
- who will be given to Israel "for a covenant of the people, to establish the earth, to cause to inherit the desolate heritages," who will free the prisoners and enlighten those who sit in darkness, and who will shepherd the chosen people (21:8–9).

Though various specific aspects of this list could probably fit a number of individuals, taken together they apply to only two beings. One is obviously Jesus, but the other is Joseph Smith! Consider the following:

- Joseph Smith was indeed called "from the womb," or foreordained.
- He knew through revelation, now recorded as Doctrine and Covenants 127:2, that he had been chosen to be the prophet of the Restoration. On another occasion he also said: "Every man who has a calling to minister to the inhabitants of the world was ordained to that very purpose in the Grand Council of heaven before this world was. I suppose that I was ordained to this very office in that Grand Council. It is the testimony that I want that I am God's servant, and this people His people."[60]
- Joseph Smith spoke as a "sharp sword" because he spoke the words of the Lord (D&C 18:35–36; 21:5), which are described in modern revelation as "quick and powerful, sharper than a two-edged sword, to the dividing asunder of both joints and marrow" (D&C 6:2).

- Joseph Smith was "hid" by the Lord (D&C 86:9).
- Joseph Smith became a "polished shaft" in the quiver of the Almighty, as his own characterization of himself testifies (see commentary at 1 Nephi 21:2).
- Joseph Smith at times became discouraged and felt that he labored in vain (D&C 121:2).
- Not only did Joseph Smith have the authority to speak for God but on numerous occasions he validated his messages by uttering the very words Isaiah predicted he would say: "Thus saith the Lord" (for example, D&C 52:1; 54:1; 60:1; 87:1).
- Joseph Smith's life work was to bring the house of Israel again to the Lord (Mormon 8:16; D&C 5:9–10; 6:6; 109:67).
- Joseph Smith was also commissioned to "raise up the tribes of Jacob" and "restore" them by overseeing the latter-day gathering of Israel (D&C 110:11).
- Joseph Smith is spoken of in the scriptures as "a light unto the Gentiles" (D&C 86:11). Only one other person can claim that distinction—the Lord himself (Isaiah 42:6).
- Joseph Smith was both despised and revered, just as the Lord had predicted (Joseph Smith–History 1:33). Joseph was also promised that the gospel he restored would be preached before "kings and rulers" (D&C 1:23).
- Joseph Smith was the servant through whom the eternal gospel covenant was reestablished (D&C 1:17–22). Surely it is not just coincidence that Doctrine and Covenants 1, the revelation by which the Lord introduces Joseph Smith to the world, begins with the same language as Isaiah 49:1. Just as Isaiah had foretold, the Prophet Joseph was also commanded to "proclaim the acceptable year of the Lord, and the gospel of salvation" (D&C 93:51).

1 Nephi 22:1–3

Nephi proceeded to interpret for his brethren the two quoted chapters of Isaiah. Is all this temporal or spiritual? Is it figurative or literal? The answer is yes. It is both.

1 Nephi 22:4–5

A large portion of the tribes of Israel has been led away from their ancient homeland, the land of Israel. The ten tribes were led away northward and then lost to history (though not lost to God). No scriptures suggest they are anywhere but scattered throughout the nations of the earth.

1 Nephi 22:6–12

The Gentiles will help nurse all parts of Israel—Nephites, Lamanites, and others. The United States of America will be raised up in the promised land, and American citizens will play a role in the scattering of the descendants of father Lehi. A marvelous work, the Restoration (including additional scripture, the gospel, the Church, and the covenant), will be "of great worth" to the remnants of Lehi. The Gentiles will be nourishing them, or carrying them, like little lambs, in their arms and on their shoulders.

This great Restoration will be valuable to all Israel and to all the Gentiles. The Lord God will "make bare his arm," or as we might say, the hand of the Lord will be in it, and all nations will know the great thing he has brought about.

After the prophesied scattering comes the necessary sequel, the prophesied gathering—both physical and spiritual. Covenant people (including those adopted or grafted in) will be gathered physically to their lands of inheritance, and they will be gathered spiritually to the knowledge that "the Lord is their Savior and their Redeemer."

1 Nephi 22:12

Inscribed on the Reformers' Wall in Geneva, Switzerland, is the motto of the Protestant Reformation, *Post Tenebras Lux,* which means, "After the darkness, light." So it is with those who are not yet members of the Church; as they come to know the truth and as they become acquainted with their Redeemer—the only Person in the universe who can take away the stain and the pain of their transgressions—"they shall be brought out of obscurity and out of darkness; and they shall know that the Lord is their Savior and their Redeemer."

1 Nephi 22:13–14

The church of the devil, also known as the great and abominable church or the whore of all the earth—that is, all those who fight against Zion, the Church of God—will factionalize itself into ruin; it will destroy itself. Remember Jesus' words that a kingdom divided against itself shall not stand (Matthew 12:25). The devil is his own worst enemy.

1 Nephi 22:15–17

The Millennium will be ushered in by power (Revelation 20:1–3; D&C 19:1–3; 84:118–19) but maintained by righteousness (see also 1 Nephi 22:26). Satan will be bound and become powerless by the power of God as well as by the righteousness of the Saints. Satan's followers will be consumed by fire, and the righteous will be preserved by fire. The fire, which can destroy or save, is the glory of the Lord (Helaman 5:23–50; 3 Nephi 25:1).

The Prophet Joseph Smith taught that the devil has no power over individuals in any age, only as they allow him to.[61] But we also realize that while the Lord's assurance that he will not allow the wicked to destroy the righteous may be true in an ultimate sense or regarding a whole righteous people, there are reasons why he does permit some righteous individuals to be killed (see commentary at Alma 14:6–11).

1 Nephi 22:18–19

Catastrophes and cataclysms, both natural and unnatural, will destroy the hard-hearted rebels who fight against God and Zion.

1 Nephi 22:20–21

"This may well be the most often-quoted messianic prophecy in scripture. It was first uttered by Moses to the children of Israel (Deuteronomy 18:15–19). Nephi quoted it to his people, Peter quoted it in his great discourse on the grounds of Herod's temple (Acts 3:22–23), Christ quoted it to the nation of the Nephites (3 Nephi 21:11), Stephen quoted it while transfigured before the Sanhedrin (Acts 7:37), Moroni quoted it to Joseph Smith (Joseph Smith–History 1:40), and we find it referred to in the revelation given as a preface to the Doctrine and Covenants (D&C 1:14) and in the revelation that was once known as its appendix (D&C 133:63)."[62]

The "prophet like unto Moses" who will be raised up is the Savior himself, the Holy One of Israel. Moses was a great lawgiver; Jesus is *the* great Lawgiver. Moses was a great deliverer; Jesus is *the* great Deliverer.

1 Nephi 22:22–23

In the long run, the righteous need not fear; the forces of evil will be overcome. The wicked—those who belong to the kingdom of the devil—are the ones who need to fear, tremble, and quake. Theirs is a pathetic and ignominious end. Here is another example of Nephi's plainness: the church of the devil consists of all churches and organizations that are built up to get gain, power over others, or acceptability in the eyes of the world or that seek to satisfy physical lusts (see also commentary at 1 Nephi 13:2–9). They will all be burned as stubble (3 Nephi 25:1).

1 Nephi 22:24–28

The time is fast approaching when the Holy One will reign in great glory (the millennial era) and the righteous will be led "as calves of the stall"; in other words, "the earth shall be given unto them for an inheritance; and they shall multiply and wax strong, and their children shall grow up without sin unto salvation" (D&C 45:58). The pastoral image is peaceful and pleasant: all the sheep are gathered into one fold and will come to know their Shepherd; "he shall feed his sheep, and in him they shall find pasture."

With the Holy One reigning and his people dwelling in righteousness, Satan has no power. He has no power over their hearts "because of the love of God which [will] dwell in the hearts of the people" (4 Nephi 1:15). The righteous don't allow the devil into their hearts because "light and truth forsake that evil one" (D&C 93:37).

President Joseph Fielding Smith wrote: "There are many among us who teach that the binding of Satan will be merely the binding which those dwelling on the earth will place upon him by their refusal to hear his enticings. This is not so. He will not have the privilege during that period of time to tempt any man."[63] Satan will be bound not only by the native righteousness of the millennial Saints but also by priesthood power that will cast him out and will not allow him the exercise of any influence. He will be *sealed* off from us by the power of God.[64]

1 Nephi 22:29–31

Notice that to Nephi, and to all other true followers of Christ, obedience is a vital matter. In the last two verses of the book of 1 Nephi and the last verse of the book of 2 Nephi, Nephi testifies that it is urgent to be obedient, and he himself sets the standard with his final words carved into the plates: "I must obey" (2 Nephi 33:15).

THE SECOND BOOK
OF NEPHI

2 Nephi 1–4

The Second Book of Nephi is one of the grandest doctrinal books ever compiled. Three of the main writers are father Lehi and his two prophet-sons, Nephi and Jacob. The other main writer is the great prophet who wrote during the eighth century B.C.: Isaiah. He is quoted at length by Nephi. Main themes are the Creation, the Fall, the Atonement, the scattering and gathering of Israel, and prophecies of the last days.

The first four chapters initiate what comes to be a familiar pattern: blessings and counsel from fathers to their sons; for example, Lehi to his sons (2 Nephi 1–4), King Benjamin to his sons (Mosiah 1), Alma to his sons (Alma 36–42), and Mormon to his son (Moroni 8–9).

2 Nephi 1:5–6

The Lord covenanted to give Lehi's posterity an everlasting possession of land in what we call the Americas, along with "all those who should be led out of other countries by the hand of the Lord." That same Lord comments on the immigration of groups of people to this land of the Americas, "There shall none come into this land save they shall be brought by the hand of the Lord." America is for all the good and righteous people of the world. President Anthony W. Ivins of the First Presidency taught in 1932 that the Lord "brought the faith of the devoted Puritans of New England; he brought the patriotism of the Dutch at New York; he brought the gallantry of the cavaliers of Virginia; the light-hearted energy of the French of New Orleans. Just the kind of composite body of men to establish a government that could not be dominated by any particular race or tongue, but made composite, that all men might be welcomed to it, live under and enjoy its privileges."[1]

The God of this land, who is Jesus Christ, describes this land as "choice above all other lands" (v. 5; see also Ether 1:42; 2:10, 12), and the covenant includes divine title to the land, plus security in the land, based on the inhabitants' obedience. See "The Promised Land—All of the Americas," accompanying the commentary at Ether 2:7–12.

2 Nephi 1:7–11

This land is consecrated to its righteous residents. *Consecrate* comes from Latin *sacrare,* meaning "to make holy"; in other words, this becomes a holy land to them, a land of liberty, a refuge against captivity—all based on their faithfulness.

The God of this land was actually protecting it for a time, "that this land should be kept as yet from the knowledge of other nations." Otherwise, "many nations would overrun the land, that there would be no place for an inheritance" for those whom he specially guided to it. In later centuries the Lord allowed the Spanish, the Portuguese, and the English in particular to overrun the land so that the restored gospel could be spread primarily in these three languages instead of the hundreds of diverse languages of the native peoples.

The promise was that upon obedience to the Lord the inhabitants would be blessed. They would prosper and be kept safe, or as the biblical covenant stipulated, upon obedience they would be able to live "long upon the land which the Lord thy God giveth thee" (Exodus 20:12).

If the people turn away from their Lord, they will suffer his judgments, he will bring other peoples to displace them, and they will be "scattered and smitten."

2 Nephi 1:12–14

Lehi waxed eloquent in his warnings and encourage-ment; he called his sons to action with such verbs as *remem-ber, hearken, awake,* and *arise.* The prophet uses poetry and euphemism to describe his imminent departure from this life: a "trembling parent, whose limbs ye must soon lay down in the cold and silent grave, from whence no traveler can return; a few more days and I go the way of all the earth." Similar poetic expressions appear in the King James Bible and in the works of Shakespeare and other great writers, but Lehi pre-cedes and exceeds most of them.

A euphemism is a figure of speech in which a harsh or indelicate word or concept is softened. Note how Book of Mormon authors spoke of dying: "go the way of all the earth" (2 Nephi 1:14; Alma 1:1; Helaman 1:2); "be carried out of this time" (1 Nephi 18:18); "gave up the ghost" (Jacob 7:20–21); "go to the place of my rest" (Enos 1:27); "yield up this mortal frame" (Mosiah 2:26); "gone to dwell with . . . God" (Alma 24:22); "taste of death" (3 Nephi 28:7); "pass away" (Ether 10:17); and "sleep" (Mormon 9:13).

2 Nephi 1:15

It is clear that Lehi knew his calling and election—his citi-zenship in God's eternal kingdom—had been made sure; he was sealed up to exaltation. Compare other such declarations among his posterity: Jacob (2 Nephi 2:3); Enos (Enos 1:27); Alma I (Mosiah 26:20); Alma II (Alma 36:28); Mormon (Mormon 2:19); and Moroni (Ether 12:37). See also com-mentary at Alma 36:28.

2 Nephi 1:16–25

Lehi continued to give patriarchal blessings and counsel to his sons (the word *patriarch* means "father," so he gave father's blessings to his children). His great anxiety through-out their lives was that they and their descendants would be righteous, favored, and prospered, and not cut off, cursed, hated, and killed. It was their choice. He hoped they would "arise . . . and be men, and be determined in one mind and in one heart," that is, live in the condition called Zion (compare Moses 7:18).

All of us should "put on the armor of righteousness." As the apostle Paul counseled, "Wherefore take unto you the whole armour of God, that ye may be able to withstand in the evil day, and having done all, to stand" (Ephesians 6:13). He further implores us to stand firmly clothed with truth, wearing the breastplate of righteousness, the preparation of the gospel of righteousness, the helmet of salvation, and the sword of the Spirit—which is the word of God. "Above all, taking the shield of faith, wherewith ye shall be able to quench all the fiery darts of the wicked" (Ephesians 6:16). In other words, the gospel of Jesus Christ is real protection!

Lehi commanded his sons not to rebel any more against their righteous brother Nephi, "whose views have been glorious." Give Nephi some credit; were it not for him, Lehi told the others, they would never have made it to this promised land. Nephi's motives were pure; he had sought only the glory of God and the welfare of his relatives.

2 Nephi 1:26–27

Nephi, under the direction of the Spirit, had used sharpness with his brothers, which sharpness was the directness of the truth and the power of the word. The Spirit had mandated the strong language of rebuke. Nephi had also appeared angry, and even though Lehi, in a fatherly way, defended Nephi's forceful approach with his brothers, later we will see that Nephi did feel real anger; he knew that such an intense feeling was wrong, and he desired to repent of it. The message was true and correct and delivered under the influence of the Spirit of God, but Nephi felt that his own feelings accompanying it were a little out of control (see commentary at 2 Nephi 4:17–29).

2 Nephi 2:1–2

Lehi taught his son Jacob, who had experienced a rough childhood because of certain older brothers. Notice that the prophet doesn't say that God will consecrate *blessings* for our gain, but "he shall consecrate thine *afflictions* for thy gain." The Lord has taught, "All things wherewith you have been afflicted shall work together for your good" (D&C 98:3). Lehi's instruction in 2 Nephi 2 constitutes one of the most profound and powerful doctrinal discourses in all of scripture.

Verse 2 contains a figure of speech called periphrasis, in which a description is used instead of the name: "my first-born in the wilderness" instead of Jacob (also v. 11). Other examples in the Book of Mormon include "a far better land of promise" instead of heaven and "vale of sorrow" instead of mortality (Alma 37:45); "the author of all sin" (Helaman 6:30), "him who is seeking to hurl away your souls" (Helaman 7:16), and "the evil one who seeketh to destroy the souls of men" (Helaman 8:28) instead of Satan; and "him who knoweth all things" (2 Nephi 2:24) and "my Well Beloved, who was from the foundation of the world" (Helaman 5:47) instead of Jesus Christ.

2 Nephi 2:3–4

As with Jacob, so with every Latter-day Saint: "thy days shall be spent in the service of thy God." Lehi knew that Jacob would be exalted and have eternal life, and all this because of the Redeemer, who would come both in the meridian of time and in the fulness of time to provide salvation. Notice the emphasis: Christ's righteousness is what redeems Jacob (and all of us). We do not, actually we cannot, redeem ourselves. The apostle Paul made a similar point: sometimes in our zeal to be righteous (certainly a worthy aspiration) we forget that it is God's righteousness that makes salvation possible, "and going about to establish [our] own righteousness, have not submitted [our]selves unto the righteousness of God" (Romans 10:3).

From the Fall, the way to salvation has been prepared; that is, from the beginnings of mortality the plan has been in place to save all who will. Salvation is free in two senses. First, the Atonement, which makes salvation possible, is a free gift. As Paul taught, "For by grace are ye saved through faith; and that not of yourselves: it is the gift of God: Not of works, lest any man should boast" (Ephesians 2:8–9). Salvation cannot be earned; it comes only through the merits, mercy, and grace of Christ, as Lehi explained. By definition, mercy is unearned, unmerited. Second, redemption has been provided for all humankind from the consequences of the transgression of Adam and Eve: death and hell. Death is totally overcome and immortality guaranteed for all by Jesus' resurrection. Jacob later described how resurrection itself is redemption (2 Nephi 9:6–10). In addition, sin and hell may be completely overcome by repenting and keeping His commandments.

2 Nephi 2:5–7

Lehi explains that all mortals are "instructed sufficiently" through the Spirit of Christ (see also Moroni 7:16). The law is given to everyone, but by the law no person is justified because no one can live it perfectly. As Paul taught, "Therefore by the deeds of the law there shall no flesh be justified in his sight: for by the law is the knowledge of sin" (Romans 3:20). The law of justice demands payment for all sin committed (see left side of accompanying chart). Because of our natural-man inclination to sin (Mosiah 3:19), we are cut off from the presence of our Heavenly Father, and we pile up a mountain of sins here in mortality, thus precluding our ever again living with the purest and holiest Beings in the universe. By temporal and spiritual law we would be consigned to misery forever. Therefore, our Savior, the Holy Messiah, came to offer Himself as payment for the demands of the law and to provide the way back (see right side of accompanying chart; see also 2 Nephi 25:23, 26).

2 Nephi 2:8–10

"How great the importance to make these things known unto the inhabitants of the earth"—that is why we serve missions. But what things, specifically, are so important for us to make known? Second Nephi 2 and 9 are two of the most important chapters in all of scripture. Lehi and Jacob taught about the greatness of God in providing redemption from our fallen condition. The following chart lays out side-by-side the points of the glorious plan of redemption.

Note that all things on the left side of the chart take us down (into a fallen condition), and all things on the right side of the chart take us back up (towards a redeemed condition).

What a great and glorious message we take to the world! With infinite mercy, grace, and love, our Father and our Savior have provided a way for us to escape all the consequences of the Fall. The consequences include becoming sinners, heaping more and more sin upon ourselves (and justice demanding suffering for all of it), eventually having our bodies and spirits separated by death, and being out of God's presence, with no possible way for us to resolve our own plight and get back to him. All of these consequences would otherwise have been irreversible and permanent were it not for the intercession or intervention of God himself. No wonder we are so anxious to bring everyone to Christ—because "there is no flesh that can dwell in the presence of God, save it be through the merits, and mercy, and grace of the Holy Messiah."

TWO INSEPARABLE PARTS OF THE PLAN

Adam fell that men might be; and men are,
that they might have joy. And the Messiah cometh
in the fulness of time, that he may redeem the
children of men from the fall.
2 Nephi 2:25–26

Adam and Eve in Eden	Jesus in Gethsemane and on Golgotha
The Fall	The Atonement, or redemption
Our first parents brought blood into the world, which makes all humankind corruptible; we are "conceived in sin" (Moses 6:55), meaning born into a sinful world, and by nature we become sinners.	What the world calls "original sin" (which was not sin but transgression) was completely paid for by the Savior, who took on flesh and blood and then shed his blood to redeem everyone from sin and make possible incorruptible bodies for all. His sacrifice was infinite and eternal.
The law of justice demands payment for all sin.	The law of mercy and grace provides payment for sin in our behalf.
Physical death—our bodies and spirits are separated from each other.	Resurrection, immortality—our bodies and spirits are permanently reunited.
Spiritual death—all are out of God's presence.	Exaltation, eternal life—all are taken back into God's presence (for judgment) (2 Nephi 2:10; 9:22; Alma 42:23; Mormon 9:13–14; Helaman 14:15–17).

Christ intercedes for everyone, and those who believe in him will be saved. They are saved by his grace—that is, his loving kindness and enabling power—and his merits (see commentary at Alma 24:1–11).

Through Jesus' intercession on our behalf, every child of Heavenly Father will be taken back into the presence of God for judgment. The Book of Mormon is clear that spiritual death is overcome by every soul returning to the presence of God. But then it is also clear that "no unclean thing can dwell with God"; therefore, those who are not worthy, those who do not have sufficient light in them in order to endure God's glorious company, must be immediately escorted back out of his presence and be "cast off forever" (1 Nephi 10:21).

Again, as the preceding chart illustrates, the glorious message of the gospel of Jesus Christ (which is originally and forever the gospel of God the Father) is that *all* the consequences of the Fall are resolved through the atonement of our Savior, Jesus Christ. He has made it possible to overcome all of the otherwise devastating and permanent effects of our fallen condition. It remains for us to do our part by keeping his commandments and receiving and living all of his teachings, laws, principles, ordinances, and covenants so that we will merit eternal life with him and our Father.

2 Nephi 2:11

There must be opposition, or opposites, in all things. Bad is the absence of good. Darkness is the absence of light. Sorrow is the absence of joy. How could we ever understand warmth if we never experienced cold? God is the author or provider of light, life, truth, joy, and good. The adversary can provide only the opposites because *he takes away.* He can provide darkness (the absence of light), death (the absence of life), falsehood (the absence of truth), misery (the absence of joy), and evil (the absence of good). The devil actually *provides nothing;* he just sees to it that all who cooperate with him are devoid of the blessings that God does provide. The unrighteous may not be miserable according to their perspective, but they do not know real happiness.

2 Nephi 2:12–14

With no opposition, or opposites, the creation of physical bodies for Heavenly Father's children would have been meaningless and purposeless, "a thing of naught." God's eternal plan would be annulled, along with his wisdom, power, mercy, and justice.

Lehi laid out his argument like a master philosopher. The pure logic is the following: no law, no sin; no sin, no righteousness; no righteousness, no happiness; no righteousness nor happiness, no punishment nor misery; and if all these principles do not exist, then God does not exist either—nor do we, nor the earth. But Lehi testified that God does exist, as evidenced by all his creations.

2 Nephi 2:15–16, 26

There must be opposites. Consider the trees in Eden: some encouraged, one forbidden; some fruit sweet, other bitter. To "act for themselves" was God's eternal plan; "to be acted upon" was Satan's plan.

If only one course were available to us, there would be no choice, no agency. There must be opposites, and that is why two seemingly contradictory commandments were given: "man could not act for himself save it should be that he was enticed by the one or the other." Choice must always be preserved. If we are forced to do what is right, the choice is not ours, and the principle of obedience is irrelevant.

2 Nephi 2:17–18, 27

Because Lucifer "had fallen from heaven, and had become miserable forever, he sought also the misery of all mankind. . . . He seeketh that all men might be miserable like unto himself." And what is his misery? That he can never be with God? No, he hates God. He has already decided that he does not want to be with his Father and his Brother, the Savior. His misery is that he can never have a physical body, never be a husband, and never have children or posterity. He particularly wants us to abuse the sacred procreative powers so that we will be denied those powers in the next life and live singly forever—and be miserable as he is.

Lucifer became a *devil,* which word derives from Greek *diabolos,* meaning "slanderer"; and he became a *satan,* which is a Hebrew word meaning "adversary." He took on other descriptive name-titles, such as "serpent," "father of lies," and many others throughout scripture, including the evil one, dragon, perdition ("lost one") and Beelzebub (literally, "lord of the flies").

Satan specializes in subtle half-truths, such as "partake of the forbidden fruit, and ye shall not die"—which was a lie—"but ye shall be as God, knowing good and evil"—which would become the truth.

2 Nephi 2:21–22

What Adam and Eve did was transgress, or break, a commandment, but that action was not imputed to them as sin. President Joseph Fielding Smith explained: "What did Adam do? The very thing the Lord wanted him to do. I hate to hear anybody call it a sin, for it wasn't a sin. . . . Now this is the way I interpret that: The Lord said to Adam, 'Here is the tree of the knowledge of good and evil. If you want to stay here, then you cannot eat of that fruit. If you want to stay here, I forbid you to eat it. But you may act for yourself and you may eat if you want to. And if you do eat it, you will die."[2]

President Smith also wrote: "I never speak of the part Eve took in this fall as a sin, nor do I accuse Adam of a sin. . . . It is not always a sin to transgress a law. . . . This was a transgression of the law, but not a sin in the strict sense, for it was something that Adam and Eve had to do!"[3]

The 1828 *American Dictionary of the English Language*

defines *transgression* as "the act of passing over or beyond any law or rule of moral duty."

2 Nephi 2:23–25

The Fall was a planned event, and it was a noble thing Adam and Eve did. Otherwise they would have remained in the Garden, and they would have had no children ("the family of all the earth"). That would have frustrated the whole plan of God to provide for his children's education a probation—a time of testing, learning, experiencing, growing, and becoming like the Father and the Son. Living innocently in Eden would have denied them the opportunity to acquire godlike goodness and real joy.

So Adam and Eve purposefully brought about the Fall to provide mortal life for all the Father's children and to facilitate their opportunity to learn joy. Notice in Moses 5:10–11 that both Adam and Eve specifically refer to their potential for joy:

"And in that day Adam blessed God and was filled, and began to prophesy concerning all the families of the earth, saying: Blessed be the name of God, for because of my transgression my eyes are opened, and in this life I shall have joy, and again in the flesh I shall see God.

"And Eve, his wife, heard all these things and was glad, saying: Were it not for our transgression we . . . never should have known good and evil, and the joy of our redemption, and the eternal life which God giveth unto all the obedient."

Undoubtedly, a knowledge of the great change that Adam and Eve brought about caused Lehi to feel gratitude for God's plan: "Behold, all things have been done in the wisdom of him who knoweth all things."

2 Nephi 2:26

Second Nephi 2:25 should never be quoted without also quoting verse 26. They are inextricably bound together as two pillars in the great plan of salvation. Yes, Adam fell that men might be, but "the Messiah cometh in the fulness of time, that he may redeem the children of men from the fall." It was all planned from the beginning: the Fall and the Redemption.

The children learn through righteous use of agency, through their proper choices to act for themselves and make progress toward becoming eternal fathers and mothers.

The phrase "fulness of time" refers to the fulfillment or completion of all righteous principles and practices known up to that time. The final dispensation is known as the "fulness of times" for the same reason (D&C 27:13; 121:31; 124:41). The last dispensation becomes the fulness of all other times. The period of the Messiah's mortal ministry is known as the "meridian of time," or the high point of earthly time.

2 Nephi 2:27–30

After reiterating the nature of the great gift of complete liberty and eternal life given by the great Mediator, Lehi pled with his sons to accept the atoning work of that Mediator-Messiah. A mediator is one who intercedes on behalf of another, who pleads for another, and who reconciles persons or parties who are at odds or estranged from each other. The scriptures mention two principal mediators who devoted their lives to reconciling the children of God with their God. The first, chronologically speaking, was a type and foreshadow of the second. The first interceded on behalf of the children of Israel. The second interceded on behalf of all humankind. The first was the mediator of a lesser law and covenant. The second was the mediator of an eternal law and covenant. The first was mortal and temporary. The second was God, infinite and eternal. The first was Moses. The second was Jesus Christ—the *great* Mediator, as Lehi declared.

Of these two mediators Paul wrote (sounding much like Lehi): "Wherefore then, the law was added because of transgressions, till the seed should come to whom the promise was made in the law given to Moses, who was ordained by the hand of angels to be a mediator of this first covenant, (the law).

"Now this mediator was not a mediator of the new covenant; but there is one mediator of the new covenant, who is Christ, as it is written in the law concerning the promises made to Abraham and his seed. Now Christ is the mediator of life; for this is the promise which God made unto Abraham" (JST, Galatians 3:19–20).

The Old Testament contains illustrations of Moses interceding on behalf of the children of Israel. But these pale in comparison to the deeds of Jesus Christ, the Holy Messiah, who came to earth to "make intercession for all the children of men," who was "the mediator of the new covenant, who wrought out this perfect atonement through the shedding of his own blood" (D&C 76:69). That is why the apostle Paul referred to Christ as the "one mediator between God and men" (1 Timothy 2:5). The old law and covenant administered under Moses "made nothing perfect, but was only the bringing in of a better hope" (JST, Hebrews 7:19), by which hope, that is, the new covenant or gospel of Jesus Christ, we are "made perfect" (D&C 76:69). Therefore, father Lehi earnestly encouraged his sons (and every individual really) "to choose liberty and eternal life, through the great Mediator of all men." Said he, "Look to the great Mediator, and hearken unto his great commandments; and be faithful unto his words, and choose eternal life."

It is only through the atonement of Jesus Christ that human beings can inherit eternal life. The Atonement is the very essence, the core, of Jesus' mediation and intercession (D&C 45:3–5). Lehi knew that if his sons did not choose the way of eternal life, they would, by default, choose "eternal death" and become captive to the devil, who will "reign over you."

2 Nephi 3

Why is it that there is so much success in the Americas with conversions to the restored gospel? In fact, why are there far more baptisms in the Americas than in all the rest of the world combined? What is so special about the lands of the Western Hemisphere?

To understand the remarkable reasons, we have to go back about four thousand years in time and about eight thousand miles in distance to a man called Joseph in the land of Egypt.

Father Jacob gave his twelve sons patriarchal blessings, and they are recorded, at least in part, in Genesis 49. Particularly outstanding blessings were given to Judah and to Joseph. Judah was promised that through his lineage the Messiah would come, "and unto him shall the gathering of the people be" (Genesis 49:10). Jacob then pronounced a prophetic metaphor to describe Joseph's descendants:

"Joseph is a fruitful bough, even a fruitful bough by a well; whose branches run over the wall" (Genesis 49:22).

The parallel images are clear. Joseph and his branches, or descendants, would be productive and prolific, and they would extend "over the wall"; in this case, they extended over a well or wall of water, the ocean.

Continuing his blessing to Joseph, Jacob promised, "The blessings of thy father have prevailed above the blessings of my progenitors" (Genesis 49:26). Jacob said, in essence, that the blessings that he was pronouncing on Joseph are even greater than the blessings of his fathers (Abraham and Isaac).

These blessings are "unto the utmost bound of the everlasting hills" (Genesis 29:26). And where are the "everlasting hills" to which the blessings of Joseph would extend? Only in the Western Hemisphere, spanning the continents of the Americas, is there a continuous chain of mountains—from Alaska to Patagonia—and to the "utmost bound" of these "everlasting hills" the descendants of Joseph would be spread over many centuries and into the latter days. Indeed, today there are stakes of the Church from the northernmost reaches (Fairbanks, Alaska) to the southernmost reaches (Punta Arenas, Chile) and thousands of cities, towns, and villages in between. These vast lands of Joseph—called the "Americas" today—are also designated in the Book of Mormon as "land[s] of promise" (1 Nephi 4:14; 7:13; 14:1–2; Ether 2:8–10); "precious lands" (1 Nephi 17:38; 2 Nephi 3:2); "holy land" (Enos 1:10); and lands which are "choice above all other lands" (1 Nephi 2:20; 2 Nephi 1:5; Ether 1:42; 2:7, 10, 15; 9:20; 13:2). See "The Promised Land—All of the Americas," accompanying the commentary at Ether 2:7–12 (in vol. 2 of this work).

Joseph's descendants through his sons Manasseh (Lehi and his posterity) and Ephraim (Ishmael and his posterity) would be brought to these consecrated lands because, as Lehi explained, "It must needs be that we should be led with one accord into the land of promise, unto the fulfilling of the word of the Lord, that we [remnants of Jacob or Israel] should be scattered upon *all* the face of the earth" (1 Nephi 10:13; emphasis added).

The blessings pronounced by Jacob "shall be on the head of Joseph, and on the crown of the head of him that was separate from his brethren" (Genesis 49:26). And how was Joseph separated from his brothers? We all know the story of how the other sons of Jacob were annoyed with their younger brother and his dreams of dominion over the rest of the family, of their hatred that was so intense that the brothers even entertained thoughts of killing him, and of how, in the end, they arranged to have him sold into Egypt (recounted in Genesis 37). Thus, at the tender age of seventeen Joseph was separated from his home and his brethren. He actually spent the rest of his life residing in Egypt, where he died at the age of 110 (Genesis 50:26). As far as we know, Joseph's sons Manasseh and Ephraim lived their whole lives, died, and were buried in Egypt, without ever becoming acquainted with their promised land.

Although Joseph and his immediate posterity were at first separated from the rest of the family of Jacob, the great patriarch's reference to Joseph's being "separate from his brethren" would have a much wider and grander fulfillment in Joseph's descendants. The families of Lehi and Ishmael inherited lands that were much more separated from the rest of Israel than was the land of Egypt.

Thus we see, through all this scriptural history, that what we call "the Americas" are truly lands of Joseph, inhabited at least in part by descendants of him who ultimately received the blessings—the double inheritance—of the firstborn. "Joseph obtained the birthright in Israel because he was worthy and because it was his natural right. When Reuben, the actual firstborn, lost the privilege by transgression (1 Chr. 5:1–2), Joseph, as the firstborn son of Jacob's second wife, was next in line for the blessing."[4] Joseph received the greatest inheritance, including the greatest lands of inheritance, which were "choice above all other lands."

Joseph's descendants, along with other scattered remnants of the house of Israel and those adopted into the covenant people, are now experiencing tremendous spiritual growth and blessings in direct fulfillment of the patriarchal blessing of Jacob to his son Joseph. Many of these spiritual blessings being poured out in the lands of Joseph are the result of the divinely led work of another Joseph in the latter days—a direct descendant of the original Joseph.

2 Nephi 3:4–6

Lehi taught his last-born son that "Joseph [of Egypt] truly saw our day [that is, the time of Lehi]. And he obtained a promise of the Lord, that out of the fruit of his loins the Lord God would raise up a righteous branch unto the house of Israel; not the Messiah, but a branch which was to be broken off, nevertheless, to be remembered in the covenants of the Lord that the Messiah should be made manifest unto them in the latter days, in the spirit of power, unto the bringing of them out of darkness unto light. . . . For Joseph truly testified, saying: A seer shall the Lord my God raise up, who shall be a choice seer unto the fruit of my loins."

FOUR JOSEPHS IN 2 NEPHI 3

Name	Time Period	Verses in 2 Nephi 3
Joseph, son of Jacob (Israel)	ca. 1800 B.C.	4–22
Joseph, son of Lehi	500s B.C.	1–4, 22–23, 25
Joseph Smith Sr.	A.D. 1800s	15
Joseph Smith Jr.	A.D. 1800s	6–9, 11–21, 24

2 Nephi 3:7–10

The Lord promised Joseph in Egypt that the choice latter-day seer, Joseph Smith, would be highly esteemed (respected, honored) by his righteous and loyal descendants and that the seer would help them come to a knowledge of the covenants of the fathers (Abraham, Isaac, and Jacob) and of the accompanying saving ordinances.

Following are a few lines from the patriarchal blessing that Joseph Smith Sr. gave to his son Joseph Smith Jr.:

"I bless thee with the blessings of thy fathers Abraham, Isaac and Jacob; and even the blessings of thy father Joseph, the son of Jacob. Behold he looked after his posterity in the last days . . . ; he sought diligently to know from whence the son should come who should bring forth the word of the Lord, by which they might be enlightened and brought back to the true fold, and his eyes beheld thee, my son; his heart rejoiced and his soul was satisfied, and he said, . . . 'From among my seed, scattered with the Gentiles, shall a choice seer arise . . . , whose heart shall meditate great wisdom, whose intelligence shall circumscribe and comprehend the deep things of God, and whose mouth shall utter the law of the just.' . . . Thou shalt hold the keys of this ministry, even the presidency of this church, both in time and in eternity."[5]

Joseph in Egypt knew that the latter-day seer would be "great like unto Moses," whom the Lord would raise up to deliver his people out of the land of Egypt—a remarkably specific prophecy of what would happen to Jacob's descendants, the children of Israel, within a few centuries after Joseph's lifetime and exactly who would be sent to earth to bring about their dramatic exodus from Egypt.

2 Nephi 3:11–12

The life's work of Joseph Smith would include bringing forth the Book of Mormon and also spending additional years of his prophetic career restoring, revising, correcting, augmenting, clarifying, and expounding the text of the Bible. The two volumes would help bring people to the Savior.

The Bible and the Book of Mormon *together* accomplish just what verse 12 describes: they confound false doctrine, lay down contentions, establish peace, and bring us to a knowledge of our ancestors and of the Lord's covenants.

With the coming forth of the complementary editions of the scriptures (the Bible in 1979 and the triple combination in 1981) the prophecy in 2 Nephi 3:12 and Ezekiel 37:15–17 stands fulfilled. We have witnessed a stunning fulfillment of a significant ancient prophecy in our day.

2 Nephi 3:13

"Out of weakness he [Joseph Smith] shall be made strong" is the same message Paul taught. The ancient missionary-apostle wrote:

"Lest I should be exalted above measure through the abundance of the revelations, there was given to me a thorn in the flesh, the messenger of Satan to buffet me, lest I should be exalted above measure.

"For this thing I besought the Lord thrice, that it might depart from me.

"And he said to me, My grace is sufficient for thee: for my strength is made perfect in weakness. Most gladly therefore will I rather glory in my infirmities, that the power of Christ may rest upon me.

"Therefore I take pleasure in infirmities . . . [and] in distresses for Christ's sake: for when I am weak, then am I strong" (2 Corinthians 12:7–10).

All of us have weaknesses. We are all given a "thorn in the flesh" (2 Corinthians 12:7) to make us humble, and if we allow the humility to work in us properly, we can make the weaknesses our strengths (Ether 12:27). We can actually become strong, even powerful—but the power does not originate in us. Paul wrote, "I rather glory in my infirmities, *that the power of Christ may rest upon me*" (2 Corinthians 12:9; emphasis added). Of ourselves, we are nothing; we are totally dependent upon him. The Lord is our strength. The Lord has said, "He that is weak among you hereafter shall be made strong" (D&C 50:16).

As we learn patience, long-suffering, and self-mastery, we will overcome the weaknesses and be "made perfect in weakness" (2 Corinthians 12:9) and have the power of Christ to rest upon us.

2 Nephi 3:14

Joseph, the seer, will be blessed, and his enemies—his would-be destroyers—will be confounded. Joseph in Egypt was told by the Lord that the promise of ultimate triumph of this latter-day seer was sure. The ancient Joseph attested, "Behold, I am sure of the fulfilling of this promise."

2 Nephi 3:15

Joseph in Egypt knew that the latter-day seer would bear his same name and the same name as his own father (Joseph Smith Sr.). Interestingly, the common practice in early America was for the *first* son to be named after the father, but the first two sons born to Joseph Sr. and Lucy Mack Smith were Alvin and Hyrum, reserving the name Joseph for the third son, thus unknowingly fulfilling an ancient prophecy.

"And he shall be like unto me; for the thing, which the Lord shall bring forth by his hand, by the power of the Lord shall bring my people unto salvation." The Hebrew word "salvation" is *yeshua*, which is the mortal name of the Savior. *Yeshua* is Jesus. What Joseph Smith helped restore definitely brings people to salvation, to Jesus.

2 Nephi 3:16–21

Ancient Joseph prophesied in further detail about Moses, his power, his weakness in speaking, his designated spokesman (his brother, Aaron), and his assigned task of receiving, recording, and preserving the Lord's words (the Torah, or the Law: what has come down to us as Genesis, Exodus, Leviticus, Numbers, and Deuteronomy).

Ancient Joseph also prophesied about the latter-day "Moses" (Joseph Smith), a spokesman who would be raised up to assist him (Oliver Cowdery, Sidney Rigdon, and others), and his assigned task of receiving, recording, and publishing the Lord's words given to the original Joseph's descendants in the Western Hemisphere (what has come down to us as the Book of Mormon), words that would "cry from the dust" the message of repentance to Joseph's seed. The words, given in their weakness, would be made strong in faith.

2 Nephi 3:22–25

Lehi's posterity would be blessed through "one mighty among them, who shall do much good, both in word and in deed, being an instrument in the hands of God, with exceeding faith, to work mighty wonders, and do that thing which is great in the sight of God, unto the bringing to pass much restoration unto the house of Israel, and unto the seed of thy brethren." No one in the last days fulfills that prophetic utterance more than Joseph Smith.

2 Nephi 4:1–2

Nephi resumed writing, giving us an additional, superlative remark about ancient Joseph: "The prophecies which he wrote, there are not many greater." Gospel scholar Daniel H.

Ludlow commented in reference to the papyrus manuscripts the Prophet Joseph Smith had acquired from the catacombs of Egypt, which contained writings from both Abraham and Joseph: "Evidently some of the writings of Joseph are still in existence but have not been published to the world. . . . Evidently the record of Joseph was translated by the Prophet, but perhaps the reason it was not published was because the great prophecies therein were 'too great' for the people of this day."[6] Prophecies of Joseph were also inscribed on the plates of brass, and someday we will have them (1 Nephi 5:18).

2 Nephi 4:3–14

Toward the end of their lives all righteous parents wonder, "Have I done everything I can to teach my children and grandchildren what they need most—what will help them the most to return and live with our Father in Heaven?" Like Jacob or Israel (Genesis 49), every righteous father wants to bless his posterity one more time before passing on. The things of eternity weigh on their minds. Brother Skinner saw this for himself just before the passing of his father-in-law. The experience he and his wife had with that good man, and the blessing they received under his hand, was one of the sweetest, most sublime experiences of their lives. It was truly a modern-day example of father Lehi's action as recounted in this passage.

We learn from 2 Nephi 1:15 that Lehi was sealed up to eternal life. By the sealing power he possessed, he left his blessing on his grandchildren, the sons and daughters of Laman, Lemuel, and the sons of Ishmael. Eventually the curses those grandchildren might inherit would be taken from them and placed squarely on the heads of their parents, and the children would be redeemed by the purity and holiness of their next righteous ancestors.

2 Nephi 4:15–35

The rest of chapter 4 contains one of the most personal glimpses we have in all scripture into the heart of a righteous man and prophet, who, in spite of his transcendent revelations and sterling example of righteousness, was still struggling to overcome his mortal weaknesses. This literary and spiritual masterpiece is often called the psalm of Nephi.

About Nephi's reflective declaration, Latter-day Saint scholar Sidney Sperry wrote: "This is a true psalm in both form and idea. Its rhythm is comparable to the noble cadence of David's poems. It not only praises God, but lays bare to us the very depths of Nephi's soul. A study of this psalm reveals how the scriptures delighted Nephi. The influence upon him of the books of Isaiah, Jeremiah, Lamentations, and the Psalms is very apparent."[7]

Nephi's psalm expresses the innermost sentiments many of us have probably felt. Compare, for example, the similar expression by the apostle Paul (Romans 7:14–25). Much of what Nephi, Paul, and others have said is attributable to our striving for perfection in a fallen world. Perhaps it is precisely because we possess the Spirit of the Lord, are on the correct path, and desire to be better than we have been that our sins, mistakes, and less than noble expressions stand out in stark contrast. Perhaps you have had the experience we have had. When looking at a car windshield out of the light, it may appear fairly clean. But when the car is turned toward the light, the sun perhaps, every blemish stands out in stark contrast. So it is with us. At those moments when we turn to the light directly, without wavering, we see more clearly what we have to work on. This is actually good news, though it can be painful, as it obviously was for Nephi. It means we are headed in the right direction.

2 Nephi 4:15–16

Nephi searched and pondered the scriptures, and he wrote out his impressions. What he wrote about the scriptures became scripture (see also Abraham 1:31).

There are negative examples in the Old Testament, such as those of Saul, David, and Solomon. They murdered and transgressed morally. At some point in their lives they stopped walking in the Spirit and gave way to the lusts of the flesh. Specifically, they must have stopped reading the scriptures and praying. They were weakened and succumbed to temptation. Nephi, on the other hand, is an impressive example of one who continued his walk in the Spirit; he knew what to do and did it: "My soul delighteth in the scriptures, and my heart pondereth them. . . . My soul delighteth in the things of the Lord; and my heart pondereth continually upon the things which I have seen and heard."

Joseph Smith laid out the way to walk as clearly as anyone. He wrote: "We [Latter-day Saints] believe in being honest, true, chaste, benevolent, virtuous, and in doing good to all men. . . . If there is anything virtuous, lovely, or of good report or praiseworthy, we seek after these things" (Articles of Faith 1:13).

2 Nephi 4:17–19

"Iniquities," "temptations," and "sins" of Nephi? But he's our perfect model, our hero! Here we learn that he, too, struggled with sin. Nephi got down on himself. He became depressed as he came face-to-face with his weaknesses. Did he give us any clues as to what his sins were? Yes, in verses 27–29.

2 Nephi 4:19–22

Though depressed because of his sinful nature, Nephi trusted in God (as evidenced by experiences such as obtaining the plates, slaying a man, and building a ship). In essence, Nephi exclaims, His love is more important to me than the desires of the flesh. He has delivered me, and he will yet deliver me. For all of us, our greatest desire should be to obtain the love of God (reach the tree of life and the waters of life). "'I Am a Child of God,'" Elder Dallin H. Oaks once remarked, "is a potent anti-depressant."[8] Others, too, have become depressed even though they were serving the Lord with intensity. Ammon, for example, said, "When our hearts were depressed . . . the Lord comforted us" (Alma 26:27). When a later Nephi was "much cast down," he pondered the revelations of the Lord, and a voice came to him saying, "Blessed art thou, Nephi" (Helaman 10:3–4). So it may be with us. Turning to the Lord can be a powerful anti-depressant.

2 Nephi 4:23–25

Nephi reminded himself: God has heard my cries. Because of my fervent prayers, he has sent visions and angels and great revelations. Nephi's "mighty prayer" yielded extraordinary results.

2 Nephi 4:26–29

Why get depressed and lose the Spirit and even physical health just because of trials? Why give in to Satan? Why let him win? Why get down on yourself because you have weaknesses? Stand up and be counted! Don't give in to the devil. Don't get angry with yourself just because you are struggling with weaknesses. Don't give up because things are tough.

Nephi's enemies were his own brothers. We saw in 2 Nephi 1:26 a hint of the struggle with anger that Nephi had. In 3 Nephi 12:22 (among other passages) anger is forbidden. Though we might think he was justified, Nephi knew that his intense feelings of anger were wrong and did not come from the Lord and that they were driving away the Spirit.

Elder Theodore M. Burton warned, "Whenever you get red in the face, whenever you raise your voice, whenever you get 'hot under the collar,' or angry, rebellious, or negative in spirit, then know that the Spirit of God is leaving you and the spirit of Satan is beginning to take over."[9]

2 Nephi 4:30–32

Don't worry; be happy—I know where help is! I praise him. He will deliver me and redeem me. Deliver me out of the control of my weaknesses. Help me to reject disobedience and sin. Guide me to walk humbly and strictly in the path.

2 Nephi 4:31

We should also shake with anger when we see Satan at work producing one Hollywood blockbusting crudity after another. Alma says that as we become more and more cleansed and purified we can look upon sin only with abhorrence (Alma 13:12). You just get to a point where you have zero tolerance for the trivial, the inane, and the crude.

President Thomas S. Monson cautioned: "The face of sin today often wears the mask of tolerance. Do not be deceived; behind that facade is heartache, unhappiness, and pain. You know what is right and what is wrong, and no disguise, however appealing, can change that. The character of transgression remains the same."[10]

2 Nephi 4:33–35

Please clothe me with righteousness. Make a way to escape the things that bother me and get me down. Please remove the obstacles in my way. I have faith and confidence in thee; I will not trust in the power of men. I know thou wilt bless me if I will just ask. I will pray sincerely to thee, my security and stability.

2 Nephi 5:1–4

There were many angry feelings flying back and forth between Nephi and his brothers. In fact, Nephi's brothers were so angry they could kill. Read the clear warning about anger in 3 Nephi 12:21–22.

2 Nephi 5:5–11

It became clear to Nephi that he and others in the family who "believed in the warnings and the revelations of God" must follow the Lord's admonition and separate themselves from the disobedient family members by fleeing inland to a place they designated the land of Nephi. They became "the people of Nephi" and kept the law of Moses, the old preparatory law given to the children of Israel of whom they were a part, but now a branch broken off from the main tree.

2 Nephi 5:15–16

Nephi undertook the construction of buildings by using abundant woods and metals (iron, copper, brass, steel, gold, silver, and other precious ores). He was already an accomplished craftsman, having followed the Lord's design and instructions in building a ship. Now he built a temple patterned after the temple of Solomon, with which he was well acquainted, having grown up in the land of Jerusalem. Verse 16 notes that the first Nephite temple was of "exceedingly fine" workmanship but could not be built "of so many precious things" as Solomon's temple, "for they were not to be found upon the land." Having just listed the precious building materials that were found in their new land in abundance, we are left to wonder exactly what was available to Solomon that was unavailable to Nephi.

2 Nephi 5:18–25

Nephi reluctantly acquiesced to serve as a king over his people. He had been serving as a ruler and a teacher in the entire Lehite colony, but the rebelliousness of some had caused Nephi's departure, and now the Lamanites were "cut off from the presence of the Lord." They had brought on themselves "a sore cursing," which included cutting themselves off from the Spirit of the Lord, from the use of true priesthood, and from the ordinances of the house of the Lord. A mark of that curse was "a skin of blackness" and a loathsome repulsiveness to the Nephites. The Lord God would use the Lamanites as a "scourge" to the Nephites "to stir them up in remembrance" of him. God warned that if the time ever came when the Nephites refused to remember him and be obedient to him, the Lamanites would "scourge them even unto destruction," which is exactly what happened hundreds of years later.

2 Nephi 5:26–34

Thirty years after leaving Jerusalem, Nephi wrote a felicitous description of his people: "We lived after the manner of happiness," a perfect one-sentence summary of the kind of fulfilling life our Father wants all of us to live.

Nephi reminded us of his obedience to the Lord's command to make two sets of plates, and on this one—the set that eventually came down into the hands of the Prophet Joseph Smith—Nephi engraved the things that are "pleasing unto God. And if my people are pleased with the things of God they will be pleased with mine engravings which are upon these plates."

2 Nephi 6–10

Jacob, a Melchizedek Priesthood holder and the equivalent of a general authority in his day, learned much from his father, Lehi, from his brother Nephi, and from the plates of brass. He became a great theologian. Chapters 6 through 10 may be considered a general conference talk; his assigned topic was Isaiah.

2 Nephi 6:4–5

Jacob taught "concerning things which are, and which are to come," indicating that Isaiah's prophecies have dual fulfillment and sometimes even *multiple* fulfillments. They apply to his people back then but also to our people in this final dispensation, so that we may "learn and glorify the name of [our] God." Isaiah wrote concerning all the house of Israel, and because we, too, are of Israel, we should liken or apply these things unto us. These are not just history lessons but lessons from history. History is what has already happened; scripture is what happens and will happen. "Things . . . which are to come" signifies prophecy, and prophecy is history in reverse. Jacob said the reason he read Isaiah to his audience is twofold: his brother Nephi wanted it read (he had read it to them before; see 1 Nephi 19:22–23), and Isaiah's words can be applied to the Nephites as well as all Israel. The Book of Mormon and Isaiah were both written for our day.

2 Nephi 6:6–7

We have already seen these verses in 1 Nephi 21:22–23. Jacob also used this text from Isaiah 49 to initiate his great discourse. The standard—the Savior's gospel and Church—is set up to tenderly gather the people to the truth. Even kings and queens are used as instruments in the Lord's hands to facilitate the great gathering. People will be able to see the Lord's hand in it.

2 Nephi 6:8–18

Jacob began his commentary on Isaiah by giving a quick summary of world history from his time until the end of time.

2 Nephi 6:8–10

Israelites left behind in the Lehites' former homeland, the land of Jerusalem, have now been killed or exiled (600–586 B.C.).

Some of the exiles, now generically called "Jews," would return to the land of Jerusalem (539 through the mid-400s B.C.). Jacob learned from an angel that centuries later, among the remnant of the Jews, the Messiah, the Holy One of Israel, would manifest himself in the flesh, and at the end of his ministry he would be scourged and crucified (ca. A.D. 30–33).

After the Jews reject their Holy Messiah, they will suffer his judgments, being killed and persecuted (beginning with the great Jewish-Roman War of A.D. 66–73). Regarding verse 9, see 2 Nephi 10:3.

2 Nephi 6:11–13

Although for many long centuries the surviving Jews would be scattered, hated, and physically afflicted, because of the prayers of the faithful and the mercy of the Lord, they would not be exterminated. When they finally come to a knowledge of their Redeemer, as a people they will be gathered back to their lands of inheritance.

Those who fight against the divine cause of Zion and against God's covenant people will be humbled and shamed, although the Lord's people will not be shamed. His people wait for him (the Hebrew word translated as "wait" means "look to," "hope for," "expect," "anticipate"; see references at footnote 13*b*). More importantly, the Lord patiently waits for his people to come back (the meaning of the Hebrew verb "to repent" is "to return").

When Jacob speaks of the Gentiles ("blessed are the Gentiles," v. 12), he is referring to those who come to America (1 Nephi 13:15–19) and hearken to the Lamb of God (1 Nephi 14:1). They will be numbered among the house of Israel.

2 Nephi 6:14–15

As Isaiah prophesied, the Messiah will return: he will come a second time to recover his people, but this time he will come "in power and great glory." Those who refuse to believe in the Messiah will be destroyed by fires, tempests, earthquakes, wars, pestilences, and famines. Then they will believe in him!

2 Nephi 6:16–18

The "prey" or "righteous captives"—God's covenant people—shall be delivered; the Mighty God will stand in their defense and rescue and save his people. Their antagonists and oppressors will receive their just due, and everyone on earth will unmistakably know that the Lord Jesus Christ is the Savior, the Redeemer, the Mighty One of Jacob.

2 Nephi 7 (Isaiah 50)

Jacob explained why he quoted chapters from Isaiah in the Nephite record: "I speak unto you these things that ye may rejoice, and lift up your heads forever, because of the blessings which the Lord God shall bestow upon your children" (2 Nephi 9:3).

2 Nephi 7:1

Jacob quotes Isaiah 50, where Isaiah is speaking messianically. Notice the questions the Lord raises right up front. The first question is new in the Book of Mormon; it is not in the King James Bible. If a man found uncleanness (infidelity) in his wife, he could put her away with a bill of divorcement (see the Mosaic law in Deuteronomy 24:1–4).

Here again we have marriage imagery: God is married to his people, but they had estranged themselves because of their wickedness. Recall the complaint (1 Nephi 21:14; Isaiah 49:14) that the Lord had forsaken and forgotten them—but he would show that he had not. They were separated but not divorced.

The Lord does not forsake us when we sin. We forsake him. He does not "sell" us. We sell ourselves when we decide to give up our eternal souls for the pleasures of the moment (compare Moses 8:15).

It is easy to see why Isaiah used the symbolism of divorce and slavery to describe the relationship between Christ and Israel. When the people of Israel (ancient or modern) commit sin, they are slaves in the "bondage of sin" (D&C 84:49–51). In ancient Israel, idolatry was regarded as spiritual adultery, and Jesus Christ, the Bridegroom, deserves unadulterated fidelity.

2 Nephi 7:2–3

The text of 2 Nephi makes some of Isaiah's questions declarative sentences; read also Doctrine and Covenants 133:64–73. His first coming was to his own, and he was rejected; now at his second coming he calls again, offering another opportunity for deliverance and redemption.

2 Nephi 7:4–10

Here is another Servant Song (see also commentary at 1 Nephi 21:1–6). The servant is likely not Israel as a people, because the suffering is undeserved; this could only be the Savior.

Incidents in Jesus' life are prophesied, as also in Isaiah 53:4–9 and Mosiah 14:4–9 and see also Matthew 5:39; 26:67; 27:26.

To set one's face "like a flint" (a very hard stone) means to be firm, steadfast, determined.

The "fear" spoken of in verse 10 means reverence, honor.

2 Nephi 7:11

"Walk in the light of your fire"—compare Doctrine and Covenants 1:16: "Every man walketh in his own way, and after the image of his own god."

2 Nephi 8 (Isaiah 51)

Verses 1–2: Abraham is the rock, and Sarah is the quarry. We must live up to the covenant called after Abraham. Ultimately, the covenant is centered on the Rock of our Salvation, which is Jesus Christ. Just as a rock will have the same physical properties and composition as the mountain from which it is taken, so we have the potential to become like our Father and his Son, our only sure foundation.

One student of the Book of Mormon wrote: "The image is of a quarry; we are just smaller pieces of the parental rock. We are made of the same stuff as Abraham, and we are also made of the same stuff as Christ and God since we are children of God. There is a reason why the Lord wants us to do our genealogy and know 'from whence we are digged.' We know several reasons, such as baptism, and eternal marriage for the dead. But are there other reasons? In France, a woman told me that her daughter had been counseled by a psychiatrist to do her genealogy as therapy: it would help her know who she is, and to feel more self-worth and a sense of belonging in this world. In modern genetics, we know that we physically inherit traits from our parents and that all of us contain a large number of identical genes, indicating a common ancestor. We should not forget those who went before us, because that is what links us all together as a world family. That is what makes it possible to love those around us and to love ourselves without being prideful. Therefore, 'from whence we have been digged' affects us physically, mentally, and spiritually."

2 Nephi 8:3–5

Both Isaiah and Jacob knew the future. Earth will return to paradisiacal glory, as stated in Articles of Faith 1:10. The Book of Mormon is certainly part of the law that will proceed from the Lord in the last days, a portion of the restoration of all things that will enlighten all who look for light.

Law, light, righteousness, salvation, and judge are all name-titles for the Savior of the world, the one Person in whom we can implicitly trust.

2 Nephi 8:6

Peter also saw the day when the heavens and the earth would pass away with great noise, fire, fervent heat, and melting elements (2 Peter 3:10–13). The earth is also a living entity; it must die and be resurrected. President Joseph Fielding Smith wrote, "The earth, as a living body, will have to die and be resurrected, for it, too, has been redeemed by the blood of Jesus Christ."[11] The Lord provides life for eternity.

2 Nephi 8:7–8

The Lord extends assurance and confidence to his faithful followers (compare D&C 6:33–37), whereas reviling men will be consumed.

2 Nephi 8:9–10

"Rahab" and "the dragon" also appear in the creation story of Ugarit, one of Israel's neighbors to the north in Old Testament times. In that story they represent the forces of chaos that God subdued through the order of his creations. God has power over all elements and all enemies.

"Put on strength"—"What is meant by the command in Isaiah, 52d chapter, 1st verse, which saith: Put on thy strength, O Zion—and what people had Isaiah reference to? He had reference to those whom God should call in the last days, who should hold the power of priesthood to bring again Zion, and the redemption of Israel; and to put on her strength is to put on the authority of the priesthood, which she, Zion, has a right to by lineage; also to return to that power which she had lost" (D&C 113:7–8).

ISRAEL AND ZION IN LATTER-DAY SAINT USAGE

The terms *Israel* and *Zion* can be confusing to those (for example, Jews and Muslims) who hear the Latter-day Saints use them. The word *Israel* has a host of meanings. It refers to a man, Jacob, one of the Old Testament patriarchs. It also designates a people, the descendants of Jacob, known as Israelites. Then again it refers to a nation, the northern kingdom of Israel—in contrast to Judah, the southern kingdom of Israelites in the Old Testament period. And now, in modern times, there is a modern country called Israel. As Latter-day Saints, we use the term *Israel* as a label for God's covenant people, whoever and wherever they are. That is the way the scriptures use the word: in reference to the people who are learning and living the principles of the gospel of Jesus Christ. They are the people of Israel.

144

The term *Zion* also has a variety of meanings. In the Bible the word *Zion* is used to identify the hill the Jebusites occupied, which King David conquered and made the administrative capital of his empire. Later, Mount Zion was the designation for the Temple Mount, where Solomon built the great temple. Later in history, the western hill of Jerusalem became known as Mount Zion. Today, in our scriptures, the term *Zion* has even more meanings. It is another name for the City of Enoch (Moses 7:18–19). It also refers to the future New Jerusalem in Jackson County, Missouri (Moses 7:62; Articles of Faith 1:10). Additionally, Joseph Smith expanded the definition of *Zion* to all of the Americas (his statement is cited at 2 Nephi 12:3). The Lord explains in Doctrine and Covenants 97:21 that Zion is "the pure in heart." Therefore, *Zion* means God's covenant people. Joseph Smith taught that "the building up of Zion is a cause that has interested the people of God in every age; it is a theme upon which prophets, priests and kings have dwelt with peculiar delight; they have looked forward with joyful anticipation to the day in which we live; and . . . have sung and written and prophesied of this our day; but they died without the sight; we are the favored people that God has made choice of to bring about the Latter-day glory."[12] He also taught: "We ought to have the building up of Zion as our greatest object."[13]

In the most important context, then, the Latter-day Saints and their scriptures use both terms, *Israel* and *Zion,* not in any political sense but in reference to all the children of God who want to learn of him and keep his commandments and thus become part of his special, chosen, covenant people.

See "Why Does God Have a Covenant People?" accompanying the commentary at 3 Nephi 5:21–26 (in vol. 2 of this work).

---

2 Nephi 8:11

"The redeemed of the Lord" are the true Latter-day Saints (D&C 45:71; 101:18–19), and the era of restoration and redemption and the establishment of Zion will be a joyful time for them.

2 Nephi 8:12

Do not be afraid of man. Man is compared to grass, suggesting the transitory nature of life. From a psalmist and from the prophet Isaiah, we learn the symbolism of grass, which persists through both the Old and New Testaments:

"As for man, his days are as grass: as a flower of the field, so he flourisheth. For the wind passeth over it, and it is gone; and the place thereof shall know it no more" (Psalm 103:15–16).

"All flesh is grass, and all the goodliness thereof is as the flower of the field: the grass withereth, the flower fadeth: because the spirit of the Lord bloweth upon it: surely the people is grass. The grass withereth, the flower fadeth: but the word of our God shall stand forever" (Isaiah 40:6–8).

Grass was a physical similitude of the transitoriness of mortals. With the heavy rains of wintertime, grass flourishes and even spreads its velvety green carpet over the barren desert; but with the coming of the hot, dry winds off that desert, it is gone. The blades are thriving and vigorous one day and vanished the next. So is the life of man.

But some things, like the word of God, are more timeless and permanent: "All flesh is as grass, and all the glory of man as the flower of grass. The grass withereth, and the flower thereof falleth away: but the word of the Lord endureth forever. And this is the word which by the gospel is preached unto you" (1 Peter 1:24–25).

The same image appears also in the Doctrine and Covenants: "Make a solemn proclamation of my gospel. . . . This proclamation shall be made to all the kings of the world, . . . to the honorable president-elect, and the high-minded governors of the nation in which you live, and to all the nations of the earth. . . . Call ye, therefore, upon them with loud proclamation, and with your testimony, fearing them not, for they are as grass, and all their glory as the flower thereof which soon falleth" (D&C 124:2–3, 7).

2 Nephi 8:13–16

There is no need to forget the Lord and fear the oppressor and the destroyer. Righteous captives are released from exile and protected and covered, as he says, "in the shadow of mine hand," and allowed to participate in establishing Zion.

2 Nephi 8:17–18

Jerusalem has indeed "drunk at the hand of the Lord the cup of his fury" and been "wrung out" to the very last drop. As Isaiah later tells us, "She hath received of the Lord's hand double for all her sins" (Isaiah 40:2).

But why so much suffering, and why for so long? The Lord declared, "As one generation hath been destroyed among the Jews because of iniquity, even so have they been destroyed from generation to generation according to their iniquities" (2 Nephi 25:9). If they continue to reject their God, they continue to suffer for it.

Verse 18 explains that there is no priesthood leadership in Judah; there are no prophets.

2 Nephi 8:19–20

Isaiah 51:19 has "these two things"; the Hebrew simply says "these two."

On the other hand, 2 Nephi 8:19 has "these two sons," who have the priesthood. These are the two witnesses, the two prophets in Jerusalem at the end of days, the time of Armageddon. John the Revelator also saw these two prophets.

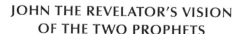

JOHN THE REVELATOR'S VISION OF THE TWO PROPHETS

Revelation 11:3

The ministry of the two witnesses or prophets in Jerusalem lasts for a period of 1,260 days (three and a half years). The number may be literal or symbolic. Three and a half is half of seven, the number of perfection or completion. Thus we understand that their mission is cut short.

Elder Bruce R. McConkie described their ministry in greater detail:

"Who are these witnesses, and when will they prophesy? 'They are two prophets that are to be raised up to the Jewish nation in the last days, at the time of the restoration, and to prophesy to the Jews after they are gathered and have built the city of Jerusalem in the land of their fathers.' (D&C 77:15.) Their ministry will take place after the latter-day temple has been built in Old Jerusalem, after some of the Jews who dwell there have been converted, and just before Armageddon and the return of the Lord Jesus. How long will they minister in Jerusalem and in the Holy Land? For three and a half years. . . . The Jews, as an assembled people, will hear again the testimony of legal administrators bearing record that salvation is in Christ and in his gospel. Who will these witnesses be? We do not know, except that they will be followers of Joseph Smith; they will hold the holy Melchizedek Priesthood; they will be members of The Church of Jesus Christ of Latter-day Saints. It is reasonable to suppose, knowing how the Lord has always dealt with his people in all ages, that they will be two members of the Council of the Twelve or of the First Presidency of the Church."[14]

Revelation 11:4–5

The prophet Zechariah also saw these two witnesses. He referred to them symbolically as two olive trees or two candlesticks (Zechariah 4:3, 11–14). Olive oil helps to heal, and candlesticks give light. The glory ("fire") of these two prophets will be miraculously displayed in protecting them and destroying their enemies.

Revelation 11:6

The two witnesses will have powers similar to two of the greatest ancient Hebrew prophets: shutting the heavens so that it does not rain, as Elijah did (1 Kings 17:1), and sending plagues on the earth, as Moses did (Exodus 7–11).

Revelation 11:7–13

The two witnesses are killed, and their bodies lie in the streets for three and a half days, with nations viewing their bodies (perhaps via satellite transmission). Then they are resurrected and ascend into heaven while a great earthquake strikes the city.

2 Nephi 8:21–23

The cup of trembling and fury passes to those who afflict God's covenant people.

2 Nephi 8:24–25

These verses come from Isaiah 52:1–2. See commentary at 3 Nephi 20:36–38.

2 Nephi 9

In 2 Nephi 2 and 9 we see clearly why Joseph Smith said a person could get closer to God by abiding by the precepts of the Book of Mormon than by the teachings of any other book. The Prophet was once asked, "What are the fundamental principles of your religion?" He replied, "The fundamental principles of our religion are the testimony of the Apostles and Prophets, concerning Jesus Christ, that He died, was buried, and rose again the third day, and ascended into heaven; and all other things which pertain to our religion are only appendages to it."[15]

In 2 Nephi 9 we have a prophet—Jacob, son of Lehi—bearing plain and powerful testimony of the Lord Jesus Christ. We are delighted to read his exclamations of pure gratitude and praise for the wisdom, mercy, grace, goodness, justice, and holiness of our God and his plan for us. Read the first sentence of verses 8, 10, 13, 17, 19, and 20. "O" is an expression of awe. This is devotional literature in its highest form. We can tell Jacob has strong feelings: "O how great . . ." and "O the greatness . . ." are similar to the sentiment of the hymn "How Great Thou Art." These teachings are given to us so that we may rejoice and lift up our heads forever (see also 2 Nephi 11:8).

It seems significant that this unsurpassed revelation (2 Nephi 9) of the place of Christ in the plan of God comes after reading Isaiah. Would not the same spiritual experience be available to each of us if we read and pondered Isaiah?

2 Nephi 9:1–3

Jacob had been quoting Isaiah to remind us of the covenants the Lord has made with all Israel and that he has spoken by his servants, the prophets, from the beginning of time (Moses 5:58–59). Isaiah and Jacob show the hand of God in history (or, *his story*) and in the covenant blessings of repentance, forgiveness, gathering, restoration, and redemption.

Verses 1–3 constitute a doctrinal bridge to verse 4 and the verses following. Jacob moved from talking about the scattering and gathering of Israel to a discussion of physical death, and then to resurrection, because they are parallel. Death is the *scattering* of elements, and resurrection is the *gathering* or *restoration* of those elements. To Jacob and other Book of Mormon prophets, the doctrines of the gospel or plan of salvation are all interconnected—one seamless web.

2 Nephi 9:4–6

In the end, the only thing that really dies is death. For inevitable as death is, yet "in our bodies we shall see God." God himself, appearing as Jesus Christ (meaning "the Anointed Savior"), would be born with a tangible body and show himself in that flesh to his own people at Jerusalem. He intentionally came to submit himself to mortal men so he could die and then be resurrected to living immortality, thus preparing the way for all the Father's children to live again—permanently. The phrase "waste away" seems an apt description of old age. The awe-inspiring power of the Atonement reverses that.

Verse 6 describes the step-by-step eternal plan of redemption: because of transgression, all are separated from God's

presence (spiritual death); because of that separation, we are
in a fallen condition; because of that fallen condition, we all
experience physical death; God's merciful plan provides resurrection for all, taking us back into God's presence for judgment and thus overcoming all consequences of the original
transgression and the Fall (see the chart accompanying the
commentary at 2 Nephi 2:8–10).

2 Nephi 9:7

Only an infinite atonement (or redemption, ransom)
could reverse the effects of the "first judgment"—death and
separation from God—and allow all to rise again, from corruption to incorruption, and make eternal life—God's kind of
life—available to everyone.

In what ways is the Atonement infinite? First, it is timeless; it affects past, present, and future. It has already operated in our premortal existence to bless us (Alma 13:3; D&C
93:38). Second, it could have been, and was, accomplished
only by an infinite Being, One who has never-ending power
and influence throughout the universe. Third, it is infinite in
that it provides immortality and potential eternal life for all of
the worlds the Savior created under the direction of his Father
and to all of the beings on those worlds:

> By him, of him, and through him, the worlds were all
>   made,
> Even all that career in the heavens so broad.
> Whose inhabitants, too, from the first to the last,
> Are sav'd by the very same Saviour of ours.[16]

Elder Bruce R. McConkie wrote: "Now our Lord's ju-
risdiction and power extend far beyond the limits of this
one small earth on which we dwell. He is, under the Father,
the Creator of worlds without number. (Moses 1:33.) And
through the power of his atonement the inhabitants of these
worlds, the revelation says, 'are begotten sons and daughters

unto God' (D. & C. 76:24), which means that the atonement of Christ, being literally and truly infinite, applies to an infinite number of earths."[17]

Thus, the atonement of Jesus Christ is infinite in time, space, and number. In the history of eternity nothing can fully compare to it.

2 Nephi 9:8–12

Were it not for God's wisdom, mercy, and grace in assuring that we will all be resurrected, our spirits "must become subject to that angel who fell," the devil, and actually become like him, become his messengers, and live forever in misery, forever "shut out" of God's presence. In other words, without the resurrection every human being would become a son (or daughter) of perdition.

Satan, the great deceiver, has power to transform himself "nigh unto an angel of light" (see also 2 Corinthians 11:14; Revelation 16:14; Alma 30:53; D&C 129:8). His purpose is to deceive, were it possible, the very elect (Joseph Smith–Matthew 1:22). The evil one stirs up people to do all kinds of secret sins in the dark. Even though the devil may seem to appear with light, he actually has no power to shine any light into anyone's life.

God is good, as evidenced by his helping all humankind to escape from evil. The greatest evil is the awful, double-headed monster, death and hell, which would keep us away from an eternal family. And resurrection relieves at least some of the damning effects of that awful monster.

2 Nephi 9:13–16

God's plan is great, as evidenced by the body and spirit being reunited or restored and made incorruptible and immortal. Every individual, whether good or bad, who has lived on this earth will rise from physical death, "this first death," unto life. All death is reversed to life (Revelation 21:4). This is incomparable power! All will rise in the resurrection

(1 Corinthians 15:21–22), and all will have a perfect knowledge of guilt, uncleanness, and nakedness; that is, unless one has repented, his sins will be exposed and he will stand naked before God. The righteous, on the other hand, will be "clothed with purity," wearing the "robe of righteousness," having been covered by the Savior's atonement. The Hebrew concept of atonement, *kippur,* means "to cover over" or "hide," so the righteous will rise with no guilt, uncleanness, or nakedness exposed, being fully clothed and endowed with virtue and goodness.

On the great day of judgment, "we shall be brought to stand before God . . . and have a bright recollection of all our guilt" (Alma 11:43). "Can ye imagine yourselves brought before the tribunal of God," Alma asked, "with your souls filled with guilt and remorse, having a remembrance of all your guilt, yea, a perfect remembrance of all your wickedness?" (Alma 5:18).

The Prophet Joseph Smith described the scene: "The great misery of departed spirits in the world of spirits, where they go after death, is to know that they come short of the glory that others enjoy and that they might have enjoyed themselves, and they are their own accusers."[18]

The Prophet declared further: "A man is his own tormenter and his own condemner. Hence the saying, They shall go into the lake that burns with fire and brimstone. The torment of disappointment in the mind of man is as exquisite as a lake burning with fire and brimstone."[19] On fire and brimstone, see commentary at Mosiah 3:27.

Everything we have ever thought, done, or said is all recorded in our brain. Most humans have a problem being able to instantly recall what has been stored there, but as Jacob and Alma teach us, when the veil is removed and our minds are quickened, we will have a perfect knowledge, a bright recollection, a perfect remembrance of all mortal experience.

President Joseph F. Smith elaborated on this phenomenon: "In reality a man cannot forget anything. He may have a lapse of memory; he may not be able to recall at the moment a thing that he knows or words that he has spoken; he may not have the power at his will to call up these events and words; but let God Almighty touch the mainspring of the memory and awaken recollection, and you will find then that you have not even forgotten a single idle word that you have spoken! I believe the word of God to be true, and, therefore, I warn the youth of Zion, as well as those who are advanced in years, to beware of saying wicked things, of speaking evil and taking in vain the name of sacred things and sacred beings. Guard your words, that you may not offend even man, much less offend God."[20]

2 Nephi 9:17–18

God is great and just, as evidenced by the lives of those who obey his strict laws and endure the crosses of the world, such as mortal sorrows, burdens, trials, temptations, calamities, struggles, and afflictions. Those who live above the shame of the world—the efforts to mock, belittle, persecute, and humiliate—will in the end receive a fulness of joy forever.

2 Nephi 9:19

God is merciful, as evidenced by his delivering his Saints from the grasp of three awful monsters: the devil, death, and hell (on "endless torment," see D&C 19:6–12; 138:59). In one sense, endless punishment or endless torment is endless because it is God's punishment and he is endless.

2 Nephi 9:20

God is holy, as evidenced by the fact that he knows all things from the beginning and that he knows all things which are to come. His knowledge is complete and perfect, which is part of what makes him a holy Man. We learn that unequivocal truth in this passage and other passages such as 1 Nephi 9:6; 2 Nephi 2:24; Words of Mormon 1:7; Moroni 7:22; Doctrine and Covenants 38:2; Moses 1:6; and Abraham

2:8; see also Jeremiah 1:5; Acts 15:18; 17:26. If God did not know all things in advance, how could he ever show all future things to prophets such as Adam, Enoch, Noah, the brother of Jared, Abraham, Moses, Isaiah, Lehi, Nephi, John, and others who were given a panoramic vision of all the world's history? Anyone who believes in prophets and prophecy must believe that God knows all things, from the beginning to the end.

Elder Bruce R. McConkie wrote: "Does God know all things? He does. Is there anything he does not know? There is not. Is he progressing in knowledge and learning new truths? He is not. He is not a student God. His knowledge and supremacy are *not* limited to a sphere or realm beyond which there are higher spheres and greater realms. He is an Eternal God, an infinite being, an omniscient man, one in whose person all knowledge, all power, and all truth center."[21]

Lectures on Faith explains, "If it were not for the idea existing in the minds of men that God had all knowledge, it would be impossible for them to exercise faith in him."[22]

2 Nephi 9:21–24

Having suffered "the pains of every living creature, both men, women, and children," Jesus Christ offers salvation to all persons who will obey him, so that every person may be resurrected and stand before him to be judged. The only way people can access the best of that salvation is by exercising faith in him, repenting of their sins, being baptized (by water and by fire), and enduring to the end; if they will not, they must be damned, or condemned.

2 Nephi 9:25–27

Any who are unaware of the laws of God are not held accountable for failing to live them. To the innocently ignorant there is no punishment or condemnation, for the atoning mercies of the Savior cover them. His merciful atonement satisfies the demands of justice for all who live on earth without a knowledge of his higher laws, and they are spared from the awful monsters of death, hell, the devil, and torment, being restored by God himself. Woe is pronounced on those who know God's laws and commandments and yet waste the days of their probation by transgressing these laws. Their condition is awful!

2 Nephi 9:28–29

Paul wrote that "knowledge puffeth up" (1 Corinthians 8:1)—much knowledge can be dangerous to us if we succumb to pride. We get in trouble when we think we know better than God, or when we think we are above some commandment. We quickly find ourselves in serious trouble when we consider ourselves an exception to a rule. On the other hand, knowledge of all kinds (especially of godly things) is commendable and desirable—if we keep our hearts open to the counsel of God (2 Nephi 9:42).

2 Nephi 9:30–38

Woes are pronounced on various kinds of people who are temporally or spiritually challenged. Those who have an abundance of worldly things—basking in wealth—often do not need God: "their treasure is their god," and "their treasure shall perish with them."

The spiritually deaf, blind, and uncircumcised of heart, along with the liars, murderers, whores, and idolaters who refuse to repent and therefore "die in their sins," will face God and punishment.

2 Nephi 9:39–41

We become what we think about, so if we are carnally minded (consumed with worldly or immoral thoughts), we are heading for death, but if we are spiritually minded, we are heading for eternal life. This is exactly what the apostle Paul taught: "For to be carnally minded is death; but to be spiritually minded is life and peace" (Romans 8:6). The carnally minded man is the natural man, a person who is of the flesh, who lives to gratify the flesh, to satisfy base impulses and debasing desires. "The natural man," the carnally minded man, "is an enemy to God" (Mosiah 3:19).

Jacob pleaded with his listeners and readers not to fight against the truths he taught: "I know that the words of truth are hard against all uncleanness." The righteous are not worried about chastisement because they stand firm in their love of the truth.

He extended the invitation to walk the path that leads to life. To get on that path requires repentance and baptism; actually, repentance and baptism are the gate to the path. Then comes remission of sins by fire and by the Holy Ghost (2 Nephi 31:17–18).

The continuing path is straight and narrow. Verse 41 uses the term *straight,* whereas other passages use *strait.* What is the difference? *Straight* means not crooked, not devious; *strait* means narrow, constricted. The terms *strait* and *narrow* mean about the same thing: constricted or tight. The juxtaposition of synonyms is an ancient Hebrew literary device.[23] We are accustomed to such dual forms, using words with related meanings; for example, joy and happiness, trials and tribulation, and sick and afflicted. As suggested in verse 41, man's path is strait (narrow), but the Lord's path is straight (see also Alma 7:9; 37:12). "For God doth not walk in crooked paths, neither doth he turn to the right hand nor to the left, . . . therefore his paths are straight" (D&C 3:2).

"The keeper of the gate is the Holy One of Israel; and he employeth no servant there." The Lord employs many servants in his kingdom: the ecclesiastical leaders who are sometimes needed to help facilitate the repentance process, the priesthood holders who perform the baptisms of water and of the Holy Ghost, and the temple workers who assist us with sacred ordinances. But in the end, all the ordinances, the instructions, and the covenants are the Lord's. Only he gives the final approvals for entrance into his heavenly kingdom and seals up each one to eternal life.

2 Nephi 9:42–43

To those who sincerely and faithfully knock, petition, and importune, the Savior will open up the mansions of his kingdom; but he will despise and turn away the wise and rich who are puffed up in the pride of their own learning and earning, unless they "consider themselves fools before God," acknowledge their own nothingness, and humble themselves to the depths (Mosiah 4:11). If they do not, they will forever miss out on the happiness of the holy ones.

Despise is a strong word, but it is a carefully chosen word here—even ironic. It means "to look down on with contempt." Those who, because of their learning or wealth, look down on others are looked down on by the Lord. President Ezra Taft Benson confirmed that the two groups of people who "have the greatest difficulty with pride are the 'learned, and the rich.' (2 Nephi 28:15.)"[24]

2 Nephi 9:44–45

Taking off his garments and shaking them was Jacob's symbolic gesture for shaking off the responsibility of his people's sins from his soul. God's "all-searching eye" is witness that Jacob ridded himself of their sins by that symbolic act. It is probably related to the priesthood ordinance of shaking off the dust from one's feet, but it is not the same. "To ceremonially shake the dust from one's feet as a testimony against another was understood by the Jews to symbolize a cessation of fellowship and a renunciation of all responsibility for consequences that might follow. It became an ordinance of accusation and testimony by the Lord's instructions to his apostles as cited in the text. In the current dispensation, the Lord has similarly directed his authorized servants to so testify against those who wilfully and maliciously oppose the truth when authoritatively presented (D&C 24:15; 60:15; 75:20;

84:92; 99:4). The responsibility of testifying before the Lord by this accusing symbol is so great that the means may be employed only under unusual and extreme conditions."[25]

Jacob admonished his brethren to do some shaking of their own—to shake off their chains of sin. Instead of being bound to the evil one, he counsels them to bind themselves to "that God who is the rock of your salvation"; the image of rock in the scriptures represents something firm, solid, and immovable.

2 Nephi 9:46–49

This life, as Amulek later taught, is the time for men to prepare to meet God (Alma 34:32). That meeting will occur at the judgment bar (Mosiah 16:10) or "judgment-seat" (Mormon 3:20, 22) or "tribunal" (Alma 5:18) of God. It will be a "glorious day when justice shall be administered unto the righteous," but the warning is out to the unrighteous to prepare and prevent, and repair and repent, so they will not have to face that day with "awful fear," "awful guilt," "awful misery," and "awful reality." Every soul will be perfectly aware of all his guilt (2 Nephi 9:13–16). In a sense, we will not even need the hierarchy of judges (the Lord Jesus Christ, the original Twelve Apostles, the dispensation heads, and our own priesthood leaders), for we will be happily or painfully aware of where we fit—which kingdom best suits our mortal performance (Mosiah 3:24–25; Alma 12:14–15).

Jacob's tenderness and compassion can be felt in verse 47 as he disclaims any intention of harrowing up souls and minds that are pure, but with his responsibility to plainly call sinners to repentance, he has to speak out. "If ye were holy I would speak unto you of holiness; but as ye are not holy, and ye look upon me as a teacher, it must needs be expedient that I teach you the consequences of sin."

2 Nephi 9:50–51

Thirsty? Come to the waters of life. Hungry? Feast upon that which perisheth not. Here is a lesson in spiritual economics, which you can apply to your everyday life: do not spend your money, your labor, or your time for that which has no value, that which cannot satisfy. Examples could be Internet surfing, television watching, video gaming, chatting, blogging, and on and on, including many things that are not evil but could distract from the things that matter most. As John Bytheway wrote, "Satan works more by distraction than confrontation."[26]

"Let your soul delight in fatness"—that is, the Lord's kind of fatness. He encourages the righteous to consume "a feast of fat things" (Isaiah 25:6; D&C 58:8), the fat things referring to the good things of the earth and of heaven.

2 Nephi 10:1–5

Jacob resumed his "conference talk," pursuing the subject of a righteous branch of father Lehi's posterity. Some of their descendants would perish in unbelief, but many would be recovered and come to a "true knowledge of their Redeemer."

Their Redeemer, as an angel revealed to Jacob, would be called Christ (*Christos* is the Greek form of the Hebrew *Mashiakh*, English *Messiah*—both language titles meaning "the Anointed One").

It was necessary for Christ, the Messiah, to come into mortality as a Jew because he came to die ("for thus it behooveth our God"). It was requisite for his divine purpose, or it was essential or imperative for him to come and die for all the children of God, and the only nation or people on earth who would crucify their own God was the Jews. However, this needs to be qualified. Not all Jews would reject and kill their God. Peter, Andrew, Matthew, James, John, Mary Magdalene, Martha, Mary, Lazarus, and many others were all Jews, and they listened intently to the Savior and loved and obeyed him. When we read in the scriptures about "the Jews" trying to entrap, condemn, and murder Jesus, we should read "some Jewish leaders," for as verse 5 reveals, it was "because of priestcrafts and iniquities [that] they at Jerusalem will stiffen their necks against him, that he be crucified."

2 Nephi 10:6

The consequence of their sins, especially the sin of killing nature's God, is that the forces of nature would be unleashed upon the Jewish nation in the form of "destructions, famines, pestilences, and bloodshed." For example, a devastating famine swept across the land a few years after Jesus' death (Acts 11:28). The Jewish historian Josephus wrote that a war with the Romans a generation after Jesus resulted in more than a million Jews losing their lives or being carried off to slavery and scattered among other nations.[27]

2 Nephi 10:7–9

In a future day, when the Jewish people as a whole come to believe that Jesus of Nazareth is indeed their long-awaited Messiah, then as a people they are promised a gathering from their long dispersion and a restoration in the flesh to the lands of their inheritance.

To be sure, a preliminary or political gathering of some Jews back to their ancient homeland has occurred already.[28] An even greater gathering of that ancient covenant people yet lies in the future, and "the nations of the Gentiles" will help facilitate it, for the kings and queens of Gentile (that is, non-Jewish) nations will be their "nursing fathers" and "nursing mothers" (see also commentary at 1 Nephi 21:14, 21, 24).

2 Nephi 10:10–17

Jacob shifted his prophetic attention to the Western Hemisphere, the lands of promise identified today as the Americas. Latter-day inhabitants of these lands, designated "Gentiles" by the ancient residents who were a branch of Israel, will be blessed and prospered. This hemisphere will be "a land of liberty unto the Gentiles, and there shall be no kings upon the land." God called this hemisphere "Zion," and he will protect and secure it from threatening encroachments from all other nations. "And he that fighteth against Zion shall perish, saith God."

Just as God counseled ancient Israel against setting up a king over them because He would be their king (1 Samuel 8:5–7), so he charged the ancient remnants of Israel inhabiting these western lands of promise against raising up any king, "for I, the Lord, the king of heaven, will be their king, and I will be a light unto them forever, that hear my words." Indeed, those who hear him and obey him will live in his kingdom when he rules and reigns as King of Kings in his millennial, and then celestial, kingdom.

Any who fight against Zion are labeled "the whore of all the earth," elsewhere also branded "the mother of harlots," "the great and abominable church," or "the church of the devil" (see also commentary at 1 Nephi 13:2–9).

2 Nephi 10:18–19

Descendants of father Lehi will be afflicted in future centuries by the "Gentiles," though the Lord will "soften the hearts of the Gentiles" that they will treat these remnants of Israel with fatherly kindness, and "the Gentiles shall be blessed and numbered among the house of Israel."

The Lord has consecrated these lands of Zion for the inheritance of those he brings to them (see commentary at 2 Nephi 1:5–6 and 7–11). Western Zion is "a choice land . . . above all other lands, wherefore I will have all men that dwell thereon that they shall worship me." That is a specific stipulation for those who live in the Americas: the God of this land, who is Jesus Christ, wants worship (adoration, reverence, devotion) centered on him—which is the only way his people can become like him and merit his kind of life, celestial and eternal life.

2 Nephi 10:20–22

Jacob's admonition applies also to every latter-day disciple: because our Lord has been merciful in giving us so much godly knowledge, let us remember him, lay aside our sins, and hold up our heads, for we, too, are not cast off. That is positive reinforcement and assurance of our good standing before the God of heaven.

Jacob noted that his family and his people were taken out of their original homeland but were now in a better land. Whatever they had to give up from before, that sacrifice was more than compensated by the richness and abundance of their new homeland.

Their journey to the promised land was through the sea, what we call the ocean, and they were then living on an "isle of the sea." The primary meaning of the term *isle* in Jacob's native Hebrew was "habitable ground" or "dry land," as opposed to water. In other words, they were now living on a very large "isle" or continent, surrounded by seas in all directions. And great are the Lord's promises to those who live on these isles or continents of the Americas.

The Lord has led various peoples of covenant lineage, groups "broken off" (such as the Jaredites, Lehites, and Mulekites) from his main concentration of covenanters, to accomplish his will and pleasure.

2 Nephi 10:23–25

Having inspired his listeners and us, his readers, with the charge to "not hang down our heads" (2 Nephi 10:20), Jacob now emboldens us with "cheer up your hearts." The Savior has taught in all ages to "be of good cheer." In a sense, the Lord, all the prophets, and all true followers are cheerleaders; we are called to promote optimism and happiness.

President Thomas S. Monson assured us, "The moral footings of society continue to slip, while those who attempt to safeguard those footings are often ridiculed and, at times, picketed and persecuted." He continued: "Fear not. Be of good cheer. The future is as bright as your faith."[29]

It is your choice—life or death, the will of God or the will of the devil—but remember that it is only by the grace of God that anyone can be saved. Only God can rescue you from physical death, by the power of the resurrection, and from spiritual death, by the power of his atonement.

Thus ends Jacob's masterful "conference talk" as recorded on the small plates of Nephi.

2 Nephi 11:1–3

Having included in his record some memorable teachings of his father, Lehi, and his brother Jacob, Nephi resumed with a desire to share more from Isaiah, because his soul delighted in that prophet's words. One of the reasons for Nephi's particular appreciation of Isaiah was the fact that the great prophet was an eyewitness of the Redeemer and, like Nephi and Jacob, he knew the great Redeemer personally. In Nephi and Jacob we see brothers who have shared the most sacred of experiences, mentoring and supporting one another.

What can we learn from these eyewitnesses? Accounts from those who know God from personal contact and experience can help prove Christ to us. The words of these three witnesses (Isaiah, Nephi, and Jacob) will "prove" or "establish" the words of God; "nevertheless, God sendeth more witnesses, and he proveth all his words."

2 Nephi 11:4–7

Nephi further described what delighted him: "My soul delighteth in proving unto my people the truth of the coming of Christ." The law of Moses and the truths given to Abraham, Enoch, and Adam all point to Christ. All things are types of Christ; all things created bear witness of the Creator.

Nephi's logic is impeccable: if there is no Christ, there is no God; if there is no God, there is no Creator and therefore

there is no creation, which means we don't exist either. But
there is ample evidence that there is a God, and he is Christ,
and he is coming "in the fulness of his own time," in what we
call the meridian or the high point of time (see also commentary at 2 Nephi 2:26).

2 Nephi 11:8

Nephi engraved thirteen of the best chapters from Isaiah
with the intent of enabling all humankind to "lift up their
hearts and rejoice," for these words of Isaiah—his teaching
and his testimony of the Savior of the world—can certainly
lift and bring joy. Anyone who will liken these words unto
themselves, and ponder them in the same Spirit with which
they were written, will find them delightful.

After these thirteen chapters of Isaiah (Isaiah 2–14;
2 Nephi 12–24), Nephi described his keys to understanding
Isaiah (2 Nephi 25:1–8).

2 Nephi 12 (Isaiah 2)

The Book of Mormon corrects and changes many verses
of Isaiah in this chapter. The joys, blessings, and peace of the
righteous in the temples of the Lord are contrasted to the sorrows, woes, and inquietude of the wicked in the day of the
Lord's coming.

2 Nephi 12:1–2

Nephi began again to write some of Isaiah's prophecies in
order to lift the spirits of his people. The "word" (Hebrew *ha
davar*) may also be translated as "thing" or "message." "Saw"
(Hebrew *khazah*) means "envisioned." Isaiah's father, whose
name is anglicized in the King James Version as Amoz, is not
the same person as the prophet Amos, Isaiah's contemporary.

Isaiah received the word concerning Jerusalem and Judah,
though his focus is Jerusalem. "*And* it shall come to pass *in
the last days* . . ." indicates dual fulfillment.

In verse 2 the italicized "that" in the King James Version

is rendered "when" in the Book of Mormon, which more properly fits the context of the previous phrase. The word "mountain" is both a literal and figurative reference to the temple of God. The mountain-temple connection in ancient Israel is well established. A common name for the temple at Jerusalem was *har ha-bayit*, "mountain of the house." Regarding the mountain abode of God and its relationship to the temple, see Psalm 68:16; Isaiah 8:18; Doctrine and Covenants 84:2–4; 133:12–13. Mountains were among God's first temples.

Isaiah's prophecies often focus on the place where God chose to put his name—that is, the temple (1 Kings 8:29; 9:3; 2 Kings 21:4; compare D&C 97:15; 109:26). The prophet saw the latter-day temple, the "mountain of the Lord's house."

The Prophet Joseph Smith asked: "What was the object of gathering the Jews, or the people of God in any age of the world? . . . The main object was to build unto the Lord a house whereby He could reveal unto His people the ordinances of His house and the glories of His kingdom, and teach the people the way of salvation; for there are certain ordinances and principles that, when they are taught and practiced, must be done in a place or house built for that purpose."[30]

This passage can have multiple meanings:

1. The Salt Lake Temple in the Rocky Mountains. President Wilford Woodruff mentioned this Isaiah passage in the prayer dedicating the Salt Lake Temple[31]
2. The New Jerusalem Temple in Independence, Missouri (D&C 57 headnote and verses 1–3)
3. The Old Jerusalem Temple (D&C 133:12–13)

Elder Bruce R. McConkie wrote: "Thus Israel gathers for the purpose of building temples in which the ordinances of salvation and exaltation are performed for the living and the dead. And thus it comes as no surprise to find the ancient prophets speaking of the temples of the Most High and doing it in the setting of the gathering of Israel. 'And it shall come to pass in the last days,' saith Isaiah, 'that the mountain of the Lord's house shall be established in the top of the mountains, and shall be exalted above the hills; and all nations shall flow unto it.' This has specific reference to the Salt Lake Temple and to the other temples built in the top of the Rocky Mountains, and it has a general reference to the temple yet to be built in the New Jerusalem in Jackson County, Missouri. Those in all nations, be it noted, shall flow to the houses of the Lord in the tops of the mountains, there to make the covenants out of which eternal life comes."[32]

Mountain may also mean meeting place as well as holy place. Compare Nephi's experience in the mountain, where the Lord showed him "great things" (1 Nephi 18:3). In a metaphorical sense, *mountain* may also mean nation or people (see commentary at 2 Nephi 12:12–18). An alternate translation of verse 2 may then be "when the nation of the Lord's house shall be established as the head of the nations."

"All nations" shall flow unto it: that is, many people from all nations. The Lord's house will be a means of unifying the peoples of the earth. In his house "all nations" may learn the mysteries of his kingdom.

2 Nephi 12:3

"Let us go up to the mountain of the Lord"—in sacred high places God teaches us of his ways, how to walk in the path to godhood.

Two Jerusalems—two headquarters—are clearly indicated (compare 3 Nephi 20) using what biblical literary scholars call synthetic or complimentary parallelism, suggesting two places. Modern prophets have explained that there are multiple fulfillments of this passage; see also, later in Isaiah, "thy holy cities . . . Zion [and] . . . Jerusalem" (Isaiah 64:10).

Several definitions of Zion have been suggested by modern prophets and apostles. Some indicate that "out of Zion shall go forth the law [teaching, doctrine]" with general conferences from the current headquarters.

President Harold B. Lee wrote: "I have often wondered what that expression meant, that out of Zion should go forth the law. Years ago I went with the brethren to the Idaho Falls Temple, and I heard in that inspired prayer of the First Presidency a definition of the meaning of that term 'out of Zion shall go forth the law.' Note what they said: 'We thank thee that thou hast revealed to us that those who gave us our constitutional form of government were men wise in thy sight and that thou didst raise them up for the very purpose of putting forth that sacred document [the Constitution of the United States; see D&C 101:80]. . . .

"'We pray that kings and rulers and the peoples of all nations under heaven may be persuaded of the blessings enjoyed by the people of this land by reason of their freedom and under thy guidance and be constrained to adopt similar governmental systems, thus to fulfill the ancient prophecy of Isaiah [and Micah] that ". . . out of Zion shall go forth the law and the word of the Lord from Jerusalem."'"[33]

The Prophet Joseph Smith explained: "You know there has been great discussion in relation to Zion—where it is, and where the gathering of the dispensation is, and which I am now going to tell you. The prophets have spoken and written upon it; but I will make a proclamation that will cover a broader ground. The whole of America is Zion itself from north to south, and is described by the Prophets, who declare that it is the Zion where the mountain of the Lord should be, and that it should be in the center of the land. When Elders shall take up and examine the old prophecies in the Bible, they will see it."[34]

Zion is also defined as the city of the living God, the New Jerusalem (D&C 76:66; 84:2; 133:12–13). See also "*Israel* and *Zion* in Latter-day Saint Usage," accompanying 2 Nephi 8:9–10.

2 Nephi 12:4–5

Swords, spears, plowshares, and pruning hooks represent instruments of war and peace. There will be an abrupt change from present political machinations: no more war! In preparing for that great day, we as individual members of the kingdom should also beat our swords of personal revenge into the plowshares of peace and reconciliation. The work of the Prince of Peace is to bring peace to nations and to individuals.

The word "come" in verse 5 is a gentle invitation to walk in the Light, to walk with him.

2 Nephi 12:6–22

These verses summarize the basic spiritual problems that troubled ancient Israel and that will prevail again before the Second Coming. Isaiah knew what will plague people in the last days because he knew what was afflicting Judah in his day, he knew basic human nature, or the nature of fallen man, and he knew the consistent strategies, themes, and tools that Satan uses to carry out his aims. For example, some seek after the philosophies of men.

2 Nephi 12:7–8

Some seek after material things. Materialism runs rampant. When people are full of the world, it is difficult to find place for God. There is no end of our "chariots" on the freeways. Could the prophet have envisioned a modern shopping mall with its myriads of stores and "treasures," the "work of their own hands"?

2 Nephi 12:9–11

Here is a change from the Isaiah text in the Old Testament: "the mean man boweth *not* down, and the great man humbleth himself *not*, therefore, forgive *him* not." Pride is always an obstacle to spiritual progress. As Malachi would later prophesy, at the Lord's second coming the proud and all that do wickedly shall be consumed as stubble (Malachi 4:1), and then the meek will inherit the earth—none of the proud will be around to contest the inheritance.

"O ye wicked ones" in verse 10 is an addition to the Isaiah text.

The Lord alone will be exalted in that day (v. 11; same as v. 17); verse 18 adds that idols are utterly abolished—the antithesis of the Lord being exalted. (How the idols are disposed of is described in verse 20.)

2 Nephi 12:12–18

The proud and lofty will be cut down in that day, the day of the Second Coming; cedars and oaks are symbolic of the proud and lofty. Mountains and towers are also symbols of the high and lofty. Verse 14 adds "and upon all the nations which are lifted up, and upon every people"—nations and people being parallel with mountains and hills.

The Greek Septuagint has one phrase from verse 16 and the traditional (Masoretic) Hebrew text the other phrase, but the Book of Mormon has both (see footnote 16a).

2 Nephi 12:19–22

The wicked flee from the God of righteousness. They separate themselves; they feel like hiding because of sins and the resultant guilt. Verse 22 counsels humans against trusting in the arm of flesh.

2 Nephi 13 (Isaiah 3)

In this chapter, historically speaking, Isaiah moved from prophesying about Ephraim's problems at the hands of the Assyrians to prophesying of Judah's and Jerusalem's demise at the hands of their oppressors, the Babylonians, beginning around 600 B.C. Verses 1–3 describe the deportation of Jerusalem's upper classes during the Babylonian siege under Jechoiachin (2 Kings 24:14–15). The second half of chapter 13 moves to a discussion of circumstances of the last days, with verse 11 perhaps being the transition. However, all of chapter 13 applies to our day as well.

2 Nephi 13:1–4

Economic prosperity is gone. Bread and water are both literal and symbolic, as Amos explained: "Not a famine of bread, nor a thirst for water, but of hearing the words of the Lord" (Amos 8:11). Leadership is also gone, with only incompetent leaders left.

2 Nephi 13:5–7

General collapse of social order ensues: lawlessness and insolence against elders, gangs of youth walking the busy streets in rebellion and violence, and families torn apart. The desperate condition of society is illustrated by the demand of one who has a simple article of clothing to rule over his peers.

2 Nephi 13:8–11

Note the use of future perfect tense verbs, as if future events and conditions are accomplished realities (see commentary at Mosiah 16:6).

Our ultimate objective, of course, is to have God's image engraven in our countenance (Alma 5:14, 19). Our outward appearance reflects our inner character. People are openly and willfully sinning, not even trying to hide it; sin is visible in their faces. Immorality is blatantly promoted in society—then and now. Some people actively endeavor to change laws to legalize so as to facilitate their sins and perversions.

The righteous and the wicked will always get what they deserve (see also D&C 29:27–28).

2 Nephi 13:12

President Ezra Taft Benson saw the fulfillment of this verse in our day: "Today the undermining of the home and family is on the increase, with the devil anxiously working to displace the father as the head of the home and create rebellion among the children. The Book of Mormon describes this condition when it states, 'As for my people, children are their oppressors, and women rule over them.' And then these words follow—and consider these words seriously when you think of those political leaders who are promoting birth control and abortion: 'O my people, they which lead thee cause thee to err, and destroy the way of thy paths' (Isaiah 3:12; 2 Nephi 13:12)."[35]

2 Nephi 13:13–15

The Lord will take the stand to accuse and prosecute the case against his people. Perhaps verse 15 refers to greedy and unconscionable institutions in the world today.

2 Nephi 13:16–24

After condemning the male leaders (2 Nephi 13:1–15), the Lord turned to rebuke the "daughters of Zion." It is clear that he expected more of the women. The pride and haughtiness that goad men in their vain ambitions are often manifested in women through their outward adornment and apparel. If women are corrupt, society is inevitably suffering its death throes. Here are described the "flirtatious fashion slaves"—those who parade the "who's wearing what" and "who's showing off what" mentality with their eyes painted and their persons bedecked with ornaments (see also Ezekiel 23:40). Name-brand clothes, earrings, nose rings, tongue rings and other body piercings, expensive haircuts, tanning salons, and plastic surgery seem to be an obsession, greater than the lasting virtues of genuine womanhood. (However, an increasing number of males in modern culture are also obsessed with manipulating the human body. Such behavior is surely not expressive of the highest ideals of manhood.) The Lord's first epithet is "haughty"; he goes on to explain in detail their offensive behavior.

Archaeologist Gabriel Barkay's 1986 report of his

excavations along the west side of Jerusalem's Hinnom Valley describes findings from the richest sepulchre opened:

"The abundant jewelry found in the tomb provides the first material evidence to support the frequent allusion in the Bible to the wealth of Jerusalem during the First Temple period. Isaiah had mocked the ostentation of Jerusalem's society ladies when he wrote: 'On that day the Lord will take away the finery of their anklets, the head bands and their crescents; the pendants, the bracelets and the scarfs; the headdresses, the armlets, the sashes, the perfume boxes and the amulets; the rings and the nose jewels.' The tomb produced six gold items and 95 silver items as well as jewelry made of rare stones, glass and faience—many of them of great beauty including earrings, rings, beads and pendants.

"This is the first time that a representative selection of jewelry worn by the women of Jerusalem at the end of the First Temple period forms part of an archaeological assemblage."[36]

The women are concerned about their physical appearance, and they are devoted to drawing attention to it. The word "wanton" in verse 16 means excessive, unrestrained, licentious. These "daughters of Zion" were also types of the future, as indicated by "in that day" in verse 18, meaning the last days. Their immodesty will result in total indecent and inhumane exposure.

In the vanity and merriment of debauchery, health is destroyed, and social diseases result.

2 Nephi 13:25–14:1

War reduces the male population; women want to remove the reproach of barrenness and childlessness. Not having seed (offspring) is deemed a curse.

Elder Wilford Woodruff recorded the following vision: "I had been reading the revelations . . . [when] a strange stupor came over me. . . . I arose to speak and said . . . I will answer you right here what is coming to pass shortly. . . . I then looked in all directions . . . and I found the same mourning in every place throughout the Land. It seemed as though I was above the earth, looking down to it as I passed along on my way east and I saw the roads full of people principally women with just what they could carry in bundles on their backs . . . It was remarkable to me that there were so few men among them. . . . Wherever I went I saw . . . scenes of horror and desolation rapine and death . . . death and destruction everywhere. I cannot paint in words the horror that seemed to encompass me around. It was beyond description or thought of man to conceive. I supposed that this was the End but I was here given to understand, that the same horrors were being enacted all over the country. . . . Then a voice said 'Now shall come to pass that which was spoken by Isaiah the Prophet 'That seven women shall take hold of one man saying &c.'"[37]

Elder Bruce R. McConkie wrote: "'And in that day'—the millennial day—'seven women shall take hold of one man, saying, We will eat our own bread, and wear our own apparel: only let us be called by thy name, to take away our reproach,' the reproach of being without a husband, without children, without a family of their own. This shall come to pass after the destruction of the wicked, and it is one of many scriptural intimations that the generality of women are more spiritual than are most men. The inference is that far more women will abide the day of his coming than will be the case with men. And they, being clean and upright, and desiring family units and children and the exaltation that grows out of all these things, will turn to the marriage discipline of Abraham their father so they may be blessed like Sarah of old."[38]

2 Nephi 14 (Isaiah 4)

At the end of time come the promised *reinstatement, restoration*, and *redemption*.

2 Nephi 14:1–3

The branch of the Lord and the fruit of the earth symbolize the Messiah himself and people who live under his rule during the millennial era. His people, the remnant of Israel, are a holy people living in a holy city in a holy land—all of which means, in the Hebrew expression, that they will be a people of holiness living in a city of holiness in a land of holiness, with the Holy One of Israel reigning among them. Those who remain to live into this glorious era are the elect, those whose names are written in the Lamb's book of life.[39]

2 Nephi 14:4

Note the strong wording: The Lord has to cleanse the *filth* of the daughters of Zion and purge the blood on the hands of his people. The people are "washed" as with the fuller's "soap" and purged by "burning" as with the refiner's "fire." Purification comes by the spirit of burning or, as we sing, "The Spirit of God like a Fire Is Burning"; the Spirit cleanses and burns away evil waste.

2 Nephi 14:5–6

On the "cloud [of] smoke" and "flaming fire," compare the cloud of smoke and fire that guided and protected the Israelites in Sinai (Exodus 13:21–22). The second image signaling protection for the righteous is a tabernacle (the Hebrew word means "booth") in the vineyard, providing shade from the harsh summer sun and cover from the pounding winter rains. The two figures depict the total safety and comfort—in all seasons, under all conditions—for those deserving of God's watchful care.

2 Nephi 15 (Isaiah 5)

Isaiah wrote this song (vv. 1–7), which is an allegory of the Lord's vineyard—the land of Israel. (Whereas a parable is a continued simile, an allegory is a continued metaphor, a series of implied comparisons.) Compare 2 Samuel 12:1–8 and Matthew 21:33–45; the meaning is hidden until the end, which is more effective than direct accusation.

2 Nephi 15:1–4

The Lord protected his vineyard by fencing it, and he gathered out the stones, or evicted the wicked previous tenants. He planted it with the finest, choicest plants (his covenant people of Israel; see also Jeremiah 2:21). The Lord does all he can, but moral agency is guaranteed; some choose to be wild.

What more could have been done? (The same question is asked in Jacob 5:41.) We have a courtroom scene again; this is a pleading question.

2 Nephi 15:5–6

Resultant curses are listed: the protective hedges and walls around his vineyard are broken down and removed, and thorns and thistles replace them. The clouds will release no rain upon the land. The ancients knew that rain came not from the sky but from heaven; spiritual rain was revelation, necessary to keep them spiritually alive (compare Deuteronomy 11:8–17).

2 Nephi 15:7

The interpretation of the allegory includes the use of paronomasia (a play on words). In Hebrew: "he looked for *mishpat*, but behold *mishpakh*; for *tsdakah*, but behold *ts'akah*." In English: "he looked for *equity*, but behold *iniquity*; for a *righteous nation*, but behold *lamentation*."[40]

2 Nephi 15:8–12

These verses describe the ills in society. The religious establishment must have considered Isaiah's prophecy as rank heresy, and the political establishment, treason. But Isaiah spoke the truth, and the truth was painful—to him as well as to the people.

Verse 8: greed in acquisition of real estate, especially the wealthy taking from the poor

Verse 9: desolated lands and properties

Verse 10: unproductive lands and properties

Verse 11: drunkenness, riotous living

Verse 12: musical revelry (compare Amos 6:5–6; Isaiah 24:8–9)

2 Nephi 15:13

The nation is taken captive and destroyed because of lack of knowledge (compare Hosea 4:6). The people are famished and thirsty because they had not turned to the Bread of Life and the Living Water (compare Amos's famine and thirst for hearing the word of the Lord in Amos 8:11). The Lord's people, of their own will and choice, were suffering from spiritual malnutrition. In our present world, which is virtually overflowing with knowledge—with the Internet and all the universal, sophisticated information and communication systems—we are, ironically, dying from a widespread famine of spiritual knowledge.

2 Nephi 15:14–19

Doom is pronounced through a host of woes and judgments.

Verse 14: A gaping hell (Hebrew *sheol*—death and spirit prison) awaits the rebels, to swallow them up.

Verses 15–16: This is the same message as 2 Nephi 12:11, 17; Isaiah 2:11, 17.

Verse 17: The once-flourishing vineyard has become mere grazing land.

Verse 18: When we willingly tie ourselves to our sins (like beasts tied to their burdens), it is difficult to later free or disentangle ourselves from those sins. "Whosoever committeth sin is the servant of sin" (John 8:34). Sin is a slave driver, and it is oppressive; 2 Peter 3:3–4 calls such people "scoffers."

Verse 19: Hypocrisy and sarcasm are offered by individuals who say, "Fine. Let this 'Holy One of Israel' bring on his work—so we can see and know for sure."

2 Nephi 15:20

The purpose of this earth life is to learn to distinguish between good and evil. Some people in the world are working hard at blurring our view of what is right and what is wrong. There *are* moral absolutes. Woe to those who call evil good, and good evil (see 2 Nephi 28:20). Examples include the following: marriage is unnecessary; homosexual marriage is acceptable; premarital and extramarital sex are admissible; movies and magazines glamorize infidelity; and abortion is justified and condoned ("pro-choice" advocates presume to do noble service in protecting and preserving women's rights). So much of what we call enlightenment is really the opposite—darkness. Much of our sophistication is really degradation.

On a very personal level, this verse is a stark warning. God knows what we know. He knows what is in our hearts, our intentions. Baptized members of the Church cannot rationalize wrong behavior on the grounds of ignorance or political correctness. President Spencer W. Kimball said, "I challenge any normal baptized person who says he did not know he was doing wrong."[41]

2 Nephi 15:21–25

Compare verse 21 to 2 Nephi 9:28–29.

Verse 22: It is ironic that Judah's men of valor were mighty not in the battle but in the bottle.

Verse 23: They acquit the wicked for a bribe and deny justice to the innocent.

Verse 24: Isaiah eloquently illustrates from nature the dire consequences of Israel's rejection of the law and the word of their God. Just as the weed or waste part of the grain is consumed by fire, so Israel's root—from which all the rest of the tree is supposed to receive nourishment—is full of rotten decay, and therefore its blossoms (its potential for fruit) are blown away by the winds of corruption. A later prophet similarly described the tragedy: "For behold, the day cometh, that shall burn as an oven; and all the proud, yea, and all that do wickedly, shall be stubble . . . , that it shall leave them neither root nor branch" (Malachi 4:1).

Verse 25: The Lord was angry with them and had smitten them with drought, famine, plague, pestilence, earthquake, and war (Amos 4:6–11). "For all this his anger is not turned away, but his hand is stretched out still" (see commentary at 2 Nephi 19:8–14).

2 Nephi 15:26–30

Hope is pronounced ("in that day," the last days).

Ensign means "standard" or "banner," something to rally around. The gospel and the Book of Mormon are to hiss forth (2 Nephi 29:2). "They [the missionaries] shall come with speed swiftly." Does sleeping without removing one's clothes suggest travel by jet aircraft?

For hissing forth through missionary work, see Doctrine and Covenants 115:5–6. Zion will be a refuge from the storm (compare Isaiah 4:5–6).

Elder LeGrand Richards interpreted these verses to mean the following: "Since there were no such things as trains and airplanes in that day, Isaiah could hardly have mentioned them by name, but he seems to have described them in unmistakable words. How better could 'their horses' hoofs be counted like flint, and their wheel like a whirlwind' than in the modern train? How better could 'Their roaring . . . be like a lion' than in the roar of the airplane? Trains and airplanes do not stop for night. Therefore, was not Isaiah justified in saying 'none shall slumber nor sleep; neither shall the girdle of their loins be loosed, nor the latchet of their shoes be broken'? With this manner of transportation the Lord can really 'hiss unto them from the end of the earth,' that 'they shall come with speed swiftly.'"[42]

2 Nephi 15:28–30

"Whose arrows are sharp and all their bows bent"—could this be an airplane from top or bottom view? Arrows, bows, horses, and prey depict war imagery. We sing about a battle that is raging in this world: "Behold! A Royal Army," "Hope of Israel," "Onward, Christian Soldiers," "We Are All Enlisted," and "We Are Marching On to Glory."

"Prey" may mean converts. Note that the missionary lions are out to rescue the prey from their enemy, to carry them away to safety.

Darkness reigns because the children of light depart, and the Lord withholds his light because of wickedness.

2 Nephi 16 (Isaiah 6)

This is Isaiah's vision of the Lord, including his call to the prophetic office. Isaiah, Nephi, and Jacob saw the Lord (2 Nephi 11:2); John had a similar vision (Revelation 4) and so did Joseph Smith (D&C 110).

2 Nephi 16:1

The year that King Uzziah died was sometime between 750 and 740 B.C. He is known by two names in the Old Testament: (1) Uzziah, which in Hebrew means "strength of the Lord," and (2) Azariah, which means "help of the Lord." More on this king of Judah is found in 2 Chronicles 26:16–21. His leprosy was the result of unauthorized assumption of priesthood functions (compare Nadab, Abihu, Uzzah, and King Saul).

"The vision was a divine revelation. It was a revelation given to the prophet in time and space upon this earth, and not in a vacuum. It is to be expected, therefore, that in a formal sense it would have a point of contact with the religious paraphernalia which the prophet would understand. In a formal sense there are relations between the contents of this vision and practices and customs to be found in other religions of antiquity. What was essentially new was the fact that this vision was a revelation from God. It must also be remembered that the pagan religions of antiquity were degenerations from the true, and indeed were imitative of it. . . .

". . . The idea of the Temple is derived from the well-known earthly Temple, and merely serves as a background for the vision."[43]

Isaiah saw the Lord (probably the experience Nephi referred to in 2 Nephi 11:2). Isaiah was an eyewitness. His vision dispels the sectarian notion of a God without body, parts, and passions; the Lord was sitting on a throne, and his train (the skirts of his robe), or his glory, filled the temple. He was "high" and "lifted up," the latter concept being especially rich in symbolism; the Savior was lifted up on the cross and then lifted up to an exalted position to rule and reign forever.

Isaiah saw an actual being. Scriptures do teach *anthropomorphism*—not "God in the image of man" but "man in the image of God." Just as Genesis 1:27 says, man was created in the image of God. We have bodies; he has a body. The Bible itself notes that God has various body parts:

Face (Exodus 33:20, 23; Deuteronomy 5:4)
Eyes (Deuteronomy 11:12)
Ears (Ezekiel 8:18)
Mouth (Numbers 12:8; Deuteronomy 8:3)
Arms (Exodus 15:16; Isaiah 52:10)
Hands (Job 10:8; 12:9; Isaiah 11:11)
Fingers (Exodus 8:19; 31:18)
Heart (Genesis 6:6; 8:21)
Feet (Isaiah 60:13; 66:1)

Paul wrote frequently about the resurrection of Jesus Christ, emphasizing that He has a glorified physical body (Romans 8:17; 1 Corinthians 15:12–29; Philippians 3:21). Luke recorded his witness of the risen Lord: "Handle me, and see; for a spirit hath not flesh and bones, as ye see me have" (Luke 24:39). The Prophet Joseph Smith testified: "That which is without body, parts and passions is nothing. There is no other God in heaven but that God who has flesh and bones."[44]

Verses 1–4 portray majesty, holiness, power, and order.

2 Nephi 16:2–3

The Book of Mormon properly uses the term *seraphim,* meaning angels in God's presence; there should be no final *s* as in the King James Version's *seraphims.*[45] Wings symbolize power and motion (D&C 77:4; 109:79).[46] The covering of the face and feet signifies reverence and obeisance toward God. Hebrew *saraph* means "fiery one" or "burning one." Those who dwell in the presence of the Lord dwell in "everlasting burnings" or, in other words, in the radiance, brilliance, or glory of that kingdom.[47]

2 Nephi 16:4

"Smoke" in Hebrew is smoke or cloud (see Exodus 19:18, where Mount Sinai was "on a smoke"; 1 Kings 8:10–11). The glory of the Lord filled his house, just as his glory fills the earth. The Lord has said that his work and glory is seeing his creations become immortal and eternal (Moses 1:39), so the earth and at least some of the Father's children will bring him additional glory.

2 Nephi 16:5

Those who see God often fear and feel unworthy. Isaiah's lips were unclean, but not his heart; he had a willing heart. One of our students wrote: "If I were to have a great vision at this very moment, I think I would become so conscious of all my weaknesses and faults that I wouldn't be able to handle the situation. The Lord has worked this problem out in a wonderful way. We can receive and learn as we are ready, willing, and worthy." Peter felt unworthy when the

Lord cleansed his feet; to a degree we all feel unworthy of the Lord's cleansing and atoning blood, but we must accept it and apply it anyway.

2 Nephi 16:6–7

A seraph (singular of *seraphim*) took a burning coal or glowing stone and touched Isaiah's mouth, symbolic of cleansing, a "baptism by fire"—the "refiner's fire." From ancient times metals have been cleansed from impurities by submitting them to extreme heat.

In this case, the cleansing was literal, but the process was symbolic or figurative. When God commissioned Jeremiah, He touched his lips (Jeremiah 1:9), symbolic of cleansing the inner man. The lips are an apt metaphor. The Savior later said that it was that which came out of the mouth, uttered by the lips, which defiled a person (Matthew 15:11). The heart and the lips are linked: "for of the abundance of the heart his mouth speaketh" (Luke 6:45).

Repentance does involve pain. If we have not suffered, we have not really repented. Isaiah's sin was "purged"; the Hebrew term *t'khuppar* means "atoned for." As he was purged, he was qualified and strengthened for the work.

2 Nephi 16:8

Isaiah's call to serve is recorded along with further instructions he received. Note the question, "Who will go for *us?*" It is the work of the Father and the Son (recall Genesis 1:26). Isaiah volunteered for missionary service, echoing Jehovah's response to the Father in the Grand Council in Heaven. Young men, women, and couples by the tens of thousands these days repeat the same sentiment when accepting mission calls: "Here am I; send me."

2 Nephi 16:9

This verse reads quite differently from Isaiah 6:9: "Hear ye indeed, but *they understood not*; and see ye indeed, but *they perceived not*" (emphasis added). This is a prophesied reaction of the people to Isaiah's preachment. It is not what the Lord desires, of course, but he knew beforehand how the people would respond to Isaiah's call to repentance. Isaiah's ministry would have the ironic effect of causing rebellious Israelites to harden their hearts. This was later true also of the Messiah.

2 Nephi 16:10

The message is presented in the form of an introverted parallelism, or chiasm:

> *a* Make the heart of this people fat,
>> *b* and make their ears heavy,
>>> *c* and shut their eyes—
>>> *c* lest they see with their eyes,
>> *b* and hear with their ears,
> *a* and understand with their heart

For more light on the rejection of the prophetic call to repent, compare Zechariah 7:11–12; Matthew 13:10–17; Jacob 4:14; Alma 12:9–11; and 3 Nephi 18:32. Isaiah was instructed to make the true doctrine so plain that his people would have to accept it or harden their hearts against it. The same would happen in these last days.

Question: Why would the Lord send a prophet to a people he knew would reject the message? *Answer:* (1) as a warning to them *and* to us in the latter-days, (2) as a testimony or witness against them, (3) so people could prove themselves *to themselves,* and (4) some would believe, and they would be grateful to Isaiah.

2 Nephi 16:11–13

The message of hope pertains both to ancient Israelite days and to the latter days. The scattering and gathering were prophesied. The tree (Israel) still has potential to grow even when its leaves have fallen and are scattered. A tenth (a remnant) will return (see footnote *b* to Isaiah 6:13).

2 Nephi 17 (Isaiah 7)

To understand this chapter of Isaiah, it is essential to read 2 Kings 15:27–17:24. Those verses contain important background material to the historical and political events recounted here.

2 Nephi 17:1–7

"In the days of Ahaz" means about 735 B.C. onward. The nations, capitals, and rulers involved are as follows:

Nation (alternate name)	Capital	Ruler
Judah	Jerusalem	Ahaz
Israel (Ephraim)	Samaria	Pekah, son of Remaliah
Syria (Aram)	Damascus	Rezin

See these place-names on Maps 9 and 10 in the Latter-day Saint edition of the King James Version of the Bible.

Syria and Israel had formed a coalition to block the armies of the Assyrian Tiglath-pileser III as they advanced westward. Ahaz, king of Judah, refused to join. Syria and Israel then decided to march on Jerusalem and replace Ahaz with a man of their own persuasion. Verse 2 says King Ahaz's "heart was moved" or shaken.

2 Nephi 17:3

"Shearjashub" means "the remnant shall return," which was a prophecy at Isaiah's call; see Isaiah 6:13. This is a familiar motif throughout Isaiah: despite the forthcoming exile, a remnant would return to the land to accomplish the

Lord's purposes (see, for example, Isaiah 10:20–22; 2 Nephi 20: 20–22).

"The end of the conduit of the upper pool in the highway of the fuller's field" meant either at the Gihon Spring or to the south near the one-time spring called En-rogel (now a well).[48] The fuller needed water for his work of cleaning and whitening cloth.

2 Nephi 17:4–7

The bold prophet commanded the king not to worry about the two kingdoms to the north, the "smoking fire-brands." If they are *smoking*, then their fire is out. The political ploy of Israel and Syria against Judah would not be accomplished; it would fail.

2 Nephi 17:8

Prophecy: Within sixty-five years, the northern tribes of Israel would be scattered.

Fulfillment: By 733–32 B.C., northeast Israel and Trans-jordanian Israel were exiled; by 722–21 B.C., the rest of Israel was exiled to Assyria and even scattered beyond there (what we often call the "lost ten tribes"). This twelve-year period was the time when the Galilee region of the Holy Land was cleaned out by the Assyrians. Most of Israel was taken away, and foreign populations were imported. This is significant because of the Messianic prophecy following in 2 Nephi 19 (Isaiah 9):1–3, which describes the religious "darkness" that engulfed the region for a long time.

2 Nephi 17:9

Again, paronomasia is used—a prophetic play on words: "If ye will not believe [*im lo taaminu*], surely ye shall not be established [*lo teamenu*]."

In English the play on words could be "If ye will not understand, ye shall not . . . stand," or "If ye have no belief, . . . ye shall have no relief," or "No confiding, no abiding."[49]

2 Nephi 17:10–13

Ahaz was told, as a command, to ask for a sign (an evidence or spiritual confirmation). He rejected the prophecy and would not trust the Lord. Why wouldn't he? He either didn't care, or he had no interest, as "Esau [who] despised his birthright" (Genesis 25:34), or else he didn't want the Lord interfering with his political plans to ally with Assyria. Ahaz intentionally set himself up as wiser and more politically astute than God.

"And he [Isaiah] said: . . . is it a small thing for you to weary men [meaning "me," Isaiah], but will ye weary my God also?" A more colloquial translation would be, "O house of David; is it not enough to try the patience of men, but will you try the patience of God also?"

Old Testament scholar Franz Delitzsch wrote: "He [King Ahaz] studiously brought down upon himself the fate denounced in [Isaiah 6; or 2 Nephi 16], and indeed not upon himself only, but upon all Judah as well. For after a few years the forces of [Assyria] would stand upon the same fuller's field . . . and demand the surrender of Jerusalem. In that very hour, in which Isaiah was standing before Ahaz, the fate of Jerusalem was decided for more than two thousand years."[50]

Biblical scholar Edward Young wrote: "Ahaz' wickedness is seen in the fact that by his stubbornness he was in fact rejecting the very foundation of the covenant. God had promised to be a God and a Deliverer to His people. Syria and Israel, therefore, will not overthrow the Davidic dynasty, for if they could succeed in so doing, the promises of God would be rendered void and salvation would not ultimately be accomplished through the Messiah. In effect, Ahaz, by his refusal, is asserting that God is not faithful to His promise."[51]

2 Nephi 17:14–15

Messianic prophecy: The apostle Matthew understood this verse to be a type or foreshadowing of Jesus. Historically it may have been talking about Isaiah's wife (2 Nephi 18:3) who bore him a second son, but Matthew was inspired to see its eternal import. The phrase "a virgin" is Hebrew *ha-alma*; that is, *the* [definite article] *young woman*, though it appears to be the only Hebrew noun that definitely applies to an *unmarried woman*. The Septuagint, the Old Testament in Greek, renders the word "virgin," and the New Testament and the Book of Mormon both refer to her as a virgin. She shall conceive and bear a son. If the birth is not a miraculous virgin birth, given as a sign, then what is so unusual about a young woman having a son? The prophecy clearly suggests miraculous and divine intervention to insure its accomplishment (see commentary at 1 Nephi 11:13–26).

Fulfillment: (1) In the spirit of 2 Nephi 11:4, all things are the typifying of Jesus Christ: a young woman in Isaiah's day (possibly his wife, the prophetess) bears a son with another symbolic name, Immanuel, which means literally "God [is] with us," fulfilling prophecy that God himself would come down, or condescend, to dwell among mortals (Isaiah 8:8, 10); and the young woman in Isaiah's day becomes a type of the young virgin in Nazareth (compare Hosea and his wife being a type or similitude of the Lord and his people; also compare the language of vv. 14 and 16 to 18:3–4); or (2) this is a direct prophecy of the virgin Mary and God the Father having a Son, Jesus (Matthew 1:23; Luke 1:27; 1 Nephi 11:13–20; Alma 7:10).

Butter (curds, yogurt) and honey are symbolic of a humble diet.

2 Nephi 17:16–25

These final verses of the chapter contain the word of the Lord concerning contemporary events.

2 Nephi 17:16

Prophecy: "Before the child [or *a* child, generic] shall know to refuse the evil, and choose the good [possibly an idiomatic reference to the age of accountability; that is, within eight years], the land that thou abhorrest shall be forsaken of both her kings."

Fulfillment: Syria and Israel were plundered. Both Pekah and Rezin were killed within three years.

2 Nephi 17:17

The nation of Judah would eventually have a Redeemer, but the king of Judah would imminently have a destroyer—the king of Assyria. What Ahaz wanted is what he got.

"The day that Ephraim departed from Judah" was in the mid-tenth century B.C., at the division of Solomon's kingdom into north and south.

Prophecy: "The Lord shall bring upon thee . . . the king of Assyria."

Fulfillment: Sennacherib laid siege to Judah and Jerusalem in 701 B.C.

2 Nephi 17:18–19

Judah was a bone of contention between Egypt (the fly, *zebub*) and Assyria (the bee, *dvorah*); they will *swarm* all over Israel. An attacking bee can sting, and a fly can carry plague.

2 Nephi 17:20

Isaiah used a metaphor to indicate that the Lord would use Assyria as an instrument of his chastisement against his chosen but wayward people. By making an alliance and paying tribute to Assyria, Ahaz hired the razor called Assyria to cut off Syria and Israel. The Lord then used the same razor to cut off part of the people of Judah. Shaving captives is symbolic of humiliation, but it is also literal: cutting off the beard was a sign of degradation to Israelites (compare 2 Samuel 10:4–5); "the hair of the *feet*" in the Hebrew text is hair of the *legs*, a euphemism for the human genital area.

2 Nephi 17:21–25

The once prosperous agricultural land would be overrun by briers and thorns and serve only as grazing land.

Isaiah had prophesied that if the people ("ye"; plural, vv. 9 and 13) did not believe and hearken, they would not be established permanently in the land, though he made it clear that Judah would not be totally destroyed; a remnant would return to the land and to their God, for the Messiah would come through Judah (which was comforting assurance of their destiny despite the temporary setbacks).

2 Nephi 18 (Isaiah 8)

Isaiah gave more messianic prophecies and prophecies for his own day.

2 Nephi 18:1–3

The name of Isaiah's child (the longest proper name in the Old Testament) means "quick to the plunder, swift to the spoil"—referring to the speed of the Assyrian destruction of Syria and Israel. The imminent future of Jerusalem was parallel to the city's future in the meridian of time, which Isaiah foreshadowed in the previous chapter.

The "witnesses" were two apparently well-known, prominent citizens, Uriah and Zechariah. The names in Hebrew mean "my light is Jehovah" and "remember Jehovah," respectively.

"The prophetess" was the prophet's wife and not necessarily a prophetic office.

2 Nephi 18:4

"As in [Isaiah] 7:15, 16 the infancy of the Messiah was made the measure of the time that Judah would suffer from her two adversaries, so here the infancy of Maher-shalal-hash-baz is made the measure of the time that would elapse before the king of Assyria would devastate Damascus and Syria. . . .

"There is thus a formal relationship between the two prophecies. There is, however, an even deeper relationship. Men could verify the prophecy concerning Isaiah's son; they could witness its fulfillment. It would thus become as it were a pledge or earnest of the prophecy of the virgin's Son. Seeing that Maher-shalal-hash-baz had been born in accordance with the prophecy, they could be sure that in His own good time God would fulfill the promise concerning the virgin, and that she would bear a son."[52]

Prophecy: "Behold, the child shall not have knowledge to cry, My father, and my mother [an idiom meaning two or three years, or a short time] before the riches of Damascus and the spoil of Samaria shall be taken away before the king of Assyria."

Fulfillment: Damascus was conquered in 732 B.C. Samaria was besieged in 733 B.C. and then destroyed in 721 B.C. The prophecy was fulfilled literally (2 Kings 16:9; 15:29–30).

2 Nephi 18:5–8

After the fall of the northern kingdom of Israel, the prophet turned to the fate of Judah. Water is life in the land of Shiloah (or Shiloh, the Messiah), and the people of Judah rejected their source of life. Jerusalem's water supply was the Gihon Spring, and the waters "that go softly" may refer to the channel that flows from that spring and waters the Kidron Valley. Instead of rejoicing in the Lord, Judah rejoiced only in the defeat of her two enemies to the north.

Contrast the "waters of Shiloah that go softly" (the blessings of the Lord) with the "strong and many waters" (the flooding Euphrates, which symbolizes the destructions of the Assyrian army).

After the flooding waters reach to the neck, the image abruptly changes to the outspread wings of a bird of prey.

Calling the land by the name of Immanuel amounts to calling it the land of Jehovah or the land of the Lord, who is Jesus. Immanuel means "God with us."

2 Nephi 18:9–10

Just as destruction was assured by the symbolic name of Isaiah's child, deliverance was assured by the symbolic name of the virgin's Child. Salvation from all enemies, mortal and spiritual, is available only when God is with us.

2 Nephi 18:11–18

Instructions are given to Isaiah and to Judah.

Verses 12–13: Judah must not rely on alliances with foreign powers for safety but rely on the Lord and reverence him.

Verses 14–15: The Lord can be a sanctuary, but he can also be a stone of stumbling, a rock of offense, for both houses of Israel (Israel and Judah). For similar descriptions, see the writings of Peter, Paul, and Jacob: 1 Peter 2:8; Romans 9:33; 1 Corinthians 1:23; and Jacob 4:15.

Verse 16: The testimony is the Prophets, and the law is the Torah, or five books of Moses. Together the testimony and the law constitute the scriptures (see also v. 20). Isaiah was to write down and seal up his own witness account.

Verses 17–18: Isaiah trusted in the Lord. He and his family were "for signs and for wonders" to the house of Israel; they constituted a message from God in the form of a similitude or a type. Just as Abraham and Isaac were types of the Father and Son, so Hosea and his unfaithful wife were types of the Lord and his unfaithful people. *Isaiah* signified that salvation was in Jehovah; *Shearjashub* meant that a remnant of Judah would return following the chastisement of exile; and *Maher-shalal-hash-baz* foreshadowed the imminent and speedy destruction of a large part of Israel.

"The Lord of Hosts . . . dwelleth in Mount Zion"—the house of the Lord was on Mount Zion, or the Temple Mount.

2 Nephi 18:19

Seeking God was commendable, of course, but not through diabolical media. In times of crisis, certain men of Judah were advocating turning to soothsayers and diviners for answers and help, rather than to the Lord's prophets. There are "witches of Endor" in all ages—those who suppose they can approach God through spiritualism instead of spirituality.

"For the living to hear from the dead?" may also be rendered, "Why consult the dead on behalf of the living?" Should we not turn to the Lord's prophets?

2 Nephi 18:20

Recall verse 16: The scriptures are the canon or standard by which we should measure the worth of all things. If our sources of information and influence do not measure up to what is written in the scriptures, it must be "because there is no light in them." Thus, verse 20 outlines the first test of any revelation: Does it speak the word of the Lord, or is it filled with light? A second test: Is it in harmony with the teachings of the only man on earth called and authorized to speak for the Lord in everything—the president of the Church? (D&C 43:1–7; 132:7). A third test: Does it come by the Holy Ghost, and can it be felt in the heart? (2 Nephi 33:1; D&C 50:17, 23; 100:5–8).

2 Nephi 18:21–22

Members of the house of Israel would be taken captive, hard-pressed and hungry, and in their distress, as they look upward, they would blame and curse their king and their God. And as they look downward, they would find no consolation on the earth—only trouble, darkness, and anguish; only gloom and depression.

2 Nephi 19:1

This verse belongs with chapter 18; it corresponds to 18:23 in the Hebrew Bible. During the period of trouble, darkness, and anguish, the tribal regions of Zebulun (the region around Nazareth) and Naphtali (the region of the Sea of Galilee) were afflicted by attacks from the Assyrian monarchs Tiglath-pileser III, Shalmaneser V, and Sargon II.

The "way of the sea" is called in Hebrew *Derekh HaYam* and in Latin *Via Maris,* the great international highway that passes along the Sea of Galilee and the Mediterranean. Why the Book of Mormon has "Red Sea" is not known.

"Beyond Jordan" in Hebrew is *Ever HaYarden* or Greek *Perea.* "Galilee of the nations" is Hebrew *Galil HaGoyim,* or "Galilee of the Gentiles," because it was formerly inhabited by noncovenant peoples.

2 Nephi 19 (Isaiah 9)

Some see fulfillment of this prophecy in Hezekiah, and others see it in some great Davidic figure before the Millennium, but note the chapter heading and footnotes, especially for verses 6–7. Isaiah is speaking of the coming Messiah.

Though the northern tribes of Zebulun, Naphtali, and others would experience the dark affliction of captivity, being vexed by Assyrian kings, the prophet proclaimed that the people who walked in darkness would see a great light. After the severe, dark blow of foreign foes, a Light would come, a Child would be born, a Son would be given. Though the tribes of Israel were carried off and lost to Israelite history, the tribe of Judah would not be totally destroyed. A remnant must return to their homeland, for the Messiah was to come through Judah and be born in Judah.

2 Nephi 19:1–2

Again, the land of Zebulun is Nazareth and its vicinity. The land of Naphtali is the Sea of Galilee region. As a result of Assyria's invasion of northern Israel in 733 B.C. and again in 722 B.C., the Israelite population of these regions was deported and the areas repopulated with Gentiles who did not know the God of Israel or anything about the true Messiah. Hence, they walked in darkness. In the second or first century B.C., Jews of a Davidic clan began resettling the region. One segment of this new Jewish population was made up of the ancestors of Joseph and Mary. Mary's infant Son, Jesus, who was the Light of the World, thus brought to the land the great light prophesied by Isaiah.

Messianic prophecy (using future perfect tense verbs as if already accomplished): the people who walked in the darkness of apostasy, those who lived in the land of the shadow of death (where the ancient armies of the Near East marched through)—those people have seen the great Light, the Messiah.

Fulfillment: Jesus is the "great light" (Matthew 4:16).

Isaiah's description of "people that walked in darkness" and "dwell in the shadow of death" refers not only to their living in the darkness of sin and apostasy but also to a very physical image. The Galilee is covered with dark volcanic basalt, spewed all over the region by several now-extinct volcanoes on the Golan, east of the lake, and the black stone casts a dark shadow across the land.

The people who dwell in the shadow of death are also all people who experience mortality, who live with the shadow of death hanging over them; it is a dark thing to us, able to be dispelled only by the Light of life.

2 Nephi 19:3–5

Second Nephi 19:3 and the Revised Standard Version of the Bible (following many ancient manuscripts) delete "not" in the second line of Isaiah 9:3. The Light brings an increase of joy to the people of Israel.

Reasons are given in verses 4–5 for the increase of joy

spoken of. The yoke and staff and rod have been broken; the oppressors—enemy armies and sin—have been taken away.

The Book of Mormon deletes "as in the day of Midian" at the end of Isaiah 9:4. Perhaps Nephi saw little relevance in that phrase for his own people or for us in the future.

The battles that the hosts of Israel, God's people, are fighting, especially in these last days, certainly are "with confused noise."

2 Nephi 19:6–7

Isaiah exults in the coming of a royal son (or descendant) of David. The oppressors of Israel—the mortal antagonists, yes, but especially the dark foes of sin and death and hell—are ultimately taken away because a Child is born, a Son is given. Verses 4, 5, and 6 all begin with "For . . ."—these are all reasons for the rejoicing among God's people noted in verse 3. Verse 6 introduces the greatest cause for rejoicing ever given and is gloriously rendered in Handel's famous oratorio *Messiah*.

Verse 6 is not specifically referred to in the New Testament. The first line refers to the first coming of Jesus, but the rest of verses 6 and 7 refer to the Second Coming. The full messianic mission was known and prophesied long before his mortal birth; it has always been important to see that mission in its complete context, what the Messiah would accomplish in his first coming and in his second coming.

Messianic prophecy: A Child is born, a Son is given.

Fulfillment: Only Jesus, the Messiah, fulfills this prophecy.[53] Yet many in the scholarly world, having no belief in the possibility of prophetic preview and disavowing any divine design, regard Hezekiah as the fulfillment of this prophecy. But was Hezekiah a great light? the mighty God? the everlasting Father? the Prince of Peace? Was there *no end* to his government and peace? Was he on the throne of David with judgment and justice *forever*?

Hezekiah might in some other ways have been a *type*

of the Messiah, but Hezekiah does not stand up to the description, nor could any mortal. This Son who was given is unique. Take away the divine Sonship, and Christianity has no foundation.

On the title *Counselor*: Think of all the money spent on counselors; if only people would turn to him, *the* Counselor, or to his agent counselor, the ward bishop. The Lord's celestial self-reparation package, called repentance, is better than all the terrestrial self-help and self-esteem-building seminars, recordings, and texts. (However, in some situations, such as with pornography and other addictions, professional counselors are absolute necessities, along with full use of the gospel of Jesus Christ, including his representatives.) Jesus is also our counselor in a legal sense. He is our advocate with the Father. He will plead our case before him (1 John 2:1; D&C 29:5; 45:3; 110:4).

The name-title *the mighty God*, apart from all others, unquestionably defines the Subject of the whole prophecy. Despite the attempts of scholars to adjust the words to mean something like "one Mighty in Valor," possibly to accommodate some private interpretation of this great prophecy, there is no allowable digression from the meaning of *El gibbor*—it means "the mighty *God*." God himself would one day come into the world as a Child.

On the title *everlasting Father*: Jesus Christ is both the Son *and* the Father—the Son because he was begotten by the Father and submitted to the will of the Father, but also the Father because he is the Creator or Father of the earth; he is the Father of our flesh because our flesh is made from the dust or elements of the earth, which he created; he is the God or Father of the Old Testament and the Father or Author of our salvation; he has all the attributes of the Father; and by divine investiture he serves the role of the Father in all things relative to our salvation. By his sacrifice he became even more than our Savior; he became our covenant Father, and as we are spiritually reborn we become the

197

children of Christ (Mosiah 5:7; 27:25; Ether 3:14; D&C 25:1; 34:3; 39:4).

On the title *Prince of Peace*: The Lord Jesus Christ is the personification of real peace; he leaves his kind of peace with us, not the world's kind of "peace" that is won at the negotiating table or on the battlefield (John 14:27). Jesus fulfilled the typology established thousands of years before his mortal life: the city to which he would eventually come was a place originally called Peace (*Shalem* or *Salem*), and the man who reigned and ministered there was Melchizedek (literally, "King of Righteousness"), who was a type of the future Messiah and who was the first referred to as "Prince of peace" (JST, Genesis 14:33). For the present time, Melchizedek's name-title is substituted, out of reverence for the name of the Son of God, when we refer to the Savior's power—the priesthood, which is the power by which all peace is established. The Prince of Peace came in the meridian of time to the City of Peace (*Uru Shalem,* or Jerusalem) but was rejected. Since then, there has been no lasting peace in that place. He will come again, and he will establish enduring peace for all lovers of peace to enjoy.

Some years ago on a BBC television program, renowned Christian theologians were interviewed, followed by Elie Wiesel, the Nobel prize–winning Jewish author. Asked about Christianity, Wiesel quipped: "One thing we know. When Messiah comes there will be peace; Jesus came, and there is no peace."[54] From this perspective, the Author of true Christianity is relegated to dismal failure due to lack of peace in this world. But Christ himself remonstrated, "Think not that I am come to send peace on earth: I came not to send peace, but a sword" (Matthew 10:34). Inherent in the great plan of happiness is a period of testing, when the war between good and evil—begun in the premortal world—continues, and the absence of total peace persists until the adversary is confined eternally to outer darkness and all flesh is brought under the Savior's dominion. The title "Prince of Peace" is, therefore, a prophecy of that millennial era, which assuredly will come.

On the expression "the throne of David" see Luke 1:32–33. Jesus, a direct descendant of David, was entitled to the throne of David, and his kingdom will last forever (see also Daniel 2:44*a*).

2 Nephi 19:8–20:4

Four evils are denounced and four warnings pronounced.

2 Nephi 19:8–14

"The Lord sent *his* word" (unlike Isaiah 9:8) to Jacob, or Israel.

Evil number one: *pride.* Israelites felt confident that they could handle any losses and that they could rebuild. They had high regard for their own abilities and little regard for God. Enemies would gather against them.

Read verse 12 as if standing in the middle of the country, looking eastward: Syrians are "before," on the east, and Philistines are "behind," on the west.

Four times (in 2 Nephi 19:12, 17, 21; and 20:4) Isaiah used the following formulaic parallelism, almost as a chorus to his poetic pronouncement of condemnation:

> *For all this his anger is not turned away;*
> *but his hand is stretched out still.*

Is this synonymous parallelism (saying the same thing twice), or is it antithetic parallelism (saying the opposite), or could it be both kinds of parallelism? Footnote 12*d* of Isaiah 9:12 says, "In spite of all, the Lord is available if they will turn to him." However, the context of this parallel thought is that since the Lord's people are still unrepentant, his anger is still directed against them (2 Nephi 15:25). Bullinger indicates that the *hand stretched out* is an idiom, meaning "to send judgments upon," "to inflict punishment."[55] And verses

13–14 say: "The people turneth not unto him. . . . Therefore will the Lord cut off from Israel head and tail, branch and rush"—that is, great and small.

Perhaps this critical couplet is either synonymous or antithetic parallelism, with the correct intent from the two opposite meanings *depending on the response of the people*. The Lord's hand, like his word, can be a sharp two-edged sword providing either protection and salvation or destruction and damnation. His hand is like a stone, which can be used to build or to crush. The Lord's hand may sometimes be construed as a hand offering relief, though here Isaiah seems to be describing the back of the Lord's hand slapping wrath against those who have rejected His open palm.

For the hand of judgment, see Isaiah 5:25; 9:12, 17, 21; 10:4; 14:26–27. For the hand of mercy, see Isaiah 59:1–2; 65:1–2.

2 Nephi 19:15–17

Evil number two: *errant leaders*. Isaiah specified some who will be cut off. The words "and honourable" in Isaiah 9:15 are deleted in 2 Nephi 19:15 because there is nothing honorable about a devious leader.

2 Nephi 19:18–21

Evil number three: *wickedness* (spreading as a forest fire). Ugly scenes of civil and family strife are envisioned.

2 Nephi 20 (Isaiah 10)

Isaiah identifies the instruments the Lord will employ to inflict punishment for evil behavior in ancient days and in the last days.

2 Nephi 20:1–4

Evil number four: *neglecting the poor and the needy*. Verse 3 asks, "What will ye do in the day of visitation, and in the desolation which shall come from far?" The Hebrew word rendered "desolation" is *shoah*, meaning holocaust.

2 Nephi 20:5–19

Doom is pronounced. Note the irony that Israel's mortal enemy, Assyria, is being used to punish her. Just as the Lord used Lamanites as a scourge against the Nephites to humble them, get them to repent, and keep them in remembrance of him, so he would use the Egyptians, then the Assyrians, then the Babylonians (the Lord even called Nebuchadnezzar "my servant"; Jeremiah 27:6), and later the Romans and others to scourge his people for the same reasons in the Old World. Assyria would punish unfaithful Israel, but Assyria would also be punished. "Behold, the judgments of God will overtake the wicked; and it is by the wicked that the wicked are punished" (Mormon 4:5).

2 Nephi 20:5–8

The footnote of Isaiah 10:5 renders this verse in parallel form:

> *Assyria is the rod of my anger,*
> *and my wrath is a staff in their hand.*

The description in Isaiah 1:2–3 portrays Judah as a disobedient child; here the parent (the Lord) punishes the child with a whipping, and Assyria is the stick he uses.[56]

"To take the spoil, and to take the prey" is related to the symbolic name Isaiah and his wife gave their son, Maher-shalal-hash-baz (2 Nephi 18:1–3). Assyrians did conquer and plunder Israel, but Assyria did not see itself as an instrument in God's hands; it boasted in its own power to overthrow many nations.

2 Nephi 20:9–11

The Lord was watching for those who needed punishment, the cities of Israel and Judah as well as other cities the Assyrians had conquered. Compare Amos 9:8: "Behold, the eyes of the Lord God are upon the sinful kingdom." Note also Assyria's arrogant attitude expressed in 2 Kings 18:33–35. Calno and Carchemish, Hamath and Arpad, Samaria and Damascus are all neighboring kingdoms destroyed by the Assyrians between 740 and 720 B.C.

2 Nephi 20:12–14

After Israel's exile, there was a scare also for Judah with the Assyrians' intent to humble the southern kingdom (the invasion in 701 B.C.). Finally, after administering justice to Jerusalem, insolent Assyria would also be punished. The Assyrian Empire, which had plucked unprotected eggs out of the nest of nations, had altered the borders of the nations more than any previous empire. And Judah could hardly make a peep or do anything about it.

2 Nephi 20:15–16

The ax, saw, rod, and staff are metaphors referring to the Lord's cutting Israel down, with Assyria serving as the tool he used. Regarding proud boasting, the Lord has said, "In nothing doth man offend God, or against none is his wrath kindled, save those who confess not his hand in all things, and obey not his commandments" (D&C 59:21).

"His fat ones" refers to the soldiers of the Assyrian king. "Under his glory" refers to the "glory" of the Assyrian. Kindling a "burning like the burning of a fire" could refer to, at least in part, the feverish plague in the Assyrian camp in the fateful year 701 B.C., when the Lord began to cut down the mighty empire.

2 Nephi 20:17–19

The Holy One of Israel, the "Light" and the "Fire" of Israel, can raise up a nation in a day, and he can destroy a nation in a day. The surviving Assyrians would be so few that a child could count them.

2 Nephi 20:20–34

Hope is proclaimed "in that day."

Verse 20: There will come a day when the remnant of Israel will cease relying on the arm of flesh and turn to the merciful arm of God. The remnant shall return, in truth. The Hebrew verb *lashuv* means both to return and to repent. The meaning of the Hebrew concept of repentance is to come back (to God).

Verse 21: "The remnant shall return" is in Hebrew *Shearjashub*, the prophetic name of Isaiah's son. There are two remnants: the historic remnant of the past and the prophetic remnant of the future. The eschatological message (the message for the last days) is embodied in the remnant's return to "the mighty God," which is a messianic prophecy already laid down in 2 Nephi 19:6. Hosea also voiced this prophetic truth: "Afterward shall the children of Israel return, and seek the Lord their God . . . and shall fear the Lord and his goodness *in the latter days*" (Hosea 3:5; emphasis added).

Verses 22–23: The hand of God is in the "consumption decreed" upon all nations in the last days (see also D&C 87:6), and though the people of Israel become numerous, yet only a remnant will truly repent and return to their God.

Verses 24–26: Consoling words from a loving God—yes, there is a consumption decreed and an overflowing scourge will be felt by all nations, but fear not. "Assyria," the figurative title for a superpower in the latter days, will again strike as an instrument in the hands of the Lord of hosts, but the smiting is measured and will, in the Lord's due time, cease.

The people that dwell in the future Zion will be rescued, and "Assyria" will be scourged just as Gideon punished the Midianites (Judges 7).

Verse 27: "The yoke shall be destroyed because of the anointing" clearly has messianic connotation. It is the Anointed One who makes all burdens or yokes light and eventually takes them away (Matthew 11:28–30).

Verses 28–32: Isaiah described, as if standing on the wall of Jerusalem, the progress of the Assyrian army toward Jerusalem, featuring in Hebrew a superb example of alliteration. "In the prophet's vision, an army is depicted as marching on Jerusalem from the north via the province of Samaria, conquering a series of towns as it passed through the district of Benjamin."[57] This idealized sequential conquest narrative apparently symbolizes also the future siege called Armageddon.

Verses 33–34: Historically this was fulfilled as leaders of Assyria were lopped off and hewn down, but the figure is also future (Zechariah 14:2; Revelation 11). The Lord of hosts will do the cutting down in both eras.

2 Nephi 21 (Isaiah 11)

Isaiah was the prophet foretelling the Restoration. Joseph Smith was the prophet fulfilling the prophecies of the Restoration. It should not surprise us, therefore, that Isaiah foresaw and wrote about the latter-day prophet who would be the Lord's instrument in fulfilling his prophecies. In fact, Isaiah may have appeared to Joseph Smith.[58] The Prophet Joseph Smith, the gathering of Israel, the restoration of the gospel, and the great Millennium would, of necessity, be significant themes in Isaiah's writings.

On 21 September 1823, Moroni quoted Isaiah 11 to Joseph Smith (Joseph Smith–History 1:40) and told him that this prophecy was "about to be fulfilled." Doctrine and Covenants 113 is important for interpretation.

2 Nephi 21:1, 10

The perpetuity of the house of Jesse is illustrated with a dramatic metaphor from the fields of Israel: "There shall come forth a rod out of the stem of Jesse, and a branch shall grow out of his roots"; or, as the parallelism translates directly from the Hebrew, "There shall come forth a branch [*khoter*] out of the trunk of Jesse: indeed, a shoot [*netzer*] from his roots shall bear fruit." The terms *khoter* and *netzer* can be used interchangeably, though in this case *khoter* is a branch or shoot from the trunk of the tree, whereas *netzer* is a shoot from the root system, and only a shoot or branch from the root can start new life.

Matthew may have referred to this prophecy when he saw in Jesus the fulfillment of what was spoken by the prophets: "He shall be called a Nazarene" (Matthew 2:23). *Nazarene* in Hebrew is *notzri*, the same root word used by Isaiah and variously translated "branch" or "shoot." The olive tree is one of the few trees that can have apparently dead branches and even a dead trunk and still produce, sometime later, new life from the root. Characteristics of the olive tree are called to bear witness that the Messiah, a descendant of David, son of Jesse, would grow from the original root of the family tree of the royal house of David.

The "stem of Jesse" (Hebrew *geza Yishai*) is Jesus Christ (D&C 113:1–2). The "rod" (Hebrew *khoter*) is Joseph Smith (a descendant of Jesse and Ephraim; D&C 113:4). In the Topical Guide under "Joseph Smith," this is the first passage listed.

The "branch" (*netzer* in Matthew 2:23) is Jesus Christ (as in other scriptures, for example, Jeremiah 23:5, all footnotes refer to the Savior).

Matthew sees fulfillment of a messianic prophecy in Jesus' connection with Nazareth. We have no specific reference in biblical literature to prophets declaring that the Messiah would be a Nazarene, unless this is an allusion to Isaiah 11:1.

Isaiah foreshadowed that a "branch" (*netzer*) would grow out of the root of Jesse—that is, from the Davidic line—and thus Jesus would be a Nazarene (*notzri*). Both Hebrew words come from the same root word.

Elder James E. Talmage taught in *Jesus the Christ*, "As made known to the prophet [Isaiah] and by him proclaimed, the coming Lord was the living Branch that should spring from the undying root typified in the family of Jesse."[59] And Elder Bruce R. McConkie taught that the Branch and the King are the Lord Jesus Christ when he returns to earth to reign as King of Kings and Lord of Lords.[60]

The "root of Jesse" (Hebrew *shoresh Yishai*, v. 10) is Joseph Smith.[61] Doctrine and Covenants 113:6 explains the fulfillment as follows:

1. A descendant of Jesse and Joseph on whom was laid much power. Brigham Young taught that "the Book of Mormon came to Ephraim, for Joseph Smith was a pure Ephraimite, and the Book of Mormon was revealed to him, and while he lived he made it his business to search for those who believed the Gospel."[62]
2. A rightful heir to the priesthood.
3. A holder of the keys of the kingdom.
4. His work would be an ensign to the nations.
5. His work would help gather Israel in the last days.

Thus in 2 Nephi 21, verses 1–5 and 10 refer to Jesus Christ and to Joseph Smith. We see this kind of multiple meaning in 1 Nephi 21 also.

The stem and the branch of Jesse are Jesus; verses 2–5 could only be Jesus. The same Being was described in 19:6. He is the personification of wisdom, understanding, counsel, might, knowledge, reverence, judgment, righteousness, equity, and faithfulness.

The rod and the root of Jesse are Joseph Smith; the description in Doctrine and Covenants 113:6 could only be Joseph Smith.

2 Nephi 21:6–9

These verses provide a refreshing description of the peacefulness of the millennial reign of Christ (compare D&C 101:24–32). The Messiah's kingdom will far exceed the peace of any and all mortal kingdoms. All enmity and hostility will cease. As in the beginning, animals and humans will be helpful to each other. "A little child shall lead them" reminds us of the Savior's injunction to become as little children.

During Zion's Camp, while journeying from Kirtland to Missouri, the Prophet Joseph Smith wrote: "In pitching my tent we found three . . . prairie rattlesnakes, which the brethren were about to kill, but I said, 'Let them alone— don't hurt them! How will the serpent ever lose its venom, while the servants of God possess the same disposition, and continue to make war upon it? Men must become harmless before the brute creation, and when men lose their vicious dispositions and cease to destroy the animal race, the lion and the lamb can dwell together, and the sucking child can play with the serpent in safety.'"[63]

2 Nephi 21:8

An asp is a viper, one of the deadly snakes in the Holy Land. The cockatrice is another venomous serpent. To appreciate the peaceful period when a little child may, without worry, play on the hole of a viper, consider the following episode.

A thirty-eight-year-old male student, large and sturdy, was working in the banana fields of a kibbutz near the Sea of Galilee. One day he tried to save a snake from the hands of other students who uncovered it and intended to kill it. When he picked it up with his fingers to remove it from danger, the viper somehow elongated itself, swung around, and sank its fangs into his forefinger.

Immediately, kibbutz personnel rushed him to a nearby hospital, where he remained for three days of observation.

They released him, and after he spent a few hours at the BYU Jerusalem Center, the pain in his finger was still so intense that he was rushed in the middle of the night to the emergency room of a Jerusalem hospital. The student remained in the hospital for twelve more days. Doctors tried every kind of painkiller to ease his periodic agony. Now and then his whole body writhed with pain from his finger. The finger increased to double its normal size, and the tissues inside turned a black color. The doctors feared that they might have to amputate his finger and maybe even his hand.

The student was released from the Jerusalem hospital to fly back to the United States with his group, and there he was admitted to another medical center. Several months passed before he recovered completely from those venomous fangs that had sunk just a fraction of an inch into his finger. The poison might well have killed a smaller, more fragile individual.

That experience with a viper highlights the extraordinary changes that will prevail in the millennial era when formerly dangerous creatures will be pacific and playful.

2 Nephi 21:9

The reason for all the remarkable changes in the new world of peace is the overflowing knowledge of the Lord, meaning that he will be seen and known and that the knowledge that he has, his wisdom, understanding, counsel, judgment, righteousness, equity, and faithfulness will be available to all his creations. They will not only know *about* him but will know him.

Elder Orson Pratt taught that "the earth will be made new, and great knowledge will be imparted to the inhabitants thereof, as predicted in the 11th chapter of the prophecy of Isaiah. The knowledge of God will then cover the earth as the waters cover the mighty deep. There will be no place of ignorance, no place of darkness, no place for those that will not serve God. Why? Because Jesus, the Great Creator, and also the Great Redeemer, will be himself on the earth, and his holy angels will be on the earth, and all the resurrected Saints that have died in former dispensations will all come forth, and they will be on the earth. What a happy earth this creation will be, when this purifying process shall come, and the earth be filled with the knowledge of God as the waters cover the great deep!"[64]

2 Nephi 21:10

In the latter days the root of Jesse, who is Joseph Smith, will stand as an ensign to the people (see commentary at 2 Nephi 21:1, 10); to him (not "it," as in the King James Version) will the Gentiles seek, and his rest will be glorious. Lucy Mack Smith, the Prophet's mother, described what happened at the viewing of her martyred sons: "I sank back, crying to the Lord in the agony of my soul, 'My God, my God, why hast thou forsaken this family!' A voice replied, 'I have taken them to myself, that they might have rest.' . . . I seemed almost to hear them say, 'Mother, weep not for us, we have overcome the world by love; . . . ours is an eternal triumph.'"[65]

2 Nephi 21:11–12

Joseph Smith taught: "The time has at last arrived when the God of Abraham, of Isaac, and of Jacob, has set His hand again the second time to recover the remnants of his people, which have been left from Assyria, and from Egypt, and from Pathros, and from Cush, and from Elam, and from Shinar, and from Hamath, and from the islands of the sea, and with them to bring in the fulness of the Gentiles, and establish that covenant with them, which was promised when their sins should be taken away."[66]

The Lord set his hand the first time to reprove his people; this second time he will recover his people and gather a remnant of them. Though in Isaiah's day there had not yet been any wide dispersion of his people, the prophet used the language of prophetic preview. Nations from antiquity were used as symbols for the future. The gathering is from all directions, from the four corners of the earth (see "To the Ends of the Earth," accompanying commentary at 3 Nephi 11:31–41 in vol. 2 of this work).

2 Nephi 21:12–13

The ensign may be the Book of Mormon (2 Nephi 29:2), or the gospel, or the Church. President Joseph Fielding Smith wrote: "In the little town of Fayette, Seneca County, New York, the Lord set up an ensign to the nations. It was in fulfillment of the prediction made by the Prophet Isaiah. . . . That ensign was the Church of Jesus Christ of Latter-day Saints, which was established for the last time, never again to be destroyed or given to other people. It was the greatest event the world has seen since the day that the Redeemer was lifted upon the cross and worked out the infinite and eternal atonement. It meant more to mankind than anything else that has occurred since that day."[67]

"Ephraim shall not envy Judah, and Judah shall not vex Ephraim" is a daring prophecy of healing, reconciliation, and cooperation, considering the bitter enmity between the two peoples in Isaiah's day. The historic rivalry between blood relatives within Israel will yet be resolved by the Messiah and his ensign. Only the eternal truths of the gospel of Jesus Christ can overcome conflict and establish peace.

A graphic illustration of this verse occurred at the dedication of the Orson Hyde Garden on the Mount of Olives in 1979. There Jewish and Latter-day Saint leaders not only shook hands but at one point were linked arm in arm as they walked down the mount. One Church leader said at that moment he could not help but think of Isaiah 11:13—"Ephraim shall not envy Judah, and Judah shall not vex Ephraim" (2 Nephi 21:13).

2 Nephi 21:14–16

Unity among the people of Israel, the covenant people of the Lord, helps to spiritually subdue surrounding peoples in the world. Again, representative nations during Isaiah's time were used as symbols for the future. The enemies of God, in the western world and in the eastern world, will be spiritually overrun by united Israel, the covenant people.

The people cannot accomplish the work of God by themselves. The Lord intervenes in miraculous ways to gather his people.

"Assyria" represents all nations from which the remnant of Israel will be gathered. The Lord will provide a way (a "highway") to deliver his people, as in the day of the great Exodus, and he will provide a way for them to come back to him. Read Doctrine and Covenants 133:25–33.

2 Nephi 22 (Isaiah 12)

Just as Moses wrote a song of praise for deliverance (Exodus 15), so Isaiah presents two psalms of praise (vv. 1–3 and 4–6) for salvation in the millennial day. In fact, one could call all of 2 Nephi 22 a millennial hymn. After writing about Jesus Christ and Joseph Smith, there was reason to sing praises! How true for our day as well. Read this short chapter *aloud* and with feeling.

2 Nephi 22:2

This verse may be translated literally as follows:

> *Behold El is my salvation,*
> *I shall trust and not be afraid;*
> *For my strength and my song is Yah, Yehovah,*
> *And he has become my salvation.*

As Jesus himself would later testify, he *was* the great Jehovah, the Law and the Light, who came to earth to provide eternal life (3 Nephi 15:5–9). He literally became salvation, as Isaiah prophesied.

El is the singular of *Elohim*, but the word seldom occurs in the Bible in singular form. In the King James Version of the Bible, both singular and plural are rendered by the word *God*. *Yah* is a contracted form of *Jehovah* or *Yehovah*, which in the Bible is usually rendered in English as *Lord*. Here, to avoid *Lord Lord*, the translators rendered it *Lord Jehovah*. This is one of the few times the name is written out fully as Jehovah in the King James Version. The short form *Yah* also occurs in Hebrew in Exodus 15:2 and Psalm 118:14, which passages reflect a similar tone of praise.

Moses, a type of the Messiah, was a great lawgiver and a great deliverer; the Messiah himself was *the* great Lawgiver and *the* great Deliverer. The Messiah is Jehovah, and Jehovah is our strength and our song; he is our salvation. It was Jesus Christ who gave his life for our salvation. Jehovah, therefore, could be none other than Jesus Christ, our Lord.

2 Nephi 22:3

In the desert world of Israelite prophets, water was life. At Sinai, Moses smote the rock, and water gushed forth to save a thirsty people. In the millennial earth the Messiah will provide the water of life; his people will symbolically draw water from the wells of salvation, water that springs up unto eternal life. Compare the language of John 4:13–14; 7:38; 1 Corinthians 10:4; and Revelation 21:6. Read also Isaiah 41:17–18.

2 Nephi 22:4–6

Hebrew *Hallelujah*, or *Hallelu Yah*, means literally "praise ye the Lord." Every tongue will praise his excellent works and cry out and shout everlasting thanksgiving, especially for the greatness of his atoning sacrifice. Read Doctrine and Covenants 84:98–102.

2 Nephi 23 (Isaiah 13)

Isaiah 13–23 are "burdens" on ten different nations— the Lord's warning voice to other peoples (Amos 3:7) and his judgments upon them. "Burden" is used to translate Hebrew *massa,* which means something lifted up, an "oracle" or "message." These oracles against the nations demonstrate that the sovereignty of the Lord God is universal and that he is involved in the history of all his people. Heavenly Father is mindful of all his children, and he is concerned about wickedness everywhere. Other nations were types for the last days; compare Amos 1–2; Jeremiah 46–51; and Ezekiel 25–32.

Isaiah 13–14, which are 2 Nephi 23–24, are about *Babylon.* Although Assyria was the superpower in Isaiah's time, through the spirit of prophecy he foresaw that mighty, wicked Babylon would threaten his homeland. These two are the only chapters of Isaiah 13–23 quoted in the Book of Mormon, which says something about their relative value.

2 Nephi 23:1

"Babylon" is a type of the whole wicked world (Revelation 14:8; D&C 133:14; see also Revelation 16:19; 17:5; 18:2–4, 10, 21; D&C 1:16; 35:11; 64:24; 86:3; 133:5, 7).

Brigham Young University professor of ancient scripture Richard D. Draper wrote: "Babylon incarnates arrogance, pride, and insatiable corruption in opposition to God and his kingdom. It stands in contrast to the heavenly city, the New Jerusalem, where the law of God thrives. . . .

". . . Babylon represents a real historical organization. . . . it is composed of more than one entity. . . . Seeing spiritual Babylon as only one association, either at its inception or today, would therefore be wrong. It symbolizes all leagues that may be properly called Antichrist, that pervert the right way of the Lord, and that promote antichristian principles and life-styles.

"The arrogant Babylonians combined purely sensual and

material principles with the lofty striving within the soul of man. Out of this grew the principle of spiritual fornication. Men mistook lust for joy, sought happiness through passion, and pursued security through materialism. The bit of graffiti, 'He who dies with the most toys wins,' could have been written as easily in Babylon as in New York, or Las Vegas. Today many still seek to find heaven through drugs, lust, money, success, or power. People continue to try to escape the deadly round of daily life through material and immoral means. . . .

"God has provided a solution: flee Babylon. The command demands a complete severing of relations. God allows no association whatsoever. There is good reason. Babylon is not to be converted but destroyed: 'We would have healed Babylon, but she is not healed: forsake her' (Jer. 51:9, KJV). Any that linger in Babylon will be taken with her plagues, 'For after today cometh the burning . . . and I will not spare any that remain in Babylon' (D&C 64:24)."[68]

2 Nephi 23:2

The Hebrew word *nes* is variously translated as "banner," "ensign," and "standard." This ensign or standard is a rallying point for God's "warriors" in a day to come.

2 Nephi 23:3–5

"Sanctified ones," "holy ones," and "saints" derive from two Hebrew words: *kadosh* or plural *k'doshim,* used ten times in the Old Testament, and *hassid* or plural *hassidim,* used nineteen times in the Old Testament.

Verse 3 corrects the statement that appears in the King James Version: "I have also called my mighty ones, for mine anger *is not upon* them that rejoice in my highness."

Can we identify the "sanctified ones," the "mighty ones" who are called and set apart (mustered) for the battle as the missionary force of the latter-day kingdom? Anyone who has been in the middle of the royal army assembled at the Missionary Training Center in Provo, Utah, has possibly felt power unequalled in any other single place in the world. These warriors of God do come from distant places ("from a far country, from the end of heaven"), and they are certainly going forth to conquer on life's great battlefield, to overthrow the whole wicked world, to destroy evil by establishing righteousness.

That "mighty army of the Lord," however, is only part of what he calls the "sanctified ones"—all the Saints, the citizens of his kingdom, are involved in the battle, including help from the other side of the veil.

2 Nephi 23:6–18

Judgments come upon earth's inhabitants at the Second Coming, "the day of the Lord."

Verses 6–8: The destructions sent forth from the Almighty (Hebrew *Shaddai*) will cause faint-heartedness in the wicked; fear, pain, and faces enflamed with embarrassment and anxiety will characterize the disobedient. Paul later envisioned the same scene: "For when they shall say, Peace and safety; then sudden destruction cometh upon them, as travail upon a woman with child; and they shall not escape" (1 Thessalonians 5:3).

Verse 9: "The day of the Lord cometh . . . and he shall destroy the sinners thereof out of it"—all telestial people and things will be removed from this earth.

Verse 10: The sun will be darkened, and the moon and the stars will give no light. Could this happen as the earth moves back into its previous orbit and becomes terrestrial? Read Doctrine and Covenants 29:14 and 133:49. Those heavenly spheres seem to act strangely—being darkened, refusing to give light—because of their relative impotence next to the Source of all light. The Lord God of heaven and earth is described as "above the brightness of the sun," whose "brightness and glory defy all description" (Joseph Smith–History 1:16–17). When he comes, those other luminaries will appear totally insignificant, just as the moon is hardly visible when the sun is shining.

Verse 11: Two sets of parallel statements detail how God's judgments will be executed. He will punish the world (meaning the wicked; compare Joseph Smith–Matthew 1:4), and he specifically identifies one type of wicked person—the proud—as the primary object of his wrath (compare Malachi 4:1).

Verse 12: The parallelism teaches that relatively few men will survive the promised judgments. Ophir, probably in the southern Arabian peninsula, was a land famous for its gold.[69]

Verse 13: Two more sets of parallel statements foreshadow God's use of earthquakes; the Hebrew phrase "remove out of her place" may be translated into English as *quake*. See also Joseph Smith–Matthew 1:29; Revelation 6:12; 16:18.

Verse 14: Like the hunted roe and the shepherdless sheep, so those who have lived without God in the world will be helpless in the day of the Lord's visitation.

Verse 15: "Everyone that is *proud* shall be thrust through; and everyone that is joined *to the wicked* shall fall by the sword" (italics indicate changes from the King James Version).

Verses 16–18: These verses, in addition to depicting horrible vengeance to be meted out at the Second Coming, take us back also to the original type, less than two centuries after Isaiah's time, when the Medes would overrun the Babylonians with viciousness and cruelty. In 539 B.C. the Lord did indeed stir up the Medes (and Persians), who, uninterested so much in monetary gain, wreaked merciless vengeance upon those who opposed them.

2 Nephi 23:19–22

"Babylon the great is falling; / God shall all her towers o'erthrow."[70] Babylon truly was "the glory of kingdoms." The Hanging Gardens of Babylon were one of the seven wonders of the ancient world. Yet, Babylon fell without a struggle before the armies of Cyrus of Persia. He and his men dug a canal into which they diverted the waters of the Euphrates, which normally flowed into Babylon, so they could penetrate into the heart of the city via the dry river bed. By this means vegetation ceased growing in the city, and the city began deteriorating, leading to the fulfillment of Isaiah's prediction that it would be uninhabited; there wouldn't even be an Arab to pitch a tent or a shepherd to make a sheepfold. Total desolation was predicted, and it was an accurate prophecy. Isaiah's prophecy was gradually but literally fulfilled within a few centuries, by the Roman period.

The vivid description of Babylon's destruction fits both the terrain at the southern end of the Dead Sea, where Sodom and Gomorrah once flourished in wickedness, and the land of Babylon. Both places foreshadow the eschatological (latter-day) devastation of spiritual Babylon.

Isaiah poetically employs two fictional beasts usually associated with superstitious traditions in this description of desolation. "Satyrs" are in Hebrew *seirim,* meaning "hairy" or "rough" ones. In Greek mythology, a satyr is half man and half goat. "Dragons" are jackals or wild dogs.

2 Nephi 24 (Isaiah 14)

Isaiah spent a lot of time describing the scattering of Israel. He then discussed the gathering in this chapter. In one of the great overriding themes of the writings of Isaiah, the prophet proclaimed his main message: Babylon, historical and symbolic, must be destroyed (chapter 23) and Israel must be gathered and saved (chapter 24). Jehovah will be just, but he will also be merciful.

Could "strangers" mean converts or proselytes? Gentiles certainly are accepting the gospel and joining spiritual Israel, being grafted or adopted into the covenant people.[71] "And I will bless them through thy name; for as many as receive this Gospel shall be called after thy name, and shall be accounted thy seed" (Abraham 2:10).

In another sense, with reference to the physical gathering to the land of Israel in the last days, could Arab Palestinians also be part of the inhabitants of the Holy Land? See Genesis 16:12 (speaking of descendants of Ishmael) and Ezekiel 47:22.

2 Nephi 24:2

This prophecy finds fulfillment in 538 B.C. and in the latter days. Other people or nations will take Israel and "bring them to their place [Joseph Smith Translation addition: *and they shall return to their lands* (plural) *of promise*]. . . . And the house of Israel shall possess them [that is, *the strangers*], and the land of the Lord shall be for servants and handmaids; and they shall take them captives unto whom they were captives; and they shall rule over their oppressors."

2 Nephi 24:3

"It shall come to pass in *that* day" (a change from Isaiah in the King James Version, which reads "*the* day"). "Hard bondage" may be literal, meaning the servitude of the Babylonian captivity (586–538 B.C.), but may also refer to the captivity and the chains with which we shackle ourselves when we serve sin. This kind of salvation, deliverance from sin, far exceeds the deliverance from captivity in ancient Egypt or Babylon.

2 Nephi 24:4–23

These verses contain a satirical or taunting song against the king of Babylon, who is Satan.

Verses 5–8: The whole earth, humankind and even the trees, rejoice when the longest-reigning, cruelest subjugator of all, the devil himself, is bound and put away (see also Revelation 20:1–3; 1 Nephi 22:15, 26; D&C 101:28).

Verses 9–11: The inhabitants of hell react as Satan is consigned there. Even the bygone, wicked rulers of nations who once were apparelled in luxurious robes note that the king of

Babylon, their evil sponsor, the devil himself, is now symbolically covered only by worms.

Verses 12–15: These verses apply to the king of Babylon, but also to Lucifer, the prototype of Babylon's king. In other words, ancient Babylon's fall is symbolic of Lucifer's fall. Undoubtedly, that is why Isaiah thought of Lucifer at this point, after describing Babylon's fall. Lucifer is the king of Babylon, meaning the whole wicked world. *Lucifer* is Latin; the Hebrew is *hellel,* both meaning "shining one." "Son of the morning" is *ben shakhar,* meaning "son of dawn." Lucifer's fall in the premortal life is recorded also in Revelation 12:7–9 and Moses 4:1–4. He sought to take away our agency—a warning to all of us not to get overanxious or overzealous in coercing or compelling others (see also Jacob 4:18; D&C 76:25–28).

The history of this world began with a war. We engaged in that war and we won, but the war continues in this world. Lucifer imports it to planet Earth. It is the longest war ever on Earth, lasting six thousand years now. We are fighting in this war with evil, and we will win again. The final battle is still ahead, and we are assured that good will always prevail. A number of our hymns teach us about the war: "Onward, Christian Soldiers" (no. 246), "Behold! A Royal Army" (no. 251), "We Are All Enlisted" (no. 250), "Hope of Israel" (no. 259), and others (see "Latter-day Saint Hymns on War," accompanying commentary at Alma 43–62). We sing about war, battles, conflicts, soldiers, armies, the foe, the battlefield, banners, swords, helmets, bucklers, shields, signals, war-cries, and victory—and we put it all in an eternal context. It is a battle not to save physical bodies, for all physical bodies will eventually be resurrected to an immortal condition, but a battle to save the souls of humankind. In a war we cannot sit back complacently while the enemy surrounds us with his formidable weaponry. Entering any day of our lives without prayer and scripture study is like a warrior charging into battle without his armor.

Verse 14: "I will be like the Most High." Ambition is pride's first cousin. Lucifer aspired to ascend to heaven, to have a throne higher than the stars of God, to be like God—all of which was ambitious indeed. It appears that he felt he could displace God. His selfish ambition ruined his life. Jesus said, "Whosoever shall exalt himself shall be abased" (Matthew 23:12) and "That which is now exalted of itself shall be laid low of power" (D&C 49:10). The higher up we are, the farther we can fall; Lucifer apparently fell from a high position. He is described as "an angel of God who was in authority in the presence of God" (D&C 76:25).

Verses 15–17: When all the children of God see Lucifer as he is consigned to his ultimate fate, they will squint at him with disgust and amazement and wonder aloud: Is this the person who caused such incredible physical and spiritual devastation in the world? this spiteful, pathetic figure of misery and degradation?

Verses 18–22: We are promised that if our eye is single to the glory of God, we can be filled with light (D&C 88:67). Lucifer wants the glory for himself and, therefore, has no light in him, only darkness. Mortal wicked people have some glory, but Satan has *none*; there is no grave for Satan—he has no body. The great irony is that he sought superior power and glory and in the end will have *none,* all of which is another warning to us.

Verse 23: Babylon will become a "possession for the bittern" and stagnant marshes, and it will be swept with the broom of destruction; that is, the world will be cleansed and renewed.

2 Nephi 24:24–27

The previous verses applied also to the evil empire Babylon. Now the scene changes back to her infamous predecessor. In the year 701 B.C., Assyria attacked Judah and succumbed to catastrophe by the hand of the Lord himself (Isaiah 36–37). Isaiah's vision of historical events is like the panoramic vision of John the Revelator in that both move back and forth through periods without too much concern for strict chronology.

The alternate parallelisms of verses 26–27 attest that God's punishing hand will inevitably fall on Assyria and on all other rebellious nations.

2 Nephi 24:28–32

In the year King Ahaz died, ca. 720 B.C., the prophet received an oracle (a revelation) against Philistia.

Verse 29: The King James Version's "Palestina" is Latin for Philistia, later called Palestine.

Some think that historically the "serpent's root" may have been Shalmaneser V, and the "cockatrice" that followed was Sennacherib.

Verse 31: The gate, and the city which it represents, will howl and cry and ultimately be dissolved by a power coming down from the north, which Assyria and then Babylon did.

Verse 32: The whole prophecy against Philistia revolves around the final thought, the central message: there is no future in any temporal state, for the Lord has founded Zion; the poor in spirit (meaning the humble) and the meek will always turn to the Lord, and Zion will be established. That foundation is sure.

2 Nephi 25:1–8

After including these writings of Isaiah in his record, Nephi gave his future readers some keys for understanding Isaiah (see "Why Study Isaiah" and "How to Understand Isaiah," preceding the commentary at 1 Nephi 20). One way to understand Isaiah, according to Nephi, is to know something "concerning the manner of prophesying among the Jews." Looking back, we can see that that manner of prophesying was at least threefold: (1) *dualistic*, where a prophecy is fulfilled two or more times across dispensations; (2) *messianic*, with prophecies fulfilled in the first or second coming of Christ; and (3) *parabolic,* where a prophecy is given in the form of a story or parable.

To emphasize the significance of his insight about the manner of Jewish prophesying, Nephi stated that he avoided teaching his people and his children very much concerning the manner of the Jews because "their works were works of darkness, and their doings were doings of abominations."

Even though Isaiah's words were not so intelligible to Isaiah's people and are still not clear to most people in our day, nevertheless, Nephi declared, "The words of Isaiah . . . are plain unto all those that are filled with the spirit of prophecy." John wrote that the spirit of prophecy is "the testimony of Jesus" (Revelation 19:10). The Jews certainly did not have the testimony of Jesus, so they could not really understand Isaiah's teachings. The same is true of us. Isaiah's words will be plain and intelligible to those who have a real testimony of the Lord Jesus Christ—which means they have the spirit of prophecy—and who make the effort to understand the prophet's words through diligent study accompanied by the Spirit of the Lord.

2 Nephi 25:5–6

Jesus of Nazareth was a master teacher. As did all the great Hebrew poets and prophets before him, Jesus consistently drew from his geographical milieu to illustrate his teachings. A favorite oratorical and literary technique of ancient writers was to demonstrate how something in nature was comparable to something in the human experience. The more people become acquainted with the land of the prophets and the Messiah, the more they will understand the imagery and symbols drawn from that holy land.

After Nephi wrote that his soul delighted in the words of Isaiah and that he understood them, he explained why: "I came out from Jerusalem, and mine eyes hath beheld the things of the Jews, and I know that . . . there is none other people that understand the things which were spoken unto the Jews like unto them, save it be that they are taught after the manner of the things of the Jews. . . . Behold, I, of myself, have dwelt at Jerusalem, wherefore I know concerning *the regions round about*" (emphasis added). Nephi could understand and appreciate Isaiah because of his personal knowledge of Isaiah's environment.

Nephi also understood his mentor-prophet because he knew the history of his homeland ("the judgments of God, which hath come to pass among the Jews") and taught those basic lessons from history so his children could learn from them.

2 Nephi 25:7–8

Contrary to the Jews' propensity to prefer teachings with apocryphal, or hidden, meaning, Nephi delighted in plainness, and he wrote so that "no man can err," so that there can be no mistaking or equivocating over his words and their meaning. He also testified that whenever Isaiah's prophecies are fulfilled, then people can see clearly and be convinced of their truthfulness. In that sense, his prophecies will be "of great worth unto them in the last days." "In that day," meaning these last days, they will finally be understood—by those who have eyes to see and ears to hear—and that is why Nephi worked hard to carve them into his record: for our benefit, for our good, in helping us become better acquainted with the Author of all these teachings.

2 Nephi 25:9

Why would the Jews experience so many centuries of suffering? And, some might ask, why would many generations of Jews have to suffer for what one generation of Jews had done in killing their Messiah? Actually, not all the Jews had opposed Jesus; his friends Peter, James, John, others of the Twelve, Mary, Martha, Lazarus, and many hundreds of other Jews accepted him for who he claimed to be—God's Son and the Savior of the world. When the scriptures, therefore, speak of "the Jews" doing this or "the Jews" doing that, we understand plainly that the intent is *certain Jewish leaders and their followers* did this or that.

Given the Latter-day Saint doctrine of personal responsibility for individual sins and not for the sins of others (Articles of Faith 1:2), can anyone rightfully assign direct culpability for the death of Jesus to succeeding generations of Jews long after his mortal life? A specific answer to this provocative question is found in this verse: "As one generation hath been destroyed among the Jews because of iniquity, even so have they been destroyed from generation to generation *according to their iniquities*." In other words, only the Jews who opposed Jesus and killed him are responsible for those actions; later generations are responsible only for their own sins.

If any people oppose or reject God, by that opposition or rejection they bring upon themselves God's punishment. One generation rejected him and suffered for it. Every succeeding generation that rejected him also suffered for it. Heavenly Father does not want any of his children to suffer, but anyone who continues to reject God will experience the natural consequence of that rejection.

Notice the use of future-perfect tense verbs—seen as completed because the prophet Nephi had already seen this tragic condition of the Jews down through the centuries (for more on the prophetic tense, see commentary at Mosiah 16:6).

The verse concludes, "And never hath any of them been destroyed save it were foretold them by the prophets of the Lord." God always issues plenty of warnings before destroying any people (Amos 3:7). "And the Lord God of their fathers sent to them by his messengers, rising up betimes, and sending; because he had compassion on his people, and on his dwelling place: But they mocked the messengers of God, and despised his words, and misused his prophets, until the wrath of the Lord arose against his people, till there was no remedy" (2 Chronicles 36:15–16).

Moses is another example of a messenger of warning. His

prophecies clearly describe the future consequences of disobedience and apostasy:

"It shall come to pass, if thou wilt not hearken unto the voice of the Lord thy God, to observe to do all his commandments and his statutes which I command thee this day; that all these curses shall come upon thee, and overtake thee. . . .

"The Lord shall send upon thee cursing, vexation, and rebuke, in all that thou settest thine hand unto. . . .

"The Lord shall smite thee with a consumption, and . . . with the sword, . . . and they shall pursue thee until thou perish. . . .

"The fruit of thy land, and all thy labours, shall a nation which thou knowest not eat up; and thou shalt be only oppressed and crushed alway. . . .

"Moreover all these curses shall come upon thee, and shall pursue thee, and overtake thee, till thou be destroyed; because thou hearkenedst not unto the voice of the Lord thy God, to keep his commandments and his statutes which he commanded thee: . . .

"The Lord shall bring a nation against thee from far, from the end of the earth, as swift as the eagle flieth [the eagle was the symbol of Rome]; a nation whose tongue thou shalt not understand;

"A nation of fierce countenance, which shall not regard the person of the old, nor shew favour to the young. . . .

"And he shall besiege thee in all thy gates, until thy high and fenced walls come down, wherein thou trustedst, throughout all thy land" (Deuteronomy 28:15, 20, 22, 33, 45, 49–50, 52).

2 Nephi 25:10–17

These verses sketch a history of the Jews from the middle of the first millennium B.C. through the Second Coming.

Verse 10: A chronicle of the destruction of the Jews and their exile to Babylon through 586 B.C.

Verse 11: Nephi's prophecy that his people (the Jews) will

return to possess "the land of Jerusalem," which happened beginning in 539 B.C.

Verse 12: The succeeding centuries of wars culminate in the coming of the Only Begotten of the Father and his ministry, around A.D. 30–33, and his rejection by some sinful, hard, and stubborn Jews.

Verse 13: Having seen all this in advance, Nephi wrote that God's Son will be crucified, buried, and after three days rise again "with healing in his wings," a figurative expression referring to his healing the wounds of mortal sorrows, pains, and death and providing salvation to believing souls. Nephi said, "I have seen his day," and because he was an eyewitness of these most glorious events in all of history, he felt to "magnify his holy name" (compare the similar sentiment of Mary, Jesus' mother, in Luke 1:46).

Verse 14: After Christ's resurrection and multiple appearances to believers, Nephi saw that the Jews will be destroyed again—which happened in the great Jewish-Roman wars of A.D. 66–70, under Vespasian and Titus, and A.D. 132–135, under Hadrian. It happened because they fought "against God and the people of his church."

Verse 15: Jews will be scattered worldwide by Babylon and by such other nations after Babylon as the Greeks, Romans, Byzantines, Islamic empires, Crusaders, and Turks.

Verses 16–17: Jews in their scattered condition (in the "dispersion," Greek *diaspora*) will be scourged by these other nations for many generations until they "shall be persuaded to believe in Christ, the Son of God" and his infinite atonement. When that day finally comes, that they "believe in Christ, and worship the Father in his name" and "look not forward any more for another Messiah," then "the Lord will set his hand again the second time to restore his people from their lost and fallen state." That restoration will be heralded as "a marvelous work and a wonder" (compare Isaiah 29:14).

2 Nephi 25:19

Prophets prophesied that the Messiah would come into the world "six hundred years from the time that my father left Jerusalem" (the names of these prophets are not noted here). The prophets and an angel (2 Nephi 10:3) also revealed that his mortal name would be *Yeshua haMashiakh* (the Hebrew equivalent of the English "Jesus Christ" or "Jesus Messiah") and that this long-awaited Messiah would be the Son of God.

2 Nephi 25:20

Nephi continued speaking in unmistakable terms. He attested to three well-known events in Israelite history: (1) the Exodus from Egypt; (2) Moses' healing of the people who looked to the serpent raised up on the pole: a type of the Messiah's healing of the people through his being raised up on the cross and the people looking to him; and (3) Moses smiting the rock and bringing forth water: a type of the Rock of our salvation offering Living Water leading to eternal life. Those events were true, and "as the Lord God liveth," salvation comes only in and through the name *Jesus Christ*.

2 Nephi 25:23

Nephi's most ardent effort was (and ours should be) to work diligently to persuade family and friends, "our children, and also our brethren," to believe in Christ and reconcile (harmonize or conform) our lives to him so we can be saved by his grace.

Do we believe in grace? The typical Latter-day Saint would hesitatingly reply, "Yes." Then why don't we talk about it more? The same typical Saint might be quick to admit, "Because *they* do!"—meaning many other Christian churches. We may not like or agree with how they use the term, at times seemingly representing "push-button salvation." Nevertheless, the fact is that we do believe in grace, "for we know that it is by grace that we are saved, *after all we can do.*" We repeat our belief, "Oh yes, we know that it is by grace that we are saved, *after all we can do*"; and we say that second phrase more loudly, by way of emphasis. That is all true, but in a sense, it really doesn't matter how much we do; it will never save us. We can accumulate a mountain of good works, and they will not save us. Thus, in one sense what Nephi seems to be saying is that it is ultimately by the grace of Christ we are saved, *apart* from what we do. Grace is not simply the finishing touch to top off our efforts at salvation. Grace is the very essence of salvation. Father Lehi declared that no flesh can dwell in God's presence—only through "the merits, and mercy, and grace of the Holy Messiah" (2 Nephi 2:8). And Moroni 6:4 states, "Relying alone upon the merits of Christ."

In the end it is by the Redeemer's grace, by his loving kindness and self-sacrifice in our behalf, that we are saved, because he paid the ultimate price to rescue us. His grace is the enabling power that justifies us to remain with the Father, and it sanctifies us to eventually become like the Father.

Elder M. Russell Ballard declared: "On our own we cannot earn the kingdom of God—no matter what we do. Unfortunately, there are some within the Church who have become so preoccupied with performing good works that they forget that those works—as good as they may be—are hollow unless they are accompanied by a complete dependence on Christ."[72]

On our willingness to be dependent on Christ, see also commentary at Mosiah 3:19.

2 Nephi 25:24–25

Verses 23 to 27 constitute one of the clearest explanations of the purpose and meaning of the Old Testament, the old covenant. The old law of Moses was given by Jehovah to point to Christ. They are, of course, the same Person: Jehovah would later come as Christ (Alma 34:14; Galatians 3:24). Everything he required his people to live, through

Moses, was to prepare them for the higher law, which came in the form of the Sermon on the Mount and other elevated teachings during his mortal and postmortal ministry, when, as he declared, "The law is fulfilled that was given unto Moses. Behold, I am he that gave the law . . . ; therefore, the law in me is fulfilled . . . ; therefore it hath an end" (3 Nephi 15:4–5). For some Nephites, more than five hundred years before the Savior's mortal mission, "the law hath become dead unto us, and we are made alive in Christ because of our faith."

2 Nephi 25:26

The former-day Saints (ancient Nephites), as well as the Latter-day Saints, talk of Christ, rejoice in Christ, preach of Christ, and prophesy of Christ for this quintessential purpose: "that our children may know to what source they may look for a remission of their sins." He is the source, and the only recourse, for taking away the stain and the pain of our sins. His is the only name under heaven whereby we can be forgiven, cleansed, strengthened, and admitted into exaltation. No wonder our lives are centered on Jesus Christ!

2 Nephi 25:27

Nephi said the old law was dead to the Nephites, which is what Paul would also forcefully express in his many epistles, especially Galatians, later written to early Christians and Gentiles. Life is in Christ.

2 Nephi 25:29–30

We go to our meetinghouses each week to worship, but what do we mean by "worship"? If we define *worship* as honor, respect, revere, adore, glorify, and venerate—who is it that we worship? We would all agree that we worship our Heavenly Father, but do we worship anyone else? Verse 29 pointedly teaches that Christ is the Holy One of Israel and that you "must bow down before him, and worship him with all your might, mind, and strength, and your whole soul," and if you do that, you will not be cast out but have life ever-lasting in him (that is clearly taught also in John 5:23 and 3 Nephi 11:17).

2 Nephi 26:1–10

Nephi prophesied of the coming of Christ to his descendants. He foresaw in vivid and heartrending detail the destructions and devastations inflicted on his own wicked descendants who would oppose the prophets and reject the Savior—all recorded in equally vivid detail in 3 Nephi 8–9 as they transpired. The language of verse 4 shows up in the writings of the later prophet Malachi (4:1) but is obviously based on a much older prophetic description of which Nephi is aware. It has multiple fulfillments, one of which occurred when the Savior appeared to the Nephites as prophesied in verse 1 (see, for example, 3 Nephi 9:3). Nephi also foresaw the merciful healing, peace, and prosperity with which his righteous descendants would be rewarded.

2 Nephi 26:11–14

The Spirit of the Lord will not always strive with human beings because they quench it through sin (Jacob 6:8; Ether 2:15). Perhaps Moroni incorporated Nephi's language in verse 12 into his title page. Verse 14 begins a discussion about the last days.

2 Nephi 26:15–16

Records of the righteous prophets were preserved, and the Nephites will yet speak to the Lamanites and Gentiles out of the ground; their words shall have a familiar sound to them, and Joseph Smith will be given power to bring their words back out of the dust of centuries.

Elder Orson Pratt testified: "One of the most marvelous things connected with this prediction is, that after the nation should be brought down, they should 'speak out of the ground.' . . . Never was a prophecy more truly fulfilled than this, in the coming forth of the Book of Mormon. Joseph Smith took that sacred history 'out of the ground.' It is the voice of the ancient prophets of America speaking 'out of the ground'; their speech is 'low out of the dust'; it speaks in a most familiar manner of the doings of bygone ages; it is the voice of those who slumber in the dust. It is the voice of prophets speaking from the dead, crying repentance in the ears of the living. In what manner could a nation, after they were brought down and destroyed, 'speak out of the ground'? Could their dead bodies or their dust, or their ashes speak? Verily, no: they can only speak by their writings or their books that they wrote while living. Their voice, speech or words, can only 'speak out of the ground,' or 'whisper out of the dust' by their books or writings being discovered."[73]

2 Nephi 26:20–22

On the "many churches" in the last days that pervert the right ways of the Lord, see commentary at 1 Nephi 13:2–9; 2 Nephi 28:1–8; 4 Nephi 1:20–49; and Mormon 8:26–41.

On the "secret combinations" that also pervert the right ways of the Lord, see commentary at Helaman 1 and Helaman 6:21–25.

2 Nephi 26:26–33

The final eight verses of 2 Nephi 26 constitute a running argument for God's graciousness in allowing all to come unto him.

Has he denied anyone entrance to his houses of worship, even to his holy temples? Has he denied anyone the opportunity to pursue salvation or to partake of his goodness? Absolutely not, Nephi exclaimed: "All men are privileged the one like unto the other, and none are forbidden."

Of course there are stipulations and requirements to attain the blessings of heaven and the glories of his kingdom: all must repent; all must have charity; all must labor to build up Zion; and all must keep his basic laws, such as the Ten Commandments.

For those willing to obey him and keep his commandments, "he inviteth them all to come unto him and partake of his goodness; and he denieth none that come unto him, black and white, bond and free, male and female; and he remembereth the heathen; and all are alike unto God, both Jew and Gentile."

God does seem to have his own timetable for various peoples to be invited to come and partake of all his heavenly gifts and blessings—for example, the gospel to covenant Israel, and then to the Gentiles; the priesthood to Aaron's family and tribe of Levi and then to all the tribes and those adopted into covenant Israel; the gospel and priesthood blessings to all other peoples and then to those of African descent; and the gospel and priesthood blessings to all nations and then to the Jews as a people.

The "first shall be last; and the last shall be first" clearly suggests a divine timetable for full accessibility to covenant blessings (Matthew 19:30; see also 1 Nephi 13:42; Ether 13:12; D&C 29:30). The same blessings offered "in this life or the next" also presuppose a schedule based on the wisdom of God.

In the meridian dispensation, Jesus said, "I am not sent but unto the lost sheep of the house of Israel" (Matthew 15:24); his apostles would later take the gospel to the Gentiles, and interestingly, conflict persisted for decades among God's people—especially between two great apostles, Peter and Paul—over the timing and conditions of Gentiles coming into the covenant people.[74]

We may not presently have all the reasons for the variables in God's timing of the dispensing of his blessings, but we trust in his perfect omniscience and wisdom as to exactly when to submit the invitation. The glorious truth, however, is that all children of Heavenly Father will—sooner or later—have full opportunity to receive all the privileges and blessings the Gods in Heaven extend to humans on earth.

Elder Dallin H. Oaks elaborated on the same concept: "Proclaiming the gospel is His work, not ours, and therefore it must be done on His timing, not ours. There are nations in the world today that must hear the gospel before the Lord will come again. We know this, but we cannot force it. We must wait upon the Lord's timing. He will tell us, and He will open the doors or bring down the walls when the time is right. . . . The Lord loves all of His children, and He desires that all have the fulness of His truth and the abundance of His blessings. He knows when groups or individuals are ready, and He wants us to hear and heed His timetable for sharing His gospel with them."[75]

The First Presidency declared on 15 February 1978: "Based upon ancient and modern revelation, The Church of Jesus Christ of Latter-day Saints gladly teaches and declares the Christian doctrine that all men and women are brothers and sisters, not only by blood relationship from common mortal progenitors but also as literal spirit children of an Eternal Father. . . .

"Consistent with these truths, we believe that God has given and will give to all peoples sufficient knowledge to help them on their way to eternal salvation, either in this life or in the life to come. . . .

"Our message therefore is one of special love and concern for the eternal welfare of all men and women, regardless of religious belief, race, or nationality, knowing that we are truly brothers and sisters because we are sons and daughters of the same Eternal Father."[76]

The Lord invites, on his schedule, all to come unto him and partake of his goodness: black and white, bond and free, male and female. We might add Germans and French, Chileans and Argentines, North Koreans and South Koreans. He remembers the Africans and the North Americans, and *all are alike unto God,* both Jew and Arab.[77]

For example, Elder Howard W. Hunter in 1979 admonished members of the Church to remember that "both the Jews and the Arabs are children of our Father. They are both children of promise, and as a church we do not take sides. We have love for and an interest in each. The purpose of the gospel of Jesus Christ is to bring about love, unity, and brotherhood of the highest order. Like Nephi of old, may we be able to say, 'I have charity for the Jew. . . . I also have charity for the Gentiles.' (2 Nephi 33:8–9)."[78]

2 Nephi 26:29

Satan is a master counterfeiter, an expert in cheap imitation. For example, whereas God always encourages his people to build sacred temples in which he can reveal the holiest instructions, covenants, and ordinances necessary for exaltation, Satan sponsors among the civilizations and peoples of the earth "temples" wherein they prostitute sacred rituals with fertility worship of false gods and goddesses.

Whereas God always encourages men to take upon themselves and use his very own power, the holy priesthood, Satan comes along sponsoring priestcraft, which means that "men preach and set themselves up for a light unto the world, that they may get gain and praise of the world; but they seek not the welfare of Zion." The early Church of Jesus Christ faced this problem. It was, in truth, at the heart of what we sometimes call the Great Apostasy (the first through the nineteenth centuries), as the apostle Paul testified: "For I know this, that after my departing shall grievous wolves enter in among you, not sparing the flock. Also of your own selves shall men arise, speaking perverse things, to draw away disciples after them" (Acts 20:29–30).

Because the Savior is the light of the world, he forbids his true followers to set themselves up "for a light unto the world" just to get money and popularity—wealth and fame—and to build up their own little kingdoms instead of the kingdom of God, the cause of Zion.

While traveling in the Yucatan Peninsula, the authors have spent hours scouring the ruins of the religious center of Chichen Itza, where Kukulcan, alias Quetzalcoatl, was worshipped. The priests certainly perverted true worship and adulterated temples. What a classic example of priestcraft. Instead of being servants of all, they set themselves above others and expected their subjects to serve them. They were adorned, as the Book of Mormon frequently notes, in luxurious apparel. Compare the high priests in the Lord's temples today. In the beginning there were true principles and true symbols, but then came perversions. None of this would have happened had they lived one principle: the greatest of all are the servants of all.

2 Nephi 26:30–31

Those who are genuinely dedicated to the welfare of Zion will seek the greatest gift of God, the gift of charity, "which charity is love." Without charity a person is nothing. With charity, we will never "suffer the laborer in Zion to perish" but will constantly be watching for the less fortunate who need help.

But the Lord extends a warning about motives to anyone who professes to work for the cause of Zion: "The laborer in Zion shall labor for Zion; for if they labor for money they shall perish." Of course there are those in God's kingdom who do receive money for their labors, but if their motive is to get rich, working to accumulate wealth instead of focusing on building the kingdom of God, they and their money will perish.

2 Nephi 27

Nephi both quotes from and paraphrases Isaiah 29. This chapter of Isaiah's writings has been quoted more often by General Authorities of the Church than any other. These verses constitute one of the great prophetic visions of Isaiah that would be understood only when it finally occurs: "In the days that the prophecies of Isaiah shall be fulfilled men shall know of a surety, at the times when they shall come to pass" (2 Nephi 25:7).

2 Nephi 27:6–11

"The book," the record from which comes the Book of Mormon, is mentioned twenty times in this chapter. It will be a blessing to Nephites and Lamanites and to Jews and Gentiles. The contents of the book, especially the sealed portion, are set forth, including an explanation of why the sealed portion has not yet been revealed to us. The book contains "a revelation from God, from the beginning of the world to the ending thereof." A portion of the book is sealed and cannot be revealed to the world because of wickedness.

The book will be delivered to a man, Joseph Smith, and he will deliver up some of the words or characters to another man, Martin Harris. The portion of the book that is sealed will be held back "until the own due time of the Lord," because it contains "all things from the foundation of the world unto the end thereof." On some future day all the sealed words will be read, by the power of Christ, "upon the house tops" (compare D&C 1:3), and all things that have ever happened—from beginning to end—will be revealed, things already seen by a select few: Adam (D&C 107:56–57), Enoch (Moses 6:36; 7:21, 67), the brother of Jared (Ether 3:21–28; 4:4–7), Abraham (Abraham 3:11–12), Moses (Moses 1:8, 28), John (Revelation 4—22), and Joseph Smith (D&C 76).

2 Nephi 27:11

"Upon the house tops"—could Isaiah be referring to television antennas, cables, satellite dishes, and other high-tech media yet to be invented that are situated on the housetops? The words of the Book of Mormon itself are broadcast by television and satellite transmission and received these days on and through the housetops of many people.

2 Nephi 27:12–14

Joseph Smith read that the gold plates were to be hidden from the world and seen by no one except "three witnesses." Those three witnesses—Oliver Cowdery, David Whitmer, and Martin Harris—would see the record "by the power of God" (their view came at the hands of the angel Moroni himself; see Ether 5:2–4). They were to "testify to the truth of the book and the things therein," which they did (see also D&C 17:1–3).[79] "The Testimony of Three Witnesses" now prefaces every copy of the Book of Mormon.

Another exception to the general rule of showing the ancient record to no one was the "few according to the will of God" (compare 2 Nephi 11:3). The testimony of eight other witnesses is also printed in the front of every copy of the Book of Mormon "to bear testimony of his word unto the children of men." The three, plus the eight, as well as the Prophet himself, constitute twelve special witnesses of the words of God preserved from ancient America.

2 Nephi 27:15–20

Martin Harris's 1828 meeting with Charles Anthon in New York City is reported in Joseph Smith–History 1:63–65. This episode in latter-day Church history was, at least in part, seen, heard, and recorded by the prophet Isaiah twenty-five hundred years before it happened.

The "learned" was the renowned professor of classical languages, Charles Anthon, from Columbia College, now Columbia University. The one "not learned" was Joseph Smith, who had received only about three years of formal education and who, during the translation of the Book of Mormon record, enlisted others to serve as scribes for him (see Joseph Smith–History 1:61–65).[80]

2 Nephi 27:21–23

Joseph Smith, the translator, received specific instruction from the Lord: (1) He was told to "Touch not the things which are sealed" and (2) when he had finished translating what he was permitted to see and had obtained the promised witnesses who would testify of the book, the Prophet was to seal up and hide the record for a future day when the Lord would reveal the balance of the engravings. In fact, the plates were delivered back into the custody of the angel Moroni until that future day (Joseph Smith–History 1:60).

One purpose for having the sealed portion remain untouched, said the Lord, was to show the world that he is able to do his own work, to reveal the sealed portion in his own way, and that he is a God of miracles. We know enough to appreciate that the Lord's ways are not our ways and that he is fully in charge.

2 Nephi 27:25

"With their lips do honor me": Lip service, without the heart, is hypocritical and insulting to the Lord (Isaiah 1:11–13). He wants righteous works as well as words.

President John Taylor warned: "We are told that 'Many will say to me in that day, Lord, Lord, have we not prophesied in Thy name and in Thy name have we cast out devils, and in Thy name done many wonderful works?' Yet to all such he will say; 'Depart from me, ye that work iniquity.' You say that means the outsiders? No, it does not. . . . This means you, Latter-day Saints, who heal the sick, cast out devils and do many wonderful things in the name of Jesus. And yet how many we see among this people . . . that become careless, and treat lightly the ordinances of God's house and the Priesthood of the Son of God; yet they think they are going by and by, to slide into the kingdom of God; but I tell you unless they are righteous and keep their covenants they will never go there. Hear it, ye Latter-day Saints!"[81]

Our scripture study, fasting, praying, partaking of the sacrament, home and visiting teaching, tithe-paying, and other spiritual duties all need to be done with full purpose of heart and not as "vain oblations"—the heart is what God wants. Inner motives are more important than outer motions. Hands that help are holier than lips that only pray.

2 Nephi 27:26

This verse speaks of the glorious restoration of the gospel in these last days. The work of the Lord will continue to flourish until it has penetrated all the lands of the earth; it will be increasingly "a marvelous work and a wonder."

"The wisdom of their wise and learned shall perish, and the understanding of their prudent shall be hid." To many scholars, this message originally from Isaiah 29 is still sealed.

2 Nephi 27:27–28

These verses describe the proud, modern atheists and antagonists of the work of God, who, like pottery vessels boasting themselves against the potter, are the created boasting themselves against their Creator. Just so, the proud and worldly "forest of Lebanon" (1 Kings 10:17, 21; 2 Chronicles 9:16, 20) will, in the final day, be replaced by the more humble and spiritually-minded "fruitful field."

2 Nephi 27:29–30

The spiritually deaf and blind will hear and see the Book of Mormon, and the meek and poor will rejoice in the Lord. This prophecy may be interpreted both symbolically and literally (for example, sophisticated hearing aids, audio recordings, scriptures in Braille, etc.).

2 Nephi 27:31–35

The Lord's promise is that Satan and his minions will be cut off. They who offend with their words, or who try to entrap those who carry out proper business transactions and legal matters (where such matters were conducted anciently, at the city gate), or who pervert justice for trivial kickbacks will all be cut off.

The descendants of Abraham and Jacob, God's covenant people, will not be embarrassed or ashamed but will sanctify the name of the Holy One of Israel and fear (revere) the God of Israel.

All who have erred and have harbored critical feelings may finally come to understanding and learn true doctrine through the Book of Mormon. "The book" is the marvelous instrument to bring people to Christ.

2 Nephi 28:1–8

Nephi began this section by bearing witness of the truth and credibility of all the prophecies he had just written about; they will be of great value to Israel at the end of time. In the last days some churches will deny the Holy Ghost (revelation) and the power of God (miracles). They will claim "there is no God today, for the Lord and the Redeemer hath done his work"—there is no more need for prophets and revelation. Some will even claim that God is dead; for example, the nineteenth-century German philosopher Nietzsche promoted that ideology. To him and all like-minded souls who deny the existence of deity, we offer the following that was found on a classroom blackboard:

> *God is dead.—Nietzsche*
> *Nietzsche is dead.—God*

Various false doctrines and beliefs of the last days are highlighted by Nephi: God is no longer a God of miracles, and such dogma is a thing of the past. That was the view of many of Joseph Smith's contemporaries: "There were no such things as visions or revelations in these days; that all such things had ceased with the apostles, and that there would never be any more of them" (Joseph Smith–History 1:21; see also 3 Nephi 29:5–6).

Others popularize the notion that we might as well relax, "eat, drink, and be merry"; when we die we might have to suffer a little for our "indiscretions," but God has "unconditional love" for his children and will punish us lightly and ultimately save us. It is normal and natural to sin; don't put yourself on a "guilt trip." It is understandable and justifiable to sin a little; there is no long-term damage done, so enjoy some minor sins now—you can always repent later. Go ahead and enjoy a little lustful indulgence in pornographic materials; go ahead and engage in a little sexual exploration, not "all the way," just a little touching, stimulation, and simulation of the act; go ahead and cheat on a few test questions or take a few insignificant items home from the workplace; go ahead and copy the videos and DVDs, the CDs, or the sheet music— "there is no harm in this; . . . and if it so be that we are guilty, God will beat us with a few stripes, and at last we shall be saved in the kingdom of God."

Can God do that? Can he perpetuate wickedness? Is he tolerant and merciful of those living in sin? He answers, "I the Lord cannot look upon sin with the least degree of allowance; nevertheless, he that repents and does the commandments of the Lord shall be forgiven" (D&C 1:31–32; see also Alma 45:16). Elder Richard G. Scott warned: "The thought of intentionally committing serious sin now and repenting later is perilously wrong. . . . Premeditated sin has greater penalties and is harder to overcome."[82]

President James E. Faust taught: "[One deception of the world] is what some erroneously call 'premeditated repentance.' There is no such doctrine in this Church. This may sound subtly appealing, but it is in fact pernicious and a false concept. Its objective is to persuade us that we can consciously and deliberately transgress with the forethought that quick repentance will permit us to enjoy the full blessings of the gospel, such as temple blessings or a mission. True repentance can be a long, painful process."[83]

Of the twisted views represented in verses 7 and 8, President Joseph Fielding Smith wrote: "Do not think that this was said of the world. . . . It is said of the members of the Church."[84]

2 Nephi 28:14

Wearing "stiff necks and high heads" refers to those who are not inclined to bow their heads in humble submission to the Lord and his authorized servants.

Another special caution is given to Latter-day Saints: In the last days all have gone astray "save it be a few, who are the humble followers of Christ; nevertheless, *they* [Latter-day Saints] *are led, that in many instances they do err because they are taught by the precepts of men*" (emphasis added). Take, for example, the widespread textbook conclusions: "history begins at Sumer," "human life on earth is millions of years old," "man evolved from lower forms," and so on. It is altogether fitting and proper to learn and even teach the world's view of pertinent issues as long as we also teach, in a believing way, the *restored truths*. Recall that it is all right to be learned if we hearken to the counsels and the teachings of God (2 Nephi 9:28–29).

2 Nephi 28:15–19

The devil hates the Book of Mormon because it exposes his tactics. The truth is laid out in plainness. The Lord rebukes the learned and wise (in their own eyes), the proud, the promoters of false doctrines or sexual perversions, and those who in any way distort the "right way of the Lord." He forewarns them that they are headed to hell.

President Joseph F. Smith also warned of three great dangers that face the modern Church of Jesus Christ and threaten it from within: (1) flattery of prominent people in the world, (2) false educational ideas, and (3) sexual impurity.[85]

Welcome to the twenty-first century! The Book of Mormon truly is for our day.

2 Nephi 28:20–22

Why is there so much about the devil and his work in a book of God? Modern prophets have told us that one of the great values of this book is that it exposes the enemies of Christ. We are informed about the evil so we can recognize it and prepare against it. The devil is the supreme rebel, the master terrorist. He stirs people up to "rage" and "anger against that which is good." He openly denounces that which is good, such as the Book of Mormon, the true Church of Jesus Christ, the power of God, marriage, family, chastity, integrity, and all things spiritual and eternal.

There is more detail on the devil's methods. These verses lay out four tactics of the adversary: (1) to stir up people to anger against that which is good; (2) to pacify Church members and give them a false sense of security based on the supposed power of humans to accomplish all they want or think is needful; (3) to flatter the prideful; and (4) to deceive people into thinking that there is no such thing as absolute truth, right and wrong, temptation, or the being known as the devil. A fifth tactic implied here is to attack doctrine and ordinances. Of tactic number four, someone once said that to believe there is no devil is roughly the equivalent of not believing in land mines while standing in the middle of a clearly marked minefield.

Note the verbs used in verses 21 and 22: *pacify, lull away, cheat, lead carefully down, flatter away, whisper,* and *grasp.* He leads some, even members of the Church, to be pacified and lulled away into a false sense of security, deceiving them to think that "all is well in Zion." Actually, in one sense, things *are* well in Zion, meaning the pure in heart, but Nephi seems to be seeing those who are apathetic and not taking a firm stand in defense of the truth; who are basking in the comforts of the world; who are ingesting the low morals of movies, music, and reading material and endorsing the low life of many Hollywood actors and actresses and professional athletes; who are enjoying a celebration of intellectualism and believing that maybe there really is no God and there is no devil—a belief that loosens morals and removes restraints.

This spawns Satan's strategy of "incremental entrapment," as John Bytheway likes to call it: "lie upon lie, decept upon decept . . . little compromises [that] eventually become large concessions."[86]

2 Nephi 28:23

On the lake of fire and brimstone, see commentary at Mosiah 3:27.

2 Nephi 28:24–29

Given the inevitable fate of those who persist in sin and refuse to repent, Nephi pronounces a series of woes. The interjection *woe* (the Book of Mormon uses the variant *wo*) is a term used to express distress, grief, and regret for a condition of ruin—deep-felt suffering for calamity or affliction. In the case of the woes Nephi enumerates here, the distress and grief are brought on the perpetrators of evil by themselves. They themselves are responsible for their lamentable destiny.

Woe to those who are "at ease in Zion," who feel that "all is well." The same expression in Amos 6:1 reads literally in Hebrew as "woe to those who feel secure in Zion." As a matter of fact, all is *not* well in Zion, even among the Saints of God, at least those who excessively indulge in and adopt the ways of the world.

Woe to those who listen to the philosophizings of men and at the same time deny God's power and the gift of the Holy Ghost. Remember, the Holy Ghost is a revelator and delights in revealing eternally tried truths that are firm, steadfast, and immovable.

Woe to anyone who says "we have received, and we need no more!" and "we have received the word of God, and we need no more . . . for we have enough!" Believing that, the Book of Mormon will be rejected out of hand.

In summary, Nephi says, woe to all those who are "angry because of the truth of God!" Anyone who is built upon the rock (that is, anyone who centers his or her life on Christ) will receive God's truth with gladness and will defend it and live it (see commentary at Helaman 5:12 and 3 Nephi 14:24–27).

2 Nephi 28:30

Second Nephi 28:30 through 29:4 is a long quotation from the Lord. Verse 30 contains words from the prophet Isaiah (Isaiah 28:9–13). The expression "line upon line, precept upon precept" suggests a need for *patience*. We are not expected to run faster than we have strength. These veiled minds of ours need time to absorb and eventually understand the mysteries of godliness. God does not give us all the principles at once, nor does he give us all the ordinances at once. If we were to receive all knowledge in one giant spoonful, we could certainly choke on it! Likewise, line upon line is the way Satan, the great imitator and great distorter, also works: little by little, until there is no turning back.

Joseph Smith taught, "When you climb up a ladder, you must begin at the bottom, and ascend step by step, until you arrive at the top; and so it is with the principles of the Gospel—you must begin with the first, and go on until you learn all the principles of exaltation."[87]

"Unto him that receiveth I will give more"—"he that will not harden his heart, to him is given the greater portion of the word, until it is given unto him to know the mysteries of God until he know them in full" (Alma 12:10). "He that receiveth light, and continueth in God, receiveth more light; and that light groweth brighter and brighter until the perfect day" (D&C 50:24).

2 Nephi 28:31

Brothers McConkie and Millet wrote: "Even among Church members, the Saints of the Most High—those who have by covenant come out of the world into the Church of God—there are those who seek to keep one foot in the world. They have a residence in Zion but visit Babylon periodically. Their membership may be in the former but their hearts are in the latter. Their ultimate trust may be in the power of God, but their interim interest is the arm of flesh."[88]

2 Nephi 29:1–11

As part of the marvelous work and recovery of the covenant people, the Lord proclaimed, "My words shall hiss forth unto the ends of the earth, for a standard unto my people." The Book of Mormon is certainly a standard by which we can measure the truth and propriety of all things. It is an ensign, or a banner, to which we can look for security, stability, and divine guidance in an unstable and untrustworthy world.

Some people will object to additional scripture, remonstrating that we already have God's words, the Bible, and we do not need any more. But the law of witnesses requires more than one testament or witness. "Know ye not that the testimony of two nations is a witness unto you that I am God, that I remember one nation like unto another? Wherefore, I speak the same words unto one nation like unto another. And when the two nations shall run together the testimony of the two nations shall run together also. And I do this that I may prove unto many that I am the same yesterday, today, and forever . . . For I command all men, both in the east [Bible lands], and in the west [Book of Mormon lands]."

2 Nephi 29:4–5

Do we really appreciate the travails, labors, and pains of the Jews in providing us with God's words? The Jews acquired a tearful past for maintaining their "peculiar" status (Exodus

19:5–6). Historically, Jews in many societies have been criticized, belittled, mocked, and persecuted, yet we would do well to remember that Isaiah, Jeremiah, Amos, Daniel, and Ezekiel were Jews. Peter was a Jew. John the Beloved, James, and Matthew were Jews. Martha, Mary, Lazarus, and Mary Magdalene were Jews. Jesus' mother, Mary, and his mortal guardian, Joseph, were Jews. Jesus was a Jew.

There are many wonderful Jewish people in our day who courageously uphold the teachings of the Hebrew Bible (the Old Testament). More important, the Lord has not forgotten his own people, and he will hold accountable those who mistreat them.

2 Nephi 29:10

The God of Israel testifies that the Bible does not contain all of his words. The prophet of the Restoration testified similarly: "Some of our friends . . . are bold to say that we have everything written in the Bible which God ever spoke to man since the world began. . . . But we ask, does it remain for a people who never had faith enough to call down one scrap of revelation from heaven, and for all they have now are indebted to the faith of another people who lived hundreds and thousands of years before them, does it remain for them to say how much God has spoken and how much He has not spoken? . . . It is nowhere said in that volume by the mouth of God, that He would not, after giving what is there contained, speak again."[89]

2 Nephi 29:11

God has placed various peoples throughout the world and spoken his words to them, and they have written those words. Out of all those written books God will judge the world, "every man according to their works." That last phrase sounds like poor grammar in English, but the use of collective nouns is a proper Hebrew construction. Revelation 20:13 has the exact same phrase.

2 Nephi 29:12–14

Jews (representing the tribe of Judah), Nephites (representing the tribes of Joseph—Ephraim and Manasseh), and "other tribes of the house of Israel" (representing all the rest) will receive the words of God. According to the law of witnesses, there will be two or three testaments of Jesus Christ, and the various peoples will at last have each others' writings. Not only will people be gathered back to their lands of inheritance, which is part of the great covenant, but God's words will be gathered together. All of this gathering—both peoples and records of the word of God—was also foreseen by Ezekiel (Ezekiel 37:16–22).

In our day, the gathering has been described in a revelation given through Joseph Smith:

"And they who are in the north countries shall come in remembrance before the Lord; and their prophets shall hear his voice, and shall no longer stay themselves; and they shall smite the rocks, and the ice shall flow down at their presence.

"And an highway shall be cast up in the midst of the great deep.

"Their enemies shall become a prey unto them,

"And in the barren deserts there shall come forth pools of living water; and the parched ground shall no longer be a thirsty land.

"And they shall bring forth their rich treasures unto the children of Ephraim, my servants.

"And the boundaries of the everlasting hills shall tremble at their presence.

"And there shall they fall down and be crowned with glory, even in Zion, by the hands of the servants of the Lord, even the children of Ephraim.

"And they shall be filled with songs of everlasting joy.

"Behold, this is the blessing of the everlasting God upon the tribes of Israel, and the richer blessing upon the head of Ephraim and his fellows" (D&C 133:26–34).

2 Nephi 30:1–7

Chapter 30 begins by teaching the doctrine of adoption as part of the gospel covenant. Adoption is a basic principle of the Abrahamic covenant. Jehovah said, "As many as receive this Gospel shall be called after thy name . . . and shall rise up and bless thee, as their father" (Abraham 2:10). Nephi taught that as many people as will repent and believe in the Messiah may become the covenant people of the Lord. Nephi then turned his prophetic eye to his own descendants.

When the Book of Mormon is distributed among father Lehi's descendants, some of them, a "remnant," will come to understand that they originated from Jerusalem and that "they are descendants of the Jews"—not in a tribal but in a national sense, or as part of the covenant people of Israel. They will be restored to a knowledge of their ancestors and their ancestors' God, Jesus Christ. Such knowledge will be a blessing, bringing them out of darkness into light, and some of them will become "a pure and a delightsome people." Thus, the doctrine of the gathering is complete: Israel is gathered to Christ through the Book of Mormon.

2 Nephi 30:9–15

Verse 9 recalls the Sermon on the Mount (Matthew 5:5) as well as the revelation called the Olive Leaf (D&C 88:17–18). Only the meek shall inherit the earth, which will become, in its celestialized state, the celestial kingdom for its inheritors and inhabitants. The wicked will be swept off. The time is quickly approaching when all inhabitants of the earth will have to declare themselves either for righteousness or against it and choose to become one of the meek or one of the wicked, causing a great division of the last days. Then comes the millennial reign of Christ. Here, Nephi once again highlights Isaiah's vision of conditions during the great Millennium, as recorded in Isaiah 11:4–9. See commentary at 2 Nephi 21:6–9.

2 Nephi 30:16–18

"In that day when the Lord shall come he shall reveal all things—things which have passed, and hidden things which no man knew" (D&C 101:32–33). "God shall give unto you knowledge by his Holy Spirit . . . that has not been revealed since the world was until now; which our forefathers have awaited with anxious expectation to be revealed in the last times, . . . a time to come in the which nothing shall be withheld" (D&C 121:26–28; see vv. 28–32 for details of great truths to be revealed).

The revelations of all dispensations will be restored in the millennial era, "and Satan shall have power over the hearts of the children of men no more, for a long time." For reasons why Satan will have no power during the Millennium, see commentary at 1 Nephi 22:24–28.

2 Nephi 31:1–3

Nephi ended his plain prophesying and his and his brother Jacob's doctrinal expositions with a few more words about the doctrine of Christ. He reminded us once again of his delight in plainness, noting that God himself speaks the same way. God speaks to men in their language, whether it be pure Adamic, Hebrew, reformed Egyptian, Greek, English, or any other tongue; he reveals at the level of humans' language ability and their spiritual understanding.

2 Nephi 31:4–12

Nephi had already previewed the ministry of John the Baptist, the prophet who would prepare the way before the Lamb of God (1 Nephi 10:7–10).

The need for everyone to be baptized is shown in the reasons why Jesus was baptized:

1. "To fulfil all righteousness"; compare Matthew 3:15: Jesus himself fulfilled all requirements for celestial glory.[90]

2. "He humbleth himself before the Father" (compare John 6:38; 8:28–29).

3. He "witnesseth unto the Father that he would be obedient unto him in keeping his commandments" (compare John 14:31; 15:9–10).

4. He "showeth unto the children of men the straitness of the path, and the narrowness of the gate, by which they should enter" (compare Matthew 7:13–14).

5. He "set the example before them" (compare John 13:15). The Savior can then say, "I am the way" (John 14:6); "Follow thou me" (compare John 21:22). And again, "Follow me, and do the things which ye have seen me do" (see also 3 Nephi 27:21). In other words, be baptized and obey all the other commandments, too.

2 Nephi 31:8

Just like Nephi, "John bare record, saying, I saw the Spirit descending from heaven like a dove, and it abode upon him" (John 1:32). John the Baptist saw the Holy Ghost descending; his spiritual eyes were opened to see pure, refined matter (D&C 131:7–8). According to the Prophet Joseph Smith, the dove is the sign of the Holy Ghost's presence and was instituted before this world was populated (see also commentary at 1 Nephi 11:27).[91] Thus, an actual dove was present at Jesus' baptism. "The sign of the dove, as an emblem for the Holy Ghost, was a pre-appointed signal by which John knew he was to recognize that he had baptized the Son of God."[92] "The personage of the Holy Ghost descended upon Christ with the grace of a dove, which imagery is chosen because the dove was present—it being the visible or outward sign of the presence of the Holy Ghost."[93]

2 Nephi 31:13

With sincere faith, repentance, baptism, and the Holy Ghost (symbolized by fire), "then can ye speak with the tongue of angels"; in other words, you are promised new language ability, the ability to speak with the facility and authority of heavenly messengers. See also 2 Nephi 32:2–5.

2 Nephi 31:17–18

Do the things your Redeemer did. He came to show us the way. The way, or the path, commences with a gate that must be entered, and the gate is faith, repentance, baptism by water, and baptism by fire—water and fire being two of the great cleansing agents we know. Doing all that, you are on the "strait and narrow path which leads to eternal life."

2 Nephi 31:19–21

Once you have entered the gate and are on the path, is that all there is to it? Have you done everything necessary? Of course not. Baptism allows you entrance into the kingdom of God, but there is more: receiving and obeying temple ordinances and covenants allows you entrance into the highest degree of the kingdom of God.

You have not even entered the gate and found yourself moving along the path except through the kindness and goodness of the Savior. Now you have to press forward, be firm and steadfast, develop hope and love for God and everyone else, feast on the Lord's words, be a faithful laborer in his temple, and *endure*. Endure what? Whatever comes, through the end of this life. Then what is the promise? "Ye shall have eternal life." And that is a promise that can be sealed or guaranteed by the Holy Spirit.

But, someone might ask, what if you slip off the path, or even intentionally deviate from it? Then recognize your error, make the course correction, repent and get back on the path, and move ahead. Knowing that we all slip—"all have sinned, and come short of the glory of God" (Romans 3:23)—the Savior has provided the way back, with full reward for anyone who comes back to him with full purpose of heart.

If you pay the price in time and effort to search the scriptures, you will see lasting benefits. "Whoso treasureth up my word, shall not be deceived" (Joseph Smith–Matthew 1:37), and "whoso would hearken unto the word of God, and would hold fast unto it, they would never perish; neither could the temptations and the fiery darts of the adversary overpower them" (1 Nephi 15:24).

Elder Bruce R. McConkie wrote: "May I suggest, based on personal experience, that faith comes and revelations are received as a direct result of scriptural study. . . . However talented men may be in administrative matters; however eloquent they may be in expressing their views; however learned they may be in worldly things—they will be denied the sweet whisperings of the Spirit that might have been theirs unless they pay the price of studying, pondering, and praying about the scriptures."[94]

2 Nephi 32

Do you want to increase your spirituality? This short chapter, which contains some of the last words of Nephi, his parting legacy to us, tells us how to do it. These verses emphasize "the doctrine of Christ," and the doctrine is given "in plainness, even as plain as word can be." You "feast upon the words of Christ," meaning daily scripture study, and you "pray always" to the Father, meaning daily prayer. But many members of the Church are not regularly studying scriptures, praying, fasting, and worshipping in the temple. Too many are nibbling but not feasting on these absolutely delicious and nutritious things God has given us to partake of. Former Salt Lake Temple president John K. Edmunds wrote, "Inactive goodness may lead to the terrestrial glory but never to the celestial."[95]

2 Nephi 32:1–5

Nephi testified that angels speak by the power of the Holy Ghost. There are two kinds of beings in heaven who are angels in the literal sense: (1) resurrected beings who have bodies of flesh and bone and (2) spirits of just men made perfect who have not yet been resurrected (D&C 129:1–3). Righteous mortals may also be called angels (JST, Genesis 19:15). All are filled with the power of the Holy Ghost.

In Hebrew the word translated into English as "angels" is *malachim,* which also means "messengers." Missionaries (which means all Latter-day Saints), for example, are messengers, so we may read this passage in this way: You, members and missionaries, speak by the power of the Holy Ghost; wherefore, you speak the words of Christ. In order to do that, you must feast upon the words of Christ; the words of Christ will guide you in all things that you should do. Now, if you do not understand these words, it is because you are not specifically asking; you are not knocking, or inquiring of God, so you are not invited into the light but instead remain out in the dark.

Regarding the power of the Holy Ghost we might ask, Is it involved in other functions and operations besides assisting angels to speak? The answer is an emphatic yes! We cannot even begin to grasp the powers and performances of the Holy Ghost.

On a personal level, this means that the power available to every baptized and confirmed member of the Church who has received the gift of the Holy Ghost is so great as to be almost incomprehensible.

Elder James E. Talmage made this stunning statement: "Through the power of the Spirit, the Father and the Son operate in their creative acts and in their general dealings with the human family. The Holy Ghost may be regarded as the minister of the Godhead, carrying into effect the decision of the Supreme Council.

"In the execution of these great purposes, the Holy Ghost directs and controls the varied forces of nature, of which indeed a few, and these perhaps of minor order wonderful as even the least of them appears to man, have thus far been investigated by mortals. Gravitation, sound, heat, light, and the still more mysterious and seemingly supernatural power of electricity, are but the common servants of the Holy Ghost in His operations. No earnest thinker, no sincere investigator supposes that he has yet learned of all the forces existing in and operating upon matter; indeed, the observed phenomena of nature, yet wholly inexplicable to him, far outnumber those for which he has devised even a partial explanation. There are powers and forces at the command of God, compared with which electricity is as the pack-horse to the locomotive, the foot messenger to the telegraph, the raft of logs to the ocean steamer. With all his scientific knowledge man knows but little respecting the enginery of creation; and yet the few forces known to him have brought about miracles and wonders, which but for their actual realization would be beyond belief. These mighty agencies, and the mightier ones still to man unknown, and many, perhaps, to the present condition of the human mind unknowable, do not constitute the Holy Ghost, but are the agencies ordained to serve His purposes."[96]

The scriptures contain answers to all problems and questions: "The words of Christ will tell you all things what ye should do." And how do the answers come? You store up the words, and when they are needed they will come. "The Holy Ghost . . . will show unto you all things what ye should do." The Beloved Apostle later recorded Jesus saying, "The Comforter, which is the Holy Ghost, . . . he shall teach you all things, and bring all things to your remembrance, whatsoever I have said unto you" (John 14:26).

THE HOLY GHOST

- **Title:** English *ghost* comes from Old High German *geist,* meaning "spirit"; *der Heilige Geist* would therefore mean "the Holy Spirit." The term *ghost* is used in the biblical phrase "give up the ghost." The Hebrew for "Holy Spirit" is *Ruakh haKodesh; ruakh* means "spirit" and "wind" (read John 3:8 for an interesting play on both meanings); *kodesh* means "holy," so the phrase signifies "the Holy Spirit."

- **Other titles:** The Spirit of God, the Spirit of the Lord, the Holy Spirit, the Spirit of Truth, and the Comforter.
- **Position:** Third member of the Godhead. He became a God without a body. He is a personage of Spirit in the form of a man.[97] He can be in only one place, though his influence can extend far and wide. Because the Holy Ghost is a male personage, he is referred to as "he," although it is proper to refer to the Spirit of God, in general, or the gift of the Holy Ghost as "it."[98]
- **Purposes:** All things are done by the *power* of the Holy Ghost (for example, "by the power of the Holy Ghost ye may know the truth of all things"; Moroni 10:5).[99] He is a revelator, a testifier, a comforter, and a sanctifier. He enlightens us to know the mysteries of godliness, and he delivers messages from the Father and the Son.
- **Definition:** The "gift of the Holy Ghost" is the right to the constant companionship of the Holy Ghost. The gift is conferred by the laying on of hands, and it operates through obedience.
- **Sign:** Dove
- **Symbol:** Fire
- **History:** From the beginning, Adam was full of the Holy Ghost (D&C 107:53–56). All the prophets had the Holy Ghost.[100] The gift was not needed when Christ was personally on earth but was received when he departed.[101]
- **Other:** The Second Comforter is Jesus Christ himself, received in conjunction with having one's calling and election made sure (receiving the more sure word of prophecy, or being sealed by the Holy Spirit of Promise).[102]

The Holy Ghost has no body of flesh and bone at present; we are instructed to avoid speculating about his origin or destiny.[103]

---

2 Nephi 32:6–7

Nephi taught the doctrine of Christ, and he noted that more of Christ's doctrine would be revealed after He came into mortality. Christ would then give teachings similar to what he gave for centuries, although there would be new doctrine, too, like vicarious work for the dead. Nephi lamented not being able to disclose more of the plain and powerful doctrine of Christ, but the Spirit would not allow him to continue because of the lack of preparation and unworthiness of men.

2 Nephi 32:8–9

"Ye must pray." President Brigham Young taught: "It matters not whether you or I feel like praying, when the time comes to pray, pray. If we do not feel like it, we should pray till we do. . . . You will find that those who wait till the Spirit bids them pray, will never pray much on this earth."[104]

2 Nephi 33:1–3

When a Latter-day Saint speaks by the power of the Holy Ghost, the power of the Holy Ghost carries the truth of the message to others' hearts. There are many who harden their hearts against the Holy Spirit, that it has no place in them, but even so we continue to work and pray continually for them, pleading that our efforts will be honored and will benefit them.

Elder David A. Bednar pointed out something important in the wording of Nephi's teaching: "Please notice how the power of the Spirit carries the message *unto* but not necessarily *into* the heart. A teacher can explain, demonstrate, persuade, and testify, and do so with great spiritual power and effectiveness. Ultimately, however, the content of a message and the witness of the Holy Ghost penetrate into the heart only if a receiver allows them to enter."[105]

2 Nephi 33:4–15

Nephi engraved his final testimony that these are the words of Christ, and to anyone who will not accept his testimony he bade "an everlasting farewell." At the last day, Christ himself will personally verify the truth of these things, and Nephi will be there at the judgment bar to confirm one final time that his testimony is true. All this is parallel to Moroni's same witness at the end of the Book of Mormon. He, too, testified of the truth of these things (Moroni 10:3–5), assuring everyone that at the last day Christ will show the truth of what is written (Moroni 10:29) Moroni, too, will be at the judgment bar to confirm one final time that his testimony is true (Moroni 10:27, 34). Nephi and Moroni stand as beginning and ending testators to this monumental testament of Jesus Christ.

THE BOOK OF JACOB

Jacob 1:1–5

Jacob was the elder of Lehi's two sons who were born in the wilderness (1 Nephi 18:7). He had endured great hardship and suffered much because of Laman and Lemuel (1 Nephi 18:19; 2 Nephi 2:1–2). Nevertheless, he was highly favored of God, for he enjoyed the visitation of angels and even saw the Lord (2 Nephi 10:3; 11:3). He was truly a kindred spirit with his brother Nephi. He stands as a model for us to follow today.

Fifty-five years after Lehi's colony left Jerusalem, Nephi instructed his brother Jacob (born ca. 595 B.C.) to continue inscribing on the small plates of Nephi the things he considered precious—sacred preachings, prophecies, and revelations. The central theme and purpose of the small plates was to focus on Christ for the sake of God's people.

Jacob 1:7

John the Revelator declared that "the testimony of Jesus is the spirit of prophecy" (Revelation 19:10), so all who have the spirit of prophecy are going to testify of Jesus and encourage all people to come unto him. Jacob confirmed, "We labored diligently among our people, that we might persuade them to come unto Christ, and partake of the goodness of God," making it possible to enter into his rest, which is the fulness of his glory (D&C 84:24).

Jacob 1:9–11

Having loved their great protector, Nephi, who had selflessly labored for their welfare all his days, the people desired to preserve his name as the revered name-title of their subsequent leaders. In much the same way, other ancient peoples had governmental rulers bearing such name-titles as Thutmose, Ramses, Ben-Hadad, Tiglath-pileser, Sargon, Darius, and Xerxes.

Jacob 1:15–19

The next generation started having serious challenges with unchastity, money, and pride, so Jacob and his brother Joseph, having been consecrated priests and teachers by Nephi and, as Jacob writes, "having obtained mine errand from the Lord," launched into a vigorous campaign to teach the doctrine of Christ and call their people to repentance. "We did magnify [amplify, strengthen] our office unto the Lord, taking upon us the responsibility, answering the sins of the people upon our own heads if we did not teach them the word of God with all diligence"; otherwise, they could be held responsible for the sins of the people by not raising the warning voice. President John Taylor taught, "If you do not magnify your callings, God will hold you responsible for those whom you might have saved had you done your duty."[1]

Similarly, the Lord reminded parents how seriously they must take the charge to teach diligently those in their care, lest their children's misdeeds be placed upon their own heads. "And again, inasmuch as parents have children in Zion, or in any of her stakes which are organized, that teach them not to understand the doctrine of repentance, faith in Christ the Son of the living God, and of baptism and the gift of the Holy Ghost by the laying on of the hands, when eight years old, the sin be upon the heads of the parents" (D&C 68:25).

Jacob 2:2–11

Chapters 1–3 constitute Jacob's temple sermon. Little wonder, then, that he spent so much time discussing marriage and family life. Stunningly, every one of the principles and doctrinal points Jacob discussed is grounded in the temple endowment as we know it today.

Jacob felt a serious responsibility, as he said, "to magnify [his] office with soberness," so he taught his people in the holy temple (Jacob 2:2; 1:17). It becomes clearer and clearer in the next verses that Jacob was a sensitive person and felt the burden of denouncing their sins: "I this day am weighed down with much more desire and anxiety for the welfare of your souls than I have hitherto been." God had revealed to him their thoughts, how they were "beginning to labor in sin" and turning to things abominable; "I must testify unto you concerning the wickedness of your hearts."

The sensitivity of Jacob's righteous soul is evident in the vocabulary he used and the way he expressed himself quite differently from any other writer in the Book of Mormon: "It grieveth me that I must use so much boldness of speech concerning you, before your wives and your children, many of whose feelings are exceedingly tender and chaste and delicate before God . . . ; and it supposeth me that they have come up hither to hear the pleasing word of God, yea, the word which healeth the wounded soul." This Book of Mormon record is indeed full of the pleasing word of God that heals wounded souls.

With some of the most gentle, sympathetic, and loving words in all of scripture, Jacob lamented, "It burdeneth my soul that I should be constrained, because of the strict commandment which I have received from God, to admonish you according to your crimes, to enlarge the wounds of those who are already wounded, instead of consoling and healing their wounds; and those who have not been wounded, instead of feasting upon the pleasing word of God have daggers placed to pierce their souls and wound their delicate minds."

As hard as it was, Jacob had to bear down on their wickedness, even in the hearing of "the pure in heart, and the broken heart, and under the glance of the piercing eye of the Almighty God."

Elder Dallin H. Oaks explained the intent of Church authorities as they teach members: "A message given by a General Authority at a general conference—a message prepared under the influence of the Spirit to further the work of the Lord—is not given to be enjoyed. It is given to inspire, to edify, to challenge, or to correct. It is given to be heard under the influence of the Spirit of the Lord, with the intended result that the listener learns from the talk and from the Spirit what he or she should *do* about it."[2]

Jacob 2:12–16

Jacob's temple discourse condemns his people's propensity to go after precious metals, become rich and prideful, be "lifted up," wear "stiff necks and high heads," and think themselves better than others. Notice a frequently mentioned manifestation of that pride from which they suffered: "the costliness of your apparel."

It seems that living in luxury may be the most severe test that any people will pass through. Knowing how luxury living distracts even covenant people from the things that matter most, cankering and destroying their souls, God soundly condemns it.

Jacob 2:17–19

In his temple discourse on pride and riches, the prophet Jacob taught this vital doctrine: what do you seek first? or, what are your priorities? Whatever they are, they determine your destiny. Your first priority should always be to build the kingdom of God (JST, Matthew 6:38). Then, if you want riches, you can have them. But you will want them to do good and help others, especially your own family. It seems like the greatest help any of us can give to others will always, in some way, point to the quest for eternal life. In this dispensation the Lord says: "Seek not for riches but for wisdom; and, behold, the mysteries of God shall be unfolded unto you, and then shall you be made rich. Behold, he that hath eternal life is rich" (D&C 11:7).

Jacob listed four proper uses of money:

1. To clothe the naked (first your family, then your relatives, then your ward, and then those lacking clothes elsewhere).

2. To feed the hungry (first your family, then your relatives, then your ward, and then those lacking food elsewhere).

3. To liberate the captive, not necessarily serving in the Church's meetinghouse in a local prison but helping to liberate those who are emotionally and spiritually captive, such as to sin or addiction.

4. To administer relief to the sick and the afflicted (in your family and among your ward members and neighbors).

King Benjamin gave a similar list of what to do with the resources with which you have been blessed (Mosiah 4:26). Wealth itself is not condemned. It is neutral. It is our attitude toward it that matters. Everything we ever get belongs to God in the first place. We must be *willing* to share all we have with others. That is consecration.

A superb illustration of compliance to the doctrine in Jacob 2:17–19 is the story of Rubén Álvarez, who in the late 1990s served as the stake president in Puerto Montt, Chile. He was a missionary from Viña del Mar who was assigned to the Osorno Mission some years before. After his mission, he studied at the university in Antofagasta and became an engineer in water agriculture in order to work in the salmon industry in Chile. When he went for an interview with one of the big salmon companies, he was one of fifty-four applicants for the job. After initial interviews he was one of four called back for another interview in Santiago. He got the job and moved to southern Chile with his bride. Before accepting the job, though, he told the managers, "I'll give you every day, even nights, except one—the Sabbath." They liked his honesty and character. The closest church was seventeen kilometers away from Rubén's home. He and his wife walked to church and back every week, even through heavy rains, because they were committed to following God. After seven months they were transferred to Chiloe, another city in the south, where he was made the branch president. They prospered financially. People told him he had good luck. He told them it was not luck; it was obedience to God's laws: faithful observance of the Sabbath and faithful payment of tithing.

One stormy night, he got a call that a four-hundred-pound sea lion had broken into the salmon cages submerged off the coast (the giant cages were worth about two million dollars each). He grabbed his big shotgun and headed to the beach. He and his crew got into their boats and made for the cages. The laws prohibited Rubén from killing any sea lion, so every time it came up for air, he shot into the water as close to it as he dared. But the shots had no effect. The company stood to lose huge sums of money; a four-hundred-pound sea lion can eat a lot of salmon.

Rubén put down his gun and walked away from the others to pray. With tears streaming down his face, he reminded the Lord that he had been faithful in all his duties as a true disciple: "I've paid my tithing; I've kept the Sabbath." He pleaded with the Lord to help him. As he got up from his knees, he felt an incredible warmth blanketing him. He walked back, and his workers grabbed him excitedly to tell him that the sea lion had left. When the scuba divers checked the damaged cages, they found them full of salmon.

Malachi 3:11 records the Lord's promise to those who are loyal to the law of tithes and offerings: "I will rebuke the devourer for your sake."

Jacob 2:20–21

How can anyone be proud? Proud of what? If we become proud because of all the things we possess, we must remember that they are not actually ours; all things belong to our Creator. If we start thinking we are better than someone else, we must remember that "the one being is as precious in [God's] sight as the other." The heavenly counsel to everyone is, as Paul wrote, "not to think of himself more highly than he ought to think" (Romans 12:3). "For if a man think himself to be something, when he is nothing, he deceiveth himself" (Galatians 6:3). And the Lord warns in our day, "If any man shall seek to build up himself, and seeketh not my counsel, he shall have no power, and his folly shall be made manifest" (D&C 136:19).

Jacob 2:22–26

After riches and pride, Jacob moved on to speak of a grosser crime. His people were trying to excuse and justify their immoral behavior by citing the examples of their royal progenitors David and Solomon, who had numerous wives and concubines. Jacob declared that "David and Solomon truly had many wives and concubines, which thing was abominable before . . . the Lord." A modern-day revelation clarifies and qualifies exactly what was abominable in their marital relationships: "David also received many wives and concubines, and also Solomon and Moses my servants, as also many others of my servants, from the beginning of creation until this time; and *in nothing did they sin save in those things which they received not of me*" (D&C 132:38; emphasis added). It is important to realize that the law of plural marriage is not condemned, but David's and Solomon's handling of the law, or their abuses of the law, is condemned (see also Deuteronomy 7:1–4; 17:17; 1 Kings 11:1–6, noting JST corrections).

Political leaders, priests, and prophets in the Near East about the same time as Jacob (for example, Ezra, Nehemiah, and Malachi) had to deal with similar abuses of marriage laws, marriages out of the covenant, divorces, and so on (Ezra 9:1–2, 12; Nehemiah 9:1–2; 13:23–27; Malachi 2:14–16).

Jacob explained the Lord's desire for the descendants of father Lehi: "I have led this people forth out of the land of Jerusalem, by the power of mine arm, that I might raise up unto me a righteous branch from the fruit of the loins of Joseph. Wherefore, I the Lord God will not suffer that this people shall do like unto them of old."

Jacob 2:27–30

The marriage law given to the Nephites was one man and one woman—one husband and one wife. Joseph Smith taught, "I have constantly said no man shall have but one wife at a time, unless the Lord directs otherwise."[3] Occasionally the Lord has directed otherwise, in ancient and in modern times. Monogamy has been the rule, and plural marriage the exception. The latter is to be practiced only when the Lord authorizes it, as in the case of the patriarchs Abraham, Isaac, and Jacob. The reason for the law of plural marriage is clearly stated in verse 30: to "raise up seed unto me."

The Biblical World: An Illustrated Atlas features an article entitled "Polygamy in the Bible," which says: "Throughout the Old Testament we read of patriarchs taking several wives. . . . Such polygamy was most likely motivated by the need to produce sufficient children to control the tribe's principal asset[s]. . . . Childbirth was fraught with danger for both new mothers and infants. Many children were carried away by disease while still in their infancy, and many women died during childbirth. Tribes practiced polygamy as a way of sustaining themselves and ensuring the survival of the clan."[4]

In modern revelation the Lord elaborates on the reasoning behind any man's being instructed to take more than one wife: "They are given unto him to multiply and replenish the earth, according to my commandment, and to fulfil the promise which was given by my Father before the foundation of the world, and for their exaltation in the eternal worlds, that they may bear the souls of men; for herein is the work of my Father continued, that he may be glorified" (D&C 132:63).

Jacob 2:31–35

In eloquently poetic but powerfully condemnatory language, the Lord rebukes and pronounces curses on the men, husbands, and fathers among the Nephites and all other peoples who have adulterated the sacred bonds of marriage, even surpassing the Lamanites in abominable behavior: "Ye have broken the hearts of your tender wives, and lost the confidence of your children, because of your bad examples before them; and the sobbings of their hearts ascend up to God against you. And because of the strictness of the word of God, which cometh down against you, many hearts died, pierced with deep wounds."

Things haven't changed much. With adultery, pornography, and various other forms of abuse, modern men continue to break the hearts of their wives.

To be absolutely clear, Alma 39:3–5 describes adultery and fornication as most serious sins, "abominable above all sins save it be the shedding of innocent blood or denying the Holy Ghost." Doctrine and Covenants 42:22–26 outlines Church discipline for adulterers.

On the other hand, it must also be made clear that there is very little, if anything, that is beyond the power of the Atonement to cleanse and heal—for those who seek it. The qualifier here is those who seek it. Those who deny the Holy Ghost will not, by definition, seek it—all the rest are able to be tucked safely under the warm blanket of the Atonement, with the assurance that the Lord will remember the sin no more. In fact, priesthood leaders who work with the repentant, even those with extraordinary memories, are blessed to remember no more the transgressions of those with whom they have counseled and who truly repent.

Elder F. Burton Howard of the Seventy told the following

story in general conference about a time when he served as bishop:

"One night, while I was in a sound sleep, the doorbell rang. I stumbled to answer it and found a young member of my priests quorum at the door. . . .

"He said, 'I have to talk to you, bishop. I've just done something serious, and I can't go home.'

"He was right. It was serious. I invited him in, and we talked. . . . He had many questions. He had committed a terrible sin. He wanted to know if there was hope. He wanted to know how to repent. . . . He wanted to know many other things.

"I didn't have all of the answers, but I told him there was hope. I told him the way back would be difficult, but it was possible. I explained what I knew about the process of repentance and helped him see what he must do. . . . Then I told him to go home, and he did.

"He made his peace with his parents. He asked forgiveness from those he had wronged. He put sin and bad company behind him and did everything he could to repent.

"A year or so later, five young men from that quorum went on missions. He was one of them. I was close to them all. . . . They all served honorable missions. Within a brief time after returning home, they all were married in the temple. My wife and I attended each of the ceremonies. I could take a piece of paper, even today, and write their names and the names of their wives and some of their children. That is how well I knew them.

"But now let me tell you something—something very private and very important. I cannot remember the name of the young man who came to my home in the middle of the night. I know he was one of the five, but I don't remember which one.

"There was a time I used to worry about that. I thought perhaps my memory might be failing. I consciously tried to recall who it was that had the problem, but I could not.

"I was eventually released, and I put the entire incident out of my mind. On a late evening walk some years later, I found myself in the ward where I had once been bishop. The shadowy quiet brought back many memories. I was deep in thought when I realized I was walking in front of a house where one of my priests had lived years before. Suddenly, the story of the young man I have mentioned came to mind, and again I tried to remember which of the five he had been. Had he lived in that house? I wondered. Why couldn't I remember?

"As I continued on my way, something happened— something difficult to explain, but real to me. I seemed to hear a voice which said: 'Don't you understand, my son? I have forgotten that. Why should you remember?'"[5]

Jacob 3:1–2

And now a few words to the pure in heart: Even though your hearts have been wounded, "lift up your heads" and "look unto God," and "he will console you" as you "feast upon his love." You can do this "if your minds are firm." Firmness of mind is a heavenly attribute. It may also be described with words such as *dependability, reliability, trustworthiness, steadfastness, unwaveringness, soundness, stability,* and *constancy.* The scriptures are clear that the Lord values this divine attribute of firmness.

While serving as a mission president in Santiago, Chile, Brother Ogden spoke with two missionaries, an elder and a sister, who expressed to him their doubts. They were not sure of the things they were teaching others, and they said they were not certain what they should do about it. He told the missionaries that they did know what to do about it: They must do exactly what they taught others to do. They must pray with more vigor than ever; they must search the scriptures diligently; they must fast with this specific purpose; and they must not doubt. It was all right that they were struggling with their testimonies—the scriptures contain a number of examples of those who struggled in the Spirit—but *they must not doubt.*

Doubt is spiritual poison. Questioning is fine; by asking questions we get answers (though not *all* answers, just what the Lord, in his wisdom, allows for now). But doubt is the opposite of what we need: faith. There is a powerful scriptural concept here: being *firm of mind* (Jacob 3:2; Moroni 7:30). Mormon wrote about "doubting nothing." He said, "Doubt not, but be believing" (Mormon 9:21, 27). And the Lord added, "Look unto me in every thought; doubt not" (D&C 6:36). We all have to grow *firmer and firmer in the faith*, nothing doubting.

Jacob 3:3–11

The Nephites were chastised and condemned for being filthy, far more than the Lamanites who held to higher family values: husbands and wives loved each other and were faithful to each other, and parents loved their children. Because the Lamanites in general showed more fidelity in basic familial relationships, "God will not destroy them . . . and one day they shall become a blessed people."

Jacob feared that unless the Nephites repented, the Lamanites would be "whiter" than they in the day of judgment—*whiter* meaning fairer, purer, and more delightsome (2 Nephi 5:21; 30:6). The prophet warned his people to avoid prejudice and to focus more on removing their own filthiness. He warned them that their filthy example might result in their children's turning from the Lord and being destroyed, with the children's sins being heaped upon the parents' heads at the last day (see also D&C 68:25).

In verse 11 Jacob issued a stern wake-up call to his brethren. Note the verbs *arouse, shake,* and *awake,* signaling that they had better do something quickly and urgently or else they were headed to a second death, a spiritual death, a prolonged and painful commitment to the devil in hell.

The first death that came upon Adam and Eve after their

transgression in Eden was a spiritual death. They were cast out of Eden and out of God's presence, becoming dead as to spiritual things. But Christ's atonement redeemed our first parents, as well as all humankind, from the first death. The realization of the blessings resulting from Christ's redemption from the first death is yet future for most of us.

The prophet Samuel the Lamanite taught:

"For behold, he surely must die that salvation may come; yea, it behooveth him and becometh expedient that he dieth, to bring to pass the resurrection of the dead, that thereby men may be brought into the presence of the Lord.

"Yea, behold, this death bringeth to pass the resurrection, and redeemeth all mankind from the first death—that spiritual death; for all mankind, by the fall of Adam being cut off from the presence of the Lord, are considered as dead, both as to things temporal and to things spiritual.

"But behold, the resurrection of Christ redeemeth mankind, yea, even all mankind, and bringeth them back into the presence of the Lord" (Helaman 14:15–17).

Jacob 3:12

The authors know from personal experience that at times a kind of carefree attitude toward morality has been exhibited by some Latter-day Saints—one that says, "Oh, I can sin now, and I can always repent later; it only takes a few months of waiting and I can go on a mission, or I can enter the temple." Our minds return to the words of Jacob, who also felt the urgency to warn his people about the inevitable outcome of their behavior: "[As] ye look upon me as a teacher, it must needs be expedient that I teach you the consequences of sin" (2 Nephi 9:48). "And now I, Jacob, spake many . . . things unto the people of Nephi, warning them against fornication and lasciviousness [looseness, lustfulness, immoral desires], and every kind of sin, telling them the awful consequences of them" (Jacob 3:12).

Jacob 4:1

Jacob said, "I cannot write but a little of my words, because of the difficulty of engraving our words upon plates," but then he engraved Jacob 5, the longest chapter in the whole Book of Mormon, which says something about the relative value he placed on that great allegory.

Jacob 4:2–3

As other ancient civilizations also discovered, whatever was engraved on metal plates could be preserved indefinitely. In contrast, our modern civilization for many years has specialized in preserving valuable records on plastic, which has a relatively brief life.

Book of Mormon scholar Paul R. Cheesman wrote that "it is evident that a knowledge of any ancient culture writing on metal, anywhere in the world, was not public knowledge at [the time of Joseph Smith]. . . .

". . . In America, Joseph Smith stood alone in his bold declaration that he had found:

- an ancient record written in an Egyptian language which had been reformed and condensed.
- a record engraved on thin sheets of gold.
- a record bound with metal rings.
- a record placed in a stone box."[6]

Every one of Joseph Smith's claims has been substantiated by archaeological evidence and the discovery of items of material culture. After a four-month tour of European and Asian museums, Brother Cheesman wrote that an "exciting feature of almost any large European museum for Latter-day Saints is the surprisingly large number of metal plates or tablets with writing engraved on them."[7] From the Louvre to the Vatican Library to repositories in Seoul, there are hundreds of samples of metal plates (gold, silver, copper, and bronze) that have survived, inscribed with ancient languages dating from the third millennium B.C. Metal rings to hold several metal leaves together have now been discovered, along with stone boxes to hold plates. Brother Cheesman wrote that the "Plates of Darius I, ruler of Persia from 518–515 B.C., are the closest parallel to the Book of Mormon yet discovered. Two tablets, one of gold and one of silver, were placed in each stone box to be buried at the four corners of his palace. They describe the boundaries of his kingdom, praise Ahuramazda, 'the greatest of all the gods,' and pray protection upon Darius 'and [his] royal house.' They were discovered by an archaeological team in 1938."[8] They are now housed in the National Archaeological Museum, Tehran, Iran.

Jacob explained his desire to record important events and lessons from his life so that his children and "beloved brethren" could "learn with joy and not with sorrow, neither with contempt, concerning their first parents." We believe that Jacob's message and example teach powerfully the value of carefully preparing a personal journal—so that many generations may come to know their parents, grandparents, great-grandparents, and so on; so that we can share something with our children that will inspire and uplift and encourage; so that they may have an example of a flawed character, a person with weaknesses, who was nevertheless trying hard to overcome his or her flaws.

Jacob 4:4

These early Nephite prophets and Saints "knew of Christ" and "had a hope of his glory many hundred years before his coming," as did "all the holy prophets which were before us." Christ's coming into mortality was not a hidden or secret thing; "to him," said Peter, "give all the prophets witness" (Acts 10:43). Those who had ears to hear were hearing the glad tidings for centuries, even millennia, before his actual arrival in person. See also commentary at Jacob 7:8–12 and Mosiah 13:33.

Jacob 4:5

The true nature of the Godhead was known for ages: the Father and the Son were known to be separate individuals, and the Father was worshiped in the name of the Son (Moses 1:17; 5:8). Even the law of Moses had as its basic purpose to point all souls to Christ. See also commentary at Mosiah 13:28–33.

Abraham's near-sacrifice of his beloved son Isaac was a similitude of the Father's sacrifice of his beloved Only Begotten Son. In fact, this is such an impressive and important likeness that in the book of Hebrews, Isaac is referred to as Abraham's "only begotten son" (Hebrews 11:17). In addition, the episode stands as a supreme example of the kind of personal, total sacrifice required of all true disciples (D&C 101:4–5). The Prophet Joseph Smith stated, "The sacrifice required of Abraham in the offering up of Isaac, shows that if a man would attain to the keys of the kingdom of an endless life; he must sacrifice all things."[9]

Elder Bruce R. McConkie wrote: "I would suppose that among faithful people in ancient Israel, through all the ages from Abraham's day onward, the favored illustration and the favored text to teach the people that the Only Begotten Son would be sacrificed to bring immortality to men would be the story of Abraham. There is nothing more dramatic than this in the whole biblical account."[10]

Jacob 4:6–8

Jacob's testimony is much like Ether's. God grants his servants great power to accomplish his work, although he also shows us our weaknesses so we will be humble and remember by whose grace we are able to exercise that power (Ether 12:27). Our unshaken faith, which comes by searching the scriptures, receiving revelations, and possessing the spirit of prophecy, empowers us to do the works of God, even to the point of miraculous control over trees, mountains, and waves of the sea. Some of the necessary understanding of the great and marvelous works of the Lord—the mysteries of godliness—is revealed to us in the holy temple.

Jacob 4:14–18

The stumblings and fall of the Jewish people in general are clarified. Some of the Jews "despised the words of plainness" and even killed their source of those plain truths, the prophets. Consequently, they became spiritually blinded. Elder Neal A. Maxwell observed that the Jews were "'looking beyond the mark' (Jacob 4:14)—the mark of Christ, who is at the center of it all."[11] So "the mark" was the Messiah, and many of them are still looking beyond him. They continue to stumble and fall because they "reject the stone upon which they might build and have safe foundation." The apostle Paul said Christ became their stumbling block rather than their foundation stone (1 Corinthians 1:22–23). The stone, or the rock, is "the great, and the last, and the only sure foundation, upon which the Jews can build." Helaman later testified, "Remember that it is upon the rock of our Redeemer, who is Christ, the Son of God, that ye must build your foundation; . . . which is a sure foundation, a foundation whereon if men build they cannot fall" (Helaman 5:12). Christ, the Redeemer, becomes for the Jews, and for all people, either a stone of building or a stone of stumbling, either a rock of salvation or a rock of offense (Isaiah 8:14 [2 Nephi 18:14]; 1 Peter 2:8). He is the "head of [our] corner," our "chief corner stone . . . in whom all [our] building fitly framed together groweth unto an holy temple in the Lord" (Ephesians 2:20–21).

The imagery of the cornerstone was so pervasive and of such significance in Israelite-Jewish culture that it forms the core of the great Hallel (Psalms 113–18), sung by Jews at Passover (Psalm 118:22; Mark 14:26). Jesus used it in his teachings (Matthew 21:42–44), and Peter referenced it as well (Acts 4:10–12).

Jacob 5

Modern prophets have acclaimed Jacob 5 as the greatest teaching story ever recorded, and it is among the greatest passages in the Book of Mormon. It contains the history of the people of Israel in an extended allegory—a story using symbols. An allegory is a continued metaphor. Unlike a parable, every object or idea in an allegory represents something. Every point can have its own meaning. The images continue to build on each other, each adding meaning and leading to a climax or a conclusion.

The overall purpose of the allegory—why Jacob went to all the work of inscribing a seventy-seven-verse exposition—is to help the Jews and everyone else to pick themselves back up after their stumbling and to repent and return to their true Messiah. Some Jewish leaders and teachers had made God into an incomprehensible mystery, an impersonal, nebulous being. Jacob unveiled the mystery of who God is and how we relate to him and potentially become as he is. This long chapter is not just about olive trees; it is about our Savior and his constant love for his people. It shows how much he loves us and what he has done to save us.

The following study outline might be helpful.

ALLEGORY OF THE OLIVE TREE

Source: The prophet Zenos, from the plates of brass. Zenos was a great prophet in the land of Israel before the time of Lehi, and he is referred to or quoted twelve times in the Book of Mormon, not only by Jacob but also by Nephi (1 Nephi 19:10, 12, 16), Alma (Alma 33:3, 13, 15), Amulek (Alma 34:7), Samuel the Lamanite (Helaman 15:11), and Mormon (3 Nephi 10:16). Zenos demonstrated tremendous literary skill in the presentation of this allegory.

Theme: The history of Israel, its people's scattering and gathering, and their centuries-long quest to know and become one with their Master, the Lord of the vineyard, Jesus Christ.

Basic stipulation of a covenant people in a promised land: Keeping the Lord's commandments results in blessings, prosperity, and safety; disobedience brings cursings, degeneration, and removal from the land (Deuteronomy 28; 2 Nephi 1:9–11; Ether 2:9–12).

Examples of removal because of disobedience: the kingdom of Israel, in 735–721 B.C. (2 Kings 15, 17); the kingdom of Judah, in 605–586 B.C. (2 Kings 24, 25); the Jaredite nation, in the first millennium B.C. (Ether 15); the Jewish nation, again, in the first and second century A.D. (Matthew 24; Luke 21:20); the Nephite nation, in the fourth century A.D. (Mormon 6).

Allegory: Throughout the scriptures and rabbinic writings the olive tree has been used as a type or symbol of the people of Israel (see commentary at 1 Nephi 10:12–14). Though it is necessary to prune, cultivate, and nourish the olive tree for ten to fifteen years before it becomes fully productive, it can then flourish and produce fruit for many centuries. Indeed, even after aging, the gnarled old trunks will continue to see fresh, new shoots coming out of the roots (compare Isaiah 11:1). In this way the olive tree can go on producing not just for hundreds but for thousands of years. Even if its trunk is cut down, with proper grafting and pruning it will persist in producing good fruit. Though the people of Israel were repeatedly cut down and seemingly destroyed, new shoots grew out of the roots.

Ancient Greece and Rome and modern America have used the symbol of an olive branch to denote peace. In the great seal of the United States, an eagle is shown clutching an olive branch in its talons.

Understanding the allegory: Note the following symbols and their meanings in the margin of your scriptures, and then read and ponder the entire story of God's covenant relationship with his people Israel.

BASIC SYMBOLS IN JACOB'S ALLEGORY

Jacob 5	Figure or Symbol	Meaning	Explanation
v. 3	tame olive tree	house of Israel (covenant Israel)	Jacob 6:1
v. 3	vineyard	the earth, the world	Jacob 6:3
v. 3	decay	wickedness, apostasy	
v. 4	master of vineyard	Jehovah/Jesus	D&C 104:86
vv. 4, 5	pruning, digging, and nourishing	work of the Master and servants to save the people	
v. 7	servant(s)	prophet(s)	Amos 3:7; Jacob 6:2; D&C 1:38
v. 7	wild olive tree	Gentiles	Romans 11:13, 17, 19
vv. 7, 9	fire, burning	judgment, exile, death, destruction	
vv. 8, 36	roots of the tree	original gospel covenants	
vv. 8, 9	grafting natural branches into wild trees	branches of Israel dispersed among Gentiles	1 Nephi 10:12–14; 15:12–13
	grafting wild branches into the tame olive tree	Gentiles adopted into Israel	
v. 17	good fruit	good works	

History of Israel in the Old Testament Period

Jacob 5:1. Zenos was a prophet of Israel sometime before the seventh century B.C. whose writings were engraved on the plates of brass.

Verse 8. Examples of branches broken off and grafted elsewhere: Ten Tribes, Lehite colony, and Mulek's group.

Verse 14. Natural branches hidden in nethermost (lowest) parts refers to the scattering of Israel. Read 2 Nephi 10:22.

Verse 15. Centuries pass.

History of Israel in the New Testament Period

Verse 16. The Lord personally comes to the vineyard to labor.

Verses 17–18. Time of the early Christian church; Jews and Gentiles together produce good fruit (the word *fruit* appears more than sixty times and is the most important word in the allegory).

Verses 19–23. Various branches of Israel visited (other sheep); much good fruit is produced.

Verses 24–25. Nephites and Lamanites (part of this tree brought forth "wild fruit"; see Helaman 15:3–4).

Verse 29. Many centuries pass (Dark Ages).

History of Israel through the Millennium

Verse 29. The servant is Joseph Smith (D&C 101:55; 103:21).

Verses 30–32. Divergent Christian churches stemming from the original, all apostate; "there is none of it which is good"; that is what the Lord told Joseph Smith (Joseph Smith–History 1:19)

Verses 33–37. Roots overpowered by wild branches, resulting in bad fruit, though the roots are still good.

Verses 38–39. The various branches of Israel again visited; all corrupt.

Verse 40. The wicked among Lehi's descendants had overcome the righteous.

Verses 41, 47, 49. Compare the very same lament in the allegory recorded by Isaiah (5:1–7).

Verse 42. Universal apostasy among all branches of the Lord's trees.

Verses 43–45. Lehite colony planted in choice land (the Americas); former inhabitants (Jaredites) removed to plant the new branch; now the bad fruit had overcome the good.

Verses 46–48. Universal apostasy caused by haughtiness and pride.

Verses 49–51. The grieving Lord relents and spares the vineyard a little longer (compare a similar decision in the parable of wheat and tares; see D&C 86:4–7).

Verses 52–56. Scattered branches of Israel brought together into a worldwide Church.

Verses 57–69. The Lord and servants labor diligently, cultivating and pruning the vineyard for the last time (Jacob 6:2–3; D&C 24:19).

Verses 70–72. Particularly important message for our day; "other servants" were relatively few (Matthew 9:37); the Lord of the vineyard labors with his servants, who are strictly obedient.

Verses 73–75. Faithful Church members in the last days; Saints rejoice with the Lord; missionaries work to help convert terrestrial-level souls until all inhabitants become obedient citizens of God's kingdom.

Verse 76. The Millennium.

Verse 77. End of the Millennium; final cleansing by fire (this earth burned at the beginning and at the end of the Millennium, meaning shifting from telestial to terrestrial, then from terrestrial to celestial).

Jacob 6:3–7, 11. Jacob's testimony about the teachings of Zenos.

Jacob 6:1–3

Chapter 6 centers on the theme of the gathering of Israel in the last days in preparation for the end of the world and the great day of burning. Jacob prophesied that the concepts in Zenos's allegory will actually become history. The Lord will recover and restore Israel, and then the end of the world will come. A blessing is pronounced on the laborers in the vineyard, among them the missionaries who labor diligently and with the Lord's power during this last time of nourishing and pruning. "Nourish" appears twenty-two times throughout Jacob's allegory, making the concept one of the main messages of Zenos's elaborate analogy. How are you helping in the nourishing process?

Jacob 6:4–11

Despite the fact that the house of Israel is stiffnecked (prideful, stubborn) and gainsaying (disagreeable, rebellious), God mercifully reaches out to them, both roots (ancestors) and branches (descendants) of his eternal family tree, promising that if they are not hard-hearted, they can be saved in his kingdom. Jacob calls on his people to repent and "cleave unto God as he cleaveth unto you." "Cleave" is an interesting word, with two quite opposite meanings: it can mean to divide asunder (Zechariah 14:4; D&C 45:48), and (as here) it can also mean to hold tight (D&C 11:19; 98:11)—in this case hold tightly to God, be reconciled to him and be at one with him (on *at-one-ment*, see commentary at Mosiah 15:2–9).

In verses 6–9, Jacob asked a series of pointed questions. His people had sobering choices to make—whether to accept or reject God's words, his power, and his great plan of redemption.

If we do not live to merit the mercy of Christ, then "justice cannot be denied," and we will suffer the consequences of hell, characterized by fire, brimstone, flames, smoke, and torment. For more on the "lake of fire and brimstone," see commentary at Mosiah 3:27.

Jacob 6:13

Jacob bade us farewell until he meets us before the pleasing bar of God; compare similar expressions from Nephi (2 Nephi 33:14) and Moroni (Ether 12:38; Moroni 10:34).

Jacob 7

It appears that Jacob had intended to conclude his writings at the end of chapter 6. But then, some years later, Sherem appeared on the scene, and Jacob added that episode and his prophetic commentary. Thus, this chapter presents the first of three classic examples of priestcraft—a man setting himself up as a light to the world and denying Christ, who is the true Light of the world (see also Nehor, in Alma 1, and Korihor, in Alma 30). Sherem was an antichrist who taught people to reject their Savior. He was eloquent and used flattery and powerful speech. He denied the gift of prophetic preview. Sherem was an idolater and adulterer; he demanded a sign (see commentary at Jacob 7:13–17).

Jacob 7:4

Flattery may be defined as excessive praise motivated by self-interest, with the intent to manipulate people for selfish purposes.

Jacob 7:5–7

Sherem attempted to arrange a meeting with Jacob for the purpose of undermining his testimony, but the prophet had received too many revelations and conducted too many interviews with angels to be dissuaded from what he knew. The Lord himself had personally spoken to Jacob, so he was unshakable—as we, too, can be as we daily feel God's love through our obedience.

Sherem approached "Brother Jacob" in a false spirit of

brotherhood and challenged his preaching of "the gospel, or the doctrine of Christ." The antichrist held up the law of Moses as "the right way" and labeled as blasphemous the future coming of a Messiah, "for no man knoweth of such things; for he cannot tell of things to come."

In fact, that is the message of secular learning today: logic dictates that there is no such thing as predictive prophecy or supernatural events. If you can't see it or quantify it, it isn't true (an unfortunate inheritance from the Age of Reason). Such is the basic premise of all unbelievers—that prophetic preview is impossible (compare Alma 30:13). Believers, on the other hand, know that God has perfect foreknowledge of all things (see commentary at 2 Nephi 9:20) and that he can and does give revelation of future events and future personalities to those who need to know and are worthy to know.

Jacob 7:8–12

Through the power of the Holy Ghost, Jacob confounded Sherem and affirmed the witness of the scriptures that all true prophets have testified of Christ. In fact, "none of the prophets have written, nor prophesied, save they have spoken concerning this Christ" (see also commentary at Mosiah 13:33).

Jacob 7:13–17

Sherem mockingly responded, "Show me a sign by this power of the Holy Ghost, in the which ye know so much." The Prophet Joseph Smith taught, "Whenever you see a man seeking after a sign, you may set it down that he is an adulterous man."[12] There is a difference, of course, between those who are sincerely seeking a sign, meaning a spiritual confirmation or witness of heavenly truth, and those who are just looking to satisfy their vain curiosity. The prophets condemn the latter.

President Joseph F. Smith wrote concerning sign-seekers: "It is a wicked and adulterous generation that seeketh after a sign. Show me Latter-day Saints who have to feed upon miracles, signs and visions in order to keep them steadfast in the Church, and I will show you members of the Church who are not in good standing before God, and who are walking in slippery paths. It is not by marvelous manifestations unto us that we shall be established in the truth, but it is by humility and faithful obedience to the commandments and laws of God."[13]

Elder George A. Smith recounted an occasion when a preacher came to Joseph Smith and, to be convinced of the Prophet's message, requested a sign, some spectacular manifestation of the power of God. Said the preacher, "I want to see a notable miracle performed; and if you perform such a one, then I will believe with all my heart and soul, and will exert all my power and all my extensive influence to convince others; and if you will not perform a miracle of this kind, then I am your worst and bitterest enemy." "Well," said Joseph, "what will you have done? Will you be struck blind, or dumb? Will you be paralyzed, or will you have one hand withered? Take your choice, choose which you please, and in the name of the Lord Jesus Christ it shall be done." That, of course, was not the kind of miracle he wanted.[14]

Jacob humbly explained to Sherem that he could see a sign only if God willed it, and it would not be to the detriment of anyone other than himself. God smote Sherem. Forced to acknowledge the hand of God in his fate, Sherem pleaded for a gathering of the people so he could admit his sins and confess the Christ, the Holy Ghost, and the ministering of angels.

Jacob 7:18–23

Sherem recognized that he had been deceived by the power of the devil. We may feel sorry for him, but he made his own choices. Satan can exercise great power over us, but only as we allow him to do so (see also commentary at 1 Nephi 22:15–17).[15] Otherwise, he has no power. There is a much greater power in the universe, and Jacob specifically asked for a manifestation of that divine power upon his people. His request was heard and his prayer answered. Once again peace and love prevailed, and the people searched the scriptures, possibly copies of the plates of brass.

Jacob 7:24–26

This is one of the most human and evocative passages in the Book of Mormon as Jacob expressed his reflections on his life and work. Efforts were made to reclaim the Lamanites but to no avail. In his old age, Jacob looked back and expressed a sentiment that appears to be quite natural as the years pass—life seems like a dream. He then described the hardships he had endured. Many of the faithful Saints of every dispensation have felt as Jacob did; they have looked to, and longed for, a return to our eternal home, confessing that we are "strangers and pilgrims on the earth" (Hebrews 11:13). The righteous, we venture, are destined to experience this divine homesickness.

Jacob 7:27

Many have pointed out the curious use of a French word at the end of the book of Jacob. The Book of Mormon is translation literature. Jacob concluded with his personal *good-bye*, which in older English is a contraction of "God be with ye"—a perfect salutation to end his writings. Joseph Smith considered the well-known French word, by that time also an English word, to be the best translation of Jacob's ancient expression. *Adieu* means literally "to God," a shortened form of *a dieu (vous) commant*, "I commend (you) to God." The Spanish *adios* means the same—otherwise, *vaya con Dios*, meaning "go with God."

THE BOOK OF ENOS

The four brief books that follow the book of Jacob—Enos, Jarom, Omni, and Words of Mormon—are the work of seven record keepers, not including Mormon, who wrote during a period of about three hundred fifty to four hundred years. Each wrote a chapter or less. If all the thousand-year history of the Book of Mormon were so abbreviated, instead of a 531-page book in English, we might have a 20-page pamphlet. Jacob's descendants kept the records for more than four hundred years.

Enos 1:1–2

Enos's father was certainly a "just man"—his father was Jacob, the sensitive scriptorian and prophet who had seen the Savior and was sealed up to eternal life. He had properly raised his son Enos and taught him about the things of God. Still, Enos had to discover for himself the value of his parents' teachings and gain his own testimony through the "wrestle" which he had before God (on "wrestling with God," see also the commentary at Alma 8:10). Enos was also "wrestling" with himself. All people, without exception, have to struggle with their own spiritual growth and come to grips with the realities and challenges of mortality.

The great patriarch Jacob (Israel) literally wrestled for a blessing from God during a time of extreme trial and anxiety. But it was also an inner struggle. He was rewarded with the presence of God (Genesis 32:7–8, 24–30). The Prophet Joseph Smith stated that Zacharias went into the temple to wrestle with God, according to the order of the priesthood, to obtain a promise of a son.[1] He was rewarded with the birth of a son, who would be the forerunner to the very Son of God. President Brigham Young said that all of us are situated "upon the same ground," in that we must "struggle, wrestle, and strive, until the Lord bursts the veil and suffers [allows] us to behold His glory, or a portion of it."[2] Thus, each of us can be rewarded with the Lord's presence in our lives. Unfortunately, many of us live below our birthright opportunities and blessings, but we do not need to.

Phillips Brooks, rector of Trinity Church in Boston, Massachusetts, in the early 1890s, wrote: "You may search all the ages for [a person who has had no struggle]. You may go through the crowded streets of heaven, asking each [one] how he came there, and you will look in vain everywhere for a man morally and spiritually strong, whose strength did not come to him in struggle. . . . Do you suppose that man has never wrestled with his own success and happiness. . . .

". . . There is no exception anywhere. Every true strength is gained in struggle."[3]

Enos 1:3–4

Although his parents may have wondered if Enos was really listening during the years of family prayers, scripture study, and "home evenings," he later admitted that the words planted in him during his younger years "sunk deep into [his] heart." As a father, Jacob blessed his children's lives by simply talking about the gospel and his testimony in an engaging, nonthreatening way. The result: Jacob trained a prophet of God—who happened to be his son. Do we realize who it is we are really training or teaching or associating with?

As a result of his father's efforts, Enos's soul hungered, and he cried unto the Lord in mighty prayer. This was not a routine sort of prayer but a fervent pleading from the depths of his soul. Other key phrases describe his profound pleading: "I did pour out my whole soul"; "I was thus struggling in the spirit"; "I prayed unto him with many long strugglings"; and "I . . . prayed and labored with all diligence."

There is a difference between saying prayers and really communicating with Heavenly Father. What do the scriptures mean when they speak of pouring out your soul to God? And when the scriptures refer to "mighty prayer"—how does it happen?

During his service as a mission president in Santiago, Chile, Brother Ogden found himself frequently in the office, staring at the picture board that contained more than two hundred photos of elders and sisters with notes about their time in the mission and where they were presently serving. He spent a lot of time on his knees in that office, pleading with Heavenly Father for guidance in doing the work of his Son. A number of times while praying, he would open his eyes, get up off his knees, stand before that picture board, and pray for each missionary by name. (That would take quite a while.) He wanted to look into the face of each and every missionary, say each person's name, and ask for blessings on each one.

We need to be specific in our prayers, mentioning the names of people we know who have special needs. They are all around us, in every ward, on every street. The Spirit will tell us for whom we can pray and how we can help them. And when we really connect with the Spirit, there can be a flow of pure intelligence. Sometimes there is a profuse flow of revelation that brings tears to the eyes, light to the mind, or joy to the heart. We find ourselves not just saying words to our God but sharing feelings with our Father.

Revelation often comes during prayer, and when the Lord tells us something, when he gives us some insight into a gospel principle or instruction about how to proceed with something or how to help someone, we need to write it down, not waiting until the end of our prayer—or we might forget it. Brother Ogden's practice on these occasions is to get up from his knees, grab a notebook and pen, and write about what came into his mind, even if it takes five or ten minutes to write. During that time, even more revelation may come. Then he gets back on his knees and resumes his prayer. Is that heresy, to get up off one's knees and do something else, thus interrupting the flow of a prayer? We believe that this is part of talking with our Father in Heaven. It is not a one-way monologue; it is two-way communication. If he tells us something, we need to write it down right away.

President Henry B. Eyring relates how he prayed through the night, and the answer came quietly and clearly: "Once . . . I prayed through the night to know what I was to choose to do in the morning. I knew that no other choice could have had a greater effect on the lives of others and on my own. I knew what choice looked most comfortable to me. I knew what outcome I wanted. But I could not see the future. I could not see which choice would lead to which outcome. So the risk of being wrong seemed too great to me.

"I prayed, but for hours there seemed to be no answer. Just before dawn, a feeling came over me. More than at any time since I had been a child, I felt like one. My heart and my mind seemed to grow very quiet. There was a peace in that inner stillness.

"Somewhat to my surprise, I found myself praying, 'Heavenly Father, it doesn't matter what I want. I don't care anymore what I want. I only want that Thy will be done. That is all that I want. Please tell me what to do.'

"In that moment I felt as quiet inside as I had ever felt. And the message came, and I was sure who it was from. It was clear what I was to do. I received no promise of the outcome. There was only the assurance that I was a child who had been told what path led to whatever He wanted for me."[4]

"All the day long" and into the night, Enos cried to God in heaven. Notice that he had to first resolve his own inner struggle, "for mine own soul," and then he could reach out to others: "I began to feel a desire for the welfare of my brethren, the Nephites"; after that: "I prayed unto him . . . for my brethren, the Lamanites." Once we have reconciled ourselves with our Father, we automatically desire to help others. Joseph Smith once said to a group of missionaries: "A man filled with the love of God, is not content with blessing his family alone, but ranges through the whole world, anxious to bless the whole human race. This has been your feeling, and caused you to forego the pleasures of home, that you might be a blessing to others, who are candidates for immortality, but strangers to truth."[5]

Sanctification involves doing all we can to get ourselves saved and help save as many others as we can.

Enos 1:5–8

Enos wrote that his "guilt was swept away"—not only that his sins were forgiven but that he was also rid of the guilt attached to the sins. "Remission" means released from guilt. Enos marveled that his sins could be completely forgiven and his guilt totally removed, and he wondered how it happens. "Because of thy faith in Christ" is the plain and powerful answer; "thy faith hath made thee whole." Sin and doubt leave us broken, but faith can make us whole again. That is the glad tidings, the best news: the first principle of the gospel is faith in the Lord Jesus Christ. When we turn to him, believe and trust in him, and look to him for a remission of our sins (see also 2 Nephi 25:26), he takes away the sin and the guilt we feel for the sin. He is the only person in the universe who can take away the stain and the pain of our transgressions, because he paid the price for them.

Enos 1:10

The voice of the Lord came into Enos's mind. This is often the way in which revelation comes to us. The Lord said to Oliver Cowdery, "I will tell you in your mind and in your heart, by the Holy Ghost" (D&C 8:2). Revelation comes as "the still small voice, which whispereth through and pierceth all things" (D&C 85:6). It comes in proportion to our diligence in keeping the commandments.

The message to Enos was familiar: God had given his people part of the land we now call the Americas, and "it is a holy land." It is holy indeed. History began on these lands, and it will end on these lands. The Garden of Eden, Adam-ondi-Ahman, Enoch's City of Holiness, the appearance of the resurrected Lord, the making of the Book of Mormon record, the latter-day Restoration—of the gospel, Church, and Abrahamic covenant—and the future New Jerusalem all center in this holy land.

The only way the land will cease to prosper, and be cursed, is if the people corrupt themselves; "their transgressions will I bring down with sorrow upon their own heads."

Enos 1:12

Two components of effective communication with God are praying and laboring with all diligence. The Hebrew word *avodah* means both "worship" and "work." True worship of God involves talking and doing: speaking while on our knees, then working while on our feet. Elder Dallin H. Oaks has taught that testimony is knowing and feeling; conversion is doing and becoming.[6]

Enos 1:13–20

Enos had likely learned from his grandfather Lehi, his uncle Nephi, and his father, Jacob, that the Nephites would eventually turn from the truth, sin, and be destroyed. Because that was the apparent future scenario, he desired that God would preserve the record of his people for his brethren, the Lamanites, so they could in some future day be brought to salvation. That is one of the purposes of the Book of Mormon. Its preface states that it is "written to the Lamanites," and Doctrine and Covenants 3:20 says the plates were preserved "that the Lamanites might come to the knowledge of their fathers, and that they might know the promises of the Lord, and that they may believe the gospel and rely upon the merits of Jesus Christ, and be glorified through faith in his name, and that through their repentance they might be saved."

Enos, along with his prophet-forefathers, asked with faith and received assurance from the Lord that he would preserve the records and eventually get them into the hands of the Lamanites. Again, the Nephites sought to reclaim the Lamanites without success. The baseness and brutality of the latter was frightening.

Enos 1:25–27

If 179 years had transpired since Lehi's departure from Jerusalem, the year would be 420 B.C., and Jacob and Enos had both lived long lives. Enos had been faithful in raising the voice of warning among his people and could look forward and rejoice at the prospect of his imminent meeting with the Savior: "Then shall I see his face with pleasure, and he will say unto me: Come unto me, ye blessed, there is a place prepared for you in the mansions of my Father." Enos had the assurance of life eternal with God, just like his grandfather Lehi and father, Jacob (2 Nephi 1:15). All possessed the "more sure word of prophecy," knowing they were sealed up to the highest heaven (D&C 131:5). As already mentioned, the "rest" of the Lord is "the fulness of his glory" (D&C 84:24).

THE BOOK OF JAROM

Jarom 1:1–3

Jarom, son of Enos, was reluctant to write much about his prophesying and revelations: "For what could I write more than my fathers have written? For have not they revealed the plan of salvation?" Moroni, the last of the Nephite record keepers, felt the same way: there was little space left on the plates, and what could he possibly add? But that was eight hundred years after Jarom! Jarom felt that all Lehi, Nephi, Jacob, and Enos had written was sufficient. Nevertheless, there was much to do among his people because they had some serious "anatomy" problems: their hearts were hard, their ears were deaf, their minds were blind, and their necks were stiff—symbolizing the fact that the merciful message of heaven was not getting through to them.

The plan of salvation (see also Alma 24:14; 42:5; Moses 6:62) is otherwise called in the Book of Mormon:

The "plan of the great Creator" (2 Nephi 9:6).

The "plan of the Eternal God" (Alma 34:9).

The "plan of mercy" (Alma 42:15, 31).

The "plan of deliverance" (2 Nephi 11:5).

The "plan of redemption" (Jacob 6:8; Alma 12:25, 26, 30, 32, 33; 17:16; 18:39; 22:13; 29:2; 34:16, 31; 39:18; 42:11, 13).

The "plan of happiness" (Alma 42:8, 16).

Jarom 1:4

The same could be said in the Church today: "There are many among us who have many revelations." And how do these revelations come? Through the Holy Spirit. Joseph Smith explained: "No man can receive the Holy Ghost without receiving revelations. The Holy Ghost is a revelator."[1]

Jarom 1:6–13

The bloodthirsty Lamanites had obviously lost a knowledge of and desire to keep the law of Moses, which prohibited the consumption of blood, teaching instead that the life of the flesh is in the blood (Genesis 9:4; Leviticus 17:11) and thus pointing to the ultimate sacrifice of the Messiah who shed his blood. Perhaps it is against this very backdrop of the blood-drinking Lamanites that the Nephite prophets, priesthood leaders, and teachers purposely taught the law of Moses with diligence and persuaded the people to "look forward unto the Messiah, and believe in him . . . as though he already was [come]." The Nephites were to look forward with perfect faith, just as we today are to look backward with perfect faith to the coming of Christ in the flesh. The requirements of faith are the same. The actual time of the Lord's coming, in a way, is irrelevant. What is not irrelevant is that he truly did come.

THE BOOK OF OMNI

The short book of Omni includes the accounts of five record keepers. The first, Jarom's son Omni, was an admittedly wicked man. The book might appropriately have been called the book of Amaleki because he wrote nearly two-thirds of the thirty verses. Also, in this short book, two new peoples are introduced: the people of Zarahemla, whom we call Mulekites (though that name is never used in the Book of Mormon), and the Jaredites.

Omni 1:1–11

Omni, a warrior, reported many seasons of war and peace. Omni's son Amaron, Amaron's brother Chemish, and Chemish's son Abinadom all inscribed brief reports.

Omni described himself as a wicked man, lax in observance of the Lord's commandments. He was not so wicked, however, that he did not take seriously his responsibility to keep the records. We sympathize with him and wonder how much of his lack of strict obedience was the result of his life as a warrior.

The destruction of "the more wicked part of the Nephites" represents the fulfillment of a prophecy given to God's people living in the new covenant land in the days of the brother of Jared—the inhabitants of this land must serve God or be swept off it "when the fulness of his wrath cometh upon them" (Ether 2:9). Verse 11 may be an indictment against the people of Abinadom in general: no new revelation or prophecy was given because they needed to live what they had already been given.

Omni 1:12–19

Abinadom's son Amaleki introduced us to a man named "Mosiah, who was made king over the land of Zarahemla," and who was warned by the Lord to take all the people still willing to listen to the voice of God and flee out of the land of Nephi into the wilderness. Guided by the prophetic voice, they journeyed to a land called Zarahemla. There they discovered the people of Zarahemla, who were immediately excited about the arrival of the people of Mosiah because they carried with them "the plates of brass which contained the record of the Jews." The excitement was mutual because Mosiah's people learned that the people of Zarahemla "came out from Jerusalem at the time that Zedekiah, king of Judah, was carried away captive into Babylon" (ca. 589 B.C.).

At this point in Book of Mormon history we see the various groups that the Lord brought out of the Old World now mixing in the New World: groups from the tribes of Joseph (Lehi's descendants from Manasseh and Ishmael's descendants from Ephraim) and these new people, who were from the tribe of Judah.

These Judahites, known as the people of Zarahemla (or Mulekites), fled Jerusalem before the Babylonians finished destroying it in 586 B.C.; they sailed to the Western Hemisphere and occupied this "land of Zarahemla" ever since, where they had become numerous. "Their language had become corrupted," and one of the main reasons was because "they had brought no records with them." Hebrew scholar and grammarian William Chomsky concluded that "two main factors generally operate as controls in the process of linguistic change: (1) isolation and (2) possession of written records."[1] Because the people of Zarahemla had been so long isolated and without written records, their language had understandably deteriorated to the point that the people of Mosiah could not communicate with them. Without scriptural records, they had lost their religious heritage and were denying the existence of their Creator.

This has to be one of the overarching lessons of the Book of Mormon: when records are lost or disregarded, language is corrupted, identity is lost, doctrinal purity is destroyed, and revelation ceases. Record keepers are the preservers of the social memory—for families and entire cultures. Without records, families, societies, and civilizations erode. This decay undermines a society's cohesion and threatens its survival. King Mosiah caused his language to be taught to the natives of Zarahemla, after which they secured from Zarahemla an oral genealogy.

Omni 1:20–22

Mosiah was a political leader and a prophet, as was his son and successor, Benjamin. When a large stone with an inscription was brought to him, he translated it or interpreted it through the gift and power of God. The inscription gave an account of Coriantumr, the last king of yet another people, the Jaredites (Ether 12:1; 13–15), who had been discovered by the people of Zarahemla and who had resided among them for "nine moons," or nine months. The inscription also contained a record of Coriantumr's ancestors who had come out from the tower of Babel (Ether 1:3) and the judgments of God that had come upon his people over many centuries, including their destruction and the scattering of their bones in a land north of the land of Zarahemla (compare Mosiah 28:11–19).

Omni 1:23–25

Amaleki continued with his own biographical sketch. He was born during the reign of Mosiah, and now, during the reign of Benjamin, he engraved a few words at the very end of the small plates of Nephi. The Lamanites invaded the land of Zarahemla, but King Benjamin's forces were able to drive them out. Approaching old age and having no posterity, Amaleki decided to deliver the sacred record into the hands of his just king, Benjamin, and he left us a brief but powerful exhortation to come to the Holy One of Israel and believe in prophecy, revelation, the ministering of angels, the gift of tongues, and every other good thing.

Omni 1:26

Amaleki, an otherwise little-known record keeper, inscribed a theological jewel into these plates of Nephi. The plan of salvation is contained in this single verse: come unto Christ, offer your whole souls as an offering unto him, continue in fasting and praying, endure to the end, and be saved. Offering your whole soul involves willingness to sacrifice all things. The *Lectures on Faith* teaches: "A religion that does not require the sacrifice of all things never has power sufficient to produce the faith necessary unto life and salvation. . . . The faith necessary unto the enjoyment of life and salvation never could be obtained without the sacrifice of all earthly things."[2]

Our English verb *sacrifice* derives from the Latin *sacer* (sacred, holy) and *ficare* (to make). The term, then, means "to make holy." Interestingly, the verb *consecrate* comes from Latin *sacrare,* which also derives from *sacer.* Therefore, both *sacrifice* and *consecrate* mean "to make holy." Our God is holy, and he wants us to be holy (Leviticus 11:44; 19:2; 20:7, 26). Sacrifice and consecration are laws that true Saints are required to live, as taught and exemplified by the Holy One of Israel in the scriptures and in his holy temple.

Omni 1:27–30

Amaleki inscribed a relatively brief but fairly comprehensive historical record of his day. He again introduced us to something new: a large group of his people with an adventurous spirit "went up into the wilderness to return to the land of Nephi," wanting to repossess their old homeland, called the land of Lehi-Nephi in Mosiah 7:1. Their leader was a strong and strong-willed man who caused fatal contention, and many of the group ended up dead in the wilderness. Fifty of them returned to the land of Zarahemla. Another large group later attempted the journey. Further on in the Book of Mormon, we learn that Zeniff left the land of Zarahemla to inherit the land of his fathers (Mosiah 7:9).

At this point Amaleki ended the record. The small plates that Nephi made some time after his family's departure from Jerusalem were now full. The date is approximately 130 B.C., which means that this set of Nephi's plates had been inscribed on and preserved for almost half a millennium.

THE WORDS OF MORMON

The prophet Mormon, living many centuries later, made an editorial insert at this point in the Book of Mormon to explain that all the preceding accounts had been taken from the small plates of Nephi (600 B.C. to about 130 B.C.). Amaleki's final words were, "These plates are full" (Omni 1:30). Mormon described the transition from small plates to large plates for the ongoing history of his people.

The books of 1 Nephi through Omni are a direct translation of original writings from Nephi, Jacob, and others; therefore, they have come to us in a first-person narration. The books of Mosiah through 4 Nephi, on the other hand, consist of Mormon's abridgment of the writings of the prophets and record keepers; therefore, they have come to us in a third-person narration—Mormon's recounting the teachings and experiences of others.

Words of Mormon 1:3–4, 6

Mormon made an abridgment of "the plates of Nephi," meaning the book of Lehi; then he found the other set of Nephi's plates (the "small plates," containing a "small account of the prophets" Nephi, Jacob, and others). He included them in the collection of records he passed on to his son Moroni. We begin to see that there were many sets of plates kept by the ancients.

Words of Mormon 1:5

Mormon tells us repeatedly that he could not include even the hundredth part of the records of his people (see also commentary at 3 Nephi 26:6–11). If he *had* included all of it, a hundred times more than what we have, we would have, in English, a 53,000-page Book of Mormon instead of a 530-page Book of Mormon.

Words of Mormon 1:7

With historical hindsight, we know that Mormon included writings from both sets of Nephi's plates because some of the record would be lost by Martin Harris fifteen hundred years later (see commentary at 1 Nephi 9 and 1 Nephi 19:1–6). The "wise purpose" of the Lord was partly to cover the loss of the 116 manuscript pages of the record of Lehi, but even more, His wise purpose was to provide us with a record that throws "greater views upon my gospel" (D&C 10:45), including powerful testimonies of Jesus Christ from Nephi, Jacob, and Isaiah.

Words of Mormon 1:10–11

More than five hundred years before the time of Mormon, King Benjamin brought the large and small plates of Nephi together to preserve them; thus they continued to be cared for over the centuries down to Mormon and Moroni.

POSSESSORS OF THE BOOK OF MORMON PLATES

Lehi	A descendant of Manasseh	1 Nephi 1:17
Nephi	Son of Lehi	1 Nephi 1:2, 17
Jacob	Son of Lehi (brother of Nephi)	Jacob 1:1–2
Enos	Son of Jacob	Jacob 7:27
Jarom	Son of Enos	Jarom 1:1
Omni	Son of Jarom	Jarom 1:15
Amaron	Son of Omni	Omni 1:4
Chemish	Son of Omni (brother of Amaron)	Omni 1:8
Abinadom	Son of Chemish	Omni 1:10
Amaleki	Son of Abinadom	Omni 1:12
Benjamin	Son of Mosiah I	Omni 1:25
Mosiah II	Son of Benjamin	Mosiah 1:16
Alma II	Son of Alma I	Mosiah 28:20
Helaman II	Son of Alma II	Alma 37:1
Shiblon	Son of Alma II	Alma 63:1
Helaman III	Son of Helaman II	Alma 63:11
Nephi II	Son of Helaman III	Helaman 3:37
Nephi III	Son of Nephi II and one of the twelve disciples of Christ (3 Nephi 12:1)	3 Nephi 1:2
Nephi IV	Son of Nephi III	4 Nephi: heading
Amos I	Son of Nephi IV	4 Nephi 1:19
Amos II	Son of Amos I	4 Nephi 1:21
Ammaron	Son of Amos I (brother of Amos II); hid up the records in Hill Shim (Mormon 1:3)	4 Nephi 1:47–48
Mormon II	Son of Mormon I; obtained records from Hill Shim (Mormon 4:23)	Mormon 1:1–5

POSSESSORS OF THE BOOK OF MORMON PLATES (CONT.)		
Moroni	Son of Mormon II, who hid all records in Hill Cumorah, except the ones he gave to Joseph Smith	Mormon 6:6
Joseph Smith Jr.	Son of Joseph Smith Sr., instructed and directed to the records by angel Moroni (Joseph Smith–History 1:30–54, 59)	2 Nephi 3:15
Moroni	Son of Mormon II; custody of record returned to Moroni	Joseph Smith–History 1:60

THE BOOK OF MOSIAH

Mosiah 1:2–7

Lehi taught his sons (1 Nephi 1:1), Jacob taught his son (Enos 1:1), and King Benjamin taught his sons (Mosiah 1:2). They learned the language and teachings of the scriptures. Were it not for the study of those sacred writings they would have "suffered in ignorance and "dwindled in unbelief." If we want to profit and prosper in life, we, too, must have the scriptures "before our eyes" and "search them diligently."

It is curious that the plates of brass taken out of Jerusalem, from which Lehi and all the succeeding prophets taught, were written in the Egyptian language (see also 1 Nephi 1:2). Historical records attest that both Hebrew and Egyptian were known in Israel during Lehi's day, and Lehi himself was a descendant of Joseph, who centuries before lived out most of his life using the Egyptian language, so perhaps this "stick of Joseph" was meant to be continued in that language. In addition, there were strong commercial and cultural ties between Judah and Egypt in the late seventh century B.C., when Egypt was growing in strength. The Book of Mormon itself reveals that Mormon and Moroni were writing in what they called "reformed Egyptian" (Mormon 9:32).

Mosiah 1:8–10

After years of teaching and training his sons, Benjamin, in his old age, conferred the kingdom on his son Mosiah, whom we designate Mosiah II because Benjamin's father was Mosiah I (see Omni 1:12).

Mosiah 1:11

King Benjamin wanted to do away with the temporal, artificial nomenclature by which his people had distinguished themselves as being from Ephraim, Manasseh, or Judah, or the people of Nephi or Zarahemla or Mosiah, etc. He wanted to bring them together under one name, to bind them all together as the family of God, to take upon them the name of Christ (see commentary at Mosiah 5:7–12).

Likewise, the most important distinction that sets us apart from the world (and from our own temporal, artificial, geopolitical designations, such as North American, European, African, Asian, Latin American, etc.) is the name of Christ, which we take upon us when we enter his kingdom. Our ultimate objective is to take upon us the name and the nature of our God, to become as Christ is.

Thus all of us become identified by the groups we associate with and the names to which we connect ourselves. On one occasion, a returned sister missionary in one of Brother Ogden's Book of Mormon classes showed him her engagement ring. He was happy for her, of course, but since an engagement is not unusual at Brigham Young University, he asked if the engagement involved anyone else he knew. She said shyly, "Well, you know that fellow who sits next to me in your class?" They had met in class two months before and begun dating. They were going to be married at the end of the semester.

Brother Ogden decided to find a fun way to announce the good news to the class. At the beginning of the next class period, he said, "Today we begin our study of King Benjamin's discourse. The king gathered his people to advise them that his son would be their new king and to give them a new name." Brother Ogden then explained that one of the young women in the class had decided to take on a new name. After the sister explained the circumstances of the engagement and after some good laughs about the whole situation, he told the students that a few days before she had whispered to him, "I love this class." He added, "Now we all know why."

Mosiah 1:12

The people of Christ can carry his name and never have that name blotted out, as long as they will continue blotting out their sins and staying clean.

Mosiah 2:1–2

For his final "general conference" address, King Benjamin wanted his numerous people to go up to the temple, or as we would do in our day, go to the Conference Center, next door to the Salt Lake Temple. In the following chapters is one of the greatest sermons ever recorded. The discourse of King Benjamin is another splendid illustration of Joseph Smith's declaration that "a man would get nearer to God by abiding by [the Book of Mormon's] precepts, than by any other book."[1]

Mosiah 2:5–8

In King Benjamin's day, families pitched their tents toward the temple, away from the world, just as their Israelite ancestors had pitched their tents around the tabernacle in Sinai (Exodus 33:8–10). Abraham's nephew Lot "pitched his tent toward Sodom" (Genesis 13:12) and lost his family. We would be wise to follow the example of the Nephite people of Christ by orienting our tents (our lives) toward the temple and the Conference Center to hear the words of the prophets and the words of God—the words of eternal life.

Because the king could not teach all who had gathered within the walls of the temple, he had a tower erected so more could hear, but the multitude was so great that many still could not hear, so Benjamin's words were written and distributed to all outside the sound of his voice. In our day, after general conference, the words of the prophets are distributed to all who will receive them.

Mosiah 2:9

King Benjamin warned his people to be serious and sober-minded; he had not gathered them together so they could trifle with his words; rather, they were to hear and hearken, to learn and obey. Today it is still true that the mysteries of God, "the mysteries of the kingdom, even the key of the knowledge of God" (D&C 84:19), and "the power of godliness" (D&C 84:20) may be unfolded to our view at the temple.

Mosiah 2:10–11

The king wanted his people to understand that he was not a bigger-than-life ruler but was only a mortal man. He was not ruling over them as did the pharaohs and other tyrants who had lorded over their subjects. "I am like as yourselves, subject to all manner of infirmities in body and mind; yet I have been chosen by this people, and consecrated by my father, and was suffered by the hand of the Lord" to be a ruler and a king. Here the word "suffered" means allowed.

Mosiah 2:11–21

In these eleven verses the words "serve" and "service" appear thirteen times. The first thing the king wanted to do was to establish clearly the reasons for which a true ruler or leader is in his position: he is called to *serve*. The Savior himself showed us how it is done. For his mortal ministry he came not to rule and reign (that is what will happen at his second coming); he came first as a servant: "I am among you as he that serveth" (Luke 22:27). He expects us to do likewise: forget ourselves and serve others.

King Benjamin had not accrued riches at the people's expense; he had not allowed the people to be lawless or lascivious; he had not been lazy but had labored along with the people with his own hands so as not to burden them with excessive taxes. Benjamin had "a clear conscience before God" in his dealings with his fellow man. In fact, through serving his people he had only been in the service of God. Out in the world, others can substitute for us (as in many humanitarian organizations and efforts), but in the kingdom of God others cannot substitute for us; each of us is called to serve.

Mosiah 2:18

"If I, whom ye call your king, do labor to serve you, then ought not ye to labor to serve one another?" These are the same sentiments Jesus expressed to his apostles a century and a half later: "Ye call me Master and Lord: and ye say well; for so I am. If I then, your Lord and Master, have washed your feet; ye also ought to wash one another's feet. For I have given you an example, that ye should do as I have done to you" (John 13:13–15). The apostles would be among the greatest men on earth and were called to be leaders over all. To be a leader simply means one has been called to serve. We are not to be self-serving but rather to be serving everyone else. President Howard W. Hunter taught, "Our focus should be on righteousness, not recognition; on service, not status."[2] Likewise, Elder Dallin H. Oaks observed, "If our service is to be most efficacious, it must be accomplished for the love of God and the love of his children."[3] It is instructive that the priesthood is given to the brethren to bless others, not themselves. We never hear of a priesthood holder laying his hands on himself and giving himself a blessing.

Mosiah 2:19

Verse 19 contains a subtle hint that while serving, we would do well to avoid accepting praise, adulation, and thanks, for all good things come from God, and we should give thanks to him. For example, we do not know the name of a single one of those two thousand young men in the army of Helaman (Alma 56); it was not important for them to receive recognition for the valiant service they rendered their people (such as getting all their names engraved into the Nephite record). The joy of serving was its own reward.

President Gordon B. Hinckley certainly deserved praise for his magnificent record of service, yet he continually counseled all of us to avoid adulation—it is poison.[4]

Elder William R. Bradford of the Seventy once spoke with the bishop of a ward whose youth had worked to earn money for an activity. The bishop asked Elder Bradford if he would help the youth get some recognition for what they had done. To the bishop's surprise, Elder Bradford said he would not. He said that he was glad that the young people had worked hard, but it was not important that they receive public recognition for that work. When the youth decided to donate their money to the Church's general missionary fund instead of using it for the activity, they wanted to have their picture taken with Elder Bradford as they made the donation, and they wanted to have the picture and an article put into the newspaper. Again Elder Bradford surprised them by saying no. He told the bishop: "You might consider helping your young people learn a higher law of recognition. Recognition from on high is silent. It is carefully and quietly recorded there. Let them feel the joy and gain the treasure in their heart and soul that come from silent, selfless service."[5]

It is a rare thing in world history to hear of a humble earthly king who acknowledges and properly gives credit and thanks to our heavenly King.

Mosiah 2:20–25, 34

If we thank our heavenly King and praise him and serve him, we still owe him far more than we can ever repay. The final lines of verse 21 put us all in our place. No matter how much good we do, we are still, in the end, "unprofitable servants"; or as Stephen Robinson, our colleague in Ancient Scripture at Brigham Young University, has said, "in a sense, we are all bad investments." We can never get God in our debt. The more we obey and serve him and others, the more he prospers us. We are always indebted to him, for our very breath even, to stay alive day to day—then how could anyone boast? How could anyone become proud? Proud of what? Without him, we are not even worth as much as the dust of the earth. Verse 34 reminds us: "Ye are eternally indebted to your heavenly Father, to render to him all that you have and are." That is a consecrated life, what the Father expects of every one of his children who will become as he is. This is the same teaching presented by Jesus during his mortal ministry (Luke 17:5–10).

Mosiah 2:26–27

King Benjamin again reminded the Saints of his day that though he was their leader he was no better than anyone else. Joseph Smith learned from the Great Jehovah that "he that is ordained of God and sent forth, the same is appointed to be the greatest, notwithstanding he is the least and the servant of all" (D&C 50:26). Having done all he could as a leader, even to the very end, Benjamin said he could walk "with a clear conscience before God." Would that it were so for all of us.

Mosiah 2:28

Regardless of what kind of vocal skill he had in mortality, King Benjamin looked forward to the next life, in which his immortal soul could join the heavenly choirs in singing praises to God. It is likely that all righteous souls will be inclined to do likewise.

Mosiah 2:36–41

Plain and strong words for those who want to withdraw from the Spirit, openly rebel, and be an enemy to God: the eternal law of justice will awaken in such a person a lively sense of guilt, pain, and anguish, the awful results being unquenchable doom and never-ending torment. On the other hand, the awesome results of faithful living are blessings and never-ending happiness.

Mosiah 3

This chapter contains the words of the Lord as delivered by an angel to King Benjamin (vv. 2, 23). The angel told him to wake up, so he woke up! The heavenly messenger described the value of the teachings we receive in the king's discourse: "I am come to declare unto you the glad tidings of great joy." It seems significant that there was an angel on each continent who was commissioned to declare "glad tidings of great joy" (compare Luke 2:10–11). Was this Gabriel? We do not know, but it was special enough news that heavenly messengers were called upon. This phrase is used three other times in the Book of Mormon (1 Nephi 13:37; Alma 13:22; Helaman 16:14), always by angels. Perhaps the use of this phrase requires a special commission.

Mosiah 3:5–11

The very first message the angel delivered, in which we certainly rejoice, is a restatement of the condescension of Deity—that Almighty God, the Lord Omnipotent himself, would come down from his throne, become mortal, and show miraculous powers of healing sick bodies, raising dead bodies, curing disabled bodies, and rescuing possessed bodies from evil spirits. But what kind of a God is willing to come down and experience temptation, pain, anguish, and suffering for the wickedness of his people? He would suffer to a greater degree than normal humans can endure, even bleeding from every pore of his body due to his deep anguish for all the sins of the Father's children (Luke 22:44; D&C 19:18).

All this was part of what Elder Neal A. Maxwell called "the awful arithmetic of the Atonement"; Jesus' suffering was "as it were, *enormity* multiplied by *infinity*."[6]

A detailed description follows, so there can be no mistaking exactly who he is: His name will be Jesus Christ, and he is the Son of God, the Father of heaven and earth (on his title of *Father* see commentary at 2 Nephi 19:6–7 and Mosiah 15:2–9), the Creator, and his mother's name will be Mary (Hebrew *Miriam*). His name is his role: *Jesus* (Hebrew *Yeshua*) means "savior" or "salvation," and *Christ* (Hebrew *Mashiakh*, or Messiah) means "Anointed One." He is, therefore, the "Anointed Savior" who rescues all humankind from physical death, and his atoning blood rescues all who will repent from spiritual death.

Mosiah 3:7

The Lord Omnipotent would "suffer temptations, . . . even more than man can suffer." Paul later explained that Jesus Christ was "in all points tempted like as we are, yet without sin" (Hebrews 4:15). Some have asked if what Jesus experienced can really be called temptation because, after all, he never committed sin. C. S. Lewis responded this way: "No man knows how bad he is till he has tried very hard to be good. A silly idea is current that good people do not know what temptation means. This is an obvious lie. Only those who try to resist temptation know how strong it is. After all, you find out the strength of [an] army by fighting against it, not by giving in. You find out the strength of a wind by trying to walk against it, not by lying down. A man who gives in to temptation after five minutes simply does not know what it would have been like an hour later. That is why bad people, in one sense, know very little about badness. They have lived a sheltered life by always giving in. We never find out the strength of the evil impulse inside us until we try to fight it: and Christ, because He was the only man who never yielded to temptation, is also the only man who knows to the full what temptation means."[7]

Lectures on Faith also describes how the Savior "descended in suffering below that which man can suffer; or, in other words, suffered greater sufferings, and was exposed to more powerful contradictions than any man can be. But, notwithstanding all this, he kept the law of God, and remained without sin."[8] Jesus undoubtedly suffered in mortality more temptations than the three recounted in Matthew 4:1–11. Alma wrote that "he shall go forth, suffering pains and afflictions and temptations of every kind" (Alma 7:11). Temptation likely pursued Jesus throughout his mortal life, just as it does us, but he "gave no heed" to it (D&C 20:22).[9]

Undoubtedly Jesus' greatest temptation came at the time of his final suffering. Elder Talmage reminded us that in Gethsemane, Christ met and overcame all the horrors that Satan, "the prince of this world," could inflict.[10] And Luke reminded us that while Jesus was hanging on the cross, He experienced a repetition of his earlier encounter with Satan after his forty-day fast. On that earlier occasion the adversary challenged the Master with at least three "if" clauses (Matthew 4:3–10). At the end, the same challenge was thrown up to him: "If thou be the king of the Jews, save thyself" (Luke 23:37).

Mosiah 3:16–18

Through the transgression of Adam and Eve, every child of God enters mortality with a natural propensity to sin. "By nature" human children are inclined to sin and worldliness, but the blood of Christ atones for their sins; he covers for them until the age of accountability (age eight; see JST, Genesis 17:11). Little children are innocent because Christ made them so, not because they do not know how to sin until age eight. Only through Jesus Christ and the cleansing and strengthening that comes through his atoning blood can anyone see the face of God, live with him, and be like him (see also D&C 84:19–22). There really is no other name, nor way, nor means to gain salvation except through the name and sacrifice of Christ, as both King Benjamin and the apostle Peter declared in almost the same language (compare Mosiah 3:17 and Acts 4:12).

Mosiah 3:19

The natural man, meaning a fallen, unregenerate, sinful person, is an enemy to God. The only way to remedy that situation is to *yield* or *submit* to the enticings of the Holy Spirit. Thus we overcome our fallen or sinful nature and become a new creature—and that happens only through the atonement of Christ.

Through the great and last sacrifice of the Holy One of Israel, we may become holy ones—which is the literal meaning of the word *saint*. As holy ones we acquire the very characteristics and attributes of the Holy One as outlined here— "child[like], submissive, meek, humble, patient, full of love, willing to submit to all things" the Lord desires. There is a vast difference between the natural or fallen man and the spiritual man living in a fallen world.

The idea of submission to God is contained in the title of one of the world's major religions—*Islam,* which word means "submission." A Muslim is one who submits to the will of *Allah* (the Arabic word meaning "God," parallel to the Hebrew *Elohim).* The doctrine of submitting ourselves to God's will and not pursuing our own will is true doctrine, as King Benjamin attests. In God's economy, everyone must submit his or her will to the Father—everyone, even the Savior.

The critical concept of submissiveness is expressed four times in this one verse in the words "yields," "submissive," and "submit" (twice). It is iterated and reiterated, possibly because it is the most difficult to live. If we are submissive to whatever God sends our way, we become as a child. In fact, we are born again; we start growing again and mature in the qualities of godliness, which are also noted in the verse.

Some years ago while Brother Ogden's children were helping at a petting farm in Mapleton, Utah, he engaged the owner in a lively conversation about the good she accomplished on her farm. She said one thing Brother Ogden will never forget. She said that if she ever had to get rid of her animals, she would still keep her horses and her sheep. Brother Ogden responded, "I can understand keeping horses, but sheep? Why would you keep an animal that seems noisy, dirty, and smelly?" The woman, who had thought a lot about the matter, replied, "Because sheep have a *willingness to be dependent.*"

The Savior is the Good Shepherd, and we are his sheep. In this life he expects us to get rid of pride, avoid any sense of self-sufficiency based on the things of this world, and be dependent on him. He expects us to humble ourselves, call on our Father daily, and stand steadfast in his goodness, willing to be submissive and dependent—like sheep—on our surest source of help.

Mosiah 3:20

Some major religions on earth do not believe human beings are in a fallen condition and, therefore, do not need any kind of savior. Benjamin, the wise king, prophesied that "the time shall come when the knowledge of a Savior shall spread throughout every nation, kindred, tongue, and people." That time has come.

Mosiah 3:25–26

This verse and others teach us that, in the end, no one else will need to judge us; "we shall have a perfect knowledge of all our guilt, and our uncleanness" (2 Nephi 9:14; see commentary at 2 Nephi 9:13–16). The Lord assures us that in that great Day of Judgment, under his direction as the great Judge, we shall have a "bright recollection" (Alma 11:43), a perfect memory, of all our words and works, and they will condemn us (Alma 12:14–15). In a sense it will be a self-judgment. Ultimately, the wicked will desire a self-imposed exile from the Lord.

But the most significant message of these verses is that the unrepentant will suffer the exact same things that the Lord suffered during the Atonement. They will shrink as Jesus shrank (D&C 19:18); they will drink out of the cup of the wrath of God, just as Jesus suffered "the wrath of Almighty God" (D&C 76:107; 88:106). Knowing this, it is difficult to understand why anyone would not want to take advantage of the vicarious punishment for broken laws suffered by the Lord on our behalf.

Mosiah 3:27

"A man is his own tormentor and his own condemner. Hence the saying, They shall go into the lake that burns with fire and brimstone. The torment of disappointment in the mind of man is as exquisite as a lake burning with fire and brimstone."[11] Brimstone is sulfur, a yellow-green, highly combustible element commonly found in Bible times along the shores of the Dead Sea. The same substance is used to make matches and gunpowder and other products in today's chemical and paper industries. When ignited, sulfur liquefies and produces a sharp and suffocating burning odor that can desolate and kill. Apparently, in ancient times no harsher picture of the hellish fate of the wicked could be portrayed than that of being thrown into a lake of fire burning with brimstone.

Mosiah 4:1-10

Verses 1–10 focus on how we may *obtain* a remission of our sins. Verses 11–26 focus on how we can *retain* a remission of our sins. The structure of the chapter is superb.

Mosiah 4:1-2

Have you ever heard a talk that so overwhelmed the listeners that they fell to the earth? King Benjamin's people had just experienced an intense encounter with reality; "they had fallen to the earth" (a phrase that has double meaning) and "viewed themselves in their own carnal state," in their fallen condition, feeling that they were "even less than the dust of the earth" to which they had fallen—because the dust or elements of the earth are obedient to their Maker, but they themselves had not always been obedient (Helaman 12:7–8). These are people who finally understand their condition without Christ.

The first thing they wanted to do when deeply touched by the Spirit was to repent. This passage describes the necessary process to repent and be forgiven: recognize your fallen condition, humble yourself, and appeal for the atoning blood of Christ in order to have your heart purified.

Just like ancient Israelites in Egypt put the blood of the lamb on their doorposts to be saved (Exodus 12:7), so we must symbolically apply the blood of Jesus Christ to cleanse and strengthen us. Just as we apply sunblock to prevent sunburn or apply lotion to soothe sunburned skin, so we cover ourselves spiritually with something that heals—he is the "balm of Gilead" that heals the sin-sick soul.[12] Recall that the Hebrew verb *kappar* means to cover (to protect, to save, to atone; see commentary at 2 Nephi 9:13–16).

President Boyd K. Packer wrote: "We all make mistakes. Sometimes we harm ourselves and seriously injure others in ways that we alone cannot repair. We break things that we alone cannot fix. It is then in our nature to feel guilt and humiliation and suffering, which we alone cannot cure. That is when the healing power of the Atonement will help."[13]

Mosiah 4:3

How do you know when your sins have been remitted and you have been forgiven? You will feel the Spirit of the Lord, you will feel joy, and you will have "peace of conscience" (the opposite of "remorse of conscience" mentioned in Alma 42:18). All of this comes about through faith in the Lord Jesus Christ. Faith is the number one principle of his gospel. It is what makes all the repentance, forgiveness, healing, joy, and peace of conscience possible.

President Boyd K. Packer explained: "Save for the

exception of the very few who defect to perdition, there is no habit, no addiction, no rebellion, no transgression, no apostasy, no crime exempted from the promise of complete forgiveness. . . .

"That great morning of forgiveness may not come at once. Do not give up if at first you fail. Often the most difficult part of repentance is to forgive yourself. Discouragement is part of that test. Do not give up. That brilliant morning will come.

"Then 'the peace of God, which passeth . . . understanding' comes into your life once again [Philippians 4:7]. Then you, like Him, will remember your sins no more. How will you know? You will know!"[14]

Mosiah 4:5, 11

We are reminded of our own nothingness, our worthless and fallen state. Why would this scripture strongly encourage us to remember our nothingness when we sing "I Am a Child of God" and quote "the worth of souls is great"? (D&C 18:10). The fact is, we *are* children of God and our souls *are* of great worth, but we must also remember that we, of ourselves, are nothing unless we yield to God and submit to him in all things. Without God we are nothing—"which thing I never had supposed," the prophet Moses exclaimed when he realized this fundamental truth (Moses 1:10). It is a truth that provides perspective.

Mosiah 4:6–7

"Book of Mormon prophets describe salvation as the journey of a lifetime rather than the ecstasy of a given moment. They use the word *salvation* as a synonym for eternal life, that which we would refer to as exaltation."[15] The central theme of these verses is that the atonement of Jesus Christ has been "prepared from the foundation of the world." Likewise, the atonement is the *foundation* of the Father's plan of salvation. It is not ancillary to, an add-on for, or an adjustment of the "real" plan. The Atonement was established in the eternity *before* this world came into being. And by it many worlds now stand, and many worlds have already passed away and are exalted (Moses 1:35). The Atonement is the core of eternal existence (Alma 13:3).

Mosiah 4:8–13

There are no other means or conditions; there is no other way to be saved. Notice all the references to "God" and "the Lord." He, not we, must be center stage in this drama of life, or else we miss our most important cues, and when the final curtain is dropped, there will be no ovation of any eternal consequence.

"There is none other salvation save this which hath been spoken of"—"We are hardly at liberty to pick and choose among various redemptive plans. While it may have been true in the ancient world that all roads led to Rome, it was equally true that there was but one entrance to the Holy of Holies. There is and can be only one salvation, and thus there is and can be only one Savior."[16]

These verses contain gospel doctrine in its purest form. They describe how to be spiritually born of God, how to get closer to God, and how to overcome the world and personal weaknesses. They specify the conditions of salvation: "Believe in God" and "repent of your sins." After having helped the Saints, both then and now, understand what must be understood and then done to obtain a remission of our sins, Benjamin turned to what can be done to retain a remission of our sins: Remember your nothingness ("acknowledge your unworthiness before God at all times"; Alma 38:14), be humble, pray daily, "be filled with the love of God," and "grow in the knowledge" of God (especially through scripture study and temple worship). Then you can "retain a remission of your sins," and here is a splendid lesson in human relations: "Ye will not have a mind to injure one another, but to live peaceably." When you are spiritually reborn and have his Spirit with you, the natural result is wanting to hurt absolutely no one and wanting to live in peace with everyone perpetually. There is a surefire way to determine if you have been spiritually reborn: Look at the way you treat others.

Mosiah 4:14–15

Parents carry huge responsibilities for their children's eternal well-being. They must provide for the temporal needs of their children. Just as important, in order for children to learn real *discipleship*, they must be *disciplined* (the two words have a common root meaning). Parents are responsible to teach their children (D&C 68:25–28), just as our Heavenly Father is the model Parent in teaching his children. Even though it is a natural propensity for beings in a fallen condition to fight and quarrel, children must be trained not to do so.

How does this scripture advise parents to prevent fighting and quarreling in the home? By teaching them to love one another. And how do parents do that? By teaching children to serve one another. That is done, at least in part, by parents themselves being an example of showing love through service.

Mosiah 4:16–22

Helping those who need our help is a characteristic sign of Zion. That is the way people lived in the cities of Enoch and Melchizedek, and it is the way it will be again in the Millennium. There is no reason we cannot start now. In fact, we are commanded to share our temporal possessions with others. Sometimes we refuse to share our possessions with others, however, and rationalize our behavior by arguing that people bring their misery on themselves; they are just suffering the natural consequences of their behavior. Anyone who thinks and acts like that has "great cause to repent." God reminds us that we are all beggars. All that we have is not ours in the first place; it all belongs to him. When we have more than we really need, we can give more fast offerings. We can assist with humanitarian projects. We can help relieve the suffering of those who lose everything in floods, fires, hurricanes, volcanic eruptions, earthquakes, tsunamis, avalanches, mudslides, and other physical disasters—not to mention all the spiritual disasters.

Mosiah 4:26

Benjamin explored in more detail how we can share what we have with others: feed the hungry, clothe the naked, visit the sick and administer to their relief—in spiritual as well as temporal ways. We do all that first with our own families, then with our neighbors, ward members, nonmembers, and other needy persons throughout our community, our nation, and the world. Giving to the needy is best done in the Lord's way (D&C 104:15–17), not by merely giving handouts but by preserving human dignity with opportunities to earn their own way. Those who are truly incapacitated, temporally or spiritually, of course have needs that we can help meet without any demands on them.

Mosiah 4:27

All things must be done in wisdom and order, without excesses or extremes. An example of going to the extreme would be if you tried to demonstrate inordinate or overzealous compliance by selling or giving away everything you have in order to bless others, but leaving your own family destitute. Life demands of each of us that we set priorities and try to stay balanced in our attitudes, actions, personal lives, and professional lives. President Harold B. Lee once gave this valuable counsel: "Most men do not set priorities to guide them in allocating their time, and most men forget that the first priority should be to maintain their own spiritual and physical strength. Then comes their family, then the Church, and then their professions—and all need time."[17]

"If you do right," taught the Prophet Joseph Smith, "there is no danger of your going too fast. He said he did not care how fast we run in the path of virtue; resist evil, and there is no danger."[18]

We must be diligent to "win the prize." What prize? "The high calling of God" (Philippians 3:14).

Mosiah 5:1

As with all the best teachers we know, it mattered to King Benjamin that his people *understood* and *believed* true doctrine. He asked for feedback. He was interested in true learning taking place.

Mosiah 5:2–7

People were deeply affected by King Benjamin's teachings. They showed their genuine conversion to those teachings by experiencing a mighty change in their hearts (see also Alma 5:14), having "no more disposition to do evil, but to do good continually." Notice that their spiritual rebirth included not only avoiding sins of commission (they had no desire to commit sin) but also avoiding sins of omission (they wanted to fill up their daily lives with good works).

At Christmastime we recall that Christ was "born to raise the sons of earth, born to give them second birth." Our spiritual rebirth comes by being willing to make a covenant to be obedient in all things and taking upon us the name and nature of Jesus Christ; our hearts are changed through faith on his name; we are born of him and become his sons and daughters, children of Christ. We take on family characteristics—in this case the attributes of Jesus Christ—just as babies adopt the traits of their families. As children of the family of Christ we come to look as well as act like our Father. The mighty change of heart also increases our desire and capacity to keep covenants and be obedient.

Mosiah 5:7–8

When we become the children of Christ, he becomes our covenant Father, and every week we remember the sacred covenant by taking upon us the name of Christ. We promise to remember him and obey him, thus showing we have truly taken upon us his name; that is, we become *Christ*ian, and our behavior is *Christ*like. We remember to *retain* his name written always in our hearts. How? By keeping all his commandments: praying, studying the scriptures, fasting, attending meetings, serving, paying tithes and offerings, maintaining healthy bodies, staying morally clean, and following all of his other instructions. We will recognize his voice to us and the name by which he calls us, which name has sacramental and temple significance.

Elder Dallin H. Oaks taught: "Willingness to take upon us the name of Jesus Christ can . . . be understood as willingness to take upon us the authority of Jesus Christ. According to this meaning, by partaking of the sacrament we witness our willingness to participate in the sacred ordinances of the temple and to receive the highest blessings available through the name and by the authority of the Savior when he chooses to confer them upon us. . . .

". . . Our witness that we are willing to take upon us the name of Jesus Christ constitutes our declaration of candidacy for exaltation in the celestial kingdom."[19]

Verse 7 declares that when we make this sacred covenant with Christ, we become his sons and daughters; with that kind of holy commitment "he hath spiritually begotten you." Of course, we are first of all sons and daughters of our Heavenly Father. He gave us our original spiritual birth, clothing our intelligences with spirit bodies. But now, in a new sense, we become "children of Christ, his sons, and his daughters." In Doctrine and Covenants 25:1, he explains that "all those who receive my gospel are sons and daughters in my kingdom" (see also Ether 3:14).

Rather than Jesus Christ being our elder Brother, as he is sometimes called by members of the Church, he has actually become our covenant Father, and we should use this more reverential title. Elder Theodore M. Burton of the Seventy explained why:

"It bothers me a little to hear members of our Church speak familiarly of Jesus Christ. They often refer to him as 'our elder Brother.' It is true that Jesus Christ was the Firstborn of all the spirit children of God the Eternal Father. In the spirit world he was known as Jehovah, the Firstborn. In that world, we were justified in referring to him as our elder Brother because we were with him there, and he was indeed our elder Brother in that existence. But that time has passed. We are now living in a new and a different world. Before we came here, we accepted Jehovah to become our Anointed Savior. We shouted with joy at the prospects of receiving him here as our Lord and Savior, our God and King, even our covenant Father.

"When we are baptized, we actually make a new covenant with God the Eternal Father to take upon us the name of his Only Begotten Son. Jesus Christ thus becomes by adoption our covenant Father. It is, therefore, in my opinion, wrong on earth after baptism to refer to him now as 'our elder Brother.' He is *now* our covenant *Father,* and we have become his covenant sons and daughters. We ought to be more respectful and show our gratitude to him for the opportunity we have to become members of his royal family."[20]

Mosiah 5:7–12

The word "name" appears eleven times in these six verses, signaling something very important and essential in the use of the term. In the Church we conclude prayers, talks, ordinances, and covenants "in the name of Jesus Christ." Moses 5 adds light on this concept: "Adam and Eve, his wife, called upon the *name* of the Lord" (Moses 5:4; emphasis added). And when the angel appeared and instructed them about the purposes of blood sacrifices, he taught: "Thou shalt do all that thou doest in the *name* of the Son, and thou shalt repent and call upon God in the *name* of the Son forevermore. . . .

And Adam and Eve blessed the *name* of God" (Moses 5:8–12; emphasis added).

In our day the Lord has warned that he will not be mocked in sacred matters: "Let all men beware how they take my *name* in their lips—For behold, . . . many there be who are under this condemnation, who use the *name* of the Lord, and use it in vain, having not authority. . . . Remember that that which cometh from above is sacred, and must be spoken with care" (D&C 63:61–64).

"There is no other *name* given whereby salvation cometh; therefore, I would that ye should take upon you the *name* of Christ, all you that have entered into the covenant with God," which all of us have done who have been baptized. We renew that covenant every time we take the sacrament, re-committing to take upon us his *name*, always remember him, and be like he is—*Christ*like. "This is the name that I said I should give unto you" (see also Mosiah 1:11). That name will never be blotted out if, when we sin, we immediately re-pent and "retain the name written always in [our] hearts," so he can ultimately "seal [us] his" (Mosiah 5:15). We receive new names at different stages of our eternal progression, par-ticularly when we enter into new, higher covenants. The new name of Jesus Christ is foundational.

Mosiah 5:15

The great king's final challenge is what the kingdom of God needs: people who are *steadfast* and *immovable,* people who are committed and trustworthy, people whom God can count on. Whatever they say they will do, they really will do. They make covenants and keep them. They abound in good works. God seals such people to eternal life.

Mosiah 6

This brief chapter describes changes in royal and eccle-siastical leadership among the people. Mosiah II follows the example of his father, Benjamin, in being a humble farmer as well as a righteous king (see "Possessors of Book of Mormon Plates," accompanying the commentary at Words of Mormon 1:10–11).

Mosiah 7:3

The Ammon who was the leader of the expedition up to the land of Nephi is not the same person as the later Ammon, son of King Mosiah, friend of Alma the Younger, and fellow missionary to the Lamanites. You may keep them straight by referring to the index of the Book of Mormon under Ammon¹ and Ammon².

Mosiah 7:6–7

Ammon, Amaleki, Helem, and Hem were cast later on into the same prison as Nephi, son of Helaman (Helaman 5:21–22).

Mosiah 7:14–15

This brief comment by Limhi, who is under tribute, is followed by a powerful discourse at the temple on the second day.

Mosiah 7:17–33

Limhi called his people together at the temple. Again we see the ancient Near Eastern pattern demonstrated of how the temple is the great place of instruction and the center of societal activity. Later, Jesus would teach daily at the temple when he was in Jerusalem (Matthew 26:55; Mark 12:35; Luke 19:47; 20:1; John 7:14). And, of course, he appeared after his resurrection to the people on the American continents at the temple in Bountiful (3 Nephi 11:1). Limhi's temple discourse emphasized an ancient principle: when the wicked rule, the people mourn (Proverbs 29:2). Limhi began by citing the Exodus as an example of God's power to release from bondage and ended by encouraging the people to turn to the Lord, trust in him, and rest assured that he would deliver them.

Mosiah 7:26–28

The people who had gone back up to the land of Nephi (or Lehi-Nephi) had seen three generations of wickedness. They had slain a prophet of the Lord, Abinadi, and the reason they had slain him was ostensibly because he taught that man was created in the image of God and that God himself would come down and live among men. Actually, it is unlikely that Abinadi was killed for those doctrinal reasons. See the commentary at Mosiah 17:8 for the more likely reasons.

Mosiah 7:29

The Lord says he will not help us if we are intentionally sinning; in fact, he will hedge up our way—put obstacles in our way—so that we do not succeed (see also Joshua 24:20; 1 Samuel 12:15). He is serious about our being obedient. "I, the Lord, am bound when ye do what I say; but when ye do not what I say, ye have no promise" (D&C 82:10).

Mosiah 7:31

The eastern Mediterranean lands of the Bible are encompassed on the east and on the south by great deserts. Barometric lows or depressions over North Africa can draw strong, dry winds off the eastern and southern deserts to blow over the land of Israel. The condition is known in Arabic as *khamsin* (which means fifty, from the tradition that a year has fifty days with *khamsin* conditions). A scientific name for the wind is *sirocco* (or *scirocco*), an Italian word that derives from the Arabic *sharkiyeh*, meaning east wind. The wind comes off the deserts carrying fine dust that impairs visibility, raises temperatures, and dissipates energy (see Genesis 41:6, 23, 27; Exodus 10:13; 14:21; Jeremiah 18:17; Ezekiel 17:10; 19:12; 27:26; Hosea 13:15; Jonah 4:8).

In the Book of Mormon, the east wind likewise represents destruction and ferocity: "If my people shall sow filthiness they shall reap the east wind, which bringeth immediate destruction"; "they shall also be smitten with the east wind" (Mosiah 12:6).

Mosiah 8:1–4

The scriptural details of all these various groups journeying back and forth throughout the lands of the Book of Mormon (Mosiah 7–24) constitute another of the great evidences of the authenticity of this sacred record. With minimal formal education, Joseph Smith could hardly have woven such an intricate historical and geographical tapestry of the several groups' movements without a single contradiction in the details. Those who knew the prophet testified that he could not have created such a complex story line out of his own head. As it was, merely translating such interrelated and interwoven narratives required Joseph Smith to depend entirely on the gift and power of God to translate, and the help of several scribes to write while he translated, without repeating previous lines when resuming the translation.

Mosiah 8:5–18

This group of Nephites, Limhi's people, had kept a record of their history during the three generations (the eighty years

MAP KEY

1. The ill-fated expedition: Omni 1:27–28; Mosiah 9:1–2
2. Zeniff's expedition: Omni 1:29; Mosiah 9:3; Mosiah 7:9
3. Expedition of 43 men to find Zarahemla: Mosiah 8:1–11
4. Alma's escape to the Waters of Mormon and establishment of the city of Helam: Mosiah 18:1–7, 30–35; Mosiah 23:1–5, 19–20
5. Ammon's expedition to find Zeniff's colony: Mosiah 7:1–6
6. Limhi's escape to Zarahemla: Mosiah 22:1–13
7. Alma's escape to Zarahemla: Mosiah 24:16–25

Journeys between lands of Zarahemla, Nephi, Waters of Mormon, and Helam

Destroyed Jaredite Nation

City of Zarahemla

IT IS NOT KNOWN HOW FAR NORTH OF ZARAHEMLA THE LAND OF THE JAREDITES WAS.

Jaredite History Book of Ether

LAND OF ZARAHEMLA

Helam

LAND OF LEHI-NEPHI

Mosiah 23:1-6

City of Lehi-Nephi

Waters of Mormon

between 200 and 121 B.C.) they had been away from the land of Zarahemla. After Ammon had read their record, Limhi recounted to him the adventures of an expedition of forty-three of his citizens who had set out to renew contact with the land of Zarahemla but had gotten lost and journeyed beyond Zarahemla to discover instead the remains of the Jaredite civilization. From that more northern land they had returned with various artifacts and objects, including twenty-four inscribed gold plates. Limhi wondered if Ammon could interpret the language on those plates.

Ammon responded that King Mosiah II in Zarahemla had a set of interpreters, a Urim and Thummim, and the gift and power to use them to decipher and translate other-language records (compare Mosiah 28:11–19). He was a seer, one who could manifest hidden things of the past as well as reveal unknown things of the future. Such a seer could, with the means God provided and with mighty faith, perform mighty miracles, thus becoming "a great benefit to his fellow beings."

To be a seer is to possess a great gift, greater than the offices of prophet or revelator. A *prophet* (from the Hebrew word meaning "to call") is one called to speak for God, as in the phrase "Thus said the Lord." A prophet is a "forthteller" more than a "foreteller"; that is, he is one who tells what the consequences of actions and events will be. A *seer* (from the Hebrew word meaning "to see") is given visions of what will be. The role of a seer was described by the Lord to Enoch: "And the Lord spake unto Enoch, and said unto him: Anoint thine eyes with clay, and wash them, and thou shalt see. And he did so. And he beheld the spirits that God had created; and *he beheld also things which were not visible to the natural eye*; and from thenceforth came the saying abroad in the land: A seer hath the Lord raised up unto his people" (Moses 6:35–36; emphasis added).

A *revelator* is one who uncovers and restores truth to the Lord's people.

Ammon's doctrinal exposition here is one of the best and most helpful scriptural descriptions of these important roles.

Mosiah 9–22

These chapters constitute the record of Zeniff, "a man who evidently was somewhat learned, had a personal knowledge of the Land of Lehi-Nephi, and also was acquainted with the language spoken by the Lamanites therein, [and] was therefore appointed a spy to learn, if possible, the size and strength of the Lamanite armies. It must always be remembered that the Nephites regarded Lehi-Nephi as the land of their father's first inheritance. The intent of the leader of this first expedition was to overwhelm the Lamanite armies and take possession of the whole land. But Zeniff, in making his report of the conditions he found among the Lamanites, told of so many good things which he saw that, he says, 'I was desirous that they should not be destroyed.'

"Instead, Zeniff advocated that a treaty be arranged with the king of the Lamanites for his people to repossess their old homes. He argued with such ardor that a great contention arose between members of the expedition who favored this peaceful settlement of their purposes and those who preferred a war-like attack, and the leader of them ordered Zeniff to be slain. But in the attempt to carry out that order a riot ensued in which all but fifty of their number perished by violence. These survivors returned to their starting place to tell the sad ending, the failure of their attempts."[21]

Mosiah 9:2–19

During the reign of King Mosiah I (the father of King Benjamin), Zeniff and his people left Zarahemla to return to the land of Nephi. Many years later, during the reign of King Benjamin's son Mosiah II, Ammon journeyed to the land of Nephi to see what had happened to Zeniff's people because they had not been heard from for so long (Mosiah 7:1–2).

This Ammon is different from the Ammon who was one of the four sons of Mosiah II.

Mosiah 9:3

A subtle warning is presented in this verse. There is nothing wrong with being zealous (which means energetic, dynamic, dedicated) in a cause, but *overzealousness* can be dangerous and an example of a strength becoming a weakness. Apparently, Zeniff was obsessed with the idea of resettling the old homeland, and he was blinded by the motives of the Lamanite king, who took advantage of him.

Wisdom suggests that we avoid becoming overzealous and instead keep things in balance.[22]

Mosiah 10:1–22

The characteristics of the Lamanites and their hatred of the Nephites reinforce a consistent, ugly picture of a people whose false traditions have led them to a cursed condition. It is a study on how ignorance and prejudice are passed on. Some of what we see in the world today, one group advocating hatred toward another group, is captured in verse 17.

Mosiah 11:1–25

The character of King Noah, one of Zeniff's sons, was not positive: he was disobedient and debauched, excessive and extravagant, sacrilegious and idolatrous, and flattering and deceiving. It is bad enough to sin but far worse to cause others to sin—which Noah did. Noah had an "edifice complex," constructing elegant public buildings and towers and a palace and temple with fine woodwork and precious metals. He heavily taxed his people to finance all his public works.

Noah and his accomplices in crime and sin spent their time in drunkenness and riotous and promiscuous living. The people became bloodthirsty and boastful, so they were ripening for destruction. In such debased conditions came the warning voice of the prophet Abinadi.

Abinadi is much like John the Baptist. The parallels are striking: lone prophets ministering to two law-of-Moses societies, both preaching repentance, both fulfilling the office of Elias in testifying of the Messiah, and both preparing the way for him. Both were bold, both were colorful, and both were killed by wicked political rulers.

Mosiah 11:24–25

The only way to extricate ourselves from any kind of bondage is to cry out to the Lord. For that reason he is called the Savior; he can rescue us from any kind of physical, spiritual, intellectual, or emotional bondage that holds us captive—but not if we are rebellious. We have to be quick to observe his light before he will be quick to respond to our plight.

Mosiah 11:27, 29

Noah reacted insolently to the prophet: "Who is Abinadi, that I and my people should be judged of him, or who is the Lord, that shall bring upon my people such great affliction?" Such words are echoes of Cain ("Who is the Lord that I should know him?"; Moses 5:16), Pharaoh ("Who is the Lord, that I should obey his voice?"; Exodus 5:2), and the people of Ammonihah ("Who is God, that sendeth no more authority than one man among this people?"; Alma 9:6). Such defiant attitudes come from blinded minds and hardened hearts.

Mosiah 12:1–12

While speaking to the people and to King Noah and his priests, Abinadi was not trying to build a relationship of trust. He was dealing with wicked, intentional sinners. He boldly denounced their sins.

While prophesying the people's fate, Abinadi used some classic similes: His countrymen would be afflicted and howl because of the burdens lashed on their backs, being "driven before like a dumb ass." The king's life would be "valued even as a garment in a hot furnace" and "as the blossoms of a thistle, which, when it is fully ripe, if the wind bloweth, it is driven forth upon the face of the land." The latter expression means that the king's life would be blown away like a worthless weed.

Mosiah 12:16–19

The scene of Abinadi before Noah's council parallels Jesus before the Jewish Sanhedrin and the Roman governor: "Behold, here is the man" (compare John 19:5). "And they began to question him, that they might cross him, . . . [and] accuse him" (compare Matthew 26:59; Luke 23:2; John 18:29). Abinadi answered boldly and "did withstand them in all their questions, and did confound them in all their words."

Mosiah 12:20–29

One of Noah's priests inquired about four verses in Isaiah, and Abinadi replied, "Are you priests, and pretend to teach this people, and to understand the spirit of prophesying, and yet desire to know of me what these things mean?" Then he condemned them: "If ye understand these things ye have not taught them," which constitutes a perversion of the ways of the Lord.

A rigorous interchange ensued.

Abinadi: "What teach ye this people?"

Priests: "We teach the law of Moses."

Abinadi: "If ye teach the law of Moses why do ye not keep it?" Then the prophet condemned their greed, their immoral behavior, and their causing the people to sin.

It is significant that Abinadi invokes "the heart" as the way to understand the things of God: "Ye have not applied your hearts [not minds] to understanding." The heart is the core of life and strength. In the ancient world it included the mind, spirit, and soul—one's entire emotional and mental makeup. As the ancient writer said, "For as he thinketh in his heart so is he" (Proverbs 23:7). But more importantly, the heart was the very thing Noah and the priests needed to have changed, and yet they would not (Alma 5:13–14).

Mosiah 13:1–24

After hearing the first two of the great commandments received on Mount Sinai (Exodus 20:3–4; Mosiah 12:35–36) and Abinadi's rebuke for failing to live them and teach their people to live them, the guilty king and his priests took the truth to be hard, for it cut them "to the very center," as Nephi had taught (see 1 Nephi 16:2). The king ordered the priests to get rid of this man, "for he is mad." The wicked do not want to hear about their sins, so they resort to name-calling: the man is crazy. The Roman governor Festus accused Paul of the very same kind of madness (Acts 26:24).

When the council members tried to lay their hands on Abinadi, he warned them not to touch him; he was full of the Spirit and shielded from any hindrance while he delivered his heaven-sent message and answered the questions they had asked him. Abinadi was transfigured before that hostile assembly the way others would be, most notably Stephen before the Sanhedrin (Acts 6:15).

The prophet also warned them that after his mission was accomplished, whatever they did to him would be a "type and a shadow," or prophetic foreshadowing, of what would also happen to them (Mosiah 17:13–15; Alma 25:9–11).

With power and authority, Abinadi boldly taught the basics. The Ten Commandments are repeated in all dispensations because they are the foundation, and foundational commandments must be written deep in our hearts.

Why would Abinadi teach such sacred doctrine to a wicked audience? One reason is that Alma was there.

Mosiah 13:28–33

Here is a concise treatise on the overall purpose of the law of Moses. Like the apostle Paul, Abinadi declared that

POINTING SOULS TO CHRIST

Following are examples of how the law of Moses helped people remember their duty to God (Mosiah 13:30), pointed their souls to Christ (Jacob 4:5), and strengthened their faith in him (Alma 25:16).

Exodus 12:5—the Passover lamb must "be without blemish, a male"	John 1:29—he is "the Lamb of God, which taketh away the sin of the world"
	1 Corinthians 5:7—"Christ, our passover, is sacrificed for us"
Exodus 16:15—"manna: . . . the bread which the Lord hath given you"	John 6:51—"the bread that I will give is my flesh"
Exodus 17:6—the rock was smitten, and water came out of it	1 Corinthians 10:4—"that Rock was Christ" (the living water), and he, too, was smitten
Exodus 30:10—"the blood of the sin offering of atonements"	Matthew 26:28—"this is my blood of the new testament"
	Mosiah 3:11—"his blood atoneth for . . . sins"
Leviticus 16:22—"the goat shall bear upon him all their iniquities"	Isaiah 53:5—"he was wounded for our transgressions, he was bruised for our iniquities"
	Mosiah 15:9—"taken upon himself their iniquity and their transgressions"
Numbers 9:12—no bone of the lamb was to be broken	John 19:36—"a bone of him shall not be broken"
Numbers 21:8—a serpent of brass was lifted up to heal the people	John 3:14—"even so must the Son of man be lifted up"

salvation does not come by the law alone (compare Galatians 2:16). Yet, earlier he was able to say with confidence that he knew that if the people would keep the commandments of the Mosaic law, they would be saved (Mosiah 12:33). How are both statements true? Because the law was conceived to bring people to the Messiah.

All those laws and practices were types of things to come; they served to strengthen the ancient disciples' faith in Christ and point their souls to him (Alma 25:16; Jacob 4:5), the only real source of salvation. The law of Moses "is a shadow of those things which are to come," and "redemption cometh through Christ the Lord" (Mosiah 16:14–15). Theirs was a very strict law with ritual performances and ordinances to observe with exactness day by day to help them remember God and their duty to him. In modern times we also have our daily and weekly performances and ordinances, reminders to keep our lives straight and our spirituality strong.

Mosiah 13:33

"All the prophets who have prophesied ever since the world began" have foretold the ministry and atonement of the Lord Jesus Christ, for as John wrote, "the spirit of prophecy is the testimony of Jesus" (Revelation 19:10); that is, testifying of Jesus is what prophesying is all about. Adam, Enoch, Noah, Melchizedek, Abraham, Joseph, Moses, Isaiah, Lehi, Nephi, and all other true prophets bore record of their Redeemer. Even the Jewish rabbis recognized the importance of that special witness. The Talmud declares, "All the prophets prophesied only of the days of the Messiah."[23]

Mosiah 13:34–35

The prophets made it clear what kind of a Messiah he would be: God himself would condescend and take up a physical body (see also Mosiah 3:5) to be oppressed and afflicted but also resurrected. This obviously led Abinadi to quote Isaiah 53.

ALL THE PROPHETS PROPHESIED OF CHRIST

Prophecy	Person Speaking or Writing	Reference
His Birth		
The Creator, Jehovah, would take a mortal body in order to redeem mankind	The brother of Jared, Nephi, Jacob, Benjamin, Abinadi, Ammon, Lamoni, John the Baptist	Isaiah 44:24; Ether 3:6–16; 1 Nephi 19:7–12; 2 Nephi 9:5; Mosiah 3:5; 7:27; 13:34; 15:1; 19:13; D&C 93:6–11
He would be the Son of God, the Only Begotten of the Father in the flesh, the God of Israel	Adam, Enoch, Moses, Isaiah, Nephi, Jacob, Abinadi, Alma, John the Baptist	Moses 1:6, 33; 2:1, 26; 6:52; Isaiah 9:6–7; 1 Nephi 11:20–21; 22:12; 2 Nephi 25:12; Jacob 4:5; Mosiah 15:2–5; Alma 5:48; 7:10; 9:26; D&C 93:11–14
His mother would be a virgin, a descendant of Jacob through King David; she would be from Nazareth, and her name would be Mary	Moses, Isaiah, Jeremiah, Nephi, Benjamin, Alma	Genesis 49:24; Isaiah 7:14; 11:1; Jeremiah 23:5–6; 33:15–16; 1 Nephi 11:13–21; Mosiah 3:8; Alma 7:10
Signs (a star, light, etc.) would attend his birth	Samuel the Lamanite	Helaman 14:3–7
His Name		
The Messiah would be called "Salvation" (in Hebrew, *Yeshua*; in English, *Jesus*)	Moses, Isaiah	Exodus 15:2; Isaiah 12:2–6
His name would be Jesus Christ	Adam, Enoch, Noah, brother of Jared, Nephi, Jacob, King Benjamin, Abinadi, Alma	Moses 6:52, 57; 8:23–24; Ether 3:14–16; 2 Nephi 10:3; 25:19; 31:10; Jacob 4:11; Mosiah 3:8, 17; 7:27; Alma 5:48

Prophecy	Person Speaking or Writing	Reference
His Time of Birth		
Jesus would be born in the meridian of time, 600 years after Lehi left Jerusalem and 5 years after Samuel's prophecy	Adam, Enoch, Moses, Lehi, Nephi, Samuel the Lamanite	Moses 5:57; 6:57, 62; 7:45–46; 1 Nephi 10:4; 19:8; 2 Nephi 25:19; Helaman 14:2
His Place of Birth		
Christ would be born among the Jews near Jerusalem at a place called Bethlehem	Micah, Jacob, Alma	Micah 5:2; 2 Nephi 10:3; Alma 7:10
Details of His Ministry		
A messenger-prophet would prepare the way for the Messiah's mission	Isaiah, Lehi	Isaiah 40:3; 1 Nephi 10:7–9
Christ would come out of Egypt	Hosea	Hosea 11:1
He would grow up in Nazareth	Nephi	1 Nephi 11:13, 20
He would be baptized by the messenger-prophet beyond Jordan near Bethabara; the prophet would testify of him, and the Holy Ghost would descend on him as a dove	Lehi, Nephi	1 Nephi 10:9–10; 11:27; 2 Nephi 31:4–8
He would suffer temptations, hunger, and thirst	Isaiah, Benjamin, Abinadi, Alma	Isaiah 53:3; Mosiah 3:7; 15:5; Alma 7:11
He would call twelve apostles in both the Old World and the New	Nephi	1 Nephi 11:29, 34; 12:8–10

PROPHECY	PERSON SPEAKING OR WRITING	REFERENCE
Details of His Ministry (continued)		
He would preach glad tidings	Isaiah	Isaiah 61:1
He would care for his followers as a shepherd	Isaiah, Ezekiel	Isaiah 40:10–11; Ezekiel 34:11–31
He would be a priest forever (after the order of Melchizedek)	Moses, David, Alma	JST, Genesis 14:25–28; Psalm 110:1–4; Alma 13:7–9
He would minister in power and glory, performing miracles	Isaiah, Nephi, Jacob, Benjamin, Abinadi, Alma	Isaiah 59:16–19; 1 Nephi 11:28, 31; 2 Nephi 10:4; Mosiah 3:5–6; 15:6; Alma 5:50
He would come to Zion (Jerusalem)	Isaiah	Isaiah 59:20
He would come as a king riding on a young ass	Zechariah	Zechariah 9:9
He would be a stumbling block to his people, who would reject him	David, Isaiah, Nephi, Jacob	Psalm 118:21–22; Isaiah 8:13–14; 53:3; 1 Nephi 19:13; 2 Nephi 10:3–5; 25:12; Jacob 4:15
He would be betrayed for thirty pieces of silver	David, Zechariah	Psalm 41:9; Zechariah 11:12–13; 13:6
Foreshadowings of his life and mission	Adam, Nephi	Moses 6:62–63; 2 Nephi 11:4
Atonement: His Suffering		
Christ would yield himself to suffer	Isaiah, Nephi, Abinadi	Isaiah 50:6; 53:7; 1 Nephi 19:9–10; Mosiah 15:5–6
He would be innocent of violence and deceit	Isaiah	Isaiah 53:9

PROPHECY	PERSON SPEAKING OR WRITING	REFERENCE
Atonement: His Suffering (continued)		
He would suffer to atone for our sins and heal our sicknesses; blood would come from every pore	Isaiah, Jacob, Benjamin, Alma, Amulek, Aaron	Isaiah 53:3–12; 2 Nephi 9:21–22; Mosiah 3:7; Alma 7:11–13; 21:9; 34:8–9
He would be judged and placed in prison	Isaiah, Nephi	Isaiah 53:8; 1 Nephi 11:32
Foreshadowings of his suffering	Abraham, Isaac, Moses, Jacob	Genesis 22:1–14; Leviticus 16:7–10; Jacob 4:5
Atonement: His Crucifixion		
Christ would die voluntarily	Isaiah, Lehi, Nephi, Abinadi	Isaiah 53:7, 9, 12; 1 Nephi 19:9–10; 2 Nephi 2:6–7; Mosiah 15:5, 7
He would be crucified for and by his people	Enoch, Zenock, Neum, Lehi, Nephi, Jacob	Moses 7:47, 55; 1 Nephi 10:11; 11:32–33; 19:10; 2 Nephi 6:9; 10:3–5; 25:13
His hands and feet would be pierced	David, Isaiah, Zechariah	Psalm 22:16; Isaiah 22:23–25; Zechariah 12:10; 13:6
He would be mocked and suffer pain and thirst	David, Isaiah	Psalm 22:7–8; Isaiah 50:6
He would be given vinegar to drink	David	Psalm 69:20–21
He would speak specific words from the cross	David	Psalm 22:1; 31:5
None of his bones would be broken	David	Psalm 34:19–20
Lots would be cast for his garments	David	Psalm 22:18

Prophecy	Person Speaking or Writing	Reference
Atonement: His Crucifixion (continued)		
He would be buried in a sepulchre	Zenos, Nephi	1 Nephi 19:10; 2 Nephi 25:13
Signs would attend his death (darkness, earthquakes, etc.)	Zenos, Nephi, Samuel the Lamanite	1 Nephi 12:4–6; 19:10–13; Helaman 14:20–28
Clear foreshadowings of his atonement and death	Adam, Eve, Enoch, Abraham, Isaac, Moses, Ezekiel, Nephi, Jacob, Alma, Nephi (son of Helaman)	Moses 5:4–7; 6:63–65; Genesis 22:1–14; Exodus 12; 16:12–35; 17:1–7; 29; Leviticus 1–17; 21–23; Numbers 19; 21:5–9; Ezekiel 43:18–27; 45:18–25; 1 Nephi 17:41; Jacob 4:4–5; Alma 33:18–23; Helaman 8:13–15
Atonement: His Resurrection		
Jesus would rise from death after three days and show himself to witnesses	Lehi, Nephi, Benjamin	1 Nephi 10:11; 2 Nephi 25:13–14; 26:1; Mosiah 3:10
Others would be resurrected because he overcame death	Enoch, Samuel, Job, David, Isaiah, Ezekiel, Hosea, Jacob, Abinadi, Alma, Amulek, Samuel the Lamanite	Moses 7:55–56, 62; 1 Samuel 2:6; Job 19:25–27; Psalm 16:9–10; Isaiah 25:8; 26:19; Ezekiel 37:12–13; Hosea 13:14; 2 Nephi 2:8; 9:4–13; Mosiah 13:33–35; 15:20–24; 16:7–11; Alma 11:42–45; 33:22; 40:2–23; Helaman 14:25
Foreshadowings of his resurrection	Jonah	Jonah 1:17; 2:1–10

PROPHECY	PERSON SPEAKING OR WRITING	REFERENCE
Atonement: Whys and Hows		
Christ's atonement would be infinite	Nephi, Jacob, Amulek	2 Nephi 9:7; 25:16; Alma 34:8–14
His sacrifice would satisfy the laws of justice and mercy	Jacob, Abinadi, Alma, Amulek	2 Nephi 9:25-26; 25:16; Mosiah 15:8–9, 26–27; Alma 34:14–18; 42:13-30
His atonement would redeem all mankind from physical death, brought by the Fall	Lehi, Jacob, Abinadi, Alma, Amulek	2 Nephi 2:8–9; 9:4–15; Mosiah 15:7–9, 20–27; Alma 11:39–45; 12:21–25; 40:23; 41:2–15
His atonement would make available the forgiveness of sins for all who have faith in him, repent, are baptized, receive the Holy Ghost, and endure; they thus become his sons and daughters and receive joy and eternal life	Adam, Eve, Noah, brother of Jared, Isaiah, Lehi, Nephi, Jacob, Benjamin, Abinadi, Alma, Amulek, Aaron, John the Baptist	Moses 5:8–11; 6:51–68; 8:23–24; Matthew 3:11; Ether 3:14; Isaiah 1:16–18; 1 Nephi 10:4–6; 2 Nephi 2:3–29; 9:10–42; 31:10–21; Mosiah 3:11–19; 4:5–30; 5:6–15; 15:10–19; Alma 5:6–62; 11:36–43; 12:12–37; 22:14; 34:2–41; 42:2–28
His Visit to the Spirit World		
The Savior's atonement would extend into the spirit world, setting the prisoners free	Enoch, Isaiah, Zechariah	Moses 7:57; Isaiah 42:6–7; 61:1; Zechariah 9:11
His Visit to a Branch of Joseph		
Christ would visit a branch of Joseph's descendants	Joseph, Nephi	JST, Genesis 50:25; 1 Nephi 12:1, 6; 2 Nephi 26:1
His Ascension into Heaven		
Jesus would ascend to the Father after his resurrection	Enoch	Moses 7:59

Isaiah and Abinadi taught that he would condescend to the form of man and provide an atoning sacrifice of himself for all humankind. The verbs they used in describing his mission paint a portrait of grief and sorrow far different than the messianic expectations of later generations of Jews. Rather than coming as a bigger-than-life political figure who would wield impressive political clout, he would come as a suffering Servant. According to five remarkable verses of Isaiah (53:3–7; Mosiah 14:3–7), He would be despised, rejected, stricken, smitten, wounded, bruised, oppressed, and afflicted.

Mosiah 14

Isaiah 53 is a prophecy of the atonement of Jesus Christ. It is one of the plain and precious things *not* taken out of the Bible, though many have tried to distort its meaning and weaken its powerful witness through humanistic and academic devices.

This chapter of Isaiah shows that the Old Testament does indeed testify of Jesus the Messiah, and it does teach the basic principles of the Atonement. Almost all of Isaiah 53 is reproduced in the New Testament, applying to Jesus.

Philip, an early Christian church leader and missionary, encountered on one occasion an officer of the Ethiopian court returning to his homeland from Jerusalem. The officer was reading Isaiah 53 when Philip met him on the road, and Philip asked him if he understood what he was reading. After looking at several verses, the officer asked Philip, "I pray thee, of whom speaketh the prophet this? of himself, or of some other man?" (Acts 8:34). It was not immediately apparent to the Ethiopian who the subject of Isaiah's prophecy was. "Then Philip opened his mouth, and began at the same scripture, and preached unto him Jesus" (Acts 8:35).

Elder Bruce R. McConkie wrote: "As our New Testament now stands, we find Matthew (Matt. 8:17), [John (John 12:37–41)], Philip (Acts 8:27–35), Paul (Rom. 4:25), and Peter (1 Pet. 2:24–25) all quoting, paraphrasing, enlarging upon, and applying to the Lord Jesus various of the verses in this great 53rd chapter of Isaiah. How many sermons have been preached, how many lessons have been taught, how many testimonies have been borne—both in ancient Israel and in the meridian of time—using the utterances of this chapter as the text, we can scarcely imagine."[24]

Mosiah 14:1

The question "who hath believed our report?" suggests that few have believed or understood the prophecies that the Messiah would come into mortality in the form of a man. This belief and understanding comes only to those to whom the "arm of the Lord," or the power of God, is revealed, for the things of God can only be understood by the Spirit of God (1 Corinthians 2:11).

Many do not respond to the Spirit because of their hard-heartedness (John 12:39–41), that is, unwillingness to listen to the prophets. Thus, the apostle John reported: "But though he had done so many miracles before them, yet they believed not on him; that the saying of Esaias the prophet might be fulfilled, which he spake, Lord, who hath believed our report? and to whom hath the arm of the Lord been revealed?" (John 12:37–38).

In the case of Abinadi and the priests of Noah, Abinadi testified that God would come in the "form of a man, and go forth in mighty power upon the face of the earth" (Mosiah 13:34), and the priests of Noah believed not his report.

Mosiah 14:2

In a chapter of the first volume of *The Mortal Messiah,* "The Soil in Which the Root Was Planted," Elder Bruce R. McConkie wrote that our Savior "was to be planted in arid soil; to grow up as a tender plant, as a root out of dry ground. Babylonia, Persia, Egypt, Syria, Greece, and Rome—each in turn—had ploughed in the fields of [Canaan, or Israel]. Each had reaped harvests without dunging the land. The early rains of revelation and the latter rains of prophetic guidance had not watered the soil for centuries. The thistles and weeds and briers of sin encumbered the vineyards. There was a famine of hearing the word of the Lord."[25]

One characteristic of dry ground that once was wet is that it becomes very hard. This is especially true of certain soils that become sun-baked; they become hardened and impenetrable. The Lord, as the fountain of living waters (Jeremiah 2:13), would come to irrigate the arid soil so that "the desert [could] rejoice, and blossom as the rose" (Isaiah 35:1).

Just as the rock was smitten to bring forth water for thirsting Israelites (Numbers 20:11), so the Lord himself was smitten to provide the living water of eternal life for all who would come and drink.

"No form . . . no beauty"—Jews expected supernatural glory in their Messiah. Some imagined that their King would be fabulously wealthy, handsome, and in every way attractive, and that he would come with great fanfare and applause. His purposes would be well-known and publicized, and there would be no question about who he was. Everyone would recognize him at a glance. President Joseph Fielding Smith wrote: "It is expressed here by the prophet that he had no form or comeliness, that is, he was not so distinctive, so different from others that people would recognize him as the Son of God. He appeared as a mortal man."[26]

Mosiah 14:3

Isaiah clearly foretold the attitude of many in Israel regarding their Savior. Ironically, in rejecting these very words as a prophecy of the Messiah, his people were fulfilling them by despising and rejecting him.

Some of his own family members failed to accept him as Messiah at first (John 7:5); people in his hometown tried to kill him (Luke 4:16–30); his own countrymen rejected him (John 1:11); one of his best friends betrayed him (Luke 22:48). In the end "all the disciples forsook him, and fled"

(Matthew 26:56), and his enemies demanded his execution (Matthew 27:22–23). The people of Israel would hide their eyes from their God and not esteem his salvation (compare 1 Nephi 19:7–9).

PROPHECIES OF THE MESSIAH

Why would Jews generally reject Jesus as their long-awaited Messiah? Glance through the following sample of prophecies to understand what concept of Messiah should have prevailed among his own people (emphasis added):

Genesis 49:10. "The *sceptre* shall not depart from Judah . . . until Shiloh come."

Numbers 24:17. "There shall come a Star out of Jacob, and a *Sceptre* shall rise out of Israel."

Psalm 22:1. "My God, my God, why hast thou forsaken me?"

Psalm 22:16. "They pierced my hands and my feet."

Psalm 34:20. "He keepeth all his bones: not one of them is broken."

Psalm 69:21. "In my thirst they gave me vinegar to drink."

Psalm 118:22. "The stone which the builders refused is become the head."

Isaiah 7:14. "A virgin shall conceive, and bear a son, . . . Immanuel."

Isaiah 9:6. "Unto us a child is born, . . . and the *government* shall be upon his shoulder."

Isaiah 9:7. "Of his government . . . there shall be no end."

Isaiah 50:6. "I gave my back to the smiters."

Isaiah 53:5. "He was wounded for our transgressions."

Isaiah 61:1. "Anointed me to preach good tidings"

Jeremiah 23:5. "A *King* shall reign and . . . execute judgment and justice."

Daniel 9:26. "Shall Messiah be cut off"

Micah 5:2. "Bethlehem . . . , out of thee shall he come forth . . . to be *ruler* in Israel."

Zechariah 9:9. "Thy *King* cometh unto thee . . . riding upon an ass."

Zechariah 11:13. "I was prised at . . . thirty pieces of silver."

Zechariah 13:6. "I was wounded in the house of my friends."

All of the prophetic suggestions of royalty, rulership, and kingship would eventually be fulfilled at the Lord's *second* coming; meanwhile, look again at the other passages for what kind of a Messiah he would be at his *first* coming.

Mosiah 14:4

This may be the single greatest verse of scripture in the Old Covenant (Old Testament) on the essential principle of the Atonement: substitution. In his vicarious sacrifice the Savior took upon himself not only all of our sins but also our pains and sorrows—in this way he knows how to succor his followers in their hour of emotional and spiritual need (compare Alma 7:11–12; Hebrews 2:18).

Some would think that the Savior was "stricken, smitten of God" because of his personal sins, but Isaiah taught otherwise: "He was wounded for *our* transgressions, he was bruised for *our* iniquities" (Isaiah 53:5; emphasis added).

Mosiah 14:5

Christ's sufferings at Gethsemane and Golgotha are described. He took upon himself the pains and sins of the world to heal and redeem mankind.

Referring to Jesus' suffering for "*our* transgressions" and "*our* iniquities," Isaiah makes us aware of our personal involvement and responsibility for the oppression and affliction of the Savior. Jacobus Revius, a Dutch poet and theologian (1586–1658), powerfully teaches the same poignant lesson that Isaiah teaches:

> It was not the Jews, Lord Jesus, who crucified you,
> Nor the traitors who dragged you to the law,

Nor the contemptuous who spit in your face
Nor those who bound you, and hit you full of wounds,
And it was not the soldiers who with evil hands
Lifted up the reed or the hammer,
Or set that cursed wood on Golgotha,
Or cast lots and gambled for your robe;
It is I, O Lord, it is I who have done it,
I am the heavy tree that overburdened you,
I am the rough bands that bound you,
The nail, the spear, and the cords that whipped you,
The bloodied crown that tore your head:
All this happened, alas! for my sins.[27]

"The chastisement of our peace was upon him"—the English word "peace" is used here to translate the Hebrew *shalom*, which carries the connotation of wholeness and reconciliation. This is not the common greeting of "shalom" that the world extends, but the deeper doctrine of justification to dwell in God's presence. The Savior suffered the chastisement so that we could be reconciled to the Father and become whole.

"With his stripes we are healed"—his "stripes" refer to his scourging, both the physical flogging and also the torturous flagellation caused by the sins of the world. Until we accept his stripes, we are spiritually sick; we need to follow the prescription of the Master Physician to be healed. It is ironic that we are healed through his stripes; our peace comes through his pain.

Mosiah 14:6

The verse "All we, like sheep, have gone astray; we have turned every one to his own way" symbolizes the need for all to be saved by the atonement of Christ (compare Matthew 9:36; Alma 5:37; D&C 1:16).

Mosiah 14:7

These images prophetically foreshadow events during the hearings or "trials" of Jesus before Jewish and Roman leaders. While being accused and interrogated by the chief priests and Pilate, Jesus gave no answer (Mark 15:3; John 19:9), and while standing before Herod Antipas, Jesus answered him nothing (Luke 23:9). When the time came for Jesus to be brought as a lamb to the slaughter, "the Lamb slain from the foundation of the world" (Revelation 13:8) opened not his mouth—just as a sheep is dumb, or mute, in the hands of the shearers.

Mosiah 14:8

The Hebrew text implies that he was taken *by arrest* and *by judgment*. Think about the combined meaning of all the adjectives Isaiah used to describe the Messiah: stricken, smitten, afflicted, wounded, bruised, and oppressed. Now the prophet even declares that he would be "cut off out of the land of the living," which was certainly not the way Jews centuries later viewed the purpose and mission of their Messiah.

In the Old Testament the value of a person's life was often measured by his posterity, who would perpetuate his name, works, and merits. Inasmuch as Christ would be "cut off" or killed, who would "declare his generation"? Who would be his posterity to carry on his work and glory? Who would declare the life and atoning mission of Jesus the Messiah? Abinadi testified "that when [Christ's] soul has been made an offering for sin he shall see his seed" or posterity (Mosiah 15:10). Abinadi then taught that Christ's seed are those who believe in him and are redeemed through him—the prophets and those who believe on their words (Mosiah 15:10–12). They become his children, his sons and daughters, who will perpetuate his words and works on the earth.

Mosiah 14:9

We read that his death was with the wicked (he was cruci-fied between two thieves; see Matthew 27:38), and he was with the rich in his grave (he was buried in the borrowed grave of wealthy Joseph of Arimathea; see Matthew 27:57–60).

This verse may give us insight into why the leaders of the Jews wanted to kill Jesus. Isaiah wrote, "He had done no violence [Abinadi: "no evil"], neither was any deceit in his mouth." Few things can stir up anger in the unrighteous as much as a good example. Recall Laman and Lemuel. Why didn't Laman and Lemuel just get up one morning and make the hike back to Jerusalem? Why was their incessant effort to kill Lehi and Nephi and *then* go back to Jerusalem? They knew that their father and brother were telling the truth, and they were angry because of it. They were jealous and envious and proud. Some of the Jewish leaders had the same problem with Jesus. No one welcomed them into the city by throwing down palm fronds in their path. Nobody was being healed by them. There were no great crowds flocking around them to hang on their every word. Something had to be done about this righteous person who always spoke the truth. They had him crucified.

Mosiah 14:10

"Yet it pleased [satisfied, gratified] the Lord to bruise him"—this phrase has at least two possible interpretations: (1) "Lord" may be a reference to Elohim, the Father, thus teaching that this was a willing offering by the Father and the Son (John 3:16) or (2) Isaiah may be differentiating between the two roles of the Savior: it pleased Jehovah, the God of the Old Testament, to bruise Jesus, pointing to the fact that the great Jehovah would come in the person of Jesus and that they are, indeed, one God (compare Mosiah 15:2–4).

"When thou shalt make his soul an offering for sin he

shall see his seed"—"his" and "he" in this verse are usually taken to mean Christ, while the pronoun "thou" is thought to refer to either God the Father or to those receiving the prophecy. In either case the message is the same for all: when one is forgiven of sins through the Atonement, one is spiritually begotten of Christ and becomes "his seed," or child (compare Mosiah 15:10–12; D&C 84:36–38).

"He shall prolong his days"—Christ will be resurrected and become immortal.

Mosiah 14:11

Luke asked, "Ought not Christ to have suffered these things, and to enter into his glory?" (Luke 24:26). Jesus' crown of thorns came before his crown of glory. Having shown the way, he later taught that "after much tribulation come the blessings" (D&C 58:4; see also Alma 26:27; 7:5; 17:11; 28:8).

The Savior will "justify many," meaning that he will make righteous and reconcile many. The use of *many* rather than *all* suggests that some, the unrepentant, will not be justified, that is, put back into a right relationship with God the Father (compare D&C 19:16–19).

Mosiah 14:12

"He shall divide the spoil with the strong"—the strong and faithful will become joint-heirs with the Savior, possessing with him the fulness of the Father (Romans 8:17; D&C 50:26–28; 76:50–60; 88:107; 93:15–30; 132:20).

Christ's atonement was active rather than passive suffering. "By saying that *he poured out his soul* unto death, Isaiah may be suggesting why it was important for him to die on the cross—for this manner of death allowed him time to do the pouring out. If he had been beheaded, hanged, run through with a sword, or stoned, he would have died instantaneously without having had any time to use his volition in giving up his life. When they put him on the cross to see that he died, all they needed to satisfy their desires was time. Given time,

THE BOOK OF MOSIAH

he would die. But by giving him time, they gave him control over the giving. He could decide at what point to lay down his life. Thus, as a priest sacrificing a lamb, he performed the sacrifice. And as a Lamb, he became his own victim. (Heb. 8:1–2; 9:11–16, esp. v. 14.) This crucial detail was known to Isaiah when he said that the righteous servant would pour out his own soul unto death."[28]

The grand purpose of Jesus' suffering is for us to become his seed and declare his generation. Jesus came to earth to be a suffering Servant, and his was a unique service to all humankind. Isaiah's description of Jesus' service is also unique; no one else could possibly fulfill such an appointed service except the Son of God himself.

Mosiah 15:1

Chapter 15 contains some of Abinadi's commentary on Isaiah 53, just quoted. It is not a verse-by-verse treatment, but thematic. Abinadi's prophecy that God himself would come down among the children of men and redeem his people is the same message the angel delivered to King Benjamin more than twenty years later (Mosiah 3:5–11). Perhaps the angel who delivered that message to the king (Mosiah 3:2) was the martyred Abinadi himself.

Mosiah 15:2–9

Eleven days before his death, Joseph Smith taught, "I have always declared God to be a distinct personage, Jesus Christ a separate and distinct personage from God the Father, and that the Holy Ghost was a distinct personage and a Spirit" (see also D&C 130:22).[29] There are three distinct persons in the Godhead. The Prophet also declared, "Everlasting covenant was made between three personages before the organization of this earth, and relates to their dispensation of things to men on the earth. These personages . . . are called God the first, the Creator; God the second, the Redeemer; and God the third, the Witness or Testator."[30]

The Book of Mormon teaches plainly the roles of the second member of the Godhead as the Old Testament Jehovah and the New Testament Jesus, but it also plainly elucidates his roles as Father and Son.

Jesus Christ is both the Son *and* the Father—the Son because he was begotten by God the Father and submitted to the will of the Father, but also the Father in the sense that he is the creator or father of the earth; he is the father of our flesh because our flesh is made from the dust or elements of the earth that he created; he is the God or Father of the Old Testament and the Father or Author of our salvation; he was and is the great Jehovah; he has all the attributes of the Father; and by divine investiture he serves the role of the Father in all things relative to our salvation. By his sacrifice, he became even more than our Savior—he became our covenant Father, and as we are spiritually reborn we become the children of Christ (for further references and explanation about becoming sons and daughters of Christ, see Mosiah 5:7; 27:25; Ether 3:14; D&C 25:1; 34:3; 39:4). The foregoing is a summary of a statement issued in 1916, "The Father and the Son: A Doctrinal Exposition by the First Presidency and the Twelve."

Jehovah of the Old Testament and Jesus of the New Testament are explained and distinguished. The phrase "they are one God" in verse 4 refers to Jehovah and Jesus as one God—the same Person.

In addition, all of the Gods constituting the Godhead are one God in the sense that they are of exactly the same mind and heart in everything they do with us here on earth. The concept of unity or oneness is foundational in the gospel of Jesus Christ. It is the basic and essential message inherent in the otherwise abstract English word *atonement,* "at-*one*-ment," or the idea of becoming one. So much alike are the three members of the Godhead that if we know one, we know the others. The Father, the Son, and the Holy Ghost

354

are *one God* (2 Nephi 31:21; Alma 11:44; 3 Nephi 11:36; D&C 20:28).[31]

Brigham Young University professors Stephen Robinson and Dean Garrett clarify: "We tend to focus on the distinctions between the Father, Son, and Holy Ghost in order to understand them as individuals. But the message of [D&C 93:3: 'I am in the Father, and the Father in me, and the Father and I are one'] is that such a neat division between their respective roles is sometimes difficult to make—for their complete unity of thought, personality, and purpose usually makes them better understood by their oneness, by their 'alikeness,' than by their differences. This unity of the Godhead is so perfect that it sometimes confuses us, as when Christ speaks as the Father, or when the Holy Ghost speaks as the Son (see Moses 1:6; 5:9; D&C 29:1, 42). As we teach the truth concerning the separate physical natures of the Father and the Son, we must be careful not to separate them in any other sense, for the Father and the Son are 'in' each other (John 14:10) and are one in a way difficult for mortals to fully appreciate, though in a way that does not compromise their separate and individual being."[32]

Mosiah 15:5–9 describes in considerable detail Christ's perfect willingness to come down and perform mighty miracles and yet experience rejection, suffering, and death, all according to the will of the Father, to intercede for all the children of men and resolve all the consequences of the Fall. Thus, Jesus the Messiah is the great Mediator (see D&C 76:69). He pleads our case before God the Father (see D&C 45:3–5). See commentary at 2 Nephi 2:8–10 and the accompanying chart.

Mosiah 15:10–13

Abinadi continued to answer questions about Isaiah's teachings. Upon offering his soul as an offering for sin, Christ will see his seed (Mosiah 14:10). The seed or children of Christ are they who covenant with him and are born of him—spiritually begotten by him—and "changed from their carnal and fallen state, to a state of righteousness, being redeemed of God, becoming his sons and daughters" (Mosiah 27:25; see also 5:7). The seed of Christ, and heirs of the kingdom of God, include all the holy prophets.

Mosiah 15:14–18

The holy prophets have preached and published the good tidings of peace and salvation, and they have testified that God lives and reigns in his heaven. Blessings on their feet! The feet, in scriptural symbolism, are the parts of the body that carry God's messengers out into the mountains (the nations) of the world. Mission doctors worldwide know that missionaries have as many problems with their well-used feet as with any other part of their bodies. How beautiful, and how indispensable, are those feet! How beautiful, especially, are the feet of him who is the Prince of Peace, the founder and provider of peace and redemption for all who truly desire to become his children.

Isaiah's words "how beautiful upon the mountains" appear seven times in the Book of Mormon: four times here, and also in 1 Nephi 13:37; Mosiah 12:21; and 3 Nephi 20:40. The beginning phrase, "how beautiful," is in Hebrew *mah nauvoo*; see commentary at 3 Nephi 20:40 for the significance of "nauvoo" to the Latter-day Saints.

Mosiah 15:20–27

The Old Testament, as it presently stands, has very few references to the resurrection of the dead. No instances of resurrection occurred during the entire Old Testament period, and few scriptural references to it have survived from the world of the Bible. In the more enlightening world of Book of Mormon prophets, however, we have a glorious exposition on the resurrection taught and inscribed in the middle of the second century B.C.

Abinadi spoke of the "first resurrection," occurring immediately following the resurrection of Christ, who is "the firstfruits of them that slept" (1 Corinthians 15:20). Those resurrected were the righteous who lived from Adam to Christ, the prophets, followers of the prophets, those obedient to the commandments, little children who lived from the time of Adam to Christ but died before the age of accountability, and those who died in ignorance but who would have received Christ and the gospel with all their hearts (D&C 137:7).

There are different subsequent times of the resurrection from the dead. There is a continuation of the first resurrection at the second coming of Christ (D&C 76:50–70; 88:95–98). These are the inheritors of the celestial glory. There is a resurrection at the time of the second trump at Christ's coming (D&C 76:71–80; 88:99). These are inheritors of the terrestrial glory. There is a resurrection at the end of the thousand years of the Millennium (D&C 76:81–85; 88:100–101). These are inheritors of the telestial glory. And then there are those resurrected at the sounding of the fourth trump, the sons of perdition, who "remain filthy still" (D&C 88:102; see also 43:18; 76:43–44).

Concerning Abinadi's remarkable statement, "little children also have eternal life," we have the powerful words of Elder Bruce R. McConkie:

"Joseph Smith taught, 'Children will be enthroned in the presence of God and the Lamb; . . . they will there enjoy the fullness of that light, glory, and intelligence, which is prepared in the celestial kingdom.' (*Teachings of the Prophet Joseph Smith*, p. 200.)

"President Joseph Fielding Smith spoke very expressly on this point: 'The Lord will grant unto these children the privilege of all the sealing blessings which pertain to the exaltation. We were all mature spirits before we were born, and the bodies of little children will grow after the resurrection to the full stature of the spirit, and all the blessings will be theirs through their obedience, the same as if they had lived to maturity and received them on the earth. The Lord is just and will not deprive any person of a blessing, simply because he dies before the blessing can be received. It would be manifestly unfair to deprive a little child of the privilege of receiving all the blessings of exaltation in the world to come simply because it died in infancy. . . . Children who die in childhood will not be deprived of any blessing. When they grow, after the resurrection, to the full maturity of the spirit, they will be entitled to all the blessings which they would have been entitled to had they been privileged to tarry here and receive them.' (*Doctrines of Salvation*, 2:54.)

"Will children be married and live in the family unit?

"Certainly. There can be no question about this. If they gain salvation, which is eternal life, which is exaltation, it means that they are married and live in the family unit. President Joseph Fielding Smith has so stated in plain words, and it is something that must necessarily be so. (See *Doctrines of Salvation*, 2:49–57)."[33]

Mosiah 15:28–31

Abinadi answered the question asked by one of Noah's priests (in Mosiah 12:21–24). Isaiah's words are fulfilled as the watchmen, the Lord's earthly leaders and messengers, lift up their voices to declare salvation to every nation, kindred, tongue, and people. The Lord reestablishes Zion, causing joyful singing, and redeems Jerusalem. All nations will see the power, glory, and salvation of the Lord.

Mosiah 16

The day of resurrection and judgment will be dramatic for all, but traumatic for many. "The ten thousand times ten thousand lies, excuses, rationalizations, and evasions that served the unrepentant so well in mortality will have been left behind in the grave. All masks will be stripped away. All [the wicked] will stand naked and defenseless before the all-seeing eye of the Almighty."[34]

Abinadi tied together the pillars of the plan of salvation, just as Lehi did (2 Nephi 2:25–26), showing that because of the Fall, all humans are lost and become carnal, rebellious, and fallen, needing to be redeemed, which is why Christ came. He broke the bands of death through resurrection. Now the grave has no victory, and "the sting of death is swallowed up in Christ." Mortality ends, and immortality goes on forever.

How long Abinadi's sermon and testimony lasted, we don't know; but in these few verses recounted for us by Mormon, Abinadi covered the whole plan: fall—redemption—resurrection—judgment—immortality with salvation or damnation. The most crucial part of the message for Noah and his courtiers (and all the rest of us) is, "Repent of your sins, and remember that only in and through Christ ye can be saved." And just for emphasis, "If ye teach the law of Moses, also teach that it is a shadow of those things which are to come—Teach them that redemption cometh through Christ the Lord" (vv. 14–15; see also Alma 25:15–16).

Mosiah 16:6

"And now if Christ had not come into the world, speaking of things to come as though they had already come . . ."—notice the use of past tense verbs, which are actually the future perfect tense.

The grammatical and prophetic use of the past tense in place of the future occurs when an action is "not yet completed but so viewed by the speaker. Hence he speaks as though it were already completed. A perfect certainty even though not yet done in time."[35] This usage is frequent in the poetic discourse of prophets (compare Numbers 24:17; Isaiah 5:13; especially Isaiah 9:1–6; also Genesis 15:15; and Judges 15:3).

"This is put when the speaker views the action as being as good as done. This is very common in the Divine prophetic utterances: where, though the sense is literally future, it is regarded and spoken of as though it were already accomplished."[36]

Such use of the prophetic tense shows the absolute

certainty of things spoken. "The great Jehovah contemplated the whole of the events connected with the earth, pertaining to the plan of salvation, before it rolled into existence . . . ; the past, the present, and the future were and are, with Him, one eternal 'now'."[37] The implications of this fact are staggering and must cause some of us to readjust our thinking. If God the Father knew of the certainty of the Savior's atoning act millennia before it physically occurred—and he did—it means that one aspect of the concept of predestination is true. All those who will be saved can be saved only through the atonement of Jesus Christ (Ephesians 1:5). There is no other way.

Mosiah 17:2–4

One young priest, Alma, believed Abinadi, pleaded his cause, and was threatened with death and banished. Fortunately for us, Alma went into hiding and wrote everything he remembered that Abinadi taught—another example of the value of record-keeping, writing a personal journal (see "The Importance of Record-Keeping," accompanying the commentary at Alma 37).

Mosiah 17:8

Was Abinadi sentenced to be executed for believing God would become mortal? No. Doctrinal issues are almost always a cover-up for underlying issues. The real cause for which Noah and his priests wanted Abinadi put to death was that he was a threat to their power and influence; they were jealous and angry, not wanting to hear about their sins. Notice their demand to "recall all the words which thou hast spoken evil concerning me and my people." It is the same with other prophets and with Jesus himself (compare, for example, 1 Kings 22:8; Matthew 14:3–4; 27:18).

Mosiah 17:9–10

Abinadi said, in effect, that he would seal his testimony with his blood rather than recant that testimony, and in so doing he would become a martyr for the truth. The term *martyr* is a Greek loan word that originally meant "witness." Such witnesses were willing to give all they possessed for the kingdom of God. In the early Christian period such resolve gave rise to the famous statement of Tertullian: "The blood of martyrs is the seed of the church."

Mosiah 17:20

Abinadi "sealed the truth of his words by his death" (see also Hebrews 9:16). He died seemingly without baptisms, but he did have one convert (Mosiah 18:1). That one convert's baptism would lead to many generations of great leaders: Alma—Alma II—Helaman—Helaman II—Nephi—Nephi II (chief disciple of the resurrected Savior). Also, for the first time in ancient America's history, thousands of Lamanites would be converted and led by their own prophets. The Savior was later greeted by worthy descendants of every branch of Lehi's family, all as a result of Abinadi's testimony!

Mosiah 18:1–7

Even great prophets have need of repentance, which is perhaps why they are able to teach the power of the Atonement with such conviction. Alma taught people privately, away from wicked King Noah, after having become a consecrated vessel.

Mosiah 18:8–10

The covenants of baptism include demonstrating a willingness to (1) come into the fold of God, (2) be called his people, (3) bear one another's burdens, (4) mourn with those that mourn, (5) comfort those who stand in need of comfort,

(6) stand as a witness of God at all times and in all things and in all places, and (7) serve God and keep his commandments.

The promises of baptism include (1) being redeemed of God, (2) being numbered with those of the first resurrection, (3) having eternal life, and (4) having his Spirit poured out more abundantly upon you.

Now Alma asks his perfect question: If all of the above is the sincere desire of your heart, "what have you against being baptized in the name of the Lord"? That simple rite is the logical manifestation of your real intent to obey God. The ordinance is very brief in time but eternal in significance.

Embedded in Alma's description of our responsibilities regarding the baptismal covenant is the essence of the Atonement—to suffer vicariously the pains of others and provide them comfort. We do what the Savior does for us: help others and try to relieve their distress (Alma 7:10–14). This is also the essence of charity (Moroni 7:45–47).

Mosiah 18:13

The record we currently have does not specify when or where Alma received his authority to baptize and perform other priesthood functions, but he repeatedly attested that he had "authority from the Almighty God" (see also Mosiah 18:18: "having authority from God"; Mosiah 23:17: "none received authority . . . except it were by him from God"; and Alma 5:3: "having power and authority from God"). The Prophet Joseph Smith made this interesting statement: "All the prophets had the Melchizedek Priesthood and were ordained by God himself."[38]

Mosiah 18:14

As in the Bible, the Book of Mormon clearly teaches baptism by immersion, which is a similitude of the burial of the old person of sin and rising up to newness of life, or being born again (Romans 6:3–6).[39]

Mosiah 18:16, 35

Abinadi's one convert, Alma, went on to baptize 204 souls on one occasion. Alma's whole colony of believers consisted of 450 souls, which would be a good-sized ward in today's Church. The rest of the Book of Mormon traces the impact of this one convert and his descendants.

Mosiah 18:19–27

Valuable counsel and warning about what to teach the people: stay with the teachings of the living prophets and the scriptures. Doctrines and practices of the Church of Jesus Christ in the second century B.C. consisted of (1) teaching the basics (faith, repentance, redemption in the Lord; see also Mosiah 25:22); (2) being united and loving, with no contention allowed (one faith, one baptism); (3) observing the Sabbath day and expressing gratitude to God daily, including gathering together to worship; and (4) working and sharing one's substance with others.

Mosiah 18:30

There are "waters of Mormon" in the wilderness of our lives. Whether it is Provo, Utah; Boston, Massachusetts; Denver, Colorado; the Sea of Galilee or Jerusalem, Israel; or Santiago, Chile—we often have a particular place that becomes sacred because it is there that we came to a knowledge of our Redeemer, having experiences that changed our life. To use Isaiah's words, *mah nauvoo*—"how beautiful" are those places and those experiences to us!

There are also "Almas" in our lives—those whom we look upon as providing the beginnings of our experience in the Lord's Church. A synopsis of Alma's activities recounted in this chapter alone is impressive: (1) he continued Abinadi's preaching in private; (2) he baptized 204 individuals; (3) he established the Church of Jesus Christ in his area; (4) he ordained priesthood holders; (5) he established a lay ministry, not a paid one; and (6) he instituted the laws or practices of a Zion society (compare Moses 7:18). Who are the Almas in your life? Are you striving to be an Alma to someone else?

Mosiah 21:1–12

These verses discuss the fulfillment of Abinadi's prophecy regarding the people of the city of Nephi. Their plight sounds a bit like the circumstances of ancient Israel in Egypt. As they sought to fight against their oppressors, their situation went from bad to worse.

Mosiah 21:14–24

What do you do when you are in the middle of painful trials and suffering afflictions? You cry mightily to God. If you are disobedient or living in sin, he may be slow to hear your cries, as he was with Limhi's people, but if you persist, he will see your determination to return to him (that is, repent) and will eventually hear your cries. Don't give up or despair; keep asking. As Joseph Smith encouraged, "Come to God [and] weary him until he blesses you."[40] Alma said, "After much tribulation, the Lord did hear my cries, and did answer my prayers" (Mosiah 23:10). It is important to know that our sorrows and afflictions are purposeful. Alma also said, "The Lord seeth fit to chasten his people; yea, he trieth their patience and their faith." And when we are struggling and our head is hanging down, Alma reminded us, we should remember that "whosoever putteth his trust in him [the Lord] the same shall be lifted up" (Mosiah 23:21–22).

After a time, the Lord caused the burdens of the people to be eased. And though he did not fully deliver them all at once, he blessed them bit by bit, and they began to practice true religion by looking after the widows and orphans (compare James 1:27). As a result of their increasing righteousness, Lamanite disruptions of their society ceased.

Mosiah 21:25–28

Before Ammon arrived in the land, Limhi had sent out a search party to find Zarahemla. The searchers got lost, found a desolate land, and returned with twenty-four gold plates that turned out to be the record of the ancient Jaredites prepared by Ether (Ether 1:2; Mosiah 8:9).

Mosiah 21:29–36

With Ammon's arrival, one of the final steps in the rehabilitation of Limhi's people occurred. They were converted, entered into a covenant with God, and desired to be baptized; however, there was no one in the land who had authority. Therefore, they did not form a branch of the Church but waited for the Spirit of the Lord to direct them; they demonstrated their willingness to live according to the baptismal covenant that Alma had taught to his people (Mosiah 18:8–10).

Mosiah 22:1–16

Even though the people of Limhi were not immediately set free, valuable lessons had been learned and eternal changes had taken place. The people had humbled themselves and become converted. With the help of Ammon, King Limhi began to make plans to escape from Lamanite bondage. The "voice of the people" was consulted. The Lord blessed them, and they were successful. They returned to Zarahemla and became subjects of King Mosiah II.

Mosiah 23:1–5

This chapter and the one following take the reader back to the account of Alma and his people. Having successfully fled from King Noah and his armies, they established their society in a beautiful and pleasant land. As with every other society, the availability of pure water was of paramount importance.

The Lord strengthened them because of their righteousness. As Isaiah said:

"He giveth power to the faint; and to them that have no might he increaseth strength. . . .

"But they that wait upon the Lord shall renew their strength; they shall mount up with wings as eagles; they shall run, and not be weary; and they shall walk, and not faint" (Isaiah 40:29, 31).

People possessing the Spirit of the Lord are naturally industrious, in contrast to the Lamanites, who are described as lazy (Mosiah 9:12), and to the priests of Noah, who were supported in their laziness by taxes imposed on the people (Mosiah 11:6).

Mosiah 23:6–15

Because of his righteous leadership, Alma was beloved of his people, who asked him to be their king. He refused and in so doing outlined doctrinal principles of political and religious leadership: kingship is not the Lord's system because it places one individual in unchecked authority over all others (Alma seemed to have in mind 1 Nephi 17:35). Kingship would be a good system of governance if the king could be guaranteed to be just, but this guarantee is rarely possible—just look at King Noah. We should cherish the liberty that has been given of God and refrain from seeking the faulty system of kingship. In fact, as with political leaders, so with other leaders and teachers—follow no one except he be a man of God (Mosiah 29).

Significantly, the elders of ancient Israel lobbied Samuel the prophet for a king, but for a different reason: They wanted to be like the surrounding nations. Through Samuel, the Lord told the people of Israel essentially the same thing Alma told his people: a king would rule over them in tyranny. Still, the people refused to obey the Lord. Therefore, the Lord gave them what they wanted (1 Samuel 8:4–22), which is another important lesson for us.

The Lord's principles of governance eschew kingship—in

every dispensation. By Alma's refusal of kingship, Jacob's prophecy of centuries earlier continued to be fulfilled: "And this land shall be a land of liberty unto the Gentiles, and there shall be no kings upon the land, who shall raise up unto the Gentiles" (2 Nephi 10:11). See commentary at Mosiah 29 for an exception to this general principle.

Mosiah 23:16

Here is another specific reference to an organized Church in the Book of Mormon (see also Mosiah 18:17; 25:21). The question is often asked, where did Alma get his authority to baptize and organize the Church of God? It is clear that he received it directly from God (or through one of God's messengers), though the time, place, and circumstances of the conferral and ordination are not given (see also commentary at Mosiah 18:13).

Mosiah 23:17

Priests in Nephite society were what we today call high priests in the Melchizedek Priesthood (see also Mosiah 25:21). It seems clear that Alma acted as the president of the Church.

Mosiah 23:21–22

"The Lord seeth fit to chasten his people; yea, he trieth their patience and their faith." In a modern revelation, the Lord worded the same lesson in slightly different terms: "They must needs be chastened and tried, even as Abraham. . . . For all those who will not endure chastening, but deny me, cannot be sanctified" (D&C 101:4–5). To chasten means to discipline, chastise, rebuke, and correct. Chastening cleanses and refines. It usually comes because of our sins, but even when we are not sinning, the Lord will still put us through trials, difficulties, and ordeals, which, if we respond properly, tend to polish us and teach us the best lessons we need for eternity. Verse 22 assures us that "whosoever putteth his trust in him the same shall be lifted up at the last day."

Notice we are not told we will be lifted up out of our devastating and depressing circumstances *the next day*, but at the last day. Until then we just have to endure and endure well.

Mosiah 23:23—24:25

The rest of chapter 23, as well as chapter 24, is the story of the people of Alma being greatly tried and tested, even though they had made covenants with the Lord and tried to live by them. The purpose of mortality is twofold: to gain a body and learn to control it, and to be tested. This is accomplished by trials and tribulations, tragedy, and temptation. Sometimes the test is filled with contradiction, as in Alma's case; sometimes the purpose of the test is to teach us that none can deliver us except the Lord, again as was the case with Alma and his people (23:23).

Regarding contradiction, when people experience unnerving, unfair, and unjust circumstances in their lives, they may know that they are in good company. Refer back to the statement of the Prophet Joseph Smith regarding the contradictions Christ suffered (see commentary at Mosiah 3:7). This has to be one of the great principles of mortality. We, like Jesus, suffer contradictions as part of our probation on this earth; there is no doubt of that. It is what we do in the face of those contradictions, how we react, that demonstrates our commitment to God and thus determines our place in eternity.

As the patriarch Abraham learned, the contradictions of mortality serve a great purpose. Not only do they act as the Lord's refining fire but they precede great and marvelous blessings. Said Moroni, a prophet who knew a great deal about trials, tribulations, and contradictions, "Ye receive no witness until after the trial of your faith" (Ether 12:6). We can state the principle in another way: the greater the contradiction, faithfully endured, the greater the blessing enjoyed afterward.

Alma and his people did finally escape their bondage and awful circumstances with the Lord's help. They ended up in

Zarahemla, where they were received joyfully by King Mosiah
II.

Mosiah 24:10–15

In these verses the theme is brought home: finding meaning in suffering. Once again, "so great were their afflictions
that they began to cry mightily to God"; they "did pour out
their hearts to him." The Lord encouraged them: "Lift up
your heads and be of good comfort. . . . I will also ease the
burdens which are put upon your shoulders."

The great lesson they learned? "The voice of the Lord
came to them in their afflictions." And he gave them this
comforting assurance and promise: "I, the Lord God, do visit
my people in their afflictions." In turn, the people "did submit cheerfully and with patience to all the will of the Lord."
Our greatest spiritual growth often comes during times
of trial and affliction, and we should express our gratitude
for our life-changing trials and their accompanying lessons.
"They poured out their thanks to God . . . [and] lifted their
voices in the praises of their God."

Following is a remarkable account of learning lessons
from suffering and affliction in modern Church history.
President David O. McKay spoke of a Sunday School class
late in the nineteenth century that was discussing the Willie
and Martin handcart companies: "Some sharp criticism of the
Church and its leaders was being indulged in for permitting
any company of converts to venture across the plains with no
more supplies or protection than a handcart caravan afforded.

"An old man [Francis Webster] in the corner sat silent
and listened as long as he could stand it, then he arose and
said things that no person who heard him will ever forget. His
face was white with emotion, yet he spoke calmly, deliberately, but with great earnestness and sincerity.

"In substance [he] said, 'I ask you to stop this criticism. . . . Mistake to send the handcart company out so late
in the season? Yes. But I was in that company and my wife

was in it. . . . We suffered beyond anything you can imagine, and many died of exposure and starvation, but did you ever hear a survivor of that company utter a word of criticism? . . . Every one of us came through with the absolute knowledge that God lives, for we became acquainted with him in our extremities. . . .

"'Was I sorry that I chose to come by handcart? No. Neither then nor any minute of my life since. The price we paid to become acquainted with God was a privilege to pay, and I am thankful that I was privileged to come in the Martin handcart company.'"[41]

That modern pioneering experience parallels the trials Alma and his people endured, along with the accompanying lesson: The Lord, instead of removing the burdens, strengthens his people's backs to bear the burdens that are placed on them. As is taught in the film *The Other Side of Heaven*, "sometimes he calms the storm, and sometimes he calms the sailor."

Mosiah 25:1–12

This chapter recounts a time of unity in Zarahemla. Mosiah called all the people together. He was now king over four different groups: Mulekites, Nephites, the people of Zeniff, and the people of Alma. King Mosiah used the various historical records to teach valuable lessons to his greatly increased group—namely, the goodness of God and his power, for which everyone was to give thanks. Thus, we see that history has a vital purpose in God's plan. When the people thought of their brethren slain at the hands of the Lamanites, they "shed many tears of sorrow." Here we think of the Lord's injunction to the Latter-day Saints: "Thou shalt live together in love, insomuch that thou shalt weep for the loss of them that die, and more especially for those that have not hope of a glorious resurrection" (D&C 42:45).

Mosiah 25:13–24

Alma preached to the members of the many churches in the land of Zarahemla on the Lord's saving grace. King Limhi and his people were finally baptized by Alma long after they expressed a desire for it (compare Mosiah 21:33–35). The unity of all the people brought to them the Spirit of the Lord. Perhaps their righteousness resulted from the constant theme of their meetings: "For there was nothing preached in all the churches except it were repentance and faith in God."

Mosiah 26:1–9

The rising generation disbelieved the doctrines of faith in the coming of a Redeemer, the need to repent of sins, and the resurrection of the dead. They refused to join the Church and be baptized, and their numbers increased "because of the dissensions among the brethren" of the Church. Members of the Church caught up in worldliness were called in to disciplinary councils before their priesthood leaders. Alma, the presiding authority of the Church, did not know about those who were rebelling against the Church, sinning, and luring away others. He was not aware, then, that his own son was among the rebels.

Mosiah 26:13–20

Alma was concerned about what to do with the divisiveness in the Church. "After he had poured out his whole soul to God, the voice of the Lord came to him." The same can happen to us if we need and really want revelation: we pour out our whole souls to God, and then the voice of the Lord may come to us, too.

The Lord reassured Alma and pronounced blessings on him, including a covenant that he would be sealed up to eternal life.

Mosiah 26:29–30, 35–36

These verses contain instructions on how to determine, during Church disciplinary councils, what course of action should be followed. We want people in the Church not out of it, of course, but they must be in it *on the Lord's conditions*. It is essential to maintain the integrity of the Church. Elder Dallin H. Oaks explained: "The objective of church discipline is to facilitate repentance," at the same time "protecting the flock and preserving the good name and influence of the Church." He observed that "the principal purpose . . . [is] not to punish the transgressor, but to aid his repentance and save his soul." Moreover, "the most important single fact bearing on what church discipline is needed [is] the extent of repentance of the transgressor."[42]

We are not interested in having people's names "blotted out." We truly desire to see their sins blotted out.

Mosiah 26:33

Verses 15–32 are the words of the Lord to Alma in answer to his earnest inquiry. The very next verse tells us, "When Alma had heard these words he wrote them down." That is a wonderful suggestion to every one of us. While you are studying the scriptures, you are entitled to receive the Spirit; and while feeling the Spirit, revelation may come. Keep a notebook, any kind of notebook, right alongside your scriptures, and during your reading, stop and ponder what you read. As impressions come to you, write them down. They may be thoughts about what you are reading, but maybe not. While you are "in the Spirit," the Lord may reveal something to you that has nothing to do with what is written on the page you are studying but has everything to do with the specific circumstances of your life. Sometimes as impressions come we may think, "Don't bother me, Lord, I'm studying the scriptures!"—and he can't get through to us. Do not get too busy going through the motions that you cannot receive revelation when he wants to send it. Joseph Smith once warned, "For neglecting to write these things when God had revealed them, not esteeming them of sufficient worth, the Spirit may withdraw and God may be angry."[43]

If God tells us something, we need to write it down right then, as Alma did.

Mosiah 27:1–7

Mosiah took steps to ensure freedom of worship without fear of persecution or duress on the part of worshippers. An inspired latter-day declaration of beliefs regarding governments and principles of governance supports Mosiah's actions to "secure to each individual the free exercise of conscience" (D&C 134:2). Indeed, these principles form the foundation of the United States Constitution (D&C 101:77–80). Likewise, the churches of Zarahemla commanded that no one be persecuted, that pride and haughtiness be eradicated, that complete equality prevail—that, basically, the golden rule be practiced. The result: "The Lord did visit them and prosper them, and they became a large and wealthy people." The kind of equality called for by both civil and ecclesiastical administration in Zarahemla is the backbone of Zion and the environment that will pervade the celestial kingdom (D&C 51:9; 105:3–5; 82:17–21).

It is not hard to see that the Lord desired to move this people to the point where they could be translated, as other communities had been (JST, Genesis 14:32–34). Such was not to be, however, partly due to the children of the very men who possessed this higher vision of the purpose of mortality.

Mosiah 27:8–37

These verses give us a detailed account of the conversion of Alma, son of Alma (whom we often call Alma the Younger), and his friends, the four sons of King Mosiah (another account is given in Alma 36). These young men are characterized as "very wicked" and "idolatrous"; "they were the very vilest of sinners" (Mosiah 28:4).

We do not have a catalog of all their crimes and sins, but in modern terms any one of these young men might be portrayed something like this: He does illegal things, violating the laws of the land (for example, experimenting with and becoming addicted to illicit substances); he does immoral things, violating the laws of God (including using pornography and fathering children outside the bonds of marriage); he lies to his parents; he cannot be trusted; he steals things from his parents and siblings to support his evil habits; he seeks out the wrong kind of friends and takes others down with him; he refuses to work, sleeping during the day and drinking and partying at night, living in a world of darkness, where everything is secretive—he is always vague about where he is, who he is with, and what he is doing; he denies and rejects God and makes light of the things of God.

Mosiah 27:11

The angel spoke to the sinners in a voice of thunder because in their wicked and rebellious condition they could no longer hear the still, small voice of the Spirit.

Mosiah 27:14

Why did an angel come to help such vile sinners? Why would there be a miraculous intervention on behalf of those who were willfully rebelling and therefore apparently unworthy of heavenly intercession? The angel was sent because of the mighty prayers of many righteous members of the Church—especially the prayers of two fathers, the king and the prophet. One immediately recalls the feelings of the father of the prodigal son (Luke 15:10–32), which are a thinly veiled reflection of our Heavenly Father's feelings for each of us. One can imagine the intensity of affection possessed by Alma and Mosiah for their sons.

There is great power in the prayer of faith and in the

pleading of the righteous. God answered their prayers, and he will answer our prayers—not always exactly like we would hope and expect but "in his own time, and in his own way, and according to his own will" (D&C 88:68). Like the prodigal son, the sons of Alma and Mosiah would feel the Spirit and come to themselves (Luke 15:17). Thus, we know that even those in the deepest throes of wickedness can feel the Spirit of the Lord.

Mosiah 27:22–23

Fasting and praying are always involved in saving souls. One might question how Alma could thoroughly repent of all his sins in just three days and three nights (Alma 36:10, 16; 38:8). We do not know how to explain that, but we can ponder the fact that the Savior, in some grand and far-reaching way, took upon himself the sins and pains of the world in just *one* night—the darkest night of eternity.

Mosiah 27:24–29

These verses, along with Alma 36:12–26, provide what is likely the most graphic description we have in all of scripture of how to repent. Alma gave us intimate details of the process of repentance, recounting step-by-step the way he was spiritually born of God. Though he did not have to record all this in such detail, notice his painstaking effort to help us understand what he went through to become a new person.

Mosiah 27:28–29

We learn from Alma and the four sons of Mosiah that godly sorrow and suffering are essential parts of the true repentance process. "They suffered much anguish of soul because of their iniquities" (Mosiah 28:4). We have not repented if we have not suffered. (Paul also taught that godly sorrow brings repentance unto salvation; 2 Corinthians 7:10; see also Psalm 38:17–18; Ezekiel 16:61.) Alma wrote about "wading through much tribulation," "repenting nigh unto death," "an everlasting burning," "the gall of bitterness," "bonds of iniquity," "the darkest abyss," and being "racked with eternal torment." In his other account (Alma 36:12–19), he added other terms of anguish: "tormented with the pains of hell," "inexpressible horror," "pains of a damned soul," "harrowed up by the memory of my many sins" and "everlasting chains of death."

A rack is an instrument of torture, and a harrow is a farm tool used to break up hard earth to make it cultivable—therefore, symbolically also an instrument of torture or torment. Alma used vivid terminology to portray to us this scene of godly suffering. Today we might use terms such as *ugly, rotten, dirty, despicable, sick,* and *gross* to sum up our innermost contempt toward the sins that we have committed.

Through all the darkness and desperation he felt, Alma had to turn to the Light; his mind caught hold on the thought of Jesus Christ, the Light of the world, who atoned for sins and takes them away (Alma 36:17–20). That Light brought exquisite joy to displace the dark feelings of anguish and despair. The Holy Ghost brings to our minds and hearts the uplifting desire to come to the Savior. The Holy Ghost will cause our souls to be bothered by our sins until we either chase the Spirit away or we repent. Alma would later teach his son, "Let your sins trouble you, with that trouble which shall bring you down unto repentance" (Alma 42:29).

True repentance is not merely feeling guilty for being discovered in our sins or the shame or embarrassment for having to confess—it is a deep-felt sorrow and suffering, our part of the cleansing and strengthening process to remove sin from our lives. At the same time, we turn to our Redeemer for the rest of the process of permanent removal of those sins—to make us a new person and a different person, one who would never again commit those sins.

Mighty change had occurred in a gloriously monumental way. Whereas sinful Alma admitted that "the very thought of coming into the presence of my God did rack my soul with

inexpressible horror" (Alma 36:14), when his genuine repentance was complete his feelings about God were dramatically altered. Said he, "There can be nothing so exquisite and
sweet as was my joy" (Alma 36:21), and when he saw God
in his heaven he exclaimed, "My soul did long to be there"
(Alma 36:22).

Mosiah 27:35

Confession and restitution, or restoring that which has
been taken or lost, are also part of true repentance. Alma and
the sons of Mosiah went out among the people, "zealously
striving to repair all the injuries which they had done."

Mosiah 28:1–9

Upon experiencing real conversion, the sons of Mosiah
wanted more than anything to bring others to the knowledge
of the Lord—even their inveterate enemies, the Lamanites.
These enemies were also children of Heavenly Father, and the
transformed brothers could not bear the thought of any soul
having to endure the endless torment of which they had had
a profound taste. The Spirit of the Lord had indeed changed
the hearts of these formerly vile sinners. We have already seen
how Enos desired the welfare of his brethren after the gospel
had provided a sure anchor to his soul (Enos 1:9).

Their father, Mosiah, who was a prophet and a seer as well
as a king (Mosiah 8:13–17), inquired of the Lord if his sons
should go up to the Lamanites, and the word came back that
not only would the Lord protect and preserve them during
their mission but he sealed them up to eternal life. The account
of their miraculous missionary labors is found in Alma 17–26.

Mosiah 28:11–14, 20

King Mosiah gathered together the sacred things in his
possession—the plates of brass, the plates of Nephi (both
sets), the twenty-four plates of gold (the Jaredite record), the
interpreters (Urim and Thummim), the sword of Laban, and

the miraculous ball (Liahona)—and conferred them upon Alma the Younger with a commission to guard them well and continue to inscribe their history.

The Urim and Thummim was an instrument of revelation prepared by God from the beginning of time and handed down from generation to generation. The appearance of the Urim and Thummim is confirmed by the Prophet Joseph Smith as "two stones in silver bows . . . fastened to a breastplate" (Joseph Smith–History 1:35). It was deposited with the gold plates found by Joseph Smith, "and the possession and use of these stones were what constituted 'seers' in ancient or former times; . . . God had prepared them for the purpose of translating the book [of Mormon]" (Joseph Smith–History 1:35).

HISTORY OF THE URIM AND THUMMIM

The history of the Urim and Thummim indicates that there was likely more than one set of interpreters. The first scriptural reference to the Urim and Thummim, though not explicitly named, appears to be in connection with the visions and revelations given to the brother of Jared. At that time, "two stones" were mentioned that he was to seal up along with the revelations that he wrote down. The Lord then indicated how the stones would be used: "For behold, the language which ye shall write I have confounded; wherefore I will cause in my own due time that these stones shall magnify to the eyes of men these things which ye shall write" (Ether 3:24). Later, "the people of Limhi brought to Mosiah a record, 'engraven on plates of ore,' [Mosiah 21:27] which record Mosiah translated, by the aid of 'two stones which were fastened into the two rims of a bow,' and which gave an account of the Jaredites [Mosiah 28:11–19]."[44] This was the Urim and Thummim hidden by Moroni and received by Joseph Smith, the same Urim and Thummim possessed by the brother of Jared (D&C 17:1).

The patriarch Abraham possessed a Urim and Thummim and learned about the nature of the physical universe by using it. Biblical references to the Urim and Thummim show it to be the means by which the Aaronic high priest inquired of the Lord. Aaron and the priests in Israel possessed it from generation to generation (Exodus 28:30; Leviticus 8:8; Numbers 27:21; Deuteronomy 33:8; 1 Samuel 28:6). Apparently, the breastplate containing the Urim and Thummim was worn over the heart. Some scholars take Ezra 2:63 and Nehemiah 7:65 to mean that the Urim and Thummim was not found in ancient Israel after the Babylonian exile.

Though Lehi and Nephi do not speak of the Urim and Thummim, it existed from the days of Ammon on, being called "interpreters," requiring divine authorization to use it, and being passed down from prophet to prophet (Mosiah 8:13, 19; 21:26–28; 28:20; Alma 37:21, 24; Ether 4:5). Ammon's comment is helpful for understanding the connection between the Urim and Thummim and those authorized to use it: "And the things are called interpreters, and no man can look in them except he be commanded, lest he should look for that he ought not and he should perish. And whosoever is commanded to look in them, the same is called seer" (Mosiah 8:13).

The Prophet Joseph Smith received the same Urim and Thummim "given to the brother of Jared upon the mount, when he talked with the Lord face to face" and of which the Three Witnesses were promised a glimpse if they trusted the Lord (D&C 17:1). President Joseph Fielding Smith stated that this Urim and Thummim was separate and distinct from the one possessed by the patriarch Abraham and by the leaders of the Aaronic Priesthood in ancient Israel.[45]

Mosiah 28:17–19

The record that Mosiah the seer translated covered the Jaredites' history from the time of their destruction, back through thousands of years to their origin at the time of the confounding of languages at the tower of Babel, and on back to the creation of Adam (compare Mosiah 8:5–18).

A condensed version of this history was later included by Moroni and is called the book of Ether.

Mosiah 29

There are various systems of government. The best is theocracy, which is government by divine guidance. Another is autocracy, also called monarchy or kingship, where one person rules with unlimited power. Verse 13 explains that if it were possible to have just men to be our kings—like Mosiah I, Benjamin, and Mosiah II—then it would be appropriate to have kings governing us, but because most monarchs are not just, verse 16 tells us that it is not wise to have kings ruling over us. Note the frequent references to 1 Samuel 8 in the footnotes of Mosiah 29. Ancient Israel had also been warned about the dangers of a king; what follows in the Bible are three tragic stories: those of Saul, David, and Solomon.

Another form of government preferable to kingship is democracy, or government by the people through a system of representation. At this point in Nephite history it was thought wise to shift to the rule of judges, a form of democracy. "Do your business by the voice of the people," Mosiah counseled. "It is not common that the voice of the people desireth anything contrary to that which is right."

"Governments are only good when the people are good. As founding father John Adams observed, 'Our Constitution was made only for a moral and religious people. It is wholly inadequate to the government of any other.'"[46] Liberty demands responsibility. Democracy can function optimally only on a foundation of decency among the citizens.

Mosiah, the great prophet-king, made an additional urgent observation about the political and moral climate of every nation: "If the time comes that the voice of the people doth choose iniquity, then is the time that the judgments of God will come upon you; yea, then is the time he will visit you with great destruction" (v. 27). As we follow the pressing political, social, and moral issues of our day, we note with concern, in these first years of the present millennium, that the views and votes of the people are hovering around fifty percent for, and fifty percent against any particular issue. On the most critical issues the nations of the world are facing (abortion, pornography, substance abuse, same-gender marriage, and so on), the proportion of the populace standing for righteous principles is often just barely over the fifty percent mark. The best armor the Latter-day Saints can use to counter the downward spiral of society is the gospel of Jesus Christ. The most important work being done on earth is the dissemination of the greatest power for lifting the souls of men—the eternal plan of salvation through the atonement of Jesus Christ.

The calendaring system of the Nephites had previously functioned according to the date of Lehi's departure from Jerusalem. Now they began calculating from the beginning of the reign of the judges. Later, the Nephite civilization would change one more time to the same system used by much of the modern world—calculating from the date of Christ's birth. For a scriptural comment on the three calendar systems, see 3 Nephi 2:5–7.

THE BOOK OF ALMA

The overall theme of the book of Alma, which also contains the record of Helaman and Shiblon (Alma 63:1, 17), is "trying the virtue of the word of God" (Alma 31:5). Alma set out to prove the value of the word of God, and the sons of Mosiah did the same. The first four chapters record challenges to the new reign of the judges.

Alma 1:1–3

Alma began by commenting on Mosiah's valiant leadership—he "warred a good warfare"—which parallels the apostle Paul's comment before his death, "I have fought a good fight" (2 Timothy 4:7). It also sets a tone for the verses that follow. Alma then moved to a description of a man whose name is not immediately disclosed but who made trouble for the Church by teaching a false but appealing doctrine. His name was Nehor (v. 15).

Alma 1:4

The idea that "all the people will be saved" in one sense is a satanic doctrine because it diminishes people's desire to do what is right for the right reasons. The notion spawns an attitude of spiritual carelessness—go ahead and do whatever your heart, your body, or your mind wants you to do; go ahead and enjoy the pleasures of sin, because God loves us and will eventually overlook our sins and save us all (see commentary at 2 Nephi 28:1–8). We see this philosophy promoted in modern times.

Alma 1:5, 16

By setting himself up as a light to the people and establishing a church, or organization, that promotes himself, Nehor was guilty of priestcraft (2 Nephi 26:29). The general public supported him and gave him money. There are occasional modern examples of televangelists and large-crowd preachers who live a profligate lifestyle on the donations of their dedicated supporters. The Lord warns, "Trust no one to be your teacher nor your minister, except he be a man of God, walking in his ways and keeping his commandments" (Mosiah 23:14).

Alma 1:6

The Book of Mormon repeatedly notes one particular sign of pride and worldliness: wearing costly apparel (see, for example, Jacob 2:13; Alma 1:32; 4:6; 5:53). Costly clothing promotes vanity and is used to show off wealth, the conspicuous consumption of the rich or those who desire to be rich. Wearing costly apparel involves the soul as much as the body. We do have a tendency to act the way we dress. Faithful Church members do not wear costly apparel, yet they are neat and comely (Alma 1:27); they wear modest, simple, and plain clothing. The issue is costliness versus comeliness (compare D&C 42:40).

Alma 1:12–19

There are historical examples of endeavoring to enforce religious beliefs on others by the sword—among Muslims, Christians, and others. In matters of religious belief and practice, the use of force is eternally proscribed. Significantly, a war was fought over this very issue in our premortal estate, and the battle then transferred to earth.

Nehor sought to perpetuate the plan of the adversary through priestcraft, but that was not his only sin. He slew a once-mighty man of God and was punished by the voice of the people—a principle now well established as a result of Mosiah's call to be forward-looking, refute kingship, choose judges, and do the business of government by the voice of the people (Mosiah 29:10–27). Verses 16–19 provide a description of how priestcraft operates.

Alma 1:20–25

Persecutions, contention, and pride arose in this religious society but this time against those who were not members of the Church of God. In our day we see that bashing anti-Mormons does not work either. Besides, all contention is contrary to God's will.

Alma 1:26

Latter-day Saints, especially missionaries, must be careful never to regard themselves as better than others—that is, not to think of themselves more highly than they should (the problem of pride). See also Romans 12:3; Galatians 6:3; and Doctrine and Covenants 136:19.

Alma 1:27–33

Because peace was restored, the Church and its members prospered, and to their credit, they did not send away the poor and needy. These verses describe a pattern for welfare assistance that the Church today embraces. Verse 30 is profound in its description of the royal law being practiced (James 2:1–9). On the other hand, wickedness and sloth abounded among those not belonging to the Church.

With Amlici's rejection by the voice of the people (Alma 2:7), we again see the truth of Mosiah's axiom that "it is not common that the voice of the people desireth anything contrary to that which is right" (Mosiah 29:26). However, the supporters of Amlici made him their king, formed another splinter group, joined the Lamanites, warred against the Nephites, and then were defeated because the Nephites were strengthened by the Lord. These episodes confirm the Lord's ancient promise to his covenant people that if they would look to him (Deuteronomy 20:1–4; Joshua 23:10), he would strengthen them and fight for them.

Alma 2:1–38

Another major challenge to the new governmental system of judges surfaced. It seems that in every generation there are those who are cunning, worldly wise, eloquent, persuasive, and flattering. That appropriately describes Sherem (Jacob 7), Nehor (Alma 1), Amlici (Alma 2), and Korihor (Alma 30).

Some kill souls spiritually, others physically. Some do both. Amlici was responsible for the deaths of more than nineteen thousand people (see also Alma 3:1–3). He did much spiritual damage as well.

Alma 3:4–5, 18

Through the ages people have marked their bodies to make themselves different from others. Our prophets have specifically counseled us against body markings. In the general conference of October 2000, President Gordon B. Hinckley taught the members of the Church to avoid "the craze of tattooing one's body. I cannot understand why any young man—or young woman, for that matter—would wish to undergo the painful process of disfiguring the skin with various multicolored representations of people, animals, and various symbols. With tattoos, the process is permanent, unless there is another painful and costly undertaking to remove it. . . . A tattoo is graffiti on the temple of the body.

"Likewise the piercing of the body for multiple rings in the ears, in the nose, even in the tongue. Can they possibly think that is beautiful? It is a passing fancy, but its effects can be permanent. Some have gone to such extremes that the ring had to be removed by surgery. The First Presidency and the Quorum of the Twelve have declared that we discourage tattoos and also 'the piercing of the body for other than medical purposes.'"[1]

In the same general conference, October 2000, President Boyd K. Packer declared: "President Hinckley has warned you not to decorate your body with pictures or symbols that will never wash off or to pierce your body with rings or jewelry after the manner of the world. . . . You would not paint a temple with dark pictures or symbols or graffiti or even initials. Do not do so with your body."[2]

Equally important is the clothing we wear. It identifies us—our aims, lifestyle, and propensities—just as the Lamanites were known by their appearance.

Alma 3:6–18

Rebellion brought certain consequences to the Lamanites. Blessings or curses (consequences) follow our actions.

Alma 3:19, 26–27

In the end, we are responsible for what rewards or punishments we receive. We get what we deserve; we reap what we sow. "Even so doth every man that is cursed bring upon himself his own condemnation." "For every man receiveth wages of him whom he listeth to obey."

Alma 4:1–7

Undesirable circumstances almost always result from war: sadness, misery, and afflictions suffered by someone; however, war can also turn people toward God. Then peace allows the Church to grow. Nonetheless, the cycle of apostasy seems to set in quickly among those who are unstable: peace brings prosperity, which brings pride, which brings division, and so on. See this cycle depicted in the commentary at Ether 9–11 (in vol. 2 of this work).

The problem of very costly apparel does not seem to go away. Do we have this problem? Do we really promote, as we have been encouraged by the prophets, a "style of our own"? This is thought-provoking language: the people were lifted up in "the pride of their eyes"; what their eyes saw, their hearts desired.

Alma 4:8–11

The conditions described here are opposite to the ideals of Zion. They represent a violation and an abrogation of the law of the celestial kingdom, which all covenant communities must learn to live. We sometimes see these problems in the missions of the Church today. Because of pride, scorn, contention, envy, inequality, and sin among the members, the investigators have a hard time believing in the Church. Because of some members' behavior and attitudes, some nonmembers are led on "from one piece of iniquity to another," and the Church begins to fail in its mission and its progress.

Alma 4:12–18

These verses describe what happens when people do not turn their backs on God even though they must live among those who have. They are, in a way, a practical illustration of Lehi's dream of the iron rod versus the great and spacious building (1 Nephi 8). We see that there is a momentary cost to true discipleship, the "suffering [of] all manner of afflictions for Christ's sake," but the rewards are everlasting.

Divisions of responsibility and labor were introduced into this society, which before had been a theocratic monarchy.

Alma 4:19–20

Alma gave up his secular job, his government post, to serve the Lord full-time. He could see no alternative other than to go among the people and "preach the word of God unto them, to stir them up in remembrance of their duty, . . . seeing no way that he might reclaim them save it were in bearing down in pure testimony against them." That is a key to success in missionary work: *bear pure testimony* of the word. Today pure testimony includes declaration of belief in the Father, in his Son, in the Prophet Joseph Smith and other living prophets, in the Book of Mormon, and in the Restoration of the true Church of Jesus Christ.

Alma 5

This chapter is another great "general conference" talk, this time by Alma (recall Jacob's in 2 Nephi 6–10 and King Benjamin's in Mosiah 2–5). It is the second longest in the Book of Mormon and unique in that it includes over forty questions. They are searching questions, the kind that cause people to examine their lives and make necessary changes.

Alma 5:1–6

Alma began his exhortation to the Church in Zarahemla by citing his authority. As "high priest over the church of God," he filled the role of president of the Church (D&C 107:8–9, 66, 91–91). Later, the apostle Paul also would begin most of his epistles with a reference to his authority.

Alma used the image of the bondage of his listeners' fathers to point to the spiritual bondage that can be removed through rebirth into the kingdom of God. The phrase "retained in remembrance the captivity of your fathers" is the same language used later with Helaman (Alma 36:29).

Alma 5:7

Alma the Younger is talking about his father's converts and how the great missionary taught them. New understanding comes to every soul who is "awakened out of a deep sleep" and illuminated by the light of the everlasting word—which may come in prayer, in scripture study, or especially in the temple. We know a couple who reported to the office of President James E. Faust of the First Presidency some years ago to receive a mission call. Here is a part of their conversation: "We told President Faust that we have been faithfully attending the temple every week for many months and it is having a dynamic effect on our personal and family lives. The sister commented with regard to the temple: 'We didn't realize it before, but we were sleeping.' President Faust leaned back in his chair and lamented: 'We've all been sleeping. Why, just three weeks ago I came to understand something new in the temple that I hadn't realized before.'" We all need to wake up and open the minds of our understanding to the priceless truths repeatedly taught us in the house of the Lord as well as through prayer and scripture study. Frequent temple attendance and attention to those other practices open our eyes.

Alma 5:8–13

Here Alma shows us just what a master teacher he was. He began a series of interrogatives, inspired questions that led to the theme of his discourse—the mighty change of heart. As he indicated, true salvation begins with faith in the possibility of salvation. He moved from speaking of the physical, temporal salvation received by his listeners' fathers to the complete salvation from death and sin afforded by spiritual rebirth. In all cases, we escape captivity through a change of heart.

Alma 5:14–29

During the first part of Alma's discourse, he presented a self-evaluation interview. It is one of the most important tests we can take. All twelve of the following questions are answered yes or no, except number 8, which is a thought question. Do take the test now. Answer honestly and sincerely.

1. "Have [you] spiritually been born of God?"
2. "Have [you] received his image in your countenances?"
3. "Have [you] experienced this mighty change in your hearts?"
4. "Do [you] exercise faith in the redemption of him who created you?"
5. "Do you look forward with an eye of faith, and view this mortal body raised in immortality . . . to stand before God to be judged?"

389

6. "Can you imagine . . . that [you] hear the voice of the Lord, saying unto you, in that day: Come unto me . . . , for behold, your works have been the works of righteousness?"

7. "Can [you] look up to God at that day with a pure heart and clean hands . . . , having the image of God engraven on your countenances?"

8. "How will . . . you feel, if [you] shall stand before the bar of God, having your garments stained with blood and all manner of filthiness?"

9. "If [you] have experienced a change of heart, and . . . felt to sing the song of redeeming love, I would ask, can [you] feel so now?"

10. "Have [you] walked, keeping yourselves blameless before God?"

11. "Could [you] say, if [you] were called to die at this time, within yourselves, that [you] have been sufficiently humble?"

12. "Are [you] stripped of pride . . . [and] envy?"

Alma 5:14

After many years of marriage, husbands and wives in some ways begin to look like each other, to think and act like each other. They may even adopt the same mannerisms. The word *countenance* derives from an old French term denoting behavior, demeanor, or conduct. With Christ's image in our countenances, we begin to look like he looks; our life becomes a reflection of the Savior's life. He never forgets us because we are engraved upon the palms of his hands (see commentary at 1 Nephi 21:14–16); we show true conversion to him by having his image engraved upon our countenance. The engraving represents permanence. Because of "a mighty change in us," we have "no more disposition to do evil, but to do good continually" (Mosiah 5:2).

Alma 5:15

Exercising faith in the Savior's redemption—having faith that his saving actions do have meaning and purpose—you can look forward "with an eye of faith" and see things that the human retina cannot normally detect. The human eye picks up only a small portion of the full electromagnetic spectrum, yet we know that there are many waves and rays surrounding us; we can see the results of harnessing them (radio waves are used to operate cell phones, microwaves are used in microwave ovens, infrared light in TV remotes, ultraviolet light in tanning booths, X-rays in medical imaging, and gamma rays in cancer radiotherapy). Likewise, if you use your eye *of faith* you can see, understand, and harness spiritual views and powers beyond this mortal sphere. The Book of Mormon tells of those who opened the eye of faith and saw beyond earthly bounds: for example, Lehi, Nephi, Jacob, both Almas, the later Nephi, the brother of Jared, Ether, Mormon, and Moroni.

Alma 5:18

Everything you have ever spoken, everything you have ever done, and everything you have ever thought—it is all there, packed away in the depths of your mind for future recall and for judgment. We all have photographic memories; we just don't have instant recall. At the great day of judgment, however, we will all have instant recall. (Someone once observed that the reason we lose our memory when we get old is so we can die with a clear conscience.) The scriptures teach us that we will have a "perfect knowledge," a "perfect remembrance," a "bright recollection" of all things except those of which we have thoroughly repented (2 Nephi 9:14; Alma 11:43). See commentary and quotes at 2 Nephi 9:13–16 and commentary at 3 Nephi 27:23–26.

Alma 5:19

This verse carries a direct temple reference and parallels the words of the psalmist (Psalm 24:3–4): who can "ascend into the hill of the Lord?" and who can "stand in his holy place?"—the one who possesses clean hands and a pure heart.

Alma 5:21, 24–25, 27

The only way you can be saved is to have your garments washed white and purified through the blood of Christ (see commentary at 1 Nephi 12:10–11). We are either cleansed by the blood of Christ or stained by the sins of the world.

Alma 5:26

"Can ye feel so now" is perhaps the most important of all Alma's questions. During spiritually elevating times of your life, if you experienced a change of heart and felt the redeeming love of the Lord, the question is, Can you feel so now? Five years after a mission, for example, or ten years, or twenty years? The one-time spiritual experience will not sustain you. You must be continually experiencing his Spirit and love. If you do not feel the Spirit regularly, the commandments become burdens, not blessings, and you may burn out and quit.

Spirituality is an ongoing process. It is the struggle for daily diligence, doing the little things by which the Savior can bring about great things in your life. The little things are actually not so little; daily sincere prayer, daily serious scripture study, regular worship in the temple, and regular service to others become a big part of your mortal life and make you a sure candidate for eternal life. Elder Marvin J. Ashton of the Quorum of the Twelve taught us that "when the Lord measures an individual, . . . He measures the heart as an indicator of the person's capacity and potential to bless others. . . . Having a 'change of heart' at one time in our lives is insufficient to give us an understanding heart today. . . . Christlike love must be continuous and contemporary."[3]

Alma 5:28–29

If you did not answer yes to all the questions (see vv. 14–29), you failed the test. You are not prepared. You must prepare quickly. By examining your responses, you will know whether or not you have been spiritually reborn of God.

Note how envy and pride are at the heart of preventing all of us from experiencing true rebirth. Even the poor must be concerned about these detrimental characteristics (D&C 56:16–17). The desire to feel superior to our fellow human beings for any reason must be eradicated from our souls.

Alma 5:33–34

The arms of the Lord are lovingly held out to you. The tree of life, the bread of life, and the waters of life are all symbols of our Redeemer, especially of his saving sacrifice, and you are invited to come to him and partake of the fruit, and eat the bread, and drink the water. You come to him, for example, during the ordinance of the sacrament, covenanting to take his name upon you and always remember him and keep his commandments, so his Spirit can always be with you (Moroni 4:3; D&C 20:77).

Alma 5:37–42

You are the sheep of someone's fold. There are two shepherds out in the wilderness of this world: the Good Shepherd and the evil shepherd. Both are calling you. Whomever you listen to will determine whose fold you will be gathered into and whose family you will eternally become a part of. Elder Jeffrey R. Holland quoted C. S. Lewis, a great Christian writer: "There is no neutral ground in the universe: every square inch, every split second, is claimed by God and counterclaimed by Satan."[4] Then Elder Holland testified, "I believe that to be absolutely true."[5] You can become a child of Christ, as King Benjamin taught (Mosiah 5:7), or you can become a child of the devil, as Alma here warned.

THE BOOK OF MORMON

In verse 40 Alma gave us a test we can apply to ourselves to determine whom we are serving. "Good" is that which brings us closer to Christ and to conversion to the fulness of his gospel. "And there are none that doeth good except those who are ready to receive the fulness of my gospel, which I have sent forth unto this generation" (D&C 35:12).

Alma 5:44–47

These verses provide a paradigm for how to teach the gospel according to the Holy Order of God, which is the Melchizedek Priesthood (D&C 84:18–19; 107:3). In part, we should use the testimonies of the apostles, prophets, and righteous souls who have gone before (D&C 52:9), bear our personal witness, and then teach others how we came to know the truth.

Suppose there were a giant sign that read: "Baptisms, Gifts of the Holy Ghost, Priesthood Ordinations, Temple Marriages—$10,000 each. Payment in Advance." How hard would you work to earn each and all of these blessings? What would you give to know the Lord? How much do you really want to know him?

Alma asks, essentially, How do you suppose I know these things are true? How did I gain my testimony? It did not come solely from my dramatic experience with the angel!

Gospel knowledge and spiritual change require a lot of work. Like Alma, you have to fast and pray many days, and then the sure knowledge comes through the Holy Ghost. It is not a matter of a single day; it is a lifetime pursuit. Most converts to the Church receive their initial testimony not through angelic visitations or visions but through the sweet, gentle, yet powerful witness from the Holy Ghost; but there's much spiritual work to be done after that.

Alma would have undoubtedly admitted at this point: I still have many questions, but I do not doubt. Doubt is spiritual poison.

Alma 5:50

The coming of the kingdom of heaven to which Alma referred was the first coming of Christ in mortality. However, this verse also has reference to the great millennial coming, when the King of Heaven will "shine forth among all the children of men."

Alma 5:52

As with most metaphors in scripture, trees represent people. The root of the tree is the essential core, the source and supplier for the body of the tree, which should bear fruit. The fruit represents "works of righteousness" (Alma 5:36). "If the root be holy, so are the branches" (Romans 11:16), but if the root system becomes corrupted by absorbing poisonous elements from its environment, then "the ax is laid at the root of the tree," and it will have to be cut down and cast into the fire. The fire into which the wicked "trees" are cast is the fire of hell—remorse and regret—which is unquenchable, not able to be put out (see also Luke 3:9; Jacob 5:46; 3 Nephi 14:19; D&C 97:7). Those who are cast into the fire are described in Alma 5:53–56.

Alma 5:57–60

Once the Good Shepherd has called you and you have entered his fold, stay away from the wicked and do not touch "their unclean things." Do not let any "ravenous wolf" enter into your life—such as pornography, indecent and violent movies, immoral behavior, substance abuse, or any other worldly perversions. If one of those wolves does try to get into your life and attack you, *drive him out* or he will destroy you.

In a general sense, the book of life is a record of all the behavior of the human family; it is kept in heaven. Specifically, it contains the names of the faithful (D&C 128:6–7; Psalm

69:28; Revelation 3:5; 21:27) who will inherit eternal life. It is also called "the book of the names of the sanctified, even them of the celestial world" (D&C 88:2).

Alma 5:62

Notice that Alma spoke to Church members by way of commandment and to nonmembers by way of invitation. Those who have been baptized, made covenants, and received the gift of the Holy Ghost can be addressed in stronger terms, but to those outside the Church we speak in more tender tones of inviting and pleading.

Alma 6

This chapter reports the fruits of Alma's pure testimony. Those who did not repent had their names "blotted out." Their names were removed from Church records and are not found in the book of life (Revelation 13:8; 17:8; 22:19).

Alma 6:5–6

"The word of God was liberal unto all"—the Book of Mormon uses the term *liberal* in the sense of "freely available" and "generous." The former-day Saints "did not set their hearts upon riches; therefore they were liberal to all, both old and young, both bond and free, both male and female, whether out of the church or in the church, having no respect to persons as to those who stood in need" (Alma 1:30). So it is in Christ's Church today; humanitarian assistance is freely given to members and nonmembers alike. True Saints are liberal, that is, open-minded and open-hearted, generous in sharing with others. "All are alike unto God" (2 Nephi 26:33).

All missionary-minded members of the kingdom attend meetings and fast and pray for those who have not yet found God.

Alma 7

This chapter contains one of the most important and profound prophecies of the coming of the Messiah, his birth, and his ministry, in all of scripture.

Alma 7:5

There is a crucial gospel principle that repeatedly appears in the book of Alma. We will discuss it here, where it first occurs. Answer the following four simple questions from these scriptures:

- Alma 7:5—Joy comes *after* what?
- Alma 17:5, 11—Saving souls comes *after* what?
- Alma 26:27—Success comes *after* what?
- Doctrine and Covenants 58:4—Blessings come *after* what?

There seems to be a clear pattern in these teachings. The eternal principle operating through this scriptural counsel is that the things we want most—joy, success, blessings, and exaltation—come *after* affliction, sorrow, long-suffering, tribulation, and adversity. Jesus is our example in all things, and Jesus' crown of glory came *after* his crown of thorns.

When confronted with interminable trials, the Prophet Joseph Smith asked not "why?" but "how long?" He understood why. The Lord told him to "endure it well." (We too will endure it, so we might as well *endure it well*.)

President Brigham Young taught that "all intelligent beings who are crowned with crowns of glory, immortality, and eternal lives must pass through every ordeal appointed for intelligent beings to pass through, to gain their glory and exaltation. Every calamity that can come upon mortal beings will be suffered to come upon the few, to prepare them to enjoy the presence of the Lord. If we obtain the glory that Abraham obtained, we must do so by the same means that he did. If we are ever prepared to enjoy the society of Enoch, Noah, Melchizedek, Abraham, Isaac, and Jacob, or of their faithful children, and of the faithful Prophets and Apostles, we must pass through the same experience, and gain the knowledge, intelligence, and endowments that will prepare us to enter into the celestial kingdom of our Father and God. . . . Every trial and experience you have passed through is necessary for your salvation."[6]

President John Taylor quoted Joseph Smith as saying: "You will have all kinds of trials to pass through. And it is quite as necessary that you be tried as it was for Abraham and other men of God, and . . . God will feel after you, and He will take hold of you and wrench your very heart strings, and if you cannot stand it you will not be fit for an inheritance in the Celestial Kingdom of God."[7]

President George Q. Cannon confirmed the same heavenly principle: "Every Latter-day Saint who gains a celestial glory will be tried to the very uttermost. If there is a point in our character that is weak and tender, you may depend upon it that the Lord will reach after that, and we will be tried at that spot for the Lord will test us to the utmost before we can get through and receive that glory and exaltation which He has in store for us."[8]

President Spencer W. Kimball wrote: "Being human, we would expel from our lives physical pain and mental anguish and assure ourselves of continual ease and comfort, but if we were to close the doors upon sorrow and distress, we might be excluding our greatest friends and benefactors. Suffering can make saints of people as they learn patience, long-suffering, and self-mastery."[9]

Alma 7:8

It is interesting to see a prophet of God admit he does not know something. Nephi confessed that he did not know the meaning of some doctrine (1 Nephi 11:17), and so did Mormon (Words of Mormon 1:7; see also 3 Nephi 28:17). And because something has not yet been revealed, prophets may also give their judgment or their opinion, as did Alma

(Alma 37:11; 40:3–4, 8, 20–21) and Paul (1 Corinthians 7:12, 25). Prophets, like all mortals, learn line upon line. They, too, have to inquire. They ask, and the answers that are revealed to them often become scripture.

Alma 7:10

Two points about Alma's wording should be noted: first, Jerusalem is referred to as a *land* rather than a city, and second, Jesus' birth would occur *at* Jerusalem. Joseph Smith, of course, knew well that Jesus was born in Bethlehem. If he himself had been writing the Book of Mormon, he would have so stated the fact, as any deviation from the well-known setting would certainly draw objection. However, Joseph Smith was merely translating a geographical note from an ancient writer, which in itself proves to be nicely packaged evidence that the Book of Mormon derives from a Semitic background.

For a major city-center such as Jerusalem to be called not a city but a *land* was standard practice anciently. El Amarna letter 287 (ancient diplomatic correspondence discovered in Egypt) mentions several times the "land of Jerusalem," and letter 290 records the complaint of Abdu-Kheba of Jerusalem to Pharaoh Akhenaton that "the land of the king went over to the 'Apiru people. But now even a town in the *land of Jerusalem*, Bit-*Lahmi* [Bethlehem] by name, a town belonging to the king, has gone over to the side of the people of Keilah."[10]

The Book of Mormon record itself is internally consistent in referring to the place from which Lehi and family had departed, where the Savior would appear as a mortal, and to which the people of Judah would eventually return as "the land of Jerusalem."[11]

Satellite towns and villages that surround larger demographic or political centers were regarded in ancient times as belonging to those larger centers. Not only Bethlehem but also Hebron (fifteen miles south of Bethlehem) were assumed to be in the "land of Jerusalem."[12]

A second point: Alma stated that Jesus would be born of Mary not *in* Jerusalem but *at* Jerusalem. A dictionary definition of the preposition *at* includes the words *on, in, within, close by,* or *near.*[13]

Regardless of our definition of the preposition *at,* Alma's declaration is true. Even if the alternate definition *in* is accepted, Jesus' birth is very properly placed *in* "Jerusalem, which is the *land* of our forefathers."

Thus, instead of Alma's prophetic preview of the setting of the Savior's birth being grossly erroneous or contradictory, it is actually quite compatible with similar biblical and extra-biblical figures of speech and constitutes an evidence of the passage's authentic ancient origin.

"A virgin"—regardless of the polemics of biblical scholars, the fact is that this young woman, Mary, would be a virgin, and still as a virgin (that is, not having intimately known any mortal man) she would have a son—the Son of the Eternal Father. She would conceive, not as Matthew's Gospel reads, "of the Holy Ghost" (Matthew 1:18), but as Alma's text reads, "by the power of the Holy Ghost." The Holy Ghost enables individuals to withstand the presence of God the Father. See also commentary at 1 Nephi 11:13–26.

Alma 7:11–13

Some of the most important purposes of Jesus' mortality are the following: he came to take upon himself our pains, sicknesses, and infirmities—to learn how to help us through our mortal debilities—and to take upon himself our sins and blot out our transgressions.

How far does the Atonement reach? What does it cover? And for whom? The Atonement is not just for sinners and not just for sins. It is for disappointment, heartache, bitterness over betrayal, unfairness, injustice, loneliness, sorrow of every kind, inadequacy, mistakes caused by unintentional carelessness, our sicknesses—physical and emotional—and many other things. The Atonement is so sweeping that Jesus suffered for his betrayers and executioners; he even suffered the suffering of victims (such as of the Holocaust).

As our colleague Stephen E. Robinson wrote: "*All* the negative aspects of human existence brought about by the Fall, Jesus Christ absorbed into himself. He experienced vicariously . . . all the private griefs and heartaches, all the physical pains and handicaps, all the emotional burdens and depressions of the human family. He knows the loneliness of those who don't fit in or who aren't handsome or pretty. He knows what it's like to choose up teams and be the last one chosen. He knows the anguish of parents whose children go wrong. He knows the private hell of the abused child or spouse. He knows all these things personally and intimately because he lived them in the Gethsemane experience. Having personally lived a perfect life, he then chose to experience our imperfect lives. In . . . the meridian of time, the center of eternity, he lived a billion billion lifetimes of sin, pain, disease, and sorrow.

"God uses no magic wand to simply wave bad things into nonexistence. The sins that he remits, he remits by making them his own and suffering them. The pain and heartaches that he relieves, he relieves by suffering them himself. These things can be shared and absorbed, but they cannot be simply wished or waved away. They must be suffered. Thus we owe him not only for our spiritual cleansing from sin, but for our physical, mental, and emotional healings as well, for he has borne these infirmities for us also. All that the Fall put wrong, the Savior in his atonement puts right. It is all part of his infinite sacrifice—of his infinite gift."[14]

Jesus was made like us (mortal) so that he could know according to the flesh how to succor us—to comfort, assist, nurture, and help us. As Paul wrote, "Wherefore in all things it behoved him to be made like unto his brethren, that he might be a merciful and faithful high priest in things pertaining to

God, to make reconciliation for the sins of the people. For in that he himself hath suffered being tempted, he is able to succour them that are tempted" (Hebrews 2:17–18).

Alma 7:14–16

Here is an invitation to show ourselves willing to repent and enter into a covenant to keep God's commandments, as evidenced by our willingness to be baptized (see also commentary at Mosiah 5:7–8; 18:8–10). On being born again, see Mosiah 5:2–7. On being promised or sealed up to eternal life, see commentary at 2 Nephi 1:15; 31:19–21; Alma 36:28.

Alma 7:20–21

God does not and cannot vary from his straight course; he never deviates to the right or to the left. His path or his course is always the same, "one eternal round" (see also 1 Nephi 10:19; Alma 37:12; D&C 3:2). In other words, God is firm, steadfast, and immovable; he is constant and totally dependable (see commentary at Jacob 3:1–2).

Only clean, kind, and loving souls can live in the presence of God; no one who is filthy can be "received into the kingdom of God." "No unclean thing can dwell with God; wherefore, ye must be cast off forever" (1 Nephi 10:21). At the last day, anyone "who is filthy shall remain in his filthiness"; Alma later taught this concept as the "plan of restoration" (Alma 41:2) or the law of the harvest (Alma 41).

Alma 7:23–24

These verses summarize the whole of the gospel; they are a master list of Christlike qualities that all true disciples should pursue and emulate. Similar lists of Christlike attributes appear in 2 Peter 1:4–7; Alma 13:28–29; D&C 4:5–6; 107:30. Doctrine and Covenants 121:36 calls these attributes the "principles of righteousness." By working hard and being obedient, we eventually acquire these divine attributes as part of our character. They are the "fruits" of the Spirit of the Lord working in our lives.

Alma 7:25

Alma blessed the people, saying, "May the Lord bless you, and keep your garments spotless . . . in the kingdom of heaven to go no more out." In other words, he blessed them that they might remain in that state of grace which attends their saved condition. He was saying, in a sense, "Your natures are changed so that your attitude is God's attitude—may that never change."

Alma 8–16

These chapters are a record of the missionary work at Ammonihah, and according to Alma 8:9, it was a very difficult mission. Before launching into this new mission, Alma returned home and rested (Alma 8:1).

Alma 8:7

"It was the custom of the people of Nephi to call their lands, and their cities . . . after the name of him who first possessed them." An example at the beginning of an older civilization is the Jaredites calling their temporary camp on the shore of the ocean Moriancumer, after the brother of Jared (Ether 2:13). It is a long-standing custom of many peoples to name a place after its first settler; for example, consider the Utah communities of Ogden, Layton, Orem, and Provo, which were named after Peter Skene Ogden, Christopher Layton, Walter C. Orem, and Etienne Provost, respectively.

Alma 8:10

Alma "labored much in the spirit, wrestling with God in mighty prayer, that he would pour out his Spirit upon the people who were in the city." On the concept of wrestling or struggling in mighty prayer, see commentary at Enos 1:1–2.

Alma 8:11–16

The people of Ammonihah reacted rudely. "They hardened their hearts" and said "we are not of thy church"; in other words, "we are not interested!" They reviled against Alma and spat on him. He was "weighed down with sorrow, wading through much tribulation and anguish of soul." Juxtapose those feelings of discouragement to Alma's next experience; an angel appeared to him (the same angel who had first appeared to him and dramatically changed his life [see v. 15; Mosiah 27:11]) and, in essence, said, You are a good, faithful soul, Alma. Now go back there and preach to them again. Missionary success is measured less by numbers of baptisms than by the missionary's obedience and diligence.

Alma 8:18–20

Alma obeyed with exactness and returned speedily, deserving the miracle that happened next: The Lord had prepared the heart of a rich and influential man (Alma 10:4); he would join the Church, become Alma's missionary companion, and quickly become a great prophet-leader. Like Alma, Paul, and other "chosen vessels," Amulek was stopped in his tracks by an angel of God and redirected in the course of his life (Alma 10:7).

The angel had told Amulek to receive into his house this missionary-messenger from God.

A zone leader wrote about the following miraculous incident in his weekly letter to his mission president in Chile: "On Monday we didn't have anything planned, so we decided to knock at a couple of houses on about every street in our proselyting area. Getting close to the end of the evening, I felt impressed to knock on a certain door. They let us in. We taught a family of six people, five of whom could be baptized. After we finished the discussion, the wife started telling us about a dream she had. She told us that three days before we knocked on their door, she had a dream of two angels appearing to her. When she saw our faces, she almost started crying because ours were the faces of the angels. I am so excited to have the opportunity to teach this family."

Did the Lord not say, "I will go before you?"

Alma 8:26–27

Amulek acted as the Savior bade his disciples, "I was an hungered, and ye gave me meat: . . . I was a stranger, and ye took me in" (Matthew 25:35). Alma remained at Amulek's home for many days to teach and train him—Amulek's "Missionary Training Center" experience.

Alma 8:30–32

The trainer and his new companion went out into their proselyting area filled with the Holy Ghost and with power. With the power of the Spirit, how did they teach? *Boldly!* (Alma 9:7). Compare their behavior with that of the early leaders and missionaries of the Church in the Holy Land after the Holy Ghost came upon them on the day of Pentecost. Peter, John, Stephen, Philip, Paul, Barnabas, and others were changed men, and they went out, like Alma and Amulek, and taught boldly. "They were all filled with the Holy Ghost, and they spake the word of God with boldness" (Acts 4:31; see also 4:18–20, 29; 5:29, 32, 40–42; 9:27, 29; 13:46; 14:3—every one of these passages declares that they were "bold" or taught "boldly" or "with boldness").

Alma 9:1–6

Alma got a cold reception and brusque rejection among the Ammonihahites. They said, in essence, Who do you think you are? We are not going to listen to you even if you were to "prophesy that this great city should be destroyed in one day"—which is literally what happened (Alma 16:1–11).

On their belligerent attitude ("Who is God?"), see commentary at Mosiah 11:27, 29.

Alma 9:7–14

Prophets always bring up the long-forgotten (or too frequently ignored) messages of the past prophets and patriarchs. The people of Ammonihah had, through wickedness, lost the ability to remember things of righteousness.

Alma 9:15, 19–23

Alma outlined the ways the people of Nephi had been blessed by God: they had (1) received knowledge of things past, present, and future according to their desires; (2) been visited by the Spirit of God; (3) conversed with angels; (4) heard the voice of the Lord; (5) received the spirit of revelation; (6) received spiritual gifts; (7) been spared destruction and delivered from bondage time after time; and (8) been given material prosperity. No wonder Alma then said, "It shall be more tolerable for [the Lamanites] in the day of judgment than for you"; compare the similar pronouncement made by Jesus on Capernaum, Chorazin, and Bethsaida (Matthew 11:21–24).[15] On falling into grave transgressions after receiving so much light and knowledge, being highly favored with the Spirit of God and many spiritual gifts, being saved from wars, famines, and diseases, and being greatly prospered, see commentary at Alma 24:30.

Alma 10:1–4

Amulek, the dynamic, new member-missionary with only a brief training experience, went out and taught great, powerful sermons. He first established his family ties as a direct descendant of Lehi and was the first to specify the tribe from which Lehi descended. From 1 Nephi 5:14 we have already learned that Lehi was from the tribe of Joseph, but here, and only here, we learn that Lehi was descended from Joseph's son Manasseh. According to apostle Erastus Snow, this truth was contained in the lost 116 pages of the book of Lehi.[16] Amulek further described himself as a self-made, independently wealthy man. He then went on to relate his conversion story.

The curious incident involving Aminadi, who interpreted a writing on the wall, is not mentioned elsewhere. It presumably finds a parallel in the Babylonian Empire of Belshazzar, recorded in Daniel 5:24–28.

Alma 10:7–11

Amulek told the story of his conversion. He and his family were blessed because he extended hospitality to a servant of the Lord. This recalls Abraham, who was blessed because of his hospitality (Genesis 18:1–10). Have you ever performed some act of kindness and been blessed for it beyond your thoughts? Brother Skinner recalls a time as a young man when his parents offered such a kindness without thinking anything about it. The kindness was returned years later at a time of family crisis when the reciprocated kindness was magnified a hundredfold. Such is the way the Lord works among his covenant people.

Alma 10:13–32; 11:20

These verses contain interesting and important comments about the potentially destructive roles of lawyers and judges in stirring up civil disturbances, contentious lawsuits, and so on for their own pecuniary benefit. Amulek actually traced "the foundation of the destruction of this people" to their lawyers and judges. Righteous lawyers can be a great blessing; unrighteous ones can wreak great havoc. This is a significant point to make for our time, considering the litigious nature of modern society.

Alma 11:1–20

Further comments about the role of judges in society and their remuneration leads to an editorial comment (perhaps Mormon's) about the system of Nephite coinage. It may have been added so that any charges about individuals taking advantage of society could be answered. Later on Korihor accused the leaders of the Nephites of glutting themselves upon the labors of the people. Those so accused, like Alma, could answer precisely. "The laborer is worthy of his hire" (D&C 31:5; 84:79; 106:3).

Alma 11:21–39

Amulek and Zeezrom (whom we might denominate the "president of the Ammonihah Bar Association") engaged in a public discussion over religious principles. Zeezrom, after employing a lie and a bribe and in his clearly litigious manner tried to trick the missionary in his teachings about the nature of God. "Is there more than one God [or Godhead, as we would say]?" No, there is only one Godhead: the Father; his Son, who would come into mortality to save his people *from* their sins; and the Holy Spirit, who would accompany that Son during his ministry in the flesh.

"Is the Son of God the very Eternal Father?" "Yea, he is the very Eternal Father [or, Creator] of heaven and earth." Amulek could have launched into a detailed treatise of the various roles of the Son as a Father, but it is seldom productive with those who are not members, and especially with antagonists, to depart from the basics. Amulek intentionally kept his teachings simple.

Alma 11:40–46

Again we note that the Hebrew Bible (the Old Testament), as presently constituted, has little instruction about the resurrection and our status in general after this life. The Book of Mormon, on the other hand, contains several discourses about Christ rescuing all humankind from the bands of death; about the permanent, indivisible restoration of body and spirit, the resurrection to immortality; and about our arraignment before the three Gods, who are one Eternal God (or, Godhead), for a final judgment (compare D&C 76:68).

The clarity and power of Amulek's teachings made a dramatic impression on the people.

Verses 40–44 perhaps constitute the clearest explanation in scripture on the relationship between universal salvation—a true doctrine—versus limited exaltation—also a true doctrine. Thus, all will be resurrected, but not all will be redeemed from their sins; Christ will come to "take upon him the transgressions of those who believe on his name; and these are they that shall have eternal life, and salvation [that is, exaltation] cometh to none else. Therefore the wicked remain as though there had been no redemption made."

Also explained is how resurrection is part of the larger doctrine of restoration. Note that here, as elsewhere, the doctrines of resurrection and judgment are usually taught together. At the final judgment, Christ will represent all three members of the Godhead because all judgment has been committed to him (compare v. 44 with John 5:22, 27).

On the perfect memory, the "bright recollection" that we will all have at the judgment bar of God, see the quotation from President Joseph F. Smith at 2 Nephi 9:13–16.

Alma 12–13

Alma expounded a complete curriculum for salvation: God, the Creation, the Fall, the Atonement, agency, revelation, the plan of redemption (including faith, repentance, baptism, and the gift of the Holy Ghost), the foreknowledge of God, foreordination, the high priesthood, ordinances, covenant people, sanctification, resurrection, and judgment. Alma taught such elevated doctrines because there was at least one soul, Zeezrom, who would respond to those deeply meaningful doctrines and change his behavior forever, not to mention the many other believers (Alma 14:1) who would suffer martyrdom because of their unwavering conversion to Alma's teachings (Alma 14:7–14). The doctrines of God have power to change peoples' hearts and minds.

Alma 12:1–8

After Amulek concluded his testimony to Zeezrom, Alma stepped in to confirm the words of Amulek and to teach the scriptures beyond what Amulek had done. Alma taught a profound principle: God cannot be fooled by anyone's outward speech, for God knows a person's inward thoughts, feelings, and intents. In fact, we know that the thoughts and intents of the heart constitute one of the criteria by which all people will be judged (D&C 137:9). Except in circumstances like this one, when the Holy Spirit reveals to God's authorized servants the thoughts and intents of another, only God knows all the thoughts and intents of our hearts (D&C 6:16).

Zeezrom had devised "a very subtle plan, as to the subtlety of the devil." The word "subtle" is used several times in the scriptures to describe something that is deceptive, elusive, shadowy, ingenious, clever, cunning, sly, tricky, or crafty (see, for example, Alma 47:4; D&C 123:12). All these terms characterize the evil one, whose constant effort is to entrap, ensnare, overpower, and destroy the souls of men and the work of God.

Alma 12:9

Gospel scholars McConkie and Millet wrote: "It is a remarkable thing how two people can be seated beside one another, hear exactly the same message preached, and come away with two different conclusions regarding the import of the declaration. To one listener the presentation is as the gibberish of alien tongues; to another, as manna from heaven. To one listener the messenger is seen as weak and unpolished, the pronouncement as unimportant and unnecessary; to the second, the messenger seems to be fired with the power of Almighty God and his sermon deep and profound. Indeed, to some it is given to know the mysteries of God and to see the power of God resting upon his servants, simply because they are prepared to so receive, because they are open to truth. . . .

"What is a mystery to one man may not be a mystery to another; it is simply a matter of preparation, readiness, and receptivity."[17]

Those who are prepared, who have proved themselves obedient and valiant, and who are determined to serve God at all cost may receive sacred knowledge, make holy covenants, and participate in holy ordinances ("the mysteries of godliness" and "the power of godliness"; see D&C 63:23; 84:19–20). They are placed under a strict command not to divulge those most sacred things (see, for example, 3 Nephi 26:16–18; 27:23; 28:13–14, 16; D&C 105:23; compare 4 Nephi 1:27). They do not go around talking about all they know.

"Some experiences are ineffable, so transcendently glorious that they defy human expression or description. Of these things it is not *possible* for man to speak. Some truths and experiences 'are not lawful for man to utter' in the sense that it is not *permitted* or appropriate to speak of them, except as led and directed by the Holy Spirit. Some special things are to be kept within the household of faith, among those who believe (see Moses 1:42; 4:32). 'Remember that that which cometh from above is sacred, and must be spoken with care, and by constraint of the Spirit . . .' (D&C 63:64).

"Just as it would be unwise and dangerous to feed strong meat to infants, so also it is unwise and dangerous to provide deeper doctrines or sacred ordinances for public display. . . . Too frequently those who encounter these things prematurely are unable to digest them properly and ultimately turn with bitterness against the very source of truth. In short, it matters a great deal not only *what* people are taught, but also *when* they are taught it."[18]

Alma 12:10

Brother Ogden's son Daniel was in Europe several years ago on an assignment from the United States government for three weeks to conduct interviews for top-secret clearance of U.S. military personnel and civilians, along with a few civilians from other countries. He described the interview questions in some detail, and in some respects, they are far more extensive than a Latter-day Saint's temple recommend interview. Before he even sat down with a person, Daniel had in his possession the person's police records, national agency records, financial records, credit reports, and so on. He probed where the individuals had been and who they had been with for business or pleasure. He inquired if they had ever used drugs or alcohol (how much and how often); if they had ever been convicted of any crime; if they had ever been divorced, been involved in any sexual misconduct, had any extramarital affairs, or been guilty of any abuse. He had to have details of any and all debt the individual had. The searching questions were to establish their loyalty and honesty. The basic idea of the interview of each individual was to answer the question: *Can this person be trusted?*

What an interesting phenomenon from a gospel perspective. Isn't that exactly what will happen to you as you pass into the eternal worlds to be judged in regard to your earth life? Are you not here to be cleared for capacity and worthiness to receive all the top secrets of godliness and to prove that you can be trusted to perform work similar to our Heavenly Father's? According to this verse in Alma, a person's worthiness to be entrusted with the mysteries of God is directly related to the hardness or softness of his heart. Living the gospel of Jesus Christ ensures that your heart will remain soft, pliable, and receptive to "the greater portion of the word" and the eventual fulness of the mysteries of godliness.

Alma 12:14–18

On our words, our works, and even our thoughts condemning us, see commentary at Mosiah 3:25–26 and at 2 Nephi 9:13–16.

Elder Dallin H. Oaks taught that "the Final Judgment is not just an evaluation of a sum total of good and evil acts— what we have *done*. It is an acknowledgment of the final effect of our acts and thoughts—what we have *become*. It is not enough for anyone just to go through the motions. The commandments, ordinances, and covenants of the gospel are not a list of deposits required to be made in some heavenly account. The gospel of Jesus Christ is a plan that shows us how to become what our Heavenly Father desires us to become."[19]

On our not daring to look up at God and wanting the mountains to fall upon us to hide us from his presence, see examples of these anxious feelings in Alma 36:14–15 and Revelation 6:16.

On spiritual death, see commentary at Jacob 3:3–11; and on torments as a lake of fire and brimstone, see commentary at Mosiah 3:27.

The rebellious and wicked will everlastingly remain "as though there had been no redemption made (see also Alma 11:41), in a state where "they cannot die"; that is, there is no annihilation or disintegration of resurrected, perfected elements, so they remain in that unredeemed condition forever. Hell is both a place and a state of mind.

Alma 12:21–26, 30

Cherubim is a plural Hebrew word referring to angelic sentinels placed in the Garden of Eden to guard "the way of the tree of life" (Genesis 3:24). A "flaming sword," the exact nature and description of which are not given in the scriptures, was also put in position to keep Adam and Eve from partaking of the fruit of that tree and living forever in a sinful condition. The biblical account gives no specific reason for these guardian agents being employed, but Alma 12:22–26 teaches that it was essential to keep the first fallen mortals from partaking of the fruit of the tree of life (representing immortality and eternal life) in order to experience this preparatory and probationary state, death, resurrection from death, and the full benefits of the plan of redemption. According to verse 30, this plan of redemption was known and accepted before we ever came to earth and is granted to us here as we exercise faith, repent, and do holy works.

Alma 12:31–37

After our original parents "transgressed the first commandments"—partaking of the forbidden fruit, which necessitated their expulsion from Eden—God gave more commandments (laws, ceremonies, and ordinances) by which to live, and mortals became "as Gods, knowing good from evil." Having choices, they learned "whether to do evil or to do good," God's commandments directing them to avoid evil and thus avoid the second death (the permanent expulsion from the presence of God after the great last judgment).

Notice that the commandments were given *after* God had first taught Adam and Eve the plan of redemption. The specifics—the do's and don'ts—followed the explanation of the larger picture—the plan. Thus, teachers and leaders today are well advised to teach the doctrinal foundation first, with the end in view, then the specific ethical components, the do's and don'ts, to show how they fit into the plan.

Verses 33–37 teach us to repent, lay claim on the Savior's mercy, have our sins remitted, and enter into his rest ("the fulness of his glory"; D&C 84:24). The key to achieving that fulness of glory is noted in every one of those five verses: not to harden your heart, but keep it soft, pliable, and receptive.

The "first provocation" was the transgression of Adam and Eve. The "last provocation" is our own, and if we harden our hearts, the consequence is the everlasting destruction of our souls.

Alma 13

This constitutes Alma's unique and powerful discourse on the Melchizedek Priesthood, which was in operation in our premortal existence. President Joseph Fielding Smith stated in general conference: "With regard to the holding of the priesthood in the preexistence, I will say that there was an organization there just as well as an organization here, and men there held authority. Men chosen to positions of trust in the spirit world held the priesthood."[20] With this understanding in mind, we more easily follow this inspiring discourse.

Alma 13:1–9

Alma began by asking his audience to project their minds forward—in which he meant forward to the beginning of time, even to the time of the earliest patriarchs who first received the higher priesthood (D&C 84:6–16; 107:2–5). He then explained why God has a special covenant people and why some are called as leaders and others are not. Some are ordained as priesthood leaders, according to God's foreknowledge of all things, in order to teach the people to look forward to the Son for redemption. In fact, all who hold the Melchizedek Priesthood were foreordained in our premortal existence to do so. When Alma uses the term *priest*, he is referring to Melchizedek Priesthood holders, who in a general sense are priests (D&C 76:56–57; 107:1–4). This foreordination was based on premortal faith and faithfulness. Foreordained leaders exercised "exceedingly great faith" in Jesus Christ and his atonement and thereby received a holy calling to continue to teach Christ's redemption here in mortality.

The Prophet Joseph Smith declared, "Every man who has a calling to minister to the inhabitants of the world was ordained to that very purpose in the Grand Council of heaven before this world was."[21]

President Spencer W. Kimball added: "In the world before we came here, faithful women were given certain assignments while faithful men were foreordained to certain priesthood tasks. While we do not now remember the particulars, this does not alter the glorious reality of what we once agreed to. You are accountable for those things which long ago were expected of you just as are those we sustain as prophets and apostles!"[22]

Alma speaks of "a preparatory redemption," which is actually the atonement of Jesus Christ that operated in our behalf in our premortal existence. If we had the opportunity to progress premortally, it is reasonable to believe we could make mistakes. Elder Orson Pratt, writing about the nature of sin in our premortal existence, said: "Among the two-thirds [of God's spirit children] who remained, it is highly probable, that, there were many who were not valiant. . . , but whose sins were of such a nature that they could be forgiven through faith in the future sufferings of the Only Begotten of the Father, and through their sincere repentance and reformation. We see no impropriety in Jesus offering himself as an acceptable offering and sacrifice before the Father to atone for the sins of his brethren, committed, not only in the second, but also in the first estate."[23]

In premortality, the atonement of Jesus Christ operated in our behalf so that we all could begin our second estate with a fresh start, free from the blemishes, mistakes, sins, and errors committed in premortality, free of the disabling and crippling spiritual baggage brought from a former life. As was revealed to the Prophet Joseph Smith, "Every spirit of man was innocent in the beginning; and God having redeemed man from the fall, men became again, in their infant state, innocent before God" (D&C 93:38). Satan and his followers would not accept our Heavenly Father's plan centered in Christ's atonement and, therefore, could not even remain with us in the first estate.

With this insight, we may read with new eyes scriptural statements that speak of Christ as "the Lamb slain from the foundation of the world" (Revelation 13:8). Or, when Adam spoke to the Lord about the necessity of baptism, the Lord said: "Behold I have [already] forgiven thee thy transgression in the Garden of Eden. Hence came the saying abroad . . .

that the Son of God hath atoned for original guilt" (Moses 6:53–54).

The tragedy of hardening the heart is noted, which kept some from enjoying the "great privilege," the holy calling of priesthood leadership.

The high priesthood after the order of the Son of God is the greatest power in the universe, and it is eternal, "without beginning of days or end of years." The high priesthood is what we now call the Melchizedek Priesthood—and the reason for that change in terminology is given in Doctrine and Covenants 107:3–4. That high priesthood is conferred upon a faithful man through "a holy ordinance." He thus becomes a high priest forever after the order of the Son, who is also "without beginning of days or end of years."

President Ezra Taft Benson explained, "To enter into the order of the Son of God is the equivalent today of entering into the fullness of the Melchizedek Priesthood, which is only received in the house of the Lord."[24]

Alma 13:10–13

By their faith, repentance, and good works, worthy individuals merited being called to the high priesthood and sanctified by the Holy Ghost, becoming pure and spotless by having their garments "washed white through the blood of the Lamb" (see commentary at 1 Nephi 12:10–11). There are an "exceedingly great many" who are exalted and enter into God's rest, which, again, is the fulness of his glory (D&C 84:24). Alma admonishes us to follow their example and become one of them, humbling ourselves and bringing forth fruit meet for repentance, laboring for the Lord and having all our sins forgiven (D&C 31:5).

Alma 13:14–19

One of the most brilliant examples of the use of faith, repentance, ordinances, and good works in the history of the world was Melchizedek. *Melchizedek* is probably a name-title rather than a personal name (Hebrew *Malki-Zedek* means "King of Righteousness"). The Savior was *the* King of Righteousness, and Melchizedek was a type of the Savior. He was a high priest after the order of the Son of God, the presiding authority on the earth in the early days of Abraham. Even the great patriarch Abraham paid his tithes to Melchizedek. After Melchizedek and his people were translated (see JST, Genesis 14:34), Abraham became the head of that dispensation.

Melchizedek was king over the land called "Peace" (*Salem*, or *Shalem*) and reigned under his father, meaning that he either ruled as a vassal king subordinate to his father, or he reigned after him. His people had become grossly sinful. All of them had departed from the ways of the Lord and had fallen into all kinds of abominable behavior, but Melchizedek exercised mighty faith and called them to repentance. So great was the impact of his message and ministry that the people did repent. We do not know how many years of intense, dedicated effort that took, but the king-prophet's faith and works resulted in extraordinary reforms, elevating his people ultimately to a temporal and spiritual level of conduct that had been paralleled only by a few, including Enoch and his people. Melchizedek and his fellow citizens established peace in their land and eventually warranted departure from this telestial world; they joined Enoch and his people in a terrestrial and translated condition (JST, Genesis 14:34).[25]

During his mortal ministry, Melchizedek, as God's presiding high priest (D&C 107:2), had also served as "keeper of the storehouse of God" (JST, Genesis 14:37), which involved also his role as administrator or president of the holy temple in the city of Salem. How could a great high priest function in his priesthood without a temple? Or how could a people establish such righteousness that they were transferred from this telestial world without having the blessings of the temple? The Prophet Joseph Smith taught that the main object of gathering the people of God in any age of the world is "to build unto the Lord a house whereby He could reveal unto His people the ordinances of His house and the glories of His kingdom, and teach the people the way of salvation; for there are certain ordinances and principles that, when they are taught and practiced, must be done in a place or house built for that purpose."[26]

It is probable that a temple or sanctuary existed in Salem during Melchizedek's ministry. The Jewish historian Josephus wrote anciently of "[Melchizedek] the Righteous King, for such he really was; on which account he was [there] the first priest of God, and first built a temple [there], and called the city Jerusalem, which was formerly called Salem."[27] Temple ordinances were given so the people could look forward to the Son of God for a remission of their sins, that they might enter into the rest or glory of the Lord (Alma 13:16).

Melchizedek was a remarkable example of one who fulfilled his premortal ordination to use God's power in order to save souls. Paul wrote, "Now consider how great this man was" (Hebrews 7:4), and Alma exclaimed, "There were many before him, and also there were many afterwards, but none were greater" (Alma 13:19).

Alma 13:20

In the scriptures, to "wrest" means to twist, distort, or pervert, in the sense of accommodating one's personal interpretation of truth.

Alma 13:24, 26

Alma announced that "angels [Hebrew *malachim*, 'messengers'] are declaring [glad tidings] unto many at this time in our land" (for example, see Alma 10:10; 39:19). These messengers could be mortals on earth or angels from heaven. Why had they come? To prepare the people's hearts to receive the Savior and his word when he would come in his glory (see also Alma 16:16) to perform the most glorious mission in the history of this, or any other, world. Angels will declare to "just and holy men" at the time of his coming that the prophecies of the holy prophets are in process of fulfillment (see "All the Prophets Prophesied of Christ," accompanying the commentary at Mosiah 13:33).

Messengers from God are declaring glad tidings—truths from heaven—now, in our day, to prepare our hearts for the Messiah's coming in glory.

Alma 14:1–3

Many people believed the teachings of Alma and Amulek and began to change their lives, although most were angry with the prophets because of the plainness of their words or their frankness and bluntness in exposing the sins of the people. Those who willfully live in sin do not like to have their sins exposed. This people wanted to kill the prophets.

Alma 14:5

Here we find an example of the voice of the people not choosing that which is right, unlike the other positive examples we have read about (Mosiah 29:27).

Alma 14:6–11

Zeezrom began the conversion process. He was "harrowed up." To harrow is to plow over hardened ground in order to break it up and make it receptive to planting. Zeezrom's heart was, in effect, plowed and broken. He felt godly sorrow and tried to repair what he had earlier wrought among the people. But the damage was not so easily undone. This is an important lesson: while true repentance guarantees that the Lord remembers sin no more, sometimes it is not possible to reverse completely the consequences of past choices in mortality. On one occasion Brother Skinner interviewed a man for advancement in the priesthood. He had made very poor choices earlier in his life but had fully repented and was by then a stalwart. Yet the earlier choices had cost him his wife, his children, his home, and his employment.

Even though he had fully turned to the Lord, he could not get back the things he had lost earlier. That would have to wait until a future day of restoration. Ironically, Zeezrom suffered the persecution he had earlier instigated. And he had to live with the knowledge that he had caused women and children to be cast into the fire.

Why doesn't choosing God here in mortality shield us from pain and suffering? When a righteous person is killed, is that death necessarily a tragedy? What are the reasons God permits the righteous to suffer? Verse 11 teaches that the Lord sometimes allows the righteous to be killed as a witness against the wicked (see also Alma 60:13; D&C 136:39). Joseph Smith declared, "It is a false idea that the Saints will escape all the judgments, whilst the wicked suffer; for all flesh is subject to suffer, and 'the righteous shall hardly escape.'"[28]

It is important for us to understand things from an eternal perspective. Though a temporary loss to us, the righteous go on to a better world and enter into God's glory (see also D&C 42:46). President Spencer W. Kimball wrote: "If all the sick for whom we pray were healed, if all the righteous were protected and the wicked destroyed, the whole program of the Father would be annulled and the basic principle of the gospel, free agency, would be ended. No man would have to live by faith. . . . Should all prayers be immediately answered according to our selfish desires and our limited understanding, then there would be little or no suffering, sorrow, disappointment, or even death, and if these were not, there would also be no joy, success, resurrection, nor eternal life and godhood."[29]

Alma 14:8

Brigham Young University religion professors McConkie and Millet, referring to the records brought forth, noted that "this is one of the evidences in the Book of Mormon that many (if not most) of the believers had scriptural records. Though there may have been only one set of metal plates (such as the brass plates), surely hundreds and thousands of other sets of records, copies—less durable but more accessible—could be found among the descendants of Lehi. See Jacob 7:23; Alma 33:2; Helaman 3:13; 3 Nephi 5:9."[30]

Alma 14:15–24

The smiting and taunting of the prophet-missionaries, and their silence before their accusers, are reminiscent of the arraignment of Jesus before religious and political rulers a century later (Matthew 26:62–68; 27:12–14, 40; John 18:22–23; 19:8–10).

Alma 14:26–28

Alma's prayer immediately calls to mind Joseph Smith's prayer in Liberty Jail (D&C 121:1–6), only with more immediate and positive results. The deliverance of Alma and Amulek from prison reminds us of Peter's experience in Jerusalem (Acts 12).

Alma 15:1–12

Zeezrom, the former antagonist, had been touched by the Spirit and was sick as he recognized the enormity of his sins. President Boyd K. Packer taught that physical illnesses can be related to spiritual ailments: "There are spiritual disorders . . . and spiritual diseases that can cause intense suffering. The body and the spirit of man are bound together. Often, very often, when there are disorders, it is very difficult to tell which is which."[31]

Zeezrom was miraculously healed, both body and spirit, and became a protagonist in the cause of Christ.

Alma 15:16

Sometimes the gospel requires us to sacrifice even family and friends, but it is worth everything we are called upon to forsake. Jesus was not uttering idle words when he said, "He that loveth father or mother more than me is not worthy of me" (Matthew 10:37).

Alma 16:1–21

The Lamanites went to war against the Nephites in the city of Ammonihah because they were angry over the converted Lamanites, the Anti-Nephi-Lehies, who were slain as a result of their covenant of peace (Alma 24:17–30; 25:1–2; on the name Anti-Nephi-Lehies, see commentary at Alma 23:16–18). Zoram, a righteous man, became chief captain over the Nephite armies and led them to victory (not the same man as the later apostate named Zoram; see Alma 30–31). Alma and Amulek continued to preach and witnessed another period in which Zion was established.

Alma 17:1–5, 9, 11

After fourteen years, five friends met again, rejoicing that they were still faithful in the Lord. Then we have a ten-chapter account of the labors of the sons of Mosiah in what we might call the Southern Lamanite Mission. These verses describe how to be a great missionary, how to receive powerful personal revelation, how to teach with authority, and how to be filled with understanding: (1) search the scriptures diligently; (2) do a lot of praying and fasting; (3) be patient while suffering physical, mental, and emotional trials and afflictions; and (4) work hard, especially spiritually. Because the five missionaries did all these things, they became men of sound understanding, they had the spirit of prophecy and revelation, they taught with power and authority, they were good examples to the people, and they had success in bringing many souls to salvation.

Alma 17:9–11

A noble ambition for all our missionaries worldwide: fast and pray that the Lord will pour out his Spirit upon the people in the various great cities, to help bring them to a realization of the incorrectness of the traditions of their fathers and to bring them to a knowledge of the truth. Actually, this is a noble ambition for every member of the Church.

Alma 17:16–18

As stated in *Preach My Gospel,* the following is every missionary's purpose: "Invite others to come unto Christ by helping them receive the restored gospel through faith in Jesus Christ and His atonement, repentance, baptism, receiving the gift of the Holy Ghost, and enduring to the end."[32] We note how Ammon blessed the others. Do we as the people of God in the latter days request and offer enough blessings?

Alma 17:20–39

What follows are excerpts from the first pages of Ammon's missionary journal. Verse 24 notes that Ammon made quite a first impression on Lamoni, the king, that he would want Ammon to marry one of his daughters.

Ammon's approach to missionary work was simple and effective. The first thing he told the king was, "I will be thy servant"—in other words, he was willing to serve. While serving, he would show forth God's power in order to win some hearts and to lead them to believe in his words. Armed with the power of God and the Lord's promise of protection given through Mosiah, Ammon smote off the arms of "not a few" of the sheep rustlers. They could not hit Ammon with their stones and "began to be astonished" at the strength of Ammon's arm.

The Lord arranged through this episode a brilliant teaching opportunity, beginning with the number-one man in the kingdom and his household. Ammon helped convert a king and, through him, a people.

Alma 18

Notice the details of Ammon's teaching approach. He was—as every missionary should be—"wise, yet harmless" (compare Matthew 10:16). Ammon served the king well. He had a spirit about him that the king had never seen or felt before. The king was ready to listen to Ammon, and Ammon knew it, so he boldly committed him to listen and believe his words. "And thus he was caught with guile"; in other words, Ammon had the king right where he wanted him. The Spanish translation of that phrase reads "*así ingeniosamente lo comprometió*": "and in that way he ingeniously committed him."

Ammon was wise in continuing to establish a relationship of confidence based in common beliefs (compare Paul, in Acts 17). His first question was: "Believest thou that there is a God?" Lamoni replied, "I do not know what that meaneth." In the late 1970s several Brigham Young University students in Jerusalem met a young Russian who had recently immigrated to Israel. After talking for a while in his broken English with the students, he asked to attend their meetings and learn more about what they believed. The students talked with him about God, but he responded that he didn't understand what they were saying. He had no concept of God; in fact, he had never heard of Adam and Eve, any of the prophets, or even of Jesus. With some it is important to begin with the basics, the essentials.

Wise missionaries start at the level of knowledge and understanding of those they are teaching. Ammon started with a primary question: Who is God? (Aaron later did the very same thing with Lamoni's father; see Alma 22:7–11.) He went from there to the three pillars of the everlasting gospel: the Creation, the Fall, and the Redemption. (Aaron taught the same principles to Lamoni's father; see Alma 22:12–13.) We continue learning of these three great doctrines as we mature in knowledge and spirituality and as we learn and worship in the holy temple.

The king asked the missionary a very pointed question, a question that every truth-seeker has a right to ask his teacher: "Art thou sent from God?" (see also Helaman 9:36). Ammon replied that he had, indeed, been called of God to teach and testify of these sacred truths.

One of his fellow servants called Ammon "Rabbanah," a title containing the Semitic root word *rab*, meaning "lord," "chief," or "great one."

Ammon had the Spirit with him, which gave him knowledge and power, according to his faith and desires. After King Lamoni listened to Ammon's first lesson, he wanted to pray.

When the king collapsed, his wife and children mourned over him "after the manner of the Lamanites"—probably meaning that the Lamanites had no knowledge of the afterlife, no understanding of redemption and resurrection. The Lord recognizes the anguish of such hopeless souls as the ancient Lamanites and has commanded in modern times, "Thou shalt live together in love, insomuch that thou shalt weep for the loss of them that die, and more especially for those that have not hope of a glorious resurrection" (D&C 42:45).

Alma 19:6–33

Verse 6 contains a succinct and powerful definition of true conversion, which involves dispelling darkness and being filled with light. We also learn that spiritual experiences (being "carried away in God") can bring about a physically weakened condition. To study this interesting phenomenon, examine the following series of scriptural passages: 1 Nephi 1:7; 17:47; 19:20; Jacob 7:21; Alma 27:17; 36:10; Moses 1:9–10; Daniel 8:27; 10:8.[33]

In verse 10, notice the Jewish form of expressing respect and honor toward a female: "I say unto thee, woman . . ."

Ammon prayed for the Spirit to touch the people, and it happened. Miracles are always involved in the conversion process. They include, in this case, a Lamanite woman had been converted through a remarkable vision of her father, a missionary could not be killed, a queen spoke words not understood by others, hearts had been changed, and many had seen and talked with angels. Which of these miracles was the greatest?

Incidentally, this Lamanite woman, Abish, is one of only four women mentioned by name in the Book of Mormon; the other three are Sariah (1 Nephi 2:5), Mary (Mosiah 3:8), and Isabel (Alma 39:3). As with the Bible, women are included by name in the scriptural narratives only when they play a significant part in a story or a teaching. The conversion of Abish played an important role in the conversion of large numbers of Lamanites and demonstrates the far-reaching effects of a righteous father on a daughter and on society.

Verse 33 further defines the process of true conversion: "hearts had been changed; that they had no more desire to do evil." President Joseph F. Smith describes his conversion: "I was indeed cleansed from sin; my heart was touched, and I felt that I would not injure the smallest insect beneath my feet. I felt as if I wanted to do good everywhere to everybody and to everything. I felt a newness of life, a newness of desire to do that which was right. There was not one particle of desire for evil left in my soul."[34]

Alma 20:1–27

Ammon and Lamoni heeded the voice of the Lord and became instruments—tools of positive change—in the Lord's hands. Marcia Ogden noted: "Ammon and King Lamoni were driving in the king's chariot to another part of the land. They met Lamoni's father, who became so furious at his son for being with a Nephite that he tried to kill him. Ammon gained the advantage such that the king found himself pleading for his life. He promised Ammon that if he would spare his life he would give him *up to half his kingdom.*

"Ammon, already having ascended quite a way up the mount of his heavenly quest, enjoying great inspiration and revelations from a heavenly kingdom, was not interested in someone's earthly kingdom. He asked only that the king allow his son to be free to run his own kingdom without interference.

"King Lamoni's father was so impressed with this display of love that when Aaron, Ammon's brother, shows up a few chapters later to teach him about the gospel he asks what he needs to do to have such great joy in his own life. What would it take to be able to have eternal life? Then he makes the stunning declaration that he would give up *his whole kingdom* to be able to have eternal life (Alma 22:15).

"See what happens to people when they get a glimpse of God's world and his life? Closer to the top of the mountain, our views become glorious. Suddenly this world and its attractions—at the foot of the mountain—become trivial by comparison."

Another key to true conversion: Lamoni's father saw love in action, and he wanted to know more.

Alma 21

Aaron is another of the five "A's"—Abinadi, Alma, Amulek, Ammon, and Aaron—great missionaries who were wise in keeping their teaching and testimony simple. They taught about the atonement of Jesus Christ (see also Alma 22:14), including his sufferings, death, and resurrection, all for the purpose of redeeming us. The Amalekites were promoting doctrines of convenience, justifying themselves in their sinning: "We do believe that God will save all men" (compare Lucifer in Moses 4:1 and Korihor in Alma 30:17–18). They said, further, "We do not believe that thou knowest of things to come" (compare Sherem in Jacob 7:7 and Korihor in Alma 30:13). They called the eternal truths "foolish traditions" (compare Alma 30:14). Many others were taught but few believed, even though the missionaries were led by the Spirit of the Lord.

Alma 22:7–13

The story of Aaron's encounter with King Lamoni's father began because Aaron followed the Spirit, as Ammon had done earlier (compare v. 1 and Alma 20:2–7). Aaron opened the door, so to speak, to a discussion by simply mentioning the role of the Lord's Spirit. He then let the king express his concerns and continued to do so throughout their exchange. Aaron and Ammon were identical twins in their teaching approach (see commentary at Alma 18).

When Aaron testified that there is a God, the king responded with another question: "Is God that Great Spirit that brought our fathers out of the land of Jerusalem?" Aaron's answer reflected his desire to build a relationship of trust based on common beliefs. The king's idea of God as the Great Spirit was sufficient to begin laying the doctrinal foundation. An incorrect or less-effective approach would have been for Aaron to reply, No way. He is not some Great Spirit. He is an exalted, glorified, resurrected, celestialized Man with a body of flesh and bones. That statement is true, but it is not information that is needed all at once. That would be trying to feed the investigator meat before milk. Rather, "when Aaron saw that the king would believe his words, he began from the creation of Adam, reading the scriptures unto the king." He taught directly from the scriptures, and he expounded the core principles of the plan of salvation—the Creation, the Fall, and the Atonement, or what Elder Bruce R. McConkie called the three pillars of eternity. This serves as an example to every teacher and leader in the Lord's Church.

Alma 22:14

"Since man had fallen he could not merit anything of himself"—McConkie and Millet explained: "We will not be saved in the highest heaven because we earn our way there. We will not be crowned with glory and eternal lives because we 'worked out our salvation' by ourselves. It is as heretical to believe that we are exalted by works as it is to teach that we are saved by grace alone. As important as our works are in evidencing our acceptance of and commitment to Christ the Lord—works such as receiving the ordinances of salvation, performing deeds of kindness and acts of Christian charity, and enduring faithfully to the end—our works will not and cannot save us. It is impossible for any human being to do enough good deeds in this mortal sphere to qualify for life in the celestial kingdom. No, ultimately we are saved not by our works but by his works—the Lord's. 'Wherefore,' Lehi said to his son Jacob, 'I know that thou art redeemed, *because of the righteousness of thy Redeemer*' (2 Nephi 2:3, italics added). That is to say, before the Father, the Lord Jesus intercedes for us on the basis of *his* works."[35]

To repeat, Aaron taught the king about the Fall and then about its necessary sequel, the Atonement. President Ezra Taft Benson explained why: "Just as a man does not really desire food until he is hungry, so he does not desire the salvation of Christ until he knows why he needs Christ.

"No one adequately and properly knows why he needs Christ until he understands and accepts the doctrine of the Fall and its effect upon all mankind."[36]

Alma 22:15

The Spirit worked in the king's heart, causing a fervent desire to be "born of God, having this wicked spirit rooted out of my breast," to have the Spirit and be filled with joy. In other words, he wanted to know more—how to attain eternal life (the same inquiry made by the rich young ruler; see Luke 18). The king had found a pearl of great price, and he was willing to sacrifice all to get it (compare Matthew 13:45–46). Reread the statement from Joseph Smith (see commentary at Omni 1:26) about the necessity of our being willing to sacrifice all things, just as the king was willing to "give up all that I possess" in order to obtain the riches of eternity.

This is one of the great ironies of God's kingdom: We

must give up all in order to gain all. The question "What shall I do?" is one found over and over in the scriptures (for example, Acts 2:37; Luke 3:10) and is even posed by the Lord himself (Ether 2:23). It is a profound question.

Alma 22:16–18

Imagine telling a king that he must *bow down* and *repent.* The process of spiritual rebirth is plain and clear for everyone: fervent desire expressed in humble prayer, combined with faith and repentance. The key to the whole process is revealed in the king's simple words: "I will give away all my sins to know thee."

Alma 22:23

Where the father ministers in the home, the household is converted and blessed.

Alma 22:27–34

These verses contain one of the most detailed descriptions of the physical geography of Book of Mormon lands (see map of the Book of Mormon lands accompanying the commentary at Alma 50). Although there is considerable detail about geographical features in the Book of Mormon, the quantity and variety of hypotheses about exactly where this thousand-year history took place make it apparent that the literary and physical evidence are insufficient for definitive answers as yet. These events did take place, and these people did live somewhere in the ancient Americas, but the specific physical locations and settings remain tentative until further identification is given from heaven.

As Latter-day Saints, interested as we are in searching out the truth of all things, we regard the continued investigation of all these historical, geographical, archaeological, cultural, and linguistic matters to be altogether fitting and proper. We should be an informed people. We should become aware of what our best researchers are finding and the conclusions they are making, but at the same time we should be careful not to be dogmatic and argumentative about issues the Lord has not seen fit to clearly reveal as yet. We continue to study the issues but hold it all in abeyance until he lays the questions to rest.

Most important is to not get lost in the thick of thin things—not get distracted by superficial issues and lose the essence of the thousand-year record: the witness of Jesus Christ.

Alma 23:1–13

The proclamation mentioned in Alma 22:27 is described. Religious freedom was proclaimed. "And thousands were brought to the knowledge of the Lord"—as in all of the Americas in recent decades. The ancient Lamanites who were brought to the knowledge of the truth through the spirit of revelation and prophecy experienced the power of God working miracles in them; that is, *their hearts were changed* and they were truly converted, and they never did fall away. Being converted in that manner there was no problem with retention (see also commentary at Alma 27:27).

Alma 23:16–18

Those Lamanites who experienced such a profound change then desired, and received, a new name: Anti-Nephi-Lehies. When any of us make life-changing covenants, we receive a new name—at baptism we take the name of Christ. We note that righteousness also brings industriousness and a desire for peace.

The first part of the term *Anti-Nephi-Lehies* may be an integral component of the name-title, not the Greek prefix meaning "against." Some have also wondered if these righteous converts wanted to be identified as descendants of Lehi, but they were not descendants of Nephi. In other words, they were Lehites but they were not Nephites; thus the name: the Lehites, or Lehies, opposite or apart from the Nephites.

Alma 24:1–11

The narrative contrasts the demeanor, outlook, purity, and power of the converts with the ugliness of those who had not been converted.

The book of Alma teaches more about the repentance process: through the merits of God's Son (that is, through his justice, mercy, compassion, love, and infinite sacrifice), we can be forgiven of all our sins—little ones and big ones. This includes having the guilt taken away from our hearts—not the memory (that stays as an early-warning system to help us keep our distance from those sins), but the guilt and stain can be totally removed.

Another pivotal concept in the cleansing of sins is "to get God to take them away from our hearts." The disposition or desire to sin can be taken away by the Savior if we ask him to do so. Bad thoughts or desires to do wrong that come into our minds or hearts may be displaced and removed by God himself if we ask him to do so. We can also help by constantly filling our minds with uplifting thoughts, good music, and memorized scriptures.

Alma 24:11–16

It may be that the converted Lamanites were anxious to bury their swords and other weapons of killing so there was no possibility of returning to the bloodlust to which they had become addicted.

Alma 24:14

"He loveth our souls"—John 3:16 says, "God so loved the world [that is, the inhabitants of the world], that he gave his only begotten Son." Psalm 8:4–5 describes how man was created a little lower than *the Gods* [*Elohim* in Hebrew], which says something about our potential to become like our Heavenly Father. Are our souls valuable? He thinks so: He

433

loveth our souls. "The worth of souls is great in the sight of God" (D&C 18:10).

Alma 24:16–26

Military action undertaken in self-defense is certainly justifiable (Alma 48:14–15, 23–25; 53:10–17), so we are made to appreciate just how great a sacrifice the Anti-Nephi-Lehies made by burying their weapons of war. Some have wondered if this act gave rise to the Native-American tradition of "burying the hatchet" as a sign of making peace. These amazing people would rather have their own lives taken than take another's life. They were firm in their convictions. God wants us to believe, then know, then remain *firm*. On the desirability of the divine attribute of firmness, see commentary at Jacob 3:1–2.

Thus we see that death can be a blessing to the righteous and also how the death of righteous souls can be a blessing to the living.

Alma 24:30

It seems to be an ever-recurring truism that after people have been enlightened by the Spirit of God and attain great knowledge of righteous things, then fall away and become sinful, they become more hardened, and their condition is worse than if they had never learned those things in the first place. Dissenters and apostates in all ages leave the Church, but they cannot leave the Church alone. According to Daniel Tyler, an early Church member, the Prophet Joseph Smith "emphasized the fact that a man or woman who had not taken sides either with Christ or [the devil] could maintain a neutral position, but when they enlisted under either the one or the other they left the neutral ground forever" (see also Alma 47:36; 2 Peter 2:20–21).[37] Of course, practically speaking, it is impossible not to take sides. Every choice we make leads us to take sides.

Alma 25:1–14

The city and people of Ammonihah were destroyed because they killed the Saints of God. Martyrs of this type are found in every age of the world (Revelation 6:9). Abinadi's prophecy was fulfilled, and the Lord was able to use the destruction for his own purposes—Lamanites were converted.

Alma 25:15–16

Regarding the purposes of the law of Moses as a type and a preparation for the coming of Christ, see commentary at Mosiah 13:28–33.

Alma 25:17

A message for every missionary and member: Success comes according to our prayers, "according to [our] petition" (D&C 90:1; see also commentary at 1 Nephi 15:10–11).

Alma 26:1–7

Ammon's words to his brethren praise the Lord and the opportunity to be his instrument of salvation. The imagery is beautiful and familiar; it occurs throughout the scriptures. The missionaries went out to work in the (mission) field; the field was ripe; they thrust in the sickle (today's instruments are the Book of Mormon, *Preach My Gospel,* area book, daily planner, and the lessons); they were out trying to reap all day long (today's schedule is usually from 6:30 A.M. to 10:30 P.M.); they gathered in many sheaves (the fruits of their labors, the converts); they brought them into the garners, the barns (today's stake centers, ward meetinghouses, homes, and temples) to protect them from being beaten down by the storms of their lives (today's storms are the "whirlwinds" and "fierce winds" of adversity and such social ills as pornography, sexually transmitted diseases, perversions of marriage and family relationships, and numerous forms of infidelity and abuse). The Lord has promised that he will provide safety for his faithful ones, "that the gathering together upon the land of Zion, and upon her stakes, may be for a defense, and for a refuge from the storm, and from wrath when it shall be poured out without mixture upon the whole earth" (D&C 115:6). Under the Lord's protection "the storm cannot penetrate to them; . . . they are in the hands of the Lord of the harvest."

Alma 26:10–13

Ammon boasted in the Lord; that is, he rejoiced or gloried in him. He knew (as every disciple knows) that he was weak and could do nothing by himself, but he also knew that in the strength of the Lord he could do all things (compare the very same message from Paul in 2 Corinthians 12:7–10.) We know, as Ammon knew, that we can do whatever is required of us "because of the power of his word which is in us."

Consider what had happened. The Nephites and Lamanites were always warring and had an intense hatred for each other—a seemingly hopeless situation, but look how that changed. The friction between the United States and the Soviet Union was intense for decades, but look at the success beginning in the 1990s in carrying the gospel to the Russians and other peoples. The animosity and antagonism between Jews and Arabs has been even more severe for many decades. Is there anything that could heal that enmity? Yes, indeed. The Savior and his gospel can heal the deep wounds of centuries of bitter hostility.

Alma 26:12

"I know that I am nothing"—think back on the crucial counsel of the prophet-king Benjamin to remember "your own nothingness" (Mosiah 4:11). See commentary at Mosiah 4:5, 11.

Regarding the phrase "as to my strength I am weak," one Brigham Young University football player was six feet eight and weighed 335 pounds. His tenacity while hitting the opposing players and while hitting the books was admirable. Someone who has both physical and spiritual strength can be particularly useful in the Lord's kingdom. Samson had the potential, but he betrayed his Coach, and he failed his courses. This football player had the potential, and was doing all he could to be a winner.

Alma 26:13–16

It is interesting that both Alma (Alma 5:26) and Ammon spoke of singing redeeming love. There is something heavenly and harmonious about divine love that redeems. It is worth praising, and that praise often comes out in song.

So Ammon asked, apparently with considerable emotion: "Who can glory too much in the Lord? Yea, who can say too much of his great power, and of his mercy, and of his long-suffering towards the children of men?" (compare the exclamations of joy and adoration from Jacob in 2 Nephi 9). Ammon continued expressing his deep feelings of exultation, his fulness of joy and rejoicing.

Alma 26:22

The success formula for the miraculous accomplishments of Ammon and his brethren is given here. The same formula will work for each of us: repent, exercise faith, work hard, pray continually without ceasing; then great knowledge and understanding of the mysteries of godliness will result (D&C 76:5–8), and through our mortal missions we can see thousands of souls begin the same process of repentance and return to God.

And if we do all of the above and do not see thousands of souls returning to God—does that mean that we have failed, that we were bad representatives of the Lord Jesus Christ? No. We are actually in good company. Noah spent many years preaching the gospel and crying repentance (Moses 8:23–27), but relatively few accepted his message. Lehi spent years preaching the gospel and crying repentance (1 Nephi 1:18–20), but relatively few accepted him, either. So it was with other ancient prophets and missionaries and with modern prophets and missionaries. President Heber J. Grant, for example, had no measurable success in Japan a hundred years ago. Many serve faithfully in numerous countries throughout the earth and experience little success by way of convert baptisms. But if we can kneel down every night and sincerely say to Heavenly Father that we have done the best we could, we are good servants of the Lord.

Alma 26:23–26

When the idea first surfaced to go save the Lamanites, people laughed at the missionaries. Some Nephites even thought, Stop all this nonsensical talk about converting them; let's kill them and rid the land of their gross wickedness. But the missionaries persisted. They wanted not to destroy but to save—even a few. The Lord had miraculously turned their own lives around; they knew he could do the same for the lost Lamanites.

Alma 26:27

So, with all their good intentions, was it easy for the missionaries to convert some Lamanites? No. They became depressed and wanted to go back home (compare Helaman 13:2–3; Samuel, the Lamanite prophet, wanted to go back home, too). But the Lord comforted them. To his servants, especially, he does send the Comforter. He gave them specific instruction, which applies to every missionary (and to every Latter-day Saint): "Bear with patience thine afflictions, and I will give unto you success." The Lord was not kidding about the afflictions; notice in verses 28–30 what kinds of privations and afflictions they had to endure. Also, refer to the commentary at Alma 7:5 for a reminder of an eternal principle: success, blessings, and joy seem to inevitably follow only after afflictions, sorrows, and tribulation. Salvation never was easy;

look at the life of Jesus, and the life of Joseph Smith, and the life of every true prophet and Saint.

Alma 26 vividly describes vintage missionary life. Of this very story Elder F. Burton Howard of the Seventy wrote: "No one but a missionary could have written this story. Joseph Smith could never have known what it was like to be a missionary to the Lamanites, for no one he knew had ever done such a thing before."[38]

Leona B. Gates put the message of Alma 26 into beautiful verse, under the title "In His Steps":

The road is rough, I said,
Dear Lord, there are stones that hurt me so.
And he said, Dear child, I understand,
I walked it long ago.

But there is a cool green path, I said,
Let me walk there for a time.
No, child, He gently answered me,
The green road does not climb.

My burden, I said, is far too great;
How can I bear it so?
My child, said he, I remember weight.
I carried my cross, you know.

But, I said, I wish there were friends with me
Who would make my way their own.
Ah, yes, he said, Gethsemane
Was hard to face alone.

And so I climbed the stony path,
Content at last to know
That where my Master had not gone
I would not need to go.

And strangely then I found new friends;
The burden grew less sore

As I remembered—long ago
He [walked this] way before.[39]

Alma 26:37

Another great lesson: God is not confined to any particular geographical location or restricted to any narrow segment of the human population. He is mindful of every people in whatever land; he loves them and yearns to bless them and save them.

Alma 27:1–15

The unwavering commitment of the Anti-Nephi-Lehies to nonviolence evoked the empathy of Ammon, who helped relocate them. Verse 4 contains a poignant description of the relationship between missionaries and their converts: "those whom they so dearly beloved, and . . . those who had so dearly beloved them—for they were treated as though they were angels sent from God to save them." For more about missionaries as angels (or messengers), see commentary at 2 Nephi 32:1–5 and Alma 8:18–20.

Alma 27:16–18

These verses contain a scene of extraordinary joy at the missionary reunion of Ammon, his brothers, and their close friend Alma. This same Ammon who was so joyful as he gloried in his God (Alma 26) was now so overcome with joy that his physical strength gave out, and he fell to the earth. For more about this loss of physical strength when immersed in the Spirit and the joy of God, see commentary at 1 Nephi 1:5–20.

Alma 27:27

What is said of the people of Ammon is what can be said of all true converts: they were known for their zeal, and "they were perfectly honest and . . . firm in the faith of Christ, even unto the end"; that is, they were solidly committed to the cause of Christ. There was no problem of inactivity among them (compare commentary at Alma 23:1–13). On the meritorious attribute of firmness, see commentary at Jacob 3:1–2.

Alma 27:28

This verse contains perceptive comments on death, as viewed by those who are "perfectly honest and upright in all things" and "firm in the faith of Christ" (v. 27). "They never did look upon death with any degree of terror, for their hope and views of Christ and the resurrection; . . . death was swallowed up to them by the victory of Christ over it." The concept of "swallowed up" appears rather frequently throughout the scriptures; for example, swallowed up in sorrow (2 Corinthians 2:7), swallowed up in pride (Alma 31:27), and swallowed up in joy (Alma 27:17; 31:38). The phrase means "overwhelmed" or "overcome." In this case, the fear of death is totally overcome because of Christ's triumph over it: "death is swallowed up in victory" (1 Corinthians 15:54); "the sting of death is swallowed up in Christ" (Mosiah 16:8); "the sting of death should be swallowed up in the hopes of glory" (Alma 22:14).

Alma 27:30

Does God favor some people? The people of Ammon were a "highly favored people of the Lord," as were others (Alma 13:23; 48:20); some "having been favored above every other nation, kindred, tongue, or people" (Alma 9:20). Nephi said he was "highly favored of the Lord in all [his] days" (1 Nephi 1:1); he was favored of the Lord because he was "faithful in keeping the commandments of the Lord" (Mosiah 10:13). The brother of Jared was also "a man highly favored of the Lord" (Ether 1:34). The Lord explains in simplicity how his kind of "favoritism" works: "he that is righteous is favored of God" (1 Nephi 17:35). God's favors are

THE BOOK OF MORMON

blessings, and "there is a law, irrevocably decreed in heaven . . . upon which all blessings are predicated—and when we obtain any blessing from God, it is by obedience to that law upon which it is predicated" (D&C 130:20–21). The law is clear: God favors, or blesses, those who obey him. He does not arbitrarily play favorites.

Alma 28

Mormon summarized lessons learned during the missions of Ammon and his brothers (Alma 17–26) and lessons learned during the first fifteen years of the reign of the judges (Alma 1–28).

Note again the eternal principle that is taught in verse 8: after sufferings, sorrows, and afflictions comes incomprehensible joy (see commentary at Alma 7:5). Having noted this phenomenon several times throughout the chapters of Alma, we may now add another dimension to the discussion: suffering and joy can exist side by side. Because of the nature of this telestial world—and the necessity of our being tried and tested here—there are many times in life when we joy in some of our loved ones and we sorrow, worry, and suffer for others. It is interesting what valuable lessons we learn from that curious mix.

Mormon highlighted his salient lessons three times with the signal words "and thus we see": (1) the inequality of man because of sin, (2) the call to labor in the Lord's vineyards, and (3) the choice of sorrow or joy, destruction or salvation, and death or life (see also Alma 29:4–5).

Alma 29:1–6

When we cannot bear the thought that any soul might perish (Mosiah 28:3) and do not want to see any more sorrow anywhere on earth (Alma 29:2), and when we have the vision of what this world is coming to and desire with all our hearts to rescue every soul possible before it is everlastingly too late, then we feel like shouting from the housetops and opening our mouths and crying repentance to everyone we meet. Actually, we do not need to aspire to do any more than what we have been called to do. As the saying goes, just "bloom where you're planted!" Your current calling may seem small or insignificant, but your glorious future lies in doing well your present work. Ponder the meaning of this simple verse:

> *"Father, where shall I work today?"*
> *And my love flowed warm and free.*
> *Then he pointed out a tiny spot,*
> *And said, "Tend that for me."*
> *I answered quickly, "Oh, no, not that!*
> *Why, no one would ever see,*
> *No matter how well my work was done.*
> *Not that little place for me."*
> *And the word he spoke, it was not stern;*
> *He answered me tenderly:*
> *"Ah, little one, search that heart of thine;*
> *Art thou working for them or for me?*
> *Nazareth was a little place,*
> *And so was Galilee."*[40]

So Alma yearned to have the capacity and the facility to "speak with the trump of God," to broadcast to all humankind the glorious news of Christ's redemption. And today, even though the Church places statues of Moroni atop numerous temples throughout the world, are not the words of Alma being disseminated throughout the earth, "cry[ing] repentance unto every people," as more than a hundred fifty million copies of the Book of Mormon have circulated worldwide? Is not Alma's testimony being spoken as "with the trump of God, with a voice [from the dead] to shake the earth," calling on the inhabitants of the earth to prepare to meet their God?

Alma 29:4

Regarding Alma's statements about his allotment in life, we have this insight from President Henry D. Moyle: "I believe that we, as fellow workers in the priesthood, might well take to heart the admonition of Alma and be content with that which God hath allotted us. We might well be assured that we had something to do with our 'allotment' in our pre-existent state. This would be an additional reason for us to accept our present condition and make the best of it. It is what we agreed to do. . . .

". . . We had our own free agency in our pre-mortal existence, and whatever we are today is likely the result of that which we willed to be heretofore."[41]

God grants to all persons just what they desire—that which will save them or destroy them: "For I know that he granteth unto men according to their desire, whether it be unto death or unto life." If one desires certain drinks, foods, drugs, or stimulants to damage himself, he can have them. It is his choice. All things good come from God, and they edify, build, lift, and inspire. Evil things come from the devil, and they demean, deceive, defile, and destroy. Whatever you really want, God may allow you to have that thing. The lesson, of course, is that you should be very careful about what you want, because you will likely get it. And you had better want the consequences of what you want, because you will get them, too.

Alma 29:8

"The Lord doth grant unto all nations, of their own nation and tongue, to teach his word"—we are seeing more and more of that: Mexican missionaries teaching Mexicans, Italian missionaries teaching Italians, Russian missionaries teaching Russians, Japanese missionaries teaching the Japanese—even Mongolians, Albanians, Ghanians, and so forth.

God the Father loves all of his children and wants them

to receive as much revelation and truth as they are capable of embracing. In a statement of the First Presidency in 1978, we read: "The great religious leaders of the world such as Mohammed, Confucius, and the Reformers, as well as philosophers including Socrates, Plato, and others, received a portion of God's light. Moral truths were given to them by God to enlighten whole nations and to bring a higher level of understanding to individuals. . . .

"We believe that God has given and will give to all peoples sufficient knowledge to help them on their way to eternal salvation."[42]

Alma 29:9

The objective of every parent, every missionary, every leader, and every teacher in the Church is to "bring some soul to repentance." Repentance and forgiveness constitute the most crucial message of the restored gospel of Jesus Christ. Those doctrines and that goal is our chief joy. Our assignment, no matter what role we fill, is to change lives and bring souls to Christ. The time is short, so we must touch them quickly and deeply.

Alma 29:14

Paul and Moroni later wrote that charity is kind, envieth not, and is not puffed up, meaning that there is no resentment or discontent over the good fortune of others; there is no contention for superiority (1 Corinthians 13:4; Moroni 7:45). Those truly converted to Christ are not threatened by others' talents, abilities, and successes. Here is a classic example. Alma declared, "I do not joy in my own success alone, but my joy is more full because of the success of my brethren."

NOTES

INTRODUCTION

1. Benson, "Book of Mormon—Keystone of Our Religion," 6.
2. Ibid., 6.
3. Ibid., 4.
4. Ibid., 6.
5. Largey, "Enemies of Righteousness," 7–11.
6. Benson, "Book of Mormon—Keystone of Our Religion," 7.
7. Romney, "Book of Mormon," 67.
8. Benson, "Flooding the Earth with the Book of Mormon," 4.
9. Benson, *Witness and a Warning*, 7.

OPENING PAGES OF THE BOOK OF MORMON

1. Smith, *History of the Church*, 1:71.
2. Cheesman, "Ancient Writing on Metal Plates," 42–47.
3. Smith, *History of the Church*, 4:537; see also Tvedtnes, "Etruscan Gold Book," 7.
4. Peterson, "Response," 68.
5. Ibid.
6. Benson, *Witness and a Warning*, 51.
7. Smith, *History of the Church*, 1:52–57.

THE FIRST BOOK OF NEPHI

1. See also Smith, *History of the Church*, 4:536.
2. Nibley, *Approach to the Book of Mormon*, 45–74.
3. *Lectures on Faith*, 66.
4. Sperry, *Book of Mormon Compendium*, 97–98.
5. Hilton and Hilton, *In Search of Lehi's Trail*, 38.
6. *Joseph Smith* [manual], 109.
7. Grant, "Dream, O Youth!" 524.

8. Woodruff, address at Weber Stake conference, Ogden, Utah, 19 Oct. 1896; cited in Ludlow, *Companion*, 191.

9. Holland, "For a Wise Purpose," 17.

10. Smith, *Gospel Doctrine*, 435–36; emphasis added.

11. Nibley, *Lehi in the Desert*, 97.

12. Smith, *History of the Church*, 5:135.

13. Lynch, *Narrative of the United States' Expedition*, 276.

14. Erastus Snow, in *Journal of Discourses*, 23:184.

15. Smith, "Message from the First Presidency," 1.

16. Hales, "With All the Feeling of a Tender Parent," 88.

17. Eyring, "True and Living Church," 22.

18. Maxwell, "Cleanse Us from All Unrighteousness," 19.

19. Daniel H. Wells, in *Journal of Discourses*, 19:367.

20. Smith, *History of the Church*, 1:21.

21. McConkie and Millet, *Doctrinal Commentary on the Book of Mormon*, 1:64–65.

22. *Joseph Smith* [manual], 81–82.

23. McConkie and Millet, *Doctrinal Commentary on the Book of Mormon*, 1:70, 89; paragraphing altered.

24. *Joseph Smith* [manual], 268.

25. Talmage, *Articles of Faith*, 144–45.

26. Benson, *Come unto Christ*, 2–4.

27. Benson, "Joy in Christ," 3–4; see also Benson, *Teachings of Ezra Taft Benson*, 7.

28. McConkie, *Mortal Messiah*, 1:314–15.

29. Ibid., 1:326–27n4.

30. *Joseph Smith* [manual], 81.

31. Ibid., 15.

32. Yarn, "Testimony of Jesus Christ," 93.

33. Stephen Robinson; cited in Nyman and Tate, eds., *Book of Mormon*, 184.

34. Wasserman, *Columbus*, 19–20; cited in Benson, *Teachings of Ezra Taft Benson*, 577.

35. Ludlow et al., *Encyclopedia of Mormonism*, "Christopher Columbus," 1:295–96

36. Woodruff, journal; cited in *My Kingdom*, 64.

37. Madison, *Federalist Papers*, no. 37; cited in Benson, *Constitution*, 23.

38. *Joseph Smith* [manual], 207.

39. Council of the Twelve Apostles, in James R. Clark, comp., *Messages of the First Presidency*, 1:257.

40. Benson, "I Testify," 87.

41. Smith, *History of the Church*, 5:342.

42. Clark, *Messages of the First Presidency*, 1:186.

43. Webster, *American Dictionary of the English Language*, "curious."

44. Scott, "Trust in the Lord," 16–17.

45. Matthews, *Behold the Messiah*, 283.

46. Packer, "Reverence Invites Revelation," 22.

47. Smith, *History of the Church*, 3:380.

48. "O Savior, Thou Who Wearest a Crown," *Hymns*, no. 197.

49. LDS Bible Dictionary, "Isaiah."

50. Bible Map 4.

51. *Joseph Smith* [manual], 419.

52. Westermann, *Isaiah 40–66*, 195.

53. McConkie and Millet, *Doctrinal Commentary on the Book of Mormon*, 1:152.

54. Brigham Young, in *Journal of Discourses*, 16:77.

55. Smith, *Answers to Gospel Questions*, 1:156–57.

56. Emerson, "Self-Reliance," in *Essays*, 31.

57. Wilford Woodruff; cited in Smith, *Signs of the Times*, 112.

58. Smith, *History of the Church*, 5:401.

59. Ibid., 4:457.

60. *Joseph Smith* [manual], 511.

61. Ibid., 214.

62. McConkie and Millet, *Doctrinal Commentary on the Book of Mormon*, 1:176.

63. Smith, *Church History and Modern Revelation*, 1:192.

64. Cannon, *Gospel Truth*, 68–69.

THE SECOND BOOK OF NEPHI

1. Ivins, in Conference Report, Oct. 1932, 108.

2. Smith, "Fall—Atonement—Resurrection—Sacrament," 124.

3. Smith, *Doctrines of Salvation*, 1:114–15; paragraphing altered.

4. LDS Bible Dictionary, "Joseph."

5. *Joseph Smith* [manual], 543.

6. Ludlow, *Companion to Your Study of The Book of Mormon*, 130–31.

7. Sperry, *Our Book of Mormon*, 111.
8. Oaks, "Powerful Ideas," 25.
9. Burton, "'Blessed Are the Peacemakers,'" 56.
10. Monson, "Examples of Righteousness," 65.
11. Smith, *Doctrines of Salvation*, 1:74.
12. Smith, *History of the Church*, 4:609–10.
13. Ibid., 3:390.
14. McConkie, *Millennial Messiah*, 390.
15. *Joseph Smith* [manual], 49.
16. Smith, "Vision," 82–83.
17. McConkie, *Mormon Doctrine*, 65.
18. *Joseph Smith* [manual], 224.
19. Ibid.
20. Smith; cited in Ludlow, *Latter-day Prophets Speak*, 56–57.
21. McConkie, *New Witness for the Articles of Faith*, 176.
22. *Lectures on Faith*, 51.
23. Ludlow et al., *Encyclopedia of Mormonism*, "Strait and Narrow," 3:1419.
24. Benson, *Witness and a Warning*, 79.
25. Talmage, *Jesus the Christ*, 321.
26. Bytheway, *Righteous Warriors*, 79.
27. Galbraith, Ogden, and Skinner, *Jerusalem*, 209–20.
28. McConkie, *Millennial Messiah*, 229, 253; see also Galbraith, Ogden, and Skinner, *Jerusalem*, 349–64.
29. Monson, "Be of Good Cheer," 89, 92.
30. Smith, *History of the Church*, 5:423.
31. Woodruff, *Discourses of Wilford Woodruff*, 337.
32. McConkie, *New Witness for the Articles of Faith*, 539.
33. Lee, *Teachings of Harold B. Lee*, 377.
34. Smith, *History of the Church*, 6:318–19.
35. Benson, *Teachings of Ezra Taft Benson*, 541.
36. Barkay, "Word for Word," 11.
37. Woodruff, journal, vision dated 16 Dec. 1877 in entry for 15 June 1878; cited in Ludlow, *Isaiah*, 109.
38. McConkie, *Millennial Messiah*, 655.
39. Topical Guide and LDS Bible Dictionary, "Book of Life."
40. Bullinger, *Figures of Speech Used in the Bible*, 313.
41. Kimball, *Love versus Lust*, 7.
42. Richards, *Marvelous Work and a Wonder*, 230.

43. Young, *Book of Isaiah,* 1:239, 250.
44. Smith, *Teachings of the Prophet Joseph Smith,* 181.
45. Topical Guide, "Cherubim."
46. LDS Bible Dictionary, "Seraphim."
47. *Joseph Smith* [manual], 53, 221.
48. Bible Map 12.
49. Bullinger, *Figures of Speech Used in the Bible,* 313.
50. Delitzsch, *Prophecies of Isaiah,* 1:215.
51. Young, *Book of Isaiah,* 1:283–84.
52. Ibid., 1:303–4.
53. Consider the footnotes to Isaiah 9:6–7 and the following Topical Guide references: "Jesus Christ, Prophecies about"; "God, Manifestations of"; "Jesus Christ, Birth of"; "Jesus Christ, Divine Sonship"; "Jesus Christ, Authority of"; "Jesus Christ, Millennial Reign"; "Jesus Christ, Mission of"; "Jesus Christ, Power of"; and "Jesus Christ, Davidic Descent of."
54. Elie Wiesel; cited in Dr. Ze'ev Harvey, in a seminar on Christ sponsored by *Shorashim* Jewish Studies Center, part of Israel's Ministry of Education and Culture, in the Galei Zohar Hotel at the Dead Sea, Israel, 23–25 Mar. 1990; author's personal notes.
55. Bullinger, *Figures of Speech Used in the Bible,* 879.
56. Hayes and Irvine, *Isaiah,* 196.
57. Aharoni, *Land of the Bible,* 339.
58. Wilford Woodruff, in *Journal of Discourses,* 16:266–67.
59. Talmage, *Jesus the Christ,* 44.
60. McConkie, *Promised Messiah,* 192–95.
61. The "root of Jesse" may also have other meanings: Romans 15:12 has the root of Jesse cross-referenced to Topical Guide, "Jesus Christ, Davidic Descent of"; Revelation 5:5 and 22:16 refer to Jesus as the "Root of David."
62. Brigham Young, in *Journal of Discourses,* 2:269; see also Smith, *Doctrines of Salvation,* 3:253.
63. Smith, *History of the Church,* 2:71.
64. Orson Pratt, in *Journal of Discourses,* 21:324–25.
65. Smith, *History of Joseph Smith,* 324–25.
66. Smith, *History of the Church,* 1:313.
67. Smith, *Doctrines of Salvation,* 3:254–55.
68. Draper, *Opening the Seven Seals,* 189–90, 204–5.
69. LDS Bible Dictionary, "Ophir."

70. "Israel, Israel, God Is Calling," *Hymns,* no. 7.
71. Topical Guide, "Conversion," and "Israel, Mission of."
72. Ballard, "Building Bridges of Understanding," 65.
73. Pratt, *Orson Pratt's Works,* 271.
74. Ogden and Skinner, *Acts through Revelation,* 162.
75. Oaks, "Timing," 189–90; see also Oaks, "Sharing the Gospel," 7–9.
76. First Presidency; cited in Palmer, *Mormons and Muslims,* 208.
77. The mention of blacks suggests that Nephi may have had some cultural contact with blacks; we wonder whether such contact may have been in the ancient Near East or in the ancient Americas.
78. Hunter, "'All Are Alike unto God,'" 74.
79. Smith, *History of the Church,* 1:52–57.
80. Ludlow et al., *Encyclopedia of Mormonism,* "Anthon Transcript," 1:43–44.
81. Taylor, address at Salt Lake Stake conference, 6 Jan. 1879; cited in Smith and Sjodahl, *Doctrine and Covenants Commentary,* 462–63.
82. Scott, "Making the Right Choices," 38–39.
83. Faust, "Enemy Within," 46.
84. Smith, *Way to Perfection,* 203.
85. Smith, *Gospel Doctrine,* 312–13.
86. Bytheway, *Righteous Warriors,* 43.
87. *Joseph Smith* [manual], 268.
88. McConkie and Millet, *Doctrinal Commentary on the Book of Mormon,* 1:344–45.
89. Smith, *History of the Church,* 2:18; see also Topical Guide, "Scriptures, Lost," and "Scriptures to Come Forth."
90. *Joseph Smith* [manual], 419.
91. Ibid., 81.
92. LDS Bible Dictionary, "John the Baptist."
93. McConkie and Ostler, *Revelations of the Restoration,* 673.
94. McConkie, *Doctrines of the Restoration,* 238; paragraphing altered.
95. Edmunds, *Through Temple Doors,* 133.
96. Talmage, *Articles of Faith,* 145–46.
97. Smith, *Doctrines of Salvation,* 1:38.
98. Ibid., 1:50.

99. Ibid., 1:18.
100. Ibid., 1:46.
101. Ibid., 1:45.
102. Ibid., 1:55.
103. Ibid., 1:39.
104. Young, *Discourses of Brigham Young,* 44.
105. Bednar, "Seek Learning by Faith," 61.

THE BOOK OF JACOB

1. John Taylor, in *Journal of Discourses,* 20:23.
2. Oaks, "Dedication of a Lifetime," 2.
3. Smith, *History of the Church,* 6:46.
4. Isbouts, *Biblical World,* 64.
5. Howard, "Come Back to the Lord," 77–78.
6. Cheesman, *Ancient Writing on Metal Plates,* 11–12.
7. Cheesman, "Ancient Writing on Metal Plates," 42.
8. Ibid., 43.
9. Smith, *History of the Church,* 5:555.
10. McConkie, "Promises Made to the Fathers," in Jackson and Millet, *Genesis to 2 Samuel,* 57; see also Galbraith, Ogden, and Skinner, *Jerusalem,* 27–33.
11. Maxwell, *"Not My Will, but Thine,"* 7.
12. Smith, *History of the Church,* 3:385.
13. Smith, *Gospel Doctrine,* 7.
14. George A. Smith, in *Journal of Discourses,* 2:326.
15. *Joseph Smith* [manual], 214.

THE BOOK OF ENOS

1. *Words of Joseph Smith,* 90n26.
2. Brigham Young, in *Journal of Discourses,* 3:192.
3. Brooks, *Twenty Sermons,* 119–20.
4. Eyring, "As a Child," 16.
5. *Joseph Smith* [manual], 330–31.
6. Oaks, "On Learning and Becoming," in Eyring, *Learning in the Light of Faith,* 75–83.

THE BOOK OF JAROM

1. Smith, *History of the Church,* 6:58.

THE BOOK OF OMNI

1. Chomsky, *Hebrew,* 30.

2. *Lectures on Faith,* 66.

THE BOOK OF MOSIAH

1. Smith, *History of the Church,* 4:461.

2. Hunter, "To the Women of the Church," 96.

3. Oaks, "Why Do We Serve?" 14.

4. Dew, *Go Forward with Faith,* ix, 271, 512.

5. Bradford, "Selfless Service," 75.

6. Maxwell, "'Willing to Submit,'" 73.

7. Lewis, *Mere Christianity,* 126.

8. *Lectures on Faith,* 57.

9. See further in Ogden and Skinner, *Four Gospels,* 90–98.

10. Talmage, *Jesus the Christ,* 569.

11. *Joseph Smith* [manual], 224.

12. LDS Bible Dictionary, "Balm."

13. Packer, "'Touch of the Master's Hand,'" 23.

14. Packer, "Brilliant Morning of Forgiveness," 20.

15. McConkie and Millet, *Doctrinal Commentary on the Book of Mormon,* 2:160.

16. Ibid.

17. Lee, *Teachings of Harold B. Lee,* 615.

18. Smith, *History of the Church,* 4:605.

19. Oaks, "Taking upon Us the Name of Jesus Christ," 81, 83.

20. Burton, "Born-Again Christian," 39.

21. Reynolds and Sjodahl, *Commentary on the Book of Mormon,* 2:107–8.

22. Faust, "Need for Balance in Our Lives," 2–5; Perry, "Tradition of a Balanced, Righteous Life," 46–53.

23. Sanhedrin 99a; cited in Edersheim, *Life and Times of Jesus the Messiah,* 1:163.

24. McConkie, *Promised Messiah,* 235.

25. McConkie, *Mortal Messiah,* 1:295.

26. Smith, *Doctrines of Salvation,* 1:23.

27. Revius, "He Bore Our Anguish," 103.

28. Meservy, "Isaiah 53," 171.

29. *Joseph Smith* [manual], 41–42.

30. Ibid., 42.

31. On the importance of the Gods being one and our being one with them, see Ogden and Skinner, *Four Gospels*, 586–88.
32. Robinson and Garrett, *Commentary on the Doctrine and Covenants*, 3:177–78.
33. McConkie, "Salvation of Little Children," 5.
34. Turner, "Two Prophets: Abinadi and Alma," 251.
35. Young, *Grammar of the Hebrew Language*, 184.
36. Bullinger, *Figures of Speech Used in the Bible*, 518.
37. *Joseph Smith* [manual], 406.
38. *Words of Joseph Smith*, 59.
39. See also Topical Guide, "Baptism, Immersion."
40. *Words of Joseph Smith*, 15.
41. David O. McKay, "The Cart Began Pushing Me," *Relief Society Magazine*, Jan. 1948, 8; cited in Price, *All Things Testify of Him*, 90.
42. Oaks, *Lord's Way*, 224–49.
43. Smith, *History of the Church*, 2:199.
44. Smith, *Doctrines of Salvation*, 3:224.
45. Ibid., 3:222.
46. John Adams, quoted in Federer, *America's God and Country*, 10–11; cited in Bytheway, *Righteous Warriors*, 33–34.

The Book of Alma

1. Hinckley, "'Great Shall Be the Peace of Thy Children,'" 52.
2. Packer, "'Ye Are the Temple of God,'" 73.
3. Ashton, "Measure of Our Hearts," 15–17.
4. Lewis, *Christian Reflections*, 33.
5. Holland, "'Sanctify Yourselves,'" 39.
6. Young, *Discourses of Brigham Young*, 345.
7. John Taylor, in *Journal of Discourses*, 24:197.
8. Cannon, *Gospel Truth*, 81.
9. Kimball, *Faith Precedes the Miracle*, 98.
10. Pritchard, *Ancient Near Eastern Texts*; emphasis added; see also Aharoni and Avi-Yonah, *Macmillan Bible Atlas*, map 39.
11. It is recorded at least thirty-three times throughout the Book of Mormon that Lehi and Nephi went out from "the land of Jerusalem" (1 Nephi 2:11; 3:9, 10; 5:6; 7:2, 7; 16:35; 17:14, 20, 22; 18:24; 2 Nephi 1:1, 3, 9, 30; Jacob 2:25, 31, 32; Omni 6; Mosiah 1:11; 2:4; 7:20; 10:12; Alma 3:11; 9:22; 10:3; 22:9;

36:29; Helaman 5:6; 7:7; 8:21; 3 Nephi 5:20; Ether 13:7). The scene of significant events in the Savior's ministry is referred to four times as "the land of Jerusalem" (Helaman 16:19; 3 Nephi 16:1; Mormon 3:18, 19); and the place to which the people of Judah would return and which they would receive as an inheritance is identified four times as "the land of Jerusalem" (2 Nephi 25:11; 3 Nephi 20:29, 33, 46).

Modern revelation perpetuates the ancient expression. Doctrine and Covenants 133:24 records that when the continents are reassembled and become again one land mass, "the land of Jerusalem and the land of Zion shall be turned back into their own place."

A host of other names we know were *cities* but were described in scripture as *lands* serves to reinforce the point. Alma 14:23 and 15:1 refer to the "land of Ammonihah." Abraham 1:20 locates an idolatrous shrine on Potiphar's Hill, which was in "the land of Ur, of Chaldea," and Abraham 2:4 has Abraham and family leaving "the land of Ur, of the Chaldees" and going to the "land of Haran."

12. Aharoni, *Land of the Bible*, 195.
13. Lehi and his family lived outside Jerusalem proper, as evidenced in the account of the sons' attempt to secure the plates with their abandoned wealth: "We went down to the land of our inheritance, and we did gather together our gold, and our silver, and our precious things. And after we had gathered these things together, we went up again unto the house of Laban" (1 Nephi 3:22–23). The record does not specify that Lehi and family lived *in* Jerusalem but, again, *at* Jerusalem: "my father, Lehi, having dwelt at Jerusalem in all his days" (1 Nephi 1:4); "he returned to his own house at Jerusalem" (1 Nephi 1:7); and "I, Nephi, have . . . dwelt at Jerusalem" (2 Nephi 25:6). Lehi could have lived several miles away and still lived at Jerusalem, just as Jesus could be born several miles away in Bethlehem but still be born at Jerusalem.
14. Robinson, *Believing Christ*, 122–23.
15. Ogden and Skinner, *Four Gospels*, 377–79.
16. Erastus Snow, in *Journal of Discourses*, 23:184.
17. McConkie and Millet, *Doctrinal Commentary on the Book of Mormon*, 3:83.

18. Ibid., 3:84.
19. Oaks, "Challenge to Become," 32.
20. Smith, in Conference Report, Oct. 1966, 84.
21. Smith, *History of the Church*, 6:364.
22. Kimball, "Role of Righteous Women," 102.
23. Pratt, "Pre-Existence of Man," 54.
24. Benson, "What I Hope You Will Teach Your Children about the Temple," 8.
25. Ogden and Skinner, *Acts through Revelation*, 251–55; see also Galbraith, Ogden, and Skinner, *Jerusalem*, 26–37.
26. *Joseph Smith* [manual], 416.
27. Josephus, *Wars of the Jews*, 6.10.1.
28. Smith, *History of the Church*, 4:11.
29. Kimball, *Faith Precedes the Miracle*, 97.
30. McConkie and Millet, *Doctrinal Commentary on the Book of Mormon*, 3:109.
31. Packer, "Balm of Gilead," 59.
32. *Preach My Gospel*, 1.
33. See also Smith, *History of the Church*, 5:303.
34. Smith, *Gospel Doctrine*, 96.
35. McConkie and Millet, *Doctrinal Commentary on the Book of Mormon*, 3:157–58.
36. Benson, "Book of Mormon and the Doctrine and Covenants," 85.
37. Tyler, in "Recollections of the Prophet Joseph Smith," 492.
38. Howard, "Ammon," 125.
39. Leona B. Gates, "In His Steps," in *Best-Loved Poems of the LDS People*, 179.
40. MacGuire, "Father, Where Shall I Work Today?" 152.
41. Moyle, in Conference Report, Oct. 1952, 71.
42. First Presidency; cited in Faust, "Communion with the Holy Spirit," 12.

SOURCES

Aharoni, Yohanan. *The Land of the Bible: A Historical Geography.* Translated by A. F. Rainey. London: Burns and Oates, 1974.

Aharoni, Yohanan, and Michael Avi-Yonah. *The Macmillan Bible Atlas.* New York: Macmillan, 1974.

Ashton, Marvin J. "The Measure of Our Hearts." *Ensign*, Nov. 1988, 15–17.

Ballard, M. Russell. "Building Bridges of Understanding." *Ensign*, June 1998, 62–68.

Barkay, Gabriel. "Word for Word." *The Jerusalem Post Magazine*, 18 July 1986, 10–12.

Bednar, David A. "Seek Learning by Faith." *Ensign*, Sept. 2007, 61–68.

Benson, Ezra Taft. "The Book of Mormon and the Doctrine and Covenants." *Ensign*, May 1987, 83–85.

———. "The Book of Mormon—Keystone of Our Religion." *Ensign*, Nov. 1986, 4–7.

———. *Come unto Christ.* Salt Lake City: Deseret Book, 1983.

———. *The Constitution: A Heavenly Banner.* Salt Lake City: Deseret Book, 1986.

———. "Flooding the Earth with the Book of Mormon." *Ensign*, Nov. 1988, 4–6.

———. "I Testify." *Ensign*, Nov. 1988, 86–87.

———. "Joy in Christ." *Ensign*, Mar. 1986, 3–5.

———. *The Teachings of Ezra Taft Benson.* Salt Lake City: Bookcraft, 1988.

———. "What I Hope You Will Teach Your Children about the Temple." *Ensign*, Aug. 1985, 6–10.

———. *A Witness and a Warning: A Modern-day Prophet Testifies of the Book of Mormon.* Salt Lake City: Deseret Book, 1988.

Book of Mormon [student manual]. Prepared by the Church Educational System. Salt Lake City: The Church of Jesus Christ of Latter-day Saints, 1979.

Bradford, William R. "Selfless Service." *Ensign*, Nov. 1987, 75–76.

Brooks, Phillips. *Twenty Sermons.* New York: Macmillan, 1886.

Bullinger, E. W. *Figures of Speech Used in the Bible.* 1898. Reprint. Grand Rapids, Mich.: Baker Book House, 1968.

Burton, Theodore M. "'Blessed Are the Peacemakers.'" *Ensign*, Nov. 1974, 54–56.

———. "A Born-Again Christian." In *Brigham Young University 1982–83 Fireside and Devotional Speeches,* 35–40. Provo, Utah: Brigham Young University, 1983.

Bytheway, John. *Righteous Warriors.* Salt Lake City: Deseret Book, 2004.

Cannon, George Q. *Gospel Truth: Discourses and Writings of George Q. Cannon.* Two volumes in one. Edited by Jerreld L. Newquist. Salt Lake City: Deseret Book, 1987.

Cheesman, Paul R. "Ancient Writing on Metal Plates." *Ensign*, Oct. 1979, 42–47.

———. *Ancient Writing on Metal Plates: Archaeological Findings Support Mormon Claims.* Bountiful, Utah: Horizon Publishers, 1985.

Chomsky, William. *Hebrew: The Eternal Language.* Philadelphia: Jewish Publication Society of America, 1957.

Clark, James R., comp. *Messages of the First Presidency of The Church of Jesus Christ of Latter-day Saints.* 6 vols. Salt Lake City: Bookcraft, 1965–75.

Delitzsch, Franz. *Biblical Commentary on the Prophecies of Isaiah.* 3d ed. Translated by James Martin. 2 vols. Grand Rapids, Mich.: Eerdmans, 1965.

Dew, Sheri L. *Go Forward with Faith: The Biography of Gordon B. Hinckley.* Salt Lake City: Deseret Book, 1996.

Draper, Richard D. *Opening the Seven Seals: The Visions of John the Revelator.* Salt Lake City: Deseret Book, 1991.

Edersheim, Alfred. *The Life and Times of Jesus the Messiah.* 2 vols. McLean, Va.: MacDonald Publishing, n.d.

Edmunds, John K. *Through Temple Doors.* Salt Lake City: Bookcraft, 1978.

Emerson, Ralph Waldo. *The Essays of Ralph Waldo Emerson.* Edited by Alfred R. Ferguson and Jean Ferguson Carr, with an introduction by Alfred Kazin. Cambridge, Mass.: Belknap Press of Harvard Press, 1987.

Eyring, Henry B. "As a Child." *Ensign*, May 2006, 14–17.

———, ed. *Learning in the Light of Faith: The Compatibility of Scholarship and Discipleship.* Salt Lake City: Bookcraft, 1999.

———. "The True and Living Church." *Ensign*, May 2008, 20–24.

Faust, James E. "Communion with the Holy Spirit." *Ensign*, May 1980, 12–15.

———. "The Enemy Within." *Ensign*, Nov. 2000, 44–46.

———. "The Need for Balance in Our Lives." *Ensign*, Mar. 2000, 2–5.

Federer, William J., comp. *America's God and Country.* Coppell, Texas: FAME Publishing, 1994.

"From W. W. Phelps to Joseph Smith: The Prophet." *Times and Seasons* 4, no. 6 (1 Feb. 1843): 81–85.

Galbraith, David B., D. Kelly Ogden, and Andrew C. Skinner. *Jerusalem, the Eternal City.* Salt Lake City: Deseret Book, 1996.

Gates, Leona B. "In His Steps." In *Best-Loved Poems of the LDS People,* edited by Jack M. Lyon et al., 179. Salt Lake City: Deseret Book, 1996.

Grant, Heber J. "Dream, O Youth! Dream Nobly and Manfully." *Improvement Era,* Sept. 1941, 524.

Hales, Robert D. "With All the Feeling of a Tender Parent: A Message of Hope to Families." *Ensign,* May 2004, 88–91.

Harvey, Ze'ev. In a seminar on Christ, sponsored by *Shorashim* Jewish Studies Center, in the Galei Zohar Hotel at the Dead Sea, 23–25 Mar. 1990.

Hayes, John H., and Stuart A. Irvine. *Isaiah, the Eighth-Century Prophet: His Times and His Preaching.* Nashville, Tenn.: Abingdon Press, 1987.

Hilton, Lynn M., and Hope Hilton. *In Search of Lehi's Trail.* Salt Lake City: Deseret Book, 1976.

Hinckley, Gordon B. "'Great Shall Be the Peace of Thy Children.'" *Ensign,* Nov. 2000, 50–53.

Holland, Jeffrey R. "For a Wise Purpose." *Ensign,* Jan. 1996, 12–19.

———. "'Sanctify Yourselves.'" *Ensign,* Nov. 2000, 38–40.

Howard, F. Burton. "Ammon: Reflections on Faith and Testimony." In *Heroes from the Book of Mormon*. Salt Lake City: Bookcraft, 1995.

———. "Come Back to the Lord." *Ensign*, Nov. 1986, 76–78.

Hunter, Howard W. "'All Are Alike unto God.'" *Ensign*, June 1979, 72–74.

———. "To the Women of the Church." *Ensign*, Nov. 1992, 95–97.

Hymns of The Church of Jesus Christ of Latter-day Saints. Salt Lake City: The Church of Jesus Christ of Latter-day Saints, 1985.

Isbouts, Jean-Pierre. *The Biblical World: An Illustrated Atlas*. Washington D.C.: National Geographic, 2007.

Ivins, Anthony W. In Conference Report, Oct. 1932, 105–12.

Jackson, Kent P., and Robert L. Millet. *Genesis to 2 Samuel*. Vol. 3 of Studies in Scripture series. Salt Lake City: Deseret Book, 1989.

Joseph Smith [manual]. Teachings of Presidents of the Church series. Salt Lake City: The Church of Jesus Christ of Latter-day Saints, 2007.

Josephus. *The Wars of the Jews*. In *Complete Works*, translated by William Whiston. Grand Rapids, Mich.: Kregel Publications, 1960.

Journal of Discourses. 26 vols. London: Latter-day Saints' Book Depot, 1854–86.

Kimball, Spencer W. *Faith Precedes the Miracle*. Salt Lake City: Deseret Book, 1972.

———. *Love versus Lust*. Brigham Young University Speeches of the Year. Provo, Utah, 5 Jan. 1965.

———. "The Role of Righteous Women." *Ensign*, Nov. 1979, 102–4.

Largey, Dennis L. "Enemies of Righteousness." *Ensign*, Dec. 1989, 7–11.

Lectures on Faith. Salt Lake City: Deseret Book, 1985.

Lee, Harold B. *The Teachings of Harold B. Lee*. Edited by Clyde J. Williams. Salt Lake City: Bookcraft, 1996.

Lewis, C. S. *Christian Reflections*. Edited by Walter Hooper. Grand Rapids, Mich.: Eerdmans, 1995.

———. *Mere Christianity*. Touchstone edition. New York: Simon & Schuster, 1996.

Ludlow, Daniel H. *A Companion to Your Study of The Book of Mormon*. Salt Lake City: Deseret Book, 1976.

———, comp. *Latter-day Prophets Speak: Selections from the Sermons and Writings of the Presidents of The Church of Jesus Christ of Latter-day Saints*. Salt Lake City: Bookcraft, 1948.

——— et al. *Encyclopedia of Mormonism*. 4 vols. New York: Macmillan, 1992.

Ludlow, Victor L. *Isaiah: Prophet, Seer, and Poet*. Salt Lake City: Deseret Book, 1982.

Lynch, W. F. *Narrative of the United States' Expedition to the River Jordan and the Dead Sea*. 6th ed. rev. Philadelphia: Lea and Blanchard, 1849.

MacGuire, Meade. "Father, Where Shall I Work Today?" In *Best-Loved Poems of the American People,* edited by Jack M. Lyon et al., 152. Salt Lake City: Deseret Book, 1996.

Madison, James. "Concerning the Difficulties of the Convention in Devising a Proper Form of Government." *The Federalist Papers,* no. 37. *Daily Advertiser,* 11 Jan. 1788. Cited in Benson, *Constitution.*

Matthews, Robert J. *Behold the Messiah*. Salt Lake City: Bookcraft, 1994.

Maxwell, Neal A. "Cleanse Us from All Unrighteousness." *Ensign,* Feb. 1986, 18–20.

———. *"Not My Will, but Thine."* Salt Lake City: Bookcraft, 1988.

———. "'Willing to Submit.'" *Ensign,* May 1985, 70–73.

McConkie, Bruce R. *The Millennial Messiah: The Second Coming of the Son of Man*. Salt Lake City: Deseret Book, 1982.

———. *Mormon Doctrine*. 2d ed. Salt Lake City: Bookcraft, 1966.

———. *The Mortal Messiah*. 4 vols. Salt Lake City: Deseret Book, 1979–81.

———. *A New Witness for the Articles of Faith*. Salt Lake City: Deseret Book, 1985.

———. *The Promised Messiah: The First Coming of Christ*. Salt Lake City: Deseret Book, 1981.

———. "The Salvation of Little Children." *Ensign,* Apr. 1977, 3–7.

McConkie, Joseph Fielding, and Robert L. Millet. *Doctrinal Commentary on the Book of Mormon*. 4 vols. Salt Lake City: Bookcraft, 1987–92.

McConkie, Joseph Fielding, and Craig J. Ostler. *Revelations of the*

Restoration: A Commentary on the Doctrine and Covenants and Other Modern Revelations. Salt Lake City: Deseret Book, 2000.

McConkie, Mark L., ed. *Doctrines of the Restoration: Sermons and Writings of Bruce R. McConkie.* Salt Lake City: Bookcraft, 1989.

Meservy, Keith. "Isaiah 53: The Richest Prophecy on Christ's Atonement in the Old Testament." In *A Witness of Jesus Christ: The 1989 Sperry Symposium on the Old Testament,* edited by Richard D. Draper, 155–77. Salt Lake City: Deseret Book, 1990.

Monson, Thomas S. "Be of Good Cheer." *Ensign,* May 2009, 89–92.

———. "Examples of Righteousness." *Ensign,* May 2008, 65–68.

Moyle, Henry D. In Conference Report, Oct. 1952, 71–73.

My Kingdom Shall Roll Forth: Readings in Church History. Salt Lake City: The Church of Jesus Christ of Latter-day Saints, 1980.

Nibley, Hugh. *An Approach to the Book of Mormon.* Edited by John W. Welch with Darrell L. Matthews and Stephen R. Callister. 3d ed. Salt Lake City: Deseret Book, 1988.

———. *Lehi in the Desert.* Edited by John W. Welch. Vol. 5 of The Collected Works of Hugh Nibley. Salt Lake City: Deseret Book, 1988.

Nyman, Monte S., and Charles D. Tate, Jr., eds. *The Book of Mormon: First Nephi, The Doctrinal Foundation.* Papers from the Second Annual Book of Mormon Symposium. Provo, Utah: Religious Studies Center, 1988.

Oaks, Dallin H. "The Challenge to Become." *Ensign,* Nov. 2000, 32–34.

———. "The Dedication of a Lifetime." CES Fireside for Young Adults, Oakland, Calif., 1 May 2005. Available at https://media.ldscdn.org/pdf/ces-firesides/2005-ces-firesides-for-young-adults/2005-05-03-the-dedication-of-a-lifetime-eng.pdf?download=true.

———. *The Lord's Way.* Salt Lake City: Deseret Book, 1991.

———. "On Learning and Becoming." In Eyring, *Learning in the Light of Faith,* 75–83.

———. "Powerful Ideas." *Ensign,* Nov. 1995, 25–27.

———. "Sharing the Gospel." *Ensign,* Nov. 2001, 7–9.

———. "Taking upon Us the Name of Jesus Christ." *Ensign*, May 1985, 80–83.

———. "Timing." In *Brigham Young University 2001–2002 Speeches*. Provo, Utah: Brigham Young University, 2002.

———. "Why Do We Serve?" *Ensign*, Nov. 1984, 12–15.

Ogden, D. Kelly, and Andrew C. Skinner. *Acts through Revelation*. Verse by Verse series. Salt Lake City: Deseret Book, 1998.

———. *The Four Gospels*. Verse by Verse series. Salt Lake City: Deseret Book, 2006.

Old Testament [student manual]. Prepared by the Church Educational System. 2 vols. Salt Lake City: The Church of Jesus Christ of Latter-day Saints, 1981.

Packer, Boyd K. "The Balm of Gilead." *Ensign*, Nov. 1977, 59–61.

———. "The Brilliant Morning of Forgiveness." *Ensign*, Nov. 1995, 18–21.

———. "Reverence Invites Revelation." *Ensign*, Nov. 1991, 21–23.

———. "'The Touch of the Master's Hand.'" *Ensign*, May 2001, 22–24.

———. "'Ye Are the Temple of God.'" *Ensign*, Nov. 2000, 72–74.

Palmer, Spencer J., ed. *Mormons and Muslims: Spiritual Foundations and Modern Manifestations*. Vol. 8 of the Religious Studies Monograph Series. Provo, Utah: Religious Studies Center, 1983.

Perry, L. Tom. "The Tradition of a Balanced, Righteous Life." *Ensign*, Aug. 2011, 46–53.

Peterson, Daniel C. "A Response: 'What the Manuscripts and the Eyewitnesses Tell Us about the Translation of the Book of Mormon.'" *Journal of Book of Mormon Studies* 11, no. 2 (2002): 67–71.

Pratt, Orson. *Orson Pratt's Works on the Doctrines of the Gospel*. Salt Lake City: Deseret News Press, 1945.

———. "The Pre-Existence of Man." *The Seer* 1, no. 4 (Apr. 1853).

Preach My Gospel: A Guide to Missionary Service. Salt Lake City: The Church of Jesus Christ of Latter-day Saints, 2004.

Price, Clark Kelley. *All Things Testify of Him: Latter-day Saint Inspirational Paintings*. Salt Lake City: Bookcraft, 1998.

Pritchard, James B. ed. *Ancient Near Eastern Texts Relating to the Old Testament*. 2d ed., corrected and enlarged. Princeton, N.J.: Princeton University Press, 1955.

Revius, Jacobus. "He Bore Our Anguish." Translated by Charles D. Tate Jr. *BYU Studies* 15, no. 1 (Autumn 1974): 103.

Reynolds, George, and Janne M. Sjodahl. *Commentary on the Book of Mormon.* Edited and arranged by Philip C. Reynolds. 7 vols. Salt Lake City: Deseret Book, 1955–61.

Richards, LeGrand. *A Marvelous Work and a Wonder.* Missionary edition. Salt Lake City: Deseret Book, 1988.

Robinson, Stephen E. *Believing Christ: The Parable of the Bicycle and Other Good News.* Salt Lake City: Deseret News, 1992.

Robinson, Stephen E., and H. Dean Garrett. *A Commentary on the Doctrine and Covenants.* 4 vols. Salt Lake City: Deseret Book, 2000–2005.

Romney, Marion G. "The Book of Mormon." *Ensign,* May 1980, 65–67.

Scott, Richard G. "Making the Right Choices." *Ensign,* Nov. 1994, 37–39.

———. "Trust in the Lord." *Ensign,* Nov. 1995, 16–18.

Smith, Hyrum M., and Janne M. Sjodahl. *Doctrine and Covenants Commentary.* Rev. ed. Salt Lake City: Deseret Book, 1978.

Smith, Joseph. *History of The Church of Jesus Christ of Latter-day Saints.* Edited by B. H. Roberts. 7 vols. 2d ed. rev. Salt Lake City: The Church of Jesus Christ of Latter-day Saints, 1932–51.

———. *Teachings of the Prophet Joseph Smith.* Selected by Joseph Fielding Smith. Salt Lake City: Deseret Book, 1976.

———. "A Vision." In *Times and Seasons* 4 (1 Feb. 1843): 82–85.

Smith, Joseph F. *Gospel Doctrine.* Salt Lake City: Deseret Book, 1986.

Smith, Joseph Fielding. *Answers to Gospel Questions.* Compiled by Joseph Fielding Smith Jr. 5 vols. Salt Lake City: Deseret Book, 1957–66.

———. *Church History and Modern Revelation.* 2 vols. Salt Lake City: The Church of Jesus Christ of Latter-day Saints, 1953.

———. *Doctrines of Salvation.* 3 vols. Compiled by Bruce R. McConkie. Salt Lake City: Bookcraft, 1954–56.

———. "Fall—Atonement—Resurrection—Sacrament." Address to religious educators, 14 Jan. 1961. In *Charge to Religious Educators,* 2d ed. Salt Lake City, Utah: The Church of Jesus Christ of Latter-day Saints, 1982.

————. In Conference Report, Oct. 1966, 83–84.

————. "Message from the First Presidency." *Ensign*, Jan. 1971, inside front cover–3.

————. *The Signs of the Times: A Series of Discussions.* Salt Lake City: Deseret Book, 1964.

————. *The Way to Perfection: Short Discourses on Gospel Themes.* Salt Lake City: Genealogical Society of Utah, 1931.

Smith, Lucy Mack. *History of Joseph Smith by His Mother, Lucy Mack Smith.* With notes and comments by Preston Nibley. Salt Lake City: Bookcraft, 1958.

Sperry, Sidney B. *Book of Mormon Compendium.* Salt Lake City: Bookcraft, 1968.

————. *Our Book of Mormon.* Salt Lake City: Stevens & Wallis, 1947.

Talmage, James E. *Articles of Faith.* Salt Lake City: The Church of Jesus Christ of Latter-day Saints, 1966.

————. *Jesus the Christ.* Salt Lake City: Deseret Book, 1983.

Taylor, John. Address at Salt Lake Stake conference, Salt Lake City, Utah, 6 Jan. 1879. Cited in Smith and Sjodahl, *Doctrine and Covenants Commentary.*

Turner, Rodney. "Two Prophets: Abinadi and Alma." In *1 Nephi to Alma 29*, edited by Kent P. Jackson. Vol. 7 of Studies in Scripture. Salt Lake City: Deseret Book, 1987.

Tvedtnes, John A. "Etruscan Gold Book from 600 B.C. Discovered." *Insights* 23, no. 5 (2003): 4, 7. https://scholarsarchive.byu.edu/cgi/viewcontent.cgi?article=1298&context=insights.

Tyler, Daniel. In "Recollections of the Prophet Joseph Smith." *Juvenile Instructor* 28, no. 16 (15 Aug. 1892): 491–92.

Wasserman, Jacob. *Columbus, Don Quixote of the Seas.* Translated by Eric Sutton. Boston: Little, Brown, and Company, 1930. Cited in Benson, *Teachings of Ezra Taft Benson.*

Watts, Pauline Moffitt. "Prophecy and Discovery: On the Spiritual Origins of Christopher Columbus's 'Enterprise of the Indies.'" *American Historical Review* 90 (1985): 73–102. Cited in Ludlow et al., *Encyclopedia of Mormonism.*

Webster, Noah. *An American Dictionary of the English Language.* 1828. Reprint. San Francisco: Foundation for American Christian Education, 1980.

Westermann, Claus. *Isaiah 40–66: A Commentary*. Translated by David M. G. Stalker. Philadelphia: Westminster Press, 1969.

Woodruff, Wilford. Address at Weber Stake conference, Ogden, Utah, 19 Oct. 1896. Cited in Ludlow, *Companion to Your Study of the Book of Mormon*.

———. *Discourses of Wilford Woodruff*. Selected by G. Homer Durham. Salt Lake City: Bookcraft, 1946.

———. Journal. Salt Lake City: Historical Department. The Church of Jesus Christ of Latter-day Saints.

The Words of Joseph Smith. Compiled and edited by Andrew F. Ehat and Lyndon W. Cook. Provo, Utah: Grandin Book, 1991.

Yarn, David H., Jr. "The Testimony of Jesus Christ." Sidney B. Sperry Symposium, Brigham Young University, Provo, Utah, 28 Jan. 1978.

Young, Brigham. *Discourses of Brigham Young*. Compiled by John A. Widtsoe. Salt Lake City: Deseret Book, 1966.

Young, Edward J. *The Book of Isaiah: The English Text, with Introduction, Exposition, and Notes*. 3 vols. Grand Rapids, Mich.: Eerdmans, 1965–72.

Young, G. Douglas. *Grammar of the Hebrew Language: A New Approach to the Hebrew Language and to Advanced Exegesis Using Hebrew and Romanized Scripts*. Grand Rapids, Mich.: Zondervan, 1951.

ABOUT THE AUTHORS

D. KELLY OGDEN is an emeritus professor of ancient scripture at Brigham Young University. His doctoral work focused on the Hebrew language and historical geography of biblical lands. He has walked the length and breadth of the Holy Land and climbed Mount Sinai eighteen times. Dr. Ogden has written numerous books and articles on the Bible, especially during the fourteen years he lived in the Near East. He was associate director of the BYU Jerusalem Center and assisted in the preparation of the Latter-day Saint edition of the King James Bible. He has served as branch president in Jerusalem, mission president in Chile, Missionary Training Center president in Guatemala, sealer in the Provo Utah Temple, and currently works on the Church's Correlation Materials Evaluation Committee. He and his wife, Marcia Hammond Ogden, are the parents of four children and have fifteen grandchildren.

ANDREW C. SKINNER, a professor emeritus of ancient scripture and Near Eastern studies, was Richard L. Evans Professor of Religious Understanding at BYU, where he served as dean of Religious Education and as the first executive director of the Neal A. Maxwell Institute for Religious Scholarship. A member of the international editorial group that translated the Dead Sea Scrolls and author or coauthor of more than two hundred articles and books on religious and historical topics, Dr. Skinner taught at the BYU Jerusalem Center and was its associate director for academics. He has served in the Church as a bishop, a counselor in three district presidencies in Israel, a member of the Correlation Evaluation Committee, and a member of the Sunday School General Board. He and his wife, Janet Corbridge Skinner, are the parents of six children and have ten grandchildren.